THE ILLUSION OF SAFETY

The Story of the Greek Jews
During the Second World War

New Edition
Revised and Expanded

Michael Matsas

Vrahori Books
Potomac, Maryland

THE ILLUSION OF SAFETY:

The Story of the Greek Jews During the Second World War

New Edition
Revised and Expanded

Copyright © 1997, first edition
Copyright © 2021, second edition
By Michael Matsas

ALL RIGHTS RESERVED

Library of Congress Control Number: 97-69837, first edition
ISBN 0-918618-66-5 first edition, Pella Publishing Co. Inc., New York

Library of Congress Control Number: 2021905905, second edition
ISBN 978-0-578-87707-5 second edition, Vrahori Books, Potomac, Maryland

Edited by Linda Esther Matsas Berger
Cover photo by Eleanor Matsas, first edition
Cover photo credit Jewish Community of Athens, second edition
All photos, unless otherwise credited, are from the collection of Michael Matsas.

Author's email: michaelmatsasillusionofsafety@gmail.com

This book is dedicated to those who lost their lives because they were Jews.

Sure enough, the nations did not interfere, nor did they protest, nor shake their heads, nor did they warn the murderers, never a murmur. It was as if the leaders of the nations were afraid that the killings might stop.

—*ITZHAK KATZNELSON*

Acknowledgments

I am grateful to the following people who helped bring this new edition into existence. I wish to thank my daughter Linda for her desire to bring my book back into circulation and for her patience, hard work, and encouragement as we worked together on the manuscript during the coronavirus pandemic. Much thanks to my daughter Alice, my sister Ninetta, and my son-in-law Ira for their thoughtful suggestions and comments. Many thanks to Drs. Mimis Cohen, Alex Levis, and Joseph (Iosif) Stroumtsa for contributing their stories and photos to the new edition, as well as to Effie Papatheodorou for sending me valuable information. In addition, I am very grateful to have reconnected with my friend Iakovos Frizis through the magic of Zoom, and I have greatly enjoyed our discussions about his heroic father Colonel Mordechai Frizis. In addition, I thank my friend Theo Pavlidis who inspired me to republish my book by showing me that many people were interested in learning about what happened to the Jews of Greece during WWII. Many thanks to the Jewish Museum of Greece and Kehila Kedosha Janina for the use of their archival photos.

I started work on the original manuscript during the 1970's and was fortunate to have the assistance of my parents Esther and Leon Matsas who shared their experiences and their wisdom with me. They both remembered many of the people and events mentioned in my book. My father became my partner in searching for material related to our project in the National Archives in Washington, DC. Further, I am indebted to the employees of the National Archives for their assistance and guidance in my research. In preparing the original draft, I wish to thank the following people: Israel Rubin for his advice, my wife Eleanor, my first editor, for her love and support, and my former dental secretary Marie Carpenti for typing the first draft.

In 1990, I was deeply obliged to Professor Steven B. Bowman of the University of Cincinnati, who recognized the potential of my work and recommended it to Leandros

Papathanasiou of the Pella Publishing Company. They suggested a different organization of the material, and Professor Bowman volunteered to edit the manuscript. My former dental secretary Gretna DeStefano deserves my thanks for typing the manuscript and then typing it again after Professor Bowman's edits, a feat far beyond her regular duties. I thank Professor Howard M. Sachar for encouraging my original work on the book at a time when I practically gave up the entire project. Thank you as well to Pella Publishing Company for publishing the first edition in 1997.

I owe special thanks to the former President of the Central Board of Jewish Communities in Greece, Joseph Lovinger, who gave me encouragement and all the assistance I requested for the original material. This Central Board is the source for the population statistics presented in the charts I include in my book. Other people who freely contributed information were Baruch Schibi, a resistance leader, and Joseph Matsas, a partisan of ELAS. Furthermore, I owe special gratitude to my childhood friend, Bishop Efthymios Acheloou, and to the resistance hero, Jack Kostis, who told me about his wartime exploits and gave me interesting short stories of Athenian Jews. I also thank my cousin Makis Matsas who interviewed survivors on my behalf, my cousins Solon Matsas and Pepos Kohen, my brother-in-law Lloyd Feldman, my uncle Dr. Nissim Cohen, and my wife's uncle Dr. Noah Cohen for collecting valuable material for me. I also thank Avi Richter for translating material from Hebrew to English. I extend my warm appreciation to all those who were kind enough to grant me personal interviews or send me letters.

I extend my thanks, posthumously, to my parents Esther and Leon Matsas, my uncle Michael Matsas, my cousins Dr. Michel Negrin, Joseph Matsas, Alberto Negrin, Jacob Alkalai, Sam Meyer, and to my friends Robert Assael, Emmanuel Velellis, Daniel Carasso, and Astro Alballa, who fortunately told me their stories before it was too late. Although they were unable to see the publication of the first edition of *The Illusion of Safety*, I am sure they would have been glad to know that their stories were not lost.

Looking at the names of those who helped me write this book, I realize that many of my relatives consider it to be a family project and certainly much more than that. I am proud of them. They felt that this book was our family's collective

Acknowledgments

expression of grief at the untimely and preventable loss of most of our relatives. Their contribution in collecting the material for this book should be understood as their expression of deep gratitude for those who helped the Jews and great contempt for those big and small, who, with their silence, indifference, or malicious motives, allowed this crime to take place. Their contribution should be interpreted as a protest against the collective conscience of the so-called civilized world of the 1930's and 1940's.

With the publication of the new edition in 2021, I am proud to report that *The Illusion of Safety* continues to be a family project. After the original publication in 1997, my family members continued to speak out about what happened to the Jews of Greece during WWII. My sister Ninetta gave lectures on the subject of Greece and the Holocaust and translated documents from Greek to English for the U.S. Holocaust Memorial Museum. She is currently writing a book on the subject for young readers. My father's brother, the late Michael Matsas, a survivor of Auschwitz, had collected the names of those from Ioannina who did not return from the concentration camps. In 1994, this alphabetical catalogue was carved into marble plaques that line the interior walls of the synagogue of Ioannina, Greece. His son Makis Matsas, who was born after the war in 1950, found his father's research in the drawers of the offices of the Central Jewish Council in Athens and published the material in Greek with photographs in 2009. His book is called *The Disappearance of a Community* (Greek). In addition, Makis' son Mihalis Matsas undertook the herculean task of translating the first edition of *The Illusion of Safety* into Greek. He did a wonderful job, and I am very proud of him. My daughter Alice Matsas Garten volunteers with the Holocaust and Remembrance Commission of the Baltimore Jewish Council and has given a lecture on our family's story. My granddaughter Leanne has presented a research paper about the Jews of Greece for her school. I am grateful for everyone's efforts to help keep the memories of the Greek Jewish community alive.

Contents

Preface.. 11

Background.. 17

Part I Events

Introduction... 37

Chapter One – The German Zone of Occupation.... 39

Chapter Two – The Bulgarian Zone of Occupation.. 87

Chapter Three – The Italian Zone of Occupation.... 95

Part II Personal Memoirs

Chapter One – The German Zone of Occupation.... 139

Chapter Two – The Bulgarian Zone of Occupation. 185

Chapter Three – The Italian Zone of Occupation... 189

Chapter Four – Memoirs of Camp Survivors......... 251

Chapter Five – Memoirs of Resistance Fighters.... 287

Part III Author's Memoirs

The Author's Memoirs...................................... 355

Epilogue... 455

Bibliographical Essay by Professor Steven Bowman........475

Preface

During a family vacation in New England in 1975, my wife Eleanor and my daughters Linda and Alice, ages 9 and 7, proved very curious about my life in Greece during the Second World War. They kept asking me questions about how I escaped to the mountains with my parents and sister, and how we lived in a cave during a German raid. They had great fun listening to my descriptions of how I, as a boy of 13, spent the year in a house without electricity, running water, a bathroom, or even toilet paper. Later my children wanted to know about my grandparents, and they asked when they were going to meet my uncles, aunts and cousins whose pictures filled the four albums in my parents' house.[1]

A day rarely passed without my mother looking at these photographs and entertaining Linda and Alice with stories about her sisters and cousins and uncles, often laughing as she relived a particularly funny moment. Linda and Alice noticed that I never joined my mother in her laughter. She talked about these relatives and friends as if they were living happily in some faraway place. I had to tell my children that I was sad at these moments because I knew that these people were not alive, in spite of how they looked in the photographs. They were "taken by the Germans." This is the way every Greek Jew describes the death of a Holocaust victim, as if the word "German" were a synonym for the mythical king of the underworld, Hades. (For me, and many others like me, the use of the word Nazis instead of the word Germans is an attempt to hide the truth. Throughout the book, I use the word Germans and Germany when describing this Axis power).

---

[1] The Germans inflicted immense and unbearable pain on my parents by killing 126 of their close relatives.

The Illusion of Safety

During this vacation, I decided to write the story of how my family and I, as Greek Jews, survived the war, so that my children could read it when they were grown. But soon my story expanded to the point where I felt it might be of interest to others as well. I quickly discovered how little information about Greek Jews existed in English, and how much of that was full of error.

A friend of mine suggested that I do research in the National Archives in Washington, D.C. I told him I did not believe I would find anything about the Greek Jews there. He insisted that I should do it, however, and since he was a high official of the American government, I decided to follow his advice. To my great surprise, I found 500 pages of documents related to the Jews of Greece, not only in the National Archives but also in the Franklin D. Roosevelt Institute and in the British Archives. In addition, I explored documents from the German Archives, which I found in the book *The Secret Archives of the SS*, written in Greek by Professor Enepekidis who did research there. I appreciate my childhood friend, Bishop Efthymios Acheloou, who sent me the professor's book.

As a child, I belonged to the very small Jewish community of Agrinion, Greece. We were just 40 people. This was the only Jewish community in German-occupied Europe that never obeyed any German regulations, and the entire community survived. We are even mentioned in the German Archives. On October 23, 1943, the German consul in Patras sent the following note to the German embassy in Athens, regarding the Jews of Agrinion: "I have the honor to respectfully report that after the local press printed the order of the obligatory registration of the Jews, they disappeared. It is said that they went to the mountains."[2] "To the mountains" meant to reach the free territory of the Partisan Resistance movement.

One should ask, to what I attribute this miraculous decision of our little community to go to the mountains? In one word, the answer is ***information.***

The three words that are the reason for my great anger and deep pain which have prompted me to write this book are **lack**

---

[2] P.K. Enepekidis, *The Secret Archives of the SS*, Athens, Papzisis Publishers, 1969. *(Greek)*

of information - information which could have saved thousands of lives.

In September 1943, conditions in Agrinion under Italian rule were normal and peaceful. The British Broadcasting Corporation (BBC), our only reliable radio source of information, was announcing how many cities were liberated every day by the Russian Army and how Germany was losing the war.

That same month, a Jewish merchant from Agrinion went to Athens to buy merchandise for his shop. He went to the three large Jewish shops where he would typically buy his goods, but he found those shops closed. This was very unusual. He did not try to find out why they were closed but immediately returned to Agrinion with this information. His brother, Yonas Mionis, a teacher, told all the men of our community, "This is not a good sign. Tomorrow morning, I will go to the mountains." He went to the nearby mountain villages, which remained free thanks to the protection of the Greek partisan movement. The rest of the small community did the same. We knew nothing more. But our desire for freedom was strong.

My family left the city by taxi on October 3, 1943. Two days after we left, the Germans went to the bank to see my father, who was an employee there. They were told that he was on vacation. It would be one year, October 3, 1944, before my family and I would return to a free Agrinion.

Thanks to the Freedom of Information Act of 1967, I discovered information I had never imagined existed in the National Archives of the United States. I became convinced that those individuals concerned with the history of the Holocaust and those who love justice and truth would be interested in reading this account.

My manuscript was finished in 1977, and a literary agent tried to find a publisher. There were publishers who wanted to publish my book provided that I would remove any criticism of the United States and Great Britain. Their excuse was that I was not a historian. I refused to do that because I suspected that this was not their main reason.

I wanted to tell the truth about what happened. Many of the documents I found were classified as "Top Secret." I know the government keeps secrets from its enemies. Therefore, the question for me became who were the enemies? Were the peaceful and innocent Jews of the Greek islands and the mainland the enemies of the United States? Why weren't they warned about the concentration camps and the killings?!

The Greek Jews did not know what was going on outside of Greece! In 1943, the BBC, in its Greek language broadcasts, mentioned every day the cities that were liberated, but never the Jews who were killed.

The Allies were safeguarding the German secret of the Holocaust from its victims: the Jews.

The following two scholars describe the Allied response. Professor Richard Breitman, in his book *Official Secrets: What the Nazis Planned, What the British and Americans Knew,* discovered that the coding system of the German Order Police that dealt with the Jews was broken by British Intelligence in September, 1939.[3] In addition, Professor David Wyman, in his book *The Abandonment of the Jews,* wrote, "The United States and Great Britain were deeply committed to a policy of NOT rescuing the Jews. A fact that particularly pains me as a Christian is that the American churches were silent."[4]

In 1997, Professor Steven Bowman of the University of Cincinnati, Ohio, found the Pella Publishing Company to publish my book. This was 52 years after the Holocaust and 20 years after my book was written.

To my great surprise, in 1997, I read in the *Washington Jewish Week* an article by William Vanden Heuvel, President of the Franklin Roosevelt Institute, with the title, "FDR Did Not Abandon European Jewry." He wrote the following, "The massacre of the Jews continued because no one could do anything to stop it and none of those proposals could have saved the Jews who perished in the Holocaust."

I responded with a letter to the editor in the *Washington Jewish Week* explaining why I did not agree at all with this gentleman. I wrote, "Many experts like to present the Holocaust as an unavoidable natural disaster that could not have been prevented. I am a Greek Jew who believes that the great majority of the 67,000 Greek Jews who were killed by the

---

3 Professor Richard Breitman, *Official Secrets: What the Nazis Planned, What the British and the Americans Knew*, New York, Hill and Wang, 1998, 84.

4 Professor David Wyman, *The Abandonment of the Jews*, New York, Pantheon Books. Co., 2007, 124.

Preface

Germans could have saved themselves if the Americans and the British let them know that deportations meant death. Neither the BBC radio broadcasts, nor the Allied missions with the Greek resistance, nor American agents, nor leaflets dropped by Allied planes exposed the German secret of the 'Final Solution of the Jewish problem'."

I wrote my book so that the truth would be known about what happened in Greece. Unfortunately, my original book is not in print anymore as the Pella Publishing Company closed in 2014. My daughter, Linda, suggested that we could publish another edition of the book so that it would be available again to the general public. With paternal pride, I accepted her suggestion. After all, out of habit and interest, I had continued to read and collect material on the subjects of the Holocaust and World War Two. This edition gives me an opportunity to include this material and to express some more of my thoughts.

I owe my enthusiasm for the updated edition of my book to my friend, Professor Theo Pavlidis. Dr. Pavlidis placed many of my writings on his website, including a lecture about the Greek Jews and the Holocaust that I gave in 2004. About my lecture, Professor Pavlidis wrote in 2005, "I read Dr. Matsas' book, and I was quite intrigued by the subject since it matched histories I had heard from non-Jewish sources in Salonica [Thessaloniki]. This lecture contains the highlights of the book, and I believe it to be required reading for any Greek or Jew and not just for Greek Jews."

After my wife died in 2015, Dr. Pavlidis, in order to "cheer" me up, told me that this lecture was visited by thousands of people! To me, this means that there is much interest in the subject, and I hope that many of these people and others would like to read more about the Jews of Greece.

The history of the Greek Jews during World War Two is not very well known, and it is my hope that I can educate the public about this subject. Sadly, I also have realized that the general history of the Holocaust and even that of the United States' role during the Second World War are not known to many of our youth and that there are even many adults who claim that the Holocaust never happened.

Having in mind those who deny the Holocaust, others who hide and distort the facts, and many who are ignorant of the history, I decided that my book is needed again for the sake of historic truth.

Background

The Jews of Greece

One of the oldest Jewish communities of Europe was in Greece. Jews first appear during the Hellenistic period as merchants or as freed slaves. By the middle of the first century, both philosopher Philo of Alexandria and Apostle Paul attest to flourishing Jewish communities throughout the Greek-speaking world of the Aegean. In addition, Roman Emperor Vespasian sent approximately 6,000 prisoners of war from Judea to assist Nero's plan to dig a canal across the Isthmus of Corinth.

During Byzantine times, Jewish communities in the cities and towns of Greece multiplied. Benjamin of Tudela (twelfth century) lists 2,000 Jews in Thebes and about 500 in Thessaloniki. In the fourteenth century, Hungarian Jews sought refuge in Greece from the persecutions following the Black Death and joined the Italian Jews and the first waves of Spanish merchants. By the year 1500, larger numbers of Spanish Jews arrived in Greece, following their expulsion by Ferdinand and Isabella in 1492 during the Spanish Inquisition. These Jews were welcomed by the new Ottoman rulers of the Aegean lands. So many Jews settled in Thessaloniki (also known as Salonika), that they made up the majority of the population, and the city was nicknamed "the Jerusalem of the Balkans." They were soon joined by fellow Portuguese Jews during the sixteenth and seventeenth centuries. While immigration continued from Sicily and Apulia, Jewish refugees from the Cossack massacres of 1648 in Poland also found their way to Greek centers.

Regardless of their place of origin, Jews assimilated into one of two traditions soon after their arrival. They were either absorbed by the Sephardic communities and spoke Ladino

(Judeo-Spanish), primarily in Thessaloniki but also in the towns along the Via Egnatia from Monastir to Edirne, or they became Greek-speaking Romaniotes in Ioannina, Arta, Preveza, Crete and other cities.

The nineteenth century witnessed a decline of Greek Jewry for many reasons. During the Greek Revolution of the 1820's, Jewish communities in the areas that would become the Greek state were massacred; this allegedly was due to the desecration of the body of Gregory V, Patriarch of Constantinople (Ottoman janissaries murdered him in 1821, then asked some passing Jews to throw his body into the sea). Over 5,000 Jews in Arta, Agrinion, Tripolitsa, Mistra, and Thebes were killed in retaliation. A few survivors converted, but most fled to British Corfu or to Ottoman Chalkis and Thessaloniki. A wave of blood libel accusations swept over Greece in the late nineteenth century and stimulated large-scale emigration from Corfu and Zakynthos. Approximately one hundred families left Larissa for Thessaloniki and Smyrna.

Background

As a result of the Balkan Wars and World War I, which increased Greek territory nearly to its present borders, the Jewish population rose to about 125,000. However, because of worsening economic conditions and the devastating fire in Thessaloniki in 1917, many Jews began to emigrate to the United States, Europe, Turkey and Palestine. By 1941, the Jewish population of Greece was approximately 77,000. The majority were Sephardic Jews who lived in Thessaloniki and were impoverished.

Greek History

In 1453, the Ottoman Turks conquered Constantinople and by 1669 occupied all of Greece except for the Ionian islands, which remained under Venetian control. After enduring nearly 400 years of occupation, the Greeks revolted in 1821 and by 1830 had created an independent state in the southern part of Greece. As a result of the Balkan Wars in 1912, the northern provinces of Epirus, Macedonia, and Thrace were liberated and added to the Greek state. This expansion included the cities of Ioannina, Salonika (Thessaloniki), and Drama.

Colonel Mordechai Frizis (1893-1940), hero of the Greek-Italian War. (Source: collection of KKJSM)

During the Second World War, on October 28, 1940, Mussolini issued an ultimatum to Greece to which Greek Prime Minister Metaxas famously responded with an emphatic refusal. As a result, Italian troops then attacked the outnumbered Greek forces on the Albanian border. The Greek people responded valiantly and drove back the Italian army.

Many Jews enlisted in the army to defend Greece, including my father. One of the heroes of the Greek-Italian war was Colonel Mordechai Frizis, a Greek Jew whose troops played a key role in stopping the advance of the Italian army on the Albanian front. Frizis fell in battle. His victory was one of the earliest Allied victories of the Second World War. Another Greek Jew, Minos Levi, a director of the Bank of Greece, was entrusted with the important mission of moving the gold reserves of Greece to Egypt where King George II of Greece relocated the Greek government-in-exile. Under his supervision, 314 boxes of gold were placed on board the cruiser *Dido* and successfully transferred to Alexandria.[5]

In October 1940, Hitler decided to attack Russia. However, because the Italians failed to conquer Greece, the Germans invaded Greece on April 6, 1941, to occupy territory where there was already a British expeditionary force. Because of this, the German attack on Russia, "Operation Barbarossa," was delayed until June 22, 1941.

The Germans entered Athens on April 27, 1941, and divided the country into three zones of occupation. Bulgaria was entrusted with part of Thrace and part of Macedonia. The rest of continental and insular Greece was given to the Italian army. The Germans took part of Macedonia, including Thessaloniki and the border zone of Thrace as well as Crete and three of the larger islands of the Aegean.[6] Thus, what would become the Greek Holocaust occurred in three distinct zones.

The Germans would have needed even more time to conquer Greece if the Greek generals accepted the British suggestion of forming a new defensive line in a narrow part of Greece at Thermopylae. According to Dr. Apostolou, "The Greek generals combined a military coup with treason by surrendering to the Germans on April 20, 1941. General Georgios Tsolakoglou and other officers had been secretly organizing a mutiny to take Greece out of the war. Tsolakoglou

---

5 M. Levi, *Chronika* (December 1990).

6 Evangelos Averoff-Tossizza, *By Fire and Axe* (New Rochelle, NY: Caratzas Bros., 1978), 31.

formed a collaborationist government, willing to make domestic concessions to the Germans."[7]

Greek Resistance

For many young Greeks, the total occupation of their country by the Axis forces meant not the end but the beginning of their struggle with the enemy. Those who felt they should join the Allied forces in the Middle East were sometimes able to do so. Many experienced Greek seamen offered them transportation from secluded and remote harbors of the mainland to the Aegean islands of Mytilini, Chios and Samos, from whose shores Turkey could be seen and easily reached by rowboat. In the cities, where newspapers were strictly censored, an underground news service appeared. Mimeographed news dispatches spread the latest news of the BBC. Messages of defiance appeared on buildings. Partisan groups formed in the mountains, and by the beginning of 1942, guerrilla leaders, although uncoordinated and disorganized, were fighting against the enemy.[8]

One of them, Aris Velouhiotis, showing his great organizational skills, quickly disarmed local police, recruited many volunteers, successfully attacked Italian units, and soon established free areas in the mountains. This force evolved into ELAS (the Greek Popular Liberation Army).[9]

In June 1942, a retired colonel, Napoleon Zervas, with the assistance of British agents, went to Epirus. Soon he was leading a group of well-armed soldiers. This became the nucleus of the right-wing organization, EDES (the National Democratic Greek Army). There were other anti-German organizations formed such as PEAN (Panhellenic Union of Fighting Youths), whose actions benefitted Jews, and EKKA (National and Social Liberation).

---

[7] Andrew Apostolou, *The Holocaust in Greece*, edited by Giorgos Antoniou and A. Dirk Moses, Cambridge University Press, 2018, 91.

[8] Tassos Bournas, *Istoria tis Synchronis Ellados* (Athens: Tolidi Brothers), 24.

[9] Markos Vafiadis, *Apomnimonevmata*, vol. 2, "Diaries" (Athens: Nea Sinora, 1985), 25.

By October 1942, the partisans of ELAS and EDES were successfully able to attack a large Italian force guarding the Gorgopotamos bridge. British commandos under Colonel Eddie Myers blew up the bridge, interrupting the flow of supplies to Rommel for six weeks.[10] EDES in Epirus and ELAS in the rest of Greece controlled vast areas in which neither the Germans nor the Italians dared enter without mounting expeditions involving hundreds or thousands of men.

On the outskirts of almost all Greek cities, the partisans of ELAS were the true rulers. Their accomplishments are best described by their most avid critic, Colonel Christopher M. Woodhouse, who succeeded Myers as head of the British Military Mission:

> EAM (the National Liberation Front) and its army, ELAS, having acquired control of almost the entire country, except the principal communications used by the Germans, they [sic] had given it things that it had never known before. Communications in the mountains, by wireless, courier and telephone, had never been as good before or since. Even motor roads were mended and used by EAM-ELAS. Their communications, including wireless, extended as far as Crete and Samos where guerrillas were already in the field. The benefits of civilization and culture trickled into the mountains for the first time. Schools, local government, law courts and public utilities, which the war had ended, worked again. Theaters, factories and parliamentary assemblies existed for the first time. Communal life was organized in place of the traditional individualism of the Greek peasant. EAM initiated the creation of something that governments in Greece had previously neglected—an organized state in the Greek mountains.[11]

The British Military Mission relocated to the village of Petrouli in the mountains of Thessaly, where ELAS

---

10 Averoff-Tossizza, op. cit., 57.
11 Christopher M. Woodhouse, *The Greek Resistance*: 19U2-UU, 374.

headquarters were located. An airstrip was built at Neraida to facilitate supply and communication with the Resistance.[12]

In September 1943, the Germans were well prepared for the Italian surrender. They relieved the Italian XI Army before it was demolished by the partisans.[13] On March 26, 1944, EAM-ELAS controlled so much of the countryside that it justified the creation of PEEA (the Political Committee of National Liberation). The Greek people considered it the "Government of the Mountains." With the exception of the cities, which were German strongholds, the rest of Greece was most of the time free.[14]

How did these developments affect the Greek Jews? When the German state decided to exterminate the Jews of Europe, Greece was the only country whose Jewish population had a place to go and save itself. The Italians welcomed any Jews who entered their zone, and, by September 1943, the Greek countryside was, for all practical purposes, free. Any Greek Jew who wished to do so could have moved his family to a remote village just as easily as before the war.

Once family members moved to partisan-controlled areas, they were usually safe under the protection of ELAS. The Greek villagers, although very religious and raised to believe that the Jews killed Jesus Christ, were also good patriots who hated the Germans. The few villagers who would have liked to betray Jews to the Germans knew very well that anyone who was even suspected of collaboration with the Germans would be summarily executed.

Free territories also existed in Yugoslavia in 1943 and 1944; however, the systematic killing of the Jews there began as early as July 1941. Out of 75,000 Yugoslav Jews, only 5,000 were in the Italian zone of occupation. "In September 1943, some of them went into hiding or joined the partisans."[15] By comparison, in France, where there was also an Italian zone, there were no equivalent free territories. The same was true in Italy.

---

12 D. Eudes, *The Kapetanios*, 57.
13 Bournas, op. cit., 264.
14 Averoff-Tossizza, op. cit., 87.
15 Nora Levin, *The Holocaust* (New York: Schocken Books, 1973), 521.

The combination of the Italian zone, the territories controlled by the partisans, easy access to neutral Turkey, and the lateness in Jewish deportations made the history of the Holocaust in Greece entirely different from that of all other countries. In fact, the deportation of the Greek Jews began in March 1943, over a year later than most of the rest of Europe, and did not end until July 20, 1944.

Western Action and Inaction

If you wish to be free, do not wish anything that depends on others or else you are bound to be a slave.

— EPICTETUS

The abandonment of the European Jews by President Franklin D. Roosevelt became obvious in 1939 when he refused to allow more than 900 German Jews aboard the ship the *MS St. Louis* to seek refuge in this immense country. Six hundred of these refugees were eventually killed by the Germans.

England deserves gratitude for accepting and saving 10,000 children of German and Austrian Jews whom the Germans allowed to leave with the Kindertransport. Among those children was my friend Alfred Rhode who came to the United States. He became a professor at George Mason University and a Pentagon consultant with the rank of General.

On August 1, 1942, a German businessman, Eduard Shulte, at the risk of his life, transmitted to the World Jewish Congress in Lausanne, Switzerland, the information that Hitler had ordered the liquidation of all Jews throughout the territories occupied by Germany. This information was transmitted to England and the United States.[16] Before that, detailed reports of mass murders of Jews in Poland and Russia had appeared in British and American newspapers. In December 1939, news stories claimed that 250,000 Polish Jews had perished. Meanwhile, the *Boston Globe* reported on June

---

16 Arthur D. Morse, *While Six Million Died* (New York: Ace Publishing Company, 1968), 13.

Background

26, 1942, that "mass murders of Jews in Poland pass [the] 700,000 mark." In addition, it was reported that 4,000 Jewish men were executed by the Germans in Belgrade, Yugoslavia, in September 1941.[17]

In a speech on September 23, 1942, the German propaganda minister Joseph Goebbels said, "There are still 48,000 Jews in Berlin.... [T]hey will be packed off to the East and delivered up to a murderous fate." The speech was obtained by the Polish government-in-exile and given to the British Foreign Office.[18]

Information about the "Final Solution" was available to many Allied governments. For example, the United States had its own varied means to collect intelligence in every European country. A document in the National Archives in Washington, D.C., identifies an American agent—code name "X"—who operated in Greece. Another agent—code name "Z"—reported: "On March 4, 1943, at 3:00am, all the Jews of Alexandroupolis together with their families were seized."[19] Another report cites Greek intelligence and "another reliable source" identifying German and Bulgarian activities in Greek Macedonia and Thrace: in particular, the arrest of the Jews of Didimotiho and Orestias, their deportation to Poland via Thessaloniki, and the seizure of their property by the Germans.[20] Further data was received from the American naval attaché in Ankara.[21]

In the National Archives and the Franklin D. Roosevelt[22] Library in Hyde Park, New York, there are over 500 pages of

---

17 David Wyman, *The Abandonment of the Jews* (New York: Pantheon Books, 1984), 20.

18 Tom Tugend, "Holocaust Evidence Hidden," *Washington Jewish* Week, 12/2/93.

19 OSS Confidential, National Archives, No. 40570.

20 OSS Confidential, National Archives, No. 39165.

21 OSS Confidential, National Archives, No. 46910.

22 Since we mention President Roosevelt, I add the following information. The son of FDR, Franklin D. Roosevelt Jr., married "Felicia Schiff Warburg Sarnoff, who came from the German Jewish gentry." FDR's grandson John Boettiger married Janet Adler, a Jewish woman. Boettiger said, "Eleanor Roosevelt was able to transcend her upbringing and the prejudices of their class." Eleanor Roosevelt was a friend of the Jews while FDR was "less able to eclipse the world he came from." John Boettiger obviously refers to anti-Jewish

reports dealing with the plight of the Greek Jews during the Second World War.[23] These reports were sent from Istanbul by American Consul Burton Berry, Brigadier General Richard Tindall (military attaché), Vice-Consul Leslie Albion Squires, and the American ambassador to Greece (who had relocated to Cairo), Lincoln MacVeagh. Most impressive for their humanitarian spirit are the reports of Consul Berry, who continuously made desperate appeals to his superiors to act to save people from a horrible fate. Suggestions were also made to assist Jews to reach the safety of the Middle East or to help them flee into the mountains.[24]

The American intelligence service received a number of reports on Greek Jewish labor battalions. In one report, Consul Berry wrote to his superiors that "the conditions in which the poor devils were made to work in the unhealthy regions of Western Macedonia and the hard labor that was required of them were of such a nature that most of the laborers became ill and the output of the work was noticeably affected."

While the Jews of Thessaloniki were preoccupied with the Jewish labor battalions, the Germans were busy planning the "Final Solution of the Jewish Problem" in Greece, starting with the deportation of the Jews to the concentration and death camps. According to Dr. Andrew Apostolou, "The German Ambassador [in Greece] Altenburg did something unusual and important – he informed the Greek Prime Minister Logothetopoulos of the deportations in the German Zone of occupation on January 26, 1943. Such advanced warning implied considerable trust. Logothetopoulos, therefore, knew of the planned deportations seven weeks before the first deportation train left Thessaloniki for Auschwitz on March 15, 1943." He continues, "Altenburg felt confident enough to tell

---

prejudices and anti-Semitism. He introduced his son Joshua to Jewish philosophers Martin Buber and Abraham Joshua Heschel. In addition, Ezra Gorodesky, of Jerusalem disliked FDR, but he liked Mrs. Eleanor Roosevelt. He remembered a radio interview where Eleanor Roosevelt was asked the question "Which man did she admire most in the world?" Her answer was, "That little man, David Ben Gurion." – International Jerusalem Post, April 17, 2020, 22.

23 War Refugee Board, No. 44786.

24 OSS Confidential, National Archives, No. 8-4016/72.

Background

Berlin on January 26, 1943, that 'from his (Logothetopoulos') side, no difficulties are expected in the execution of the action following the talk.'"

Consul Berry, did not know that his suggestion that "the Greek Jews should flee to the mountains" was classified as "top secret" and was locked in the archives. His superiors did not give his advice to the Greek Jews. After March 15, 1943, Consul Berry became busy sending to Washington eye witness accounts of the arrest and deportation of the Jews of Thessaloniki.[25] Another report Berry sent recounts the appeal of the Metropolitan of Thessaloniki to the Germans in March 1943 "to refrain from cruelties in deportations."[26]

For the remaining Greek Jews in the Italian Zone, the summer of 1943 was uneventful. However, once Italy surrendered to Germany in September, the Germans descended on the remainder of Greece. On September 11, 1943, Consul Berry in Istanbul reported the adventure of a Syrian Jew of French citizenship who had been employed by an American company in Athens for twenty years. This man explained that, after the fall of Italy and the arrival of the Germans, he was afraid that the Germans would soon start their customary persecution of the Jews. He traveled to Sofia by plane; the other 22 passengers were German officers. From Sofia he traveled by rail to Istanbul, afraid that the Germans might create difficulties at Tatoi airfield, since his permission to leave Greece was granted by the Italian authorities. He was questioned briefly but experienced no trouble. Berry concluded: "My informant left Athens on August 27 and arrived in Istanbul September 1st."[27]

On October 6, 1943, Brigadier General Richard Tindall sent a report to Washington entitled "Possible expulsion of Jews from Athens." In it he wrote: "German authorities in Athens have asked the Chief Rabbi to prepare a complete list of all Jews in Athens, which gave rise to fears that the Jews are about to be expelled from that city as they were from Thessaloniki. These latter were sent to Poland under

---

25 OSS Confidential, National Archives, No. 1601 R-1483.
26 OSS Confidential, National Archives, No. 1823 R-2285.
27 OSS Confidential, National Archives, No. 3068 R-2835.

indescribable conditions and there has been no news from them since deportation."[28]

Consul Berry, in a long report received by the State Department on October 22, 1943, stated "... it is my opinion that the one hope for the Jews is escape, for in the long run it is possible that the fear of reprisal might influence our Greek friends (who gave shelter to Jews) to change their attitude."[29] On October 15, the Office of Strategic Services (OSS) in Washington was notified of a Gestapo census in Greece.[30] On November 20, Consul Berry forwarded a copy of the appeal by the Metropolitan of Athens addressed to the Germans by Ioannis Rallis (the newly German-appointed prime minister) and Minister of Education Nikolaos Louvaris.[31]

On April 16, 1944, Consul Berry sent an extensive report in which he criticizes his superiors for their inaction: "... as was suggested in dispatch No. 2680 (R-2404) .... resulted in the seizure of all those who obeyed the order to report." In dispatch No. 2917 (R-2706), Consul Berry reports "... on March 24, 1944, an order was published stating that all Jews living in the provinces were to be arrested and brought to Athens."[32]

A most interesting document is Consul Berry's report entitled "Further information regarding the Jews of Greece," in which he describes meeting with a humanitarian Christian Greek: "Michael Boyiadjoglou, a Greek tobacco merchant, recently arrived in Turkey. On April 30, while on a train from Athens to Thessaloniki, Mr. Boyiadjoglou talked with three German SS officers who said that they were on their way to Corfu, where they were to deport all the Jews. These officers left the train at Larissa."[33] The unsuspecting Jews of Corfu were arrested on June 9, 1944, almost seventy days after Consul Berry informed Washington about the impending German action in the provinces. Of 2,000 deportees, only 187 returned from the death camps.

---

28 "Franklin D. Roosevelt Library, File No. 820.02. [henceforth: FDRL]
29 240SS Confidential, National Archives, No. 101301.
30 "National Archives, No. 2680 R-2494.
31 "Enclosure No. 3103 to dispatch No. 90 of 4/7/44 from Cairo.
32 "National Archives, Cairo, Egypt, No. 86, from Ambassador Lincoln MacVeagh to Secretary of State REC-435.
33 FDRL, War Refugee Board, Container No. 26, p. 109.

Background

Despite information available to the U.S. government, the World Jewish Congress (WJC), the most important Jewish organization in the United States at the time, knew nothing about the fate of Greek Jewry as late as April 28, 1944, one year after two-thirds of Greek Jewry were already dead. On that day the WJC in New York sent a letter to the Sephardic Chief Rabbi in Jerusalem, Benzion Uziel, requesting "some idea of the extent and gravity of the plight of Greek Jewry." On August 4, a reply was dispatched to the executive director of the War Refugee Board, John Pehle, who sent it in turn on September 14 to the WJC.[34] It had taken nearly five months merely to exchange a letter. By then, 87 percent of the Greek Jews were already dead, and the Germans were leaving Greece.

The British and American governments had known since 1942 that the Germans planned the execution of all Jews who resided in occupied territories. In November 1942, Rabbi Stephen Wise publicly announced the murder of over two million Jews. In a meeting, President Franklin D. Roosevelt declared: "The Government of the United States is very well acquainted with most of the facts that you are now bringing to our attention."[35]

John Pehle, director of the War Refugee Board, revealed that the State Department kept information about the Holocaust secret from the American people.

Officials of the Treasury Department exposed the "dirty scandal" in a report entitled, "Acquiescence of this government in the murder of the Jews of Europe." The head of "this" government was President Franklin D. Roosevelt, who was beloved by the American Jews and who received 90% of their vote.

Rabbi Joshua Boettiger, a great grandson of President Franklin D. Roosevelt, said about his famous ancestor, "If he

---

[34] FDRL, War Refugee Board, Container No. 45.

[35] Hanoch Teller, "Unfashionable Causes," *Jerusalem Post* (Inti. Ed.) 11/20/93, excerpt from *Reverence, Righteousness, and Rahmanut* (New Jersey: Jason Aronson, 1993).

knew about the slaughter of Jews in Europe and he did not act, that is very serious, inexcusable."[36]

The United States had an opportunity to save 20,000 German-Jewish children in a deal with Sweden in which Sweden agreed to receive the children provided that the United States would accept them to come to the U.S. after the war. The Congress of the United States refused to accept them (the defeat of the Wagner-Rogers Bill of 1939), so they perished. It is obvious that everyone assumed that there would not be any parents left alive to seek their children.

A cousin of President Roosevelt, Mrs. Laura Delano, did not want these children to come to the United States. She expressed her compassion for these unfortunate children by saying, "The 20,000 charming children would soon grow up to 20,000 ugly adults." [37]

By the end of the war, 1,500,000 Jewish children were murdered. Who knows how many great scientists were lost with the killing of these children? Let's not forget that "there were more than 900 individuals and organizations awarded the Nobel Prize between 1901 and 2018. Two hundred and four of them have been Jewish."[38] Proportionately, the Jewish people contributed more to this world than any other people on earth.[39]

In December 1942, in the House of Commons, Sydney Silverman asked British Foreign Affairs Secretary Anthony Eden "whether it was true that the Germans planned to deport all Jews to eastern Europe and put them to death. 'Yes sir,' Eden replied. A non-Jewish member asked whether the House might rise to express its grief. For two minutes the members stood with heads bowed. It was a gesture unprecedented in the history of the British Parliament."[40]

On the other side of the Atlantic, Secretary of the Treasury Henry Morgenthau wrote: "We knew in Washington, from

---

36 Joseph Berger, "Roosevelts and the Quirks of Destiny." *The New York Times*, Mar. 16, 2005

37 Michael Dobbs, *The Unwanted*, 102.

38 JewishVirtualLibrary.org

39 Steve Linde, "Jewish World." *International Jerusalem Post*, May 21, 2010, 16.

40 Morse, *While Six Million Died*, 35.

Background

August 1942 on, that the Nazis were planning the extermination of all the Jews of Europe. Yet, for nearly 18 months, the State Department did practically nothing. Officials dodged their grim responsibility, procrastinated, or suppressed information about atrocities. They lacked either the administrative drive or the emotional commitment."[41]

Other nations collaborated with the Germans directly like France or indirectly like Switzerland, Sweden, and Turkey. Turkey collaborated with Germany by sending food supplies. Sweden, to its credit, accepted the Jews of Denmark.

Albania also deserves credit because hundreds of German and Austrian Jews, who were not accepted by other countries, went to Albania before the Italian occupation and survived the war. This is thanks to King Zog of Albania who left for New York before the Italians arrived.

Fortunately, there were individuals who helped, like the following two Righteous Among the Nations: Sugihara Chiune, a Japanese official who issued thousands of transit visas to help Jews flee before the advancing Germans and Jan Zwartendijk, the Dutch Consul, who issued documents permitting the holders of such visas to enter the Dutch West Indies [42]

Another noble individual was the "scion of one of the most powerful families of Sweden - the 32-year-old Raoul Wallenberg. He arrived on July 9, 1944, in Budapest, empowered by the U.S. War Refugee Board and the Swedish government. Historians believe that Wallenberg and his team managed to save tens of thousands of [Jewish] lives." [43] He issued protective Swedish passports and created safe houses where Jews hid during the war. As the Russian Army was near Budapest, Wallenberg and his driver, Vilmos Langfelder, wanted to meet the Red Army commander, Marshal Rodion Malinovsky, to discuss the future of the Jewish survivors. They were arrested by the Soviet military counterintelligence unit

---

41 Ibid., 261.

42 Michael Pollak, *Mandarins, Jews, And Missionaries: Jewish Experience in The Chinese Empire*, Jewish Publication Society of America; 1st edition (1980)

43 Baruch Tenembaum, "Happy 108th Birthday, Mr. Wallenberg," *International Jerusalem Post*, Aug. 13, 2020, 19.

and nobody knows what happened to them. Baruch Tenembaum concludes by writing, "We still call upon President Putin to enable access to the relevant KGB archives."

Another savior of the Jews was Philippine President Manuel Quezon. He welcomed over 1,200 Jews from Germany and Austria. He wanted to bring tens of thousands more, but the United States limited him to accept just 1,000 Jews per year over a ten-year period.[44]

In light of the above information, the following questions need to be answered. Would any Greek Jew have waited his or her turn to be sent to Poland if he or she knew about the gas chambers? Would any man or woman have peacefully accompanied his or her children to the crematoria?

These are, of course, academic questions, since the Jews who remained in Greece learned about the death camps only after May 1945. The BBC never mentioned anything related to the Jews in all its Greek broadcasts during the Second World War.[45]

I am convinced that *great numbers of Jews had no chance to remain free and survive, relying on their own resources alone, in any German-occupied country except in Greece.* The previous statement is based on my premise that the historic background of the Holocaust in Greece was unique and totally different from that of any other European country. Only proud and benevolent Finland, with its Jewish population of 2,000, successfully resisted all German pressures. It is true that almost all Danish Jews survived, but they had to flee to Sweden. The Bulgarian Jews survived, but they lived like slaves at the mercy of a government allied with Germany. The same was true for the remnants of Romanian and Hungarian Jewry, whose total extermination was interrupted only because it had begun so late in the war.

I feel it is essential to emphasize that only in Greece could Jews have saved themselves *and* contributed greatly to the war against the Germans. The Germans could not have controlled the Greek Jews because in Greece avenues of escape existed. Until the end of 1942, Jewish families in German-occupied Greece could easily move to the Italian zone of occupation, and

---

44 Rich Tenorio, *Times of Israel*, Feb. 20, 2020.
45 Personal letter from Mr. Nathaniel of the BBC to me, 12/10/75.

from there (before September 1943, when the Italian zone was overrun by the Germans) Jews could have moved to the Resistance-controlled areas. Another avenue of escape was that of going to Turkey.

It is obvious that these possibilities did not exist in France, Holland, Italy, or in any other country except in Greece. There is little doubt in my mind that if the Allies had exposed the secret of the German plan of the "Final Solution" and the death camps, the losses in Greece would have been greatly reduced. Instead, the losses of the Jewish community of Greece were an appalling 87 percent, not to mention the untold suffering of those who returned to Greece having survived the horrors of captivity.

Part I

EVENTS

Introduction

At this point, as an American and as a Greek Jew, I want to express my gratitude to the people of the United States, to those who fought as members of the Armed Forces, to the more than 400,000 who fell in action and their families, and to those who contributed to the war effort with their labor in the farms, the factories, and the merchant marine.

Saving the Jews of Europe should have been a moral obligation for the United States and the Allies and not simply a humanitarian act. Five hundred fifty thousand American Jews served valiantly in the Armed Forces of the United States. Eleven thousand were killed, over 27,000 were wounded, and almost all of them had relatives in Europe who were abandoned to the hands of the Germans. The American government rejected thousands of applications for immigration to this enormous country. Among these applications was that of Anne Frank's family in Amsterdam. In addition, 30,000 Jews served in the British Army including 5,000 who served in the Jewish Brigade from Palestine. Michael Weizmann, son of Professor Chaim Weizmann, the first president of Israel, was a pilot in the British Royal Air Force. He fell in action fighting the Lüftwaffe in aerial combat. Chaim Weizmann was a professor of biochemistry in Great Britain. He invented a fermentation process for the manufacture of acetone which was used by the Allies during the First World War in the production of explosives. Lord Balfour, in gratitude for Weizmann's invention, issued the Balfour Declaration of 1917, which promised the establishment of a Jewish home in Palestine.

While the United States was becoming a nuclear superpower thanks to Jewish scientists like Albert Einstein, J. Robert Oppenheimer, Leo Szilard, Edward Teller, Isidor Rabi, and Admiral Hyman Rickover (inventor of the nuclear submarine), the relatives of these Jews were left to die in the gas chambers of Auschwitz and Treblinka.

German archival photos of the arrest and deportation of the Jewish community of Ioannina, Greece, March 25, 1944.
(Permissions: KKJSM)

I recognize the following family members: my cousin Sam Meyer (1), my uncle Dr. Nissim Samuel (2), great-uncle Eliasaf Matsas (3), and uncle Michael Matsas (4).

In this photo, there is Elda Levi (smiling with hand raised) who survived Auschwitz and my aunt Annetta Raphael (second to the left of the tree), who did not.
These photos were brought to my attention by Isaak Dostis.

Chapter One

The German Zone of Occupation

All that is necessary for evil to triumph is for good people to do nothing.

—EDMUND BURKE

The losses of the Greek Jewish population as a result of German persecution were as follows in the communities listed:

Communities	Population (prearrest)	Population (postwar)	Percentage of Loss	Date of Arrest
Didimotio	900	33	96%	March 1943
Florina	400	64	84%	March 1943
Chania	350	7	98%	June 1944
Katerini	30	29	3.3%	March 1943
Langada	50	—	100%	March 1943
Naoussa	50	20	60%	March 1943
Nea Orestias	197	3	98%	March 1943
Thessaloniki	56,000	1,950	96%	Mar-July 1943
Soufli	40	8	80%	March 1943
Veria	460*	131	72%	March 1943

*According to Dr. Joseph Stroumtsa, the prewar Jewish population of Veria was around 600 people.

The Illusion of Safety

In this book, I use the official statistics from the Central Board of Jewish Communities in Greece. These are depicted in the charts at the beginning of the sections in Part I Events. There are other sources of information, however, that report differing numbers. According to historian Mark Mazower, "precise figures are difficult to find, since there are no exact details either of how many Jews were in Greece when the deportations started or of how many escaped or survived the camps. At the outbreak of the war, there were between 70,000 and 80,000 Jews in Greece.... fewer than 10,000 survived."[46]

Thessaloniki

On April 8, 1941, two days after Germany attacked Greece, the Greek administration abandoned Thessaloniki. The Germans were but a few miles from the city. The Jews were in despair. They knew that within hours they would be at the mercy of the Germans, whose anti-Semitism was known to them. Some Jews, like the journalists Mentes Besantsi and Baruch Schibi, left Thessaloniki as soon as Germany invaded Greece, but almost everyone else remained in the city. Fifty-six thousand Jews fell into German hands.

On the morning of April 9, the first armored German units entered the city. A few people in the streets applauded the invading troops. During the first day of occupation, all market places, factories, and places of entertainment were closed. The Germans put up posters announcing that they came as friends of the Greek people and calling for a return to normalcy. All newspapers were closed and replaced immediately by *Nea Evropi (New Europe)*.

On April 11, many Jewish homes were confiscated. The occupants of the Hirsch Hospital were given a few hours to vacate the premises. The Jewish Community Council, after many hours of secret meetings, decided to send two representatives, Zyl Naar and Isaak Benveniste (who spoke German fluently), to the German commander to pledge their cooperation. The general refused to see them, and his secretary refused to discuss anything with them. Finally, a sergeant told

---

46 Mark Mazower, *Inside Hitler's Greece*, 1993, 256.

I. Events – The German Zone of Occupation

them arrogantly: "If the Germans want to know something, they have ways of finding the answer."[47]

On April 15, the Germans arrested most of the Jewish Community Council, including Isaak Siaki, director of the welfare institutions, and Albert Tsenio of the Masonic order, and imprisoned them under inhumane conditions. There was not enough room for all detainees to lie on the bare floor; half remained standing while the other half lay down. They were allowed to go to the lavatory only once every twenty-four hours. The president of the Jewish Community Council, Rabbi Tzevi Koretz, was in Athens and, consequently, not immediately arrested. On April 20, *Nea Evropi* published its first anti-Semitic article. The leader of the anti-Semites, Laskaris Papanaoum, placed notices at the entrances to cafes, restaurants, pastry shops, and other public gathering places, announcing: "Jews are not welcome."[48]

On April 29, 1941, the Jews were ordered to surrender their radios to the German authorities; each received a receipt. Robert Assael turned in his radio, but not before he had the chance to listen to a French broadcast that mentioned Jews were being deported to an unknown destination on "death trains." Nobody believed his story, and he was called crazy by his friends and relatives for believing the broadcast.[49]

On May 17, Rabbi Koretz was arrested by the Gestapo and sent to Vienna. The Germans charged that he had protested the bombardment of the Metropolitan church of Thessaloniki, Saint Sophia, by the Italian air force, and he had criticized the Axis powers in a lecture before the literary club Parnassos. In his place, the Germans appointed Saby Saltiel, an honest but weak man who did not know German. He appointed Jacques Alballa, a tourist guide from Vienna, as his interpreter. The members of the Community Council were soon released, and the Jews thought the worst was over. Their sense of security was reinforced when German-appointed Greek Prime Minister Georgios Tsolakoglou declared, "There is no Jewish problem in Greece. The Jews, whose patriotism I appreciated in the Greek-

---

[47] Rabbi Michael Molho, *In Memoriam* (Thessaloniki: Jewish Community of Thessaloniki, 1974), 35. Translated from Greek by the author.

[48] P. K. Enepekidis, "Ta Mystika Archia tou SS," *To Vima*, August 1966.

[49] Robert and Mimi Assael, personal interview.

Italian war, will be treated in the same way as the citizens of other religions."

The Germans took no further action against the Jews beyond arresting those individuals who were British subjects. Then, in June 1941, Dr. Johann Pohl, Director of the Hebrew Collection of the Institute for Jewish Studies in Frankfurt, arrived with his staff (known as kommando Rosenberg). Their mission was the systematic looting of rare and valuable Jewish manuscripts and religious items. Tens of thousands of books and silver ornaments were sent to Germany. (Even before the invasion of Greece, pro-Nazi Greeks in Thessaloniki had compiled a list of important book collections for the Nazis.) In 1937, for example, Hans Reegler, a Berlin electrical engineer whose mother was Greek, underwent plastic surgery in Friedenau and became an intelligence officer. He arrived in Athens as William Lions from England. In his autobiography, Reegler described his duties as the collection of military data and also the detailed study of German and other Jews who remained in Greece after their expulsion from Germany. In 1939, he was ordered by Admiral Wilhelm Canaris, head of the Abwehr, to make a complete list of the Greek Jews, their professions or occupations, and their home addresses.[50] Thirty German agents, most of them in Thessaloniki, went to work. Valentin Fischer and Egmond Kontoumas made a detailed list of all the important Jewish enterprises, which was then sent to German military attaché, Von Clem Hohenberg, in Athens. Many of Fischer's agents in Thessaloniki were considered friends of the Jews. Egmond Kontoumas, for example, was an electrical engineer before becoming an intelligence agent. Since his ancestors were Greeks living in Germany, and given his background, he easily gained employment in the Athens Telephone Company, where he developed many agents who monitored all important conversations. These included the Maissner brothers who, along with Egmond Kontoumas and especially Hans Reegler, prepared the way for the destruction of the Jews of Thessaloniki.[51]

---

50 Ant. Sarantidis, "Who Prepared the Holocaust in Thessaloniki?" *Chronika*, April 1981, 7.

51 Enepekidis, op. cit.

I. Events – The German Zone of Occupation

The private library of Joseph Nehama was the first of many to be confiscated. The religious court (Beth Din) library held 2,500 volumes, including ancient manuscripts of Maimonides and Joseph Caro. The library of Rabbi Tzevi Koretz comprised 1,000 volumes, while that of Rabbi Saoul Amarillio included in its 500 volumes an important collection of responses. Two hundred and fifty Torah scrolls were taken from the synagogues; 150 went to Germany, and the rest were burned.

A group of forty German-speaking Jewish refugees who had come from Yugoslavia and settled in Thessaloniki was sheltered and assisted by the Jewish community, but they were very demanding. The Germans supported their every request, including their move into expensive hotels and the purchase of valuable items. The Gestapo intended to use these Jews when the persecution started. The local pro-German newspapers, *Nea Evropi* and *Apoyevmatini*, continued to accuse the Jews of being communists, Masons, and enemies of the people.

On December 11, 1941, the personnel of the U.S. consulate in Thessaloniki were arrested, including two Jews, David Tiano and Emanuel Carasso, who were tortured while in prison. In February 1942, Tiano and another Jew, Michael Kazes, a former member of the Greek Parliament, were executed by firing squad. Meanwhile, Rabbi Koretz, in a Viennese prison, gained the sympathy of a German officer named Darhung who obtained his release. (At least this was the excuse for his release; most probably, the Germans assumed that Rabbi Koretz could be used by them.) He returned to his position as chief rabbi of Thessaloniki in January 1942.[52]

Life continued "as usual" for the Jews of Thessaloniki. There were no specifically anti-Jewish measures, and a false sense of security prevailed, but the winter of 1941-1942 was the worst in memory. Mortality increased four times, and some 20,000 of the poorer Jews suffered from typhoid and lice. Further, there were daily harassments: looting, insults, and even prank calls to the offices of the community by Greek Christians pretending to be Germans giving orders or making demands. Individual Jews were blackmailed and forced to give money to avoid accusations of being communists. The elderly

---

52 Molho, op. cit., 58.

rabbi Chaim Habib was beaten by Gestapo agents while a German officer shaved half the face of another rabbi. Many German officers who lived in Jewish homes, however, developed excellent relations with their hosts. An air force officer, Colonel Weber, who lived with Robert and Mimi Assael, even made a vain attempt to retrieve their confiscated radio.

In July 1942, the Germans took their first major action against the Jews. Itzhak Nehama gave the following testimony at the Eichmann trial in Jerusalem: "One day, July 11, 1942, they ordered all male Jews between the ages of eighteen to forty-five to assemble the next day, on Saturday, in the very large Liberation Square . . . about 9,000 showed up." Photos found after the war were shown to the witness: "Yes, that is the place, these are the people . . . They ordered us to exercise for hours. Whoever did not perform as the SS man wanted was beaten up until he fainted. Then water was poured on him and he was ordered back. It lasted from 8:00 a.m. until 2:30 p.m. There were German women on all the balconies around the place taking pictures. Whenever a Jew fainted and collapsed, the women applauded." Nehama was able to identify himself in one of the photographs. "This is me," he said, with understandable emotion, "bending my knees after six hours of exercises and all beaten up ... I was ill several weeks after that. For four days I was almost unconscious." The German women who took the pictures were actresses of the military theater Kraft Durch Freude. They had enormous fun observing the unfortunate Jews in the square, who were not allowed to cover their heads in the fierce sun. Many men died on the spot or succumbed a few days later from meningitis or cerebral hemorrhage.[53]

The U.S. Consul in Istanbul, Burton Berry, soon informed Washington about the events of that day:

> The people who were assembled in the square included those wounded on the Albanian front, without eyes, without arms, and without legs. At 8:00 a.m., SS officers began an inspection of the candidates for forced labor. They selected principally those persons who, from their bearing and appearance, were thought to

---

[53] Gideon Hausner, *Justice in Jerusalem* (New York, 1968), 127.

belong to the better classes. These victims were forced, under threat of being whipped or shot, to gaze fixedly at the hot July sun for minutes at a time, without being allowed to make the slightest movement, either of eyes or body. If anyone lowered his eyes or turned his gaze aside through sheer physical necessity, he was whipped until the blood ran . . . not content with the above outrages, the SS ordered their victims to go back to their homes and required them to run the first 150 meters or to go on all fours, turning somersaults or rolling in the dust. Packs of police dogs were set on mothers, wives, and children of the victims who were in the square and who could not keep from expressing their anguish by angry cries of protest.

Later in his report, he commented on the Jewish forced laborers: "The conditions of work were such that most of the laborers became ill and the output of the work was noticeably affected."[54]

While the Jews were singled out for this inhumane treatment, some Christians showed approval, but the great majority remained silent. There was no protest from the various unions in Thessaloniki. The University officially ignored the indignities forced upon its fellow citizens. Those Jews who were enrolled were given a numbered identity card. In a few days, the newspapers announced a call-up of 2,000 men for the first forced labor unit. Prior to their departure, they were sent to the Joseph Nissim School (a Jewish school) to be examined by non-Jewish physicians appointed by the medical society of Thessaloniki. "They were almost all considered suitable for work. They included even cardiac patients and invalids. Many physicians did not honor their Hippocratic oath."[55] Before departure, their hair was cut off, and they were given a bath and their clothes sterilized. In a

---

[54] Burton Berry, National Archives, dispatches Nos. 966 (R-885) of July 1943; No. 1085 (R992) of August 7, 1943; No. 1746 (R1618) of Nov. 11, 1943; No. 1823 (R1694) of Nov. 20, 1943; No. 2844 (R2642) of April 15, 1944; and No. 2917 (R2796) of April 29, 1944.

[55] Dr. J. A. Matarasso, ...and Yet All of Them Did Not Die (Athens, 1948), 24, translated by the author.

few days, however, they were filthy and swarming with body lice. On roads and airports and in mines, under the blistering summer sun, they labored on projects for which they were physically unprepared. They worked ten hours a day under strict supervision without adequate food, water, sanitation, and sleeping accommodations. They slept on the ground or in stables, and in a few weeks they were sick, exhausted, and unfit for work. The Jewish community mobilized its own physicians to help the inmates in the forced labor camps, but they worked without equipment, bandages, and medicines.

Many physicians suffered from malaria along with their patients. Many prisoners died from typhoid. The number of ill and demoralized increased with the number of conscripted Jews. Although laborers assigned to Italian military projects were treated humanely (and many were able to escape), those under German supervision suffered greatly. Some villagers sold food to the Jews at black market prices; a jacket for half a loaf of bread was not unusual. The German organization Todt treated its slaves so barbarously that many escaped; those who were recaptured were executed by firing squad.

A committee composed of Jewish attorney Yiomtov Yakouel, German contractor Johannes Miller, and General Labrano visited the forced labor camps, where they found that 60 percent of the working force was sick and 12 percent had died within two months. Those unfit for work were returned to Thessaloniki. One physician remembered the sick trying to support each other as they disembarked from the train. One fell to the ground weak from malaria; another, Pepo Beza, fell down dead. One wore only pants, another a jacket without sleeves. Others had no shoes because they had exchanged anything they could for food. All had numerous sores and lice. These were professors, merchants, and technicians, many of whom soon died after their return.

The condition of these forced laborers was dire, and a ransom was proposed to release the Jews. The German Commission sent their overseer, Johannes Miller, to the Jewish Community Committee with the offer to release the Jews from forced labor for the sum of three billion drachmas. German military administration lawyer Max Merten even signed a document that the Jews would not be disturbed for a year (that is, until September-October 1943) if the ransom was paid.

I. Events – The German Zone of Occupation

As a member of the committee, Rabbi Koretz was the liaison between the Germans and the community, and he played a leading role in the negotiations and collection of the ransom. When they were not able to collect the full sum, they had to sell the land of the ancient Jewish cemetery to complete the ransom. The Aristotle University of Thessaloniki currently stands on the site of the Jewish cemetery. Per Molho: "The Jews of Thessaloniki bled themselves white in order to pay the enormous ransom, and as soon as the last installment was paid, the Germans, in their usual manner, forgot their written promise, and in violation of their signature began other savage measures."[56]

Maurice Chaim, a resistance hero who died fighting after his escape from the Leptocaria slave labor camp, composed this dirge:

> During the cold nights
> And until dawn
> We sigh, plunged into our dreams of happiness
> The sweet dreams, die at dawn
> Oh! If it were possible for one to die also.
>
> We leave with ploughs and picks
> We march, we march
> Birds with amputated wings
> with hearts bitter like bile.
>
> In Leptocaria we dig, we dig
> a soil—hard, ungrateful
> The tenacious hunger gnaws us.
> She buried her children.
>
> The community promises, promises to help us
> Is it to send us burial coffins?
> Bodies of superb youth
> Who have barely blossomed
> Melt like wax.

---

[56] Molho, op. cit., 76.

In the cloudy sky, Oh God of kindness
Sad witness.

Consoler of solitude
Revive the hope
Rose with thorns of pain
Oh God of kindness
Sad witness.

— *"The Song of the Slaves of Leptocaria"*

In August 1942, the Germans invited the Jewish community of Thessaloniki to give a Jewish burial to an executed Jew. Within a few hours, members of the community witnessed the incongruous spectacle of a German honor guard presenting arms while a rabbi gave last rites to a man about to be executed by a German firing squad. He was a Czechoslovakian Jew who had volunteered for the German army and was sentenced after his true identity was discovered.[57]

At the end of 1942, the Germans and their Greek collaborators began the systematic looting of Jewish merchandise and confiscation of shops and warehouses. On February 2, 1943, they confiscated the Albo factory, the wealthiest in northern Greece, and the enterprises Navarro, Amaratji, Tiano, Matalon, Bernardout, Levi, Kohen, and Kapon, among others. The stolen merchandise was worth at least four million gold francs. On March 3, the Germans also confiscated the Chaim Benroubi Company, the biggest glassware and porcelain house in the Balkans, worth many million gold francs; it took an entire month for German trucks to empty its contents. The owners were imprisoned and released only after they signed documents stating the voluntary donation of their fortunes to strangers. During this period, many wealthy Jews left Thessaloniki. In October 1942, Houter, who was in charge of Jewish affairs in Berlin, complained to Joachim von Ribbentrop that because of the regulations issued by the German military administration Max Merten and the Greek Vasilis Simeonides in Thessaloniki,

---

57 Ibid.

I. Events – The German Zone of Occupation

many wealthy Jews were abandoning the German zone to find asylum in the Italian zone.[58]

Consul Berry recounted what happened next:

> Not content with attacking the living Jews of Thessaloniki, the Germans found means and excuses to attack the dead also. One fine morning the Jewish community was invited to send representatives to a commission which had been set up to expropriate the Jewish cemetery. Jews living in Thessaloniki were allowed to carry away the remains of their dear ones if they arrived in time. We want to draw attention to the fact that the Thessaloniki cemetery was of the greatest historical value, dating from the first centuries of the Christian era. There were in this cemetery very ancient grave stones with very important inscriptions. Workers set about dismantling the tombs and disinterring the dead. The work of destroying the cemetery was done in such haste that very few Jews succeeded in finding the remains of their families and relatives. Recently buried dead were thrown to the dogs.

The late Rabbi Michael Molho spent considerable effort to document the thousands of epitaphs written on the headstones dating back to the 15th century. The cemetery had over 300,000 marble memorials (mostly 2.5 x 1.2 meters and 20 centimeters thick). The remains of renowned rabbis, judges, writers, teachers, and politicians were placed in appropriate urns for reburial in a new cemetery. All gold dental work and jewelry were removed and entrusted to the safekeeping of a committee of Jewish teachers. This gold was supposed to help finance construction of a new cemetery, but it was confiscated by the Germans during the deportations. Thousands of marble tombstones were reused on sidewalks, in courtyards in front of many churches, and even in the bathroom of a public school on Philikis Etairias Street and in a swimming pool. Two elderly rabbis, the scribe Abraham Mitsi and the kindly Solomon Matalon, supervised the rituals in the Jewish cemetery; both had little education. The Germans gave them plenty of food and

---

58 Enepekidis, op. cit.

did not shave their beards. They were also exempt from all work. Their only duty was to sign the certificates that declared the Jews were well treated and lacked nothing.

In January 1943, Adolf Eichmann, Chief of the Jewish Affairs Bureau of the SS, appointed Rolf Gunther to "negotiate the Jewish affairs" in Thessaloniki. A few days later Dieter Wisliceny, a native of East Prussia and a lawyer, arrived from Bratislava with orders to replace Gunther. Wisliceny's orders were "to effect the removal of the Jews from the area of Thessaloniki," a task estimated to take six to eight weeks. Wisliceny was to work with the German Military Government of Macedonia. Another of Eichmann's assistants, Alois Brunner, was entrusted with the technical execution of all operations in Greece. By February 1943, both had arrived in Thessaloniki.[59]

A key person in the unfolding drama was Rabbi Tzevi Koretz. He was an Ashkinazi Jew from Berlin who was invited by the local community to serve as the chief Rabbi of Thessaloniki in 1933 and eventually became president of the Jewish community. He gradually became a controversial figure at odds with the local Jewish leaders. He became the lead negotiator with the Germans regarding the ransom of the Jews sent to forced labor, and he believed that if they all complied with the German orders, they would not be further harmed. Some accuse him of being a weak leader and blame him for the tragedy that befell Thessaloniki.

In his defense, Gitta Koretz, the rabbi's widow, argued his innocence after the war. A short and revealing biography was sent to me in 1975:

> The Rabbi was an intellectual and not a resistance leader. He was a specialist in Oriental studies. He spoke Polish, Yiddish, German, French, English, Hebrew, Ladino, and Greek fluently. He was a devoted religious leader who loved the Jews of Thessaloniki. In 1941 the mayor of Athens, Kotzias, invited Rabbi Koretz and his family to follow the important Greeks who went to Egypt. "Come with us," he told him. "If you

---

59 Ibid.

I. Events – The German Zone of Occupation

remain here with the Germans, you will see many bitter days." The Rabbi replied, "I thank you. My place is here and I can't even think of leaving.

Gitta Koretz insists that her husband did not know what would happen to those who were deported and felt that the best solution was "to obey the Germans."[60]

On February 8, 1943, the recently appointed president of the community, Rabbi Koretz, was summoned to the Gestapo. After a two-hour meeting, he emerged pale and depressed, having been informed that the Nuremberg laws were to be applied, which meant marking the Jews with the Star of David and ghettoization. The following orders appeared in the local newspapers:

1. All Jews residing in Thessaloniki—with the exception of Jews of foreign nationality who possess a valid passport—are obliged immediately to wear a sign that they are Jews. Their shops or offices should also have visible signs in German and Greek with the inscription *"Jüdisches Geschäft"* ("Jewish shop").
2. All Jews residing in Thessaloniki, with the exception of the above mentioned, have to move their residence without delay into a special quarter of the city.
3. All expenses incurred as a result of the above measures will be the responsibility of each Jew. The community will pay the expenses of those who are unable to do so as a form of charity.[61]

In another order dated February 12, 1943, the specification for the Star of David was described:

1. The distinguishing sign consists of a six-pointed star with a ten cm. diameter in the color yellow. It will be worn on the chest on the left side, close to the position of the heart, on the outside garments. It must be visible in all kinds of weather. The sign will be worn

---

[60] Letter to the author from Mrs. Gitta Koretz, 1975, 45 pages. This material was donated to the Museum of Jewish Heritage in New York.

[61] Enepekidis, op. cit.

by all Jews above the age of five. It should be worn even while they are inside their homes.

2. A person is considered a Jew if:

    a) He is a descendant of three generations of Jews.

    b) He is the product of a mixed marriage, has two Jewish ancestors, and he belonged to the Mosaic faith.

    c) Abandonment of the Jewish religion, no matter when it took place, does not exempt one from the sign.

    d) A Jew who is married to a Christian is not exempt even if he converted to Christianity.

    e) Children produced as a result of such marriages are considered Jews unless they were baptized prior to April 1941. The Aryan members of a family remain Aryan, while the Jewish ones have to comply with the regulations.

    f) Applications for exemptions from the sign are unnecessary.

Three Jews who were married to German women were not obliged to wear the Star of David or live in the ghetto. Max Merten also exempted Maurice Raphael, who was married to a French woman. When this became known, other Jews took advantage of this mild interpretation of the regulations. Sixteen Jews who were married to Christians ignored all German anti-Jewish regulations and survived the war, except for three who were arrested and deported to Poland.

On February 13, 1943, the Jews were informed of the following:

    1. We remind all Jews that it is forbidden to change domicile without permission. Whoever disregards this order will be considered a deserter and will be executed on the spot when he is arrested.

I. Events – The German Zone of Occupation

2. It is forbidden for Jews to use a tramway or other means of transportation. This prohibition is put into effect immediately.

3. It is forbidden for Jews to be in the streets, squares or public places after sunset.

4. It is forbidden for Jews to use private or public telephones. The Jews are obligated to return their telephones to the telephone company and pay their bills.

5. It is forbidden for Jews to sell or transfer their belongings.

6. Any citizen who purchases or safeguards items belonging to Jews will be severely punished.

7. Foreign Jews are exempt from the above order.

8. Only members of the Community Council and Jewish doctors are allowed to use telephones.[62]

The above orders were published in the newspapers and also announced from the pulpit of the Beth Saoul Synagogue by Rabbi Koretz, who tried to persuade his congregation to "obey the orders with self-discipline." He assured the Jews that the German authorities had pledged no further measures against them. The once proud Jews of Thessaloniki bent their heads, distressed and humiliated, and continued their normal work routines.

The Stars of David were made in record time and distributed to the people together with their new identity cards. Each star carried a number; the first thousand were reserved for the members of the Community Council and all those who collaborated with the Germans in the application of their racist policy. These numbers, according to rumor, defined the "privileged ones." (Rabbi Koretz was given the number "1.")

---

62 FDRL, War Refugee Board, Container No. 26.

This rumor encouraged the envy of the vast majority, who felt insulted by the Star and worried that wearing it would provoke the irony and laughter of the Christians. They soon realized that the Christians were either indifferent or felt sorry for them.

On March 1, 1943, the Germans demanded that the Jews declare all their assets: real estate, stocks, jewelry, rugs, kitchen utensils, furniture, money, and any other possessions. The head of the family had to present his declaration in duplicate; heavy penalties were imposed for false declarations. Everyone, even porters and stevedores, complied with the new order. The Germans, it is believed, never paid any attention to the avalanche of paperwork deposited in the basement of the Bank Amar. Their purpose was to keep the Jews busy and in doubt about their future. Under threat of prison or even death, the Greek Jews of Thessaloniki received new orders, studied them, quarreled among themselves over the interpretation of each point, and hoped that each order would be the last. They were in total isolation from the rest of Europe and completely ignorant of what was happening in other Jewish communities.

The Germans justified their regulations as either security measures or statistical studies. For example, a new order began: "This declaration is of a statistical nature. A special form has to be used issued by the Community Council." In the description of all jewelry, the order excluded wedding rings! In its detailed manner, it requested the description of ducks or dogs in Jewish possession; even the contents of each room had to be enumerated separately. A committee of Jewish bank employees was formed to commence its statistical work. Rumors were circulated that the real German purpose was to apply a special tax on the Jews; some people had heard that a similar measure had taken place in Bulgaria. Rare were those who submitted inaccurate declarations. Traitors were ready to denounce anyone, and German collaborators were ready to blackmail individuals.[63]

By March 25, 1943, all Jews were to be restricted to specific areas of Thessaloniki. The poor neighborhoods were already

---

63 Many of the events which took place in Thessaloniki during the German occupation were described to me by Daniel Carasso of Randallstown, Maryland.

I. Events – The German Zone of Occupation

considered ghettos. Two other zones included the area of Exohi and the center of the city. Each family took minimal necessities and moved. Three, four, and sometimes up to six families occupied one apartment. The congestion was great, and the hygienic conditions deplorable. The Germans again assured the Jewish leadership communal autonomy. All Jewish apartments were marked, and the Christians who resided in the same neighborhood were allowed to remain. The word "ghetto" never appeared in the German orders. Everything was done to give the Jews a false sense of security. Still, some Jews felt that this was but the prelude of yet another German-planned mass exile of the Jewish population. Many people escaped Thessaloniki and tried to go to Athens. Some disguised themselves as railway workers, others as villagers or porters. Some hid themselves in barrels and arrived in Athens by truck.

The Germans did not appreciate Jewish escapes. They threatened to execute hostages, but Rabbi Koretz persuaded them not to take such drastic measures and promised total submission, obedience, and discipline. This, he declared, was the only way to obtain German leniency. On March 5, Rabbi Koretz made the following appeal:

> We appeal to all our coreligionists to maintain their calmness and self-discipline. We ask them not to panic and to believe in rumors, which are all baseless. Everyone should continue his work and should have confidence in the leaders of the community.

The Germans continued to feed the rabbi with false information about the future functions of the autonomous democratic Jewish city. The Council subsequently had long meetings dealing with the organization of the "autonomous Jewish republic." Meanwhile, its building on Sarantaporou Street was always filled with people who walked up and down aimlessly. Nobody thought of work anymore since, on March 6, the Germans ordered the ghettos closed, and the great majority of Jewish shops were outside the ghettos.[64]

---

64 Matarasso, ... *Kai omos oloi tous den pethanan*, 39.

The Baron Hirsch Camp

The Hirsch neighborhood of Thessaloniki had been established by Baron Maurice de Hirsch at the beginning of the century to shelter the victims of the Kishinev and Mogilev pogroms. It contained 2,315 Jews, all Greeks, since the original inhabitants had long since left or died from malaria. The Germans enclosed this area with a tall wooden wall reinforced with a barbed wire fence, one of whose three guarded exits led to the railroad station. A sign forbade entrance to non-Jews. A day later Jews were not allowed to exit the neighborhood.[65]

The Judenordner

Rabbi Koretz invited Robert Assael (then aged 43) to his home and asked him to be one of the leaders of the new Jewish police. As he explained the work to him, Assael exclaimed, "But this means doing things against our people!"

"You are a coward," the rabbi said.

"History will show who the coward is," Assael replied. He left without another word. Mrs. Koretz accompanied him to the door and apologized for the scene.[66] A Jewish police force of 250 men commanded by Jacques Alballa and assisted by Jewish former officers and noncommissioned officers of the Greek army was subsequently formed. It included members of that Jewish refugee group whom the Germans had treated well and had preserved precisely for this collaborative task. The Jewish police wore a yellow armband with the word "*Judenordner.*" Obedient servants of the Germans who treated the people with kindness were severely beaten by their masters. Still, almost all of them assisted invalids and the aged without objection from the Germans. Rabbi Koretz and Jacques Alballa did their best to effect the German orders. The Community Council never objected to the spirit of cooperation

---

65 Molho, *In Memoriam*, 95.

66 In 1968, Robert and Mimi Assael were our friends. They lived in Washington, DC in an apartment over a liquor store. On the day of the riots after the assassination of Martin Luther King, Jr, I asked them to leave their house immediately and come to our house in Maryland, which they did.

I. Events – The German Zone of Occupation

that Rabbi Koretz imposed on them. Afraid of German reprisals, they thought that obedience was the most sensible course. Rabbi Koretz told the people: "Don't be afraid. We will recreate our community in Krakow. Obey the German orders and regulations. Do not abandon the ghetto!" Even so, hundreds of Jews from Thessaloniki continued to escape, for they anticipated that deportation meant death for the aged, the invalids, and the children and women who were not used to the cold climate of Poland.

Jews are known for their optimism, and soon a new song became popular. Sung to the lovely tune of the Mexican song "Vaya Con Dios," its first line was "Oloi mazi stin Polonia!" ("Let's all go together to Poland."). Many Jews, including Mimi Assael, bought warm clothes, woolen hats, and scarves. The sister of Emilio Neri, who was a secretary in the Italian consulate in Thessaloniki, offered to help Mrs. Assael escape. She refused rather than allow her and her husband's parents to go alone to Poland. "Who will help them there?" she replied.

In the meantime, hundreds of Jewish volunteers were at work preparing directories with names, ages and addresses, and lists of real estate and other statistics, including the inventories and catalogues that the Germans demanded. On March 15, 1943, all Jewish assets were confiscated. The Germans prepared the groundwork for the demoralization of the people, but they wanted to be sure that there would be no resistance from their victims. They forced the community to supply 102 respected people as hostages, who were threatened with execution if there were any disobedience or sabotage. Activity in the community offices was continuous, day and night without interruption. Everything had to be finished on time and in perfect order. The number of volunteers on the different committees and subcommittees was increased. Soon hundreds of the best-qualified men, those who could be the natural leaders of their people, were forced to spend all their energy processing meaningless papers. The atmosphere was tense, and a continuous war of nerves kept them in a constant state of agitation.

Rabbi Koretz galvanized this mass; he yelled, he got angry, he was present everywhere. He was obstinate, dictatorial, hard, vengeful, abrupt. He accepted neither advice nor suggestions from anybody. He received the German orders and enforced them with a determination resulting in their prompt and exact execution. Did he do that in order to gain personal favors, or did he want to persuade the Germans that the Jews too liked order and discipline, that they were indefatigable and sincere, and so in a naive way hoped to disarm their hate? Thus, the Jewish community leaders failed in their task to help save their people.[67]

In the meantime, Brunner, assisted by his traitors, applied all his efforts to extract information as to hidden treasures. Every wealthy Jew was forced to appear in front of this committee. The Armenian interpreter Agop Boudourian, who had been helped by Jews to make a living as a tobacco merchant before the war, was now the "expert." He could point out the rich Jews who had gold, foreign currency, precious carpets, or jewelry. He also participated in the torture of the victims. Soon thousands of carpets, along with boxes of jewelry and boxes of gold, passed from their hands. The villa on Velissariou Street was stocked with valuables of all kinds, destined for transfer in German cars, trains, and airplanes to Germany.

Panic enveloped the community. Each family thought of its own problems. It was too late to escape; their love for each other and their desire not to abandon their aged parents or grandparents paralyzed them into inaction. Even if they decided to escape, money was needed to pay a Christian to lead them out of the city. They had to trust that this intermediary was an honest patriot and not a collaborator who would betray them. In addition, the need for living expenses after the successful escape discouraged the many poor. There was also danger: six escapees were arrested and executed. Yet several Jewish youths, such as Sam Broudo, son of Rabbi Broudo of Thessaloniki, and Moissis Bourla, a lawyer, were in love with Christian girls who hid them.

EAM sent one of its leaders to Rabbi Koretz to inform him that EAM was ready and able to help in the salvation of the Jews.[68] Rabbi Koretz and his advisers, already servile organs of the Germans, could not contemplate any form of resistance. EAM pleaded with the Jews, asking them not to follow German orders and to leave the city. Resistance newspapers and

---

67 Ibid., 152.
68 Joseph Matsas, letter to the author, Nov.12, 1975.

pamphlets also threatened any traitors with severe punishment. An appeal was addressed to the Greek prime minister by 150 lawyers who pleaded with him to try everything possible to save the Jews: "If exile is unavoidable, insist that the Jews be interned on an Aegean island.[69]

Italians Who Helped

The Italian consul in Thessaloniki, Mr. Zambani, a fascist who admired the Germans, was not respected by his subordinates. His second-in-command was Mr. Rosenberg, a brave and sincere man, who along with his colleagues, Mr. Stabile and Emilio Neri, son-in-law of former Consul Dolfini, who had been dismissed for his anti-fascist views, were determined to save as many Jews as possible. Captain Merci, the Italian liaison to German headquarters, was also part of the rescue group.

Many Jews, hiding in secret places, pursued by traitors and German agents, waited patiently for the day when Emilio Neri's car would take them from Thessaloniki to Plati where an Italian military train would transport them to Athens. The fascist Zambani was replaced by Giuseppe Castrucci, an experienced diplomat, a noble person and a dedicated anti-fascist. Castrucci issued many certificates verifying Italian nationality to Jewish Italian women, their Greek-Jewish husbands and their dependent children. Even men aged 35 were considered as "dependent." Whoever could claim even the most distant family relationship with Italian Jews was saved. People who had similar names to those who were Italians received passports. The Gestapo, which had to approve these passports and release the captive Jews, was furious but had no choice. The Italians were still their allies.

Thirty families were allowed to travel to Athens under Italian protection. Italian officers presented Jewish women as their wives and escorted them to the safety of the Italian zone, after which they returned to their duty in Thessaloniki. When the Jews who reached Larissa presented themselves at Italian headquarters identified as Jewish refugees, the Italians sent

---

69 *Chronika*, Athens, April 1982, 6.

them to Athens on board military trains and even provided them with food. Others escaped with the aid of Greek Christians who stripped them of all their possessions and abandoned them. Some delivered Jews to the Germans; others helped them join the resistance.

Meanwhile, life in the ghetto and especially in the Baron Hirsch camp was becoming increasingly dreadful. Joseph Nehama recalled:

> It was full of dirt and lice . . . when we were told we were going to Poland to settle near Krakow to form our own community there, I said we would go . . . We were even given Polish money in exchange for our Greek drachmas. People were told to take their umbrellas with them because it was raining and snowing there . . . Had I really known what was actually awaiting us, I would have preferred to die on the spot . . . We were sent to Auschwitz.[70]

Consul Berry reported to Washington:

> Every Jew was given a form upon which he was ordered to write a complete inventory of his possessions, stating the value of all objects listed and including items which would ordinarily be considered of no value, such as pet dogs. The next day these lists had to be turned in. The Jews could see no reason for the inventories, since the SS troops paid no attention to those that were submitted but instead seized every bit of property of all Greek Jews, regardless of value.
>
> Houses were emptied, the contents carted away in trucks, and the owners were taken to the Baron Hirsch camp. Articles of value were sent to Germany, while a collection of worthless objects was stored in warehouses.
>
> A zone of fifty meters wide was established around the camp, which no Jew could enter upon any pretext whatsoever. They reinforced the guard of that section

---

70 Gideon Hausner, *Justice in Jerusalem*, 127. Testimony of Joseph Nehama.

I. Events – The German Zone of Occupation

of the city [with] SS troops and Jewish policemen. One of these policemen was shot on the spot by an SS trooper because he was seen to reply to a question asked by a member of the International Red Cross.

Suddenly it became known that 300 railway cars were ready at the station. The Jews were to be deported. Rabbi Koretz and those members of the Community Council present signed a declaration stating that the Jewish community voluntarily offered the Germans fifty percent of all their assets, including real estate, to suspend the deportations. The rabbi took the proposal to the German chief, Max Merten. Twenty-four hours later, Merten informed Rabbi Koretz that the deportations could not be stopped. He stated, "The Greek organizations of Thessaloniki had flooded Berlin with appeals demanding the removal of the Jews, and the Germans had to bow to this pressure." Since no Greek organizations ever sent such an appeal, Merten's reply was but another German lie.

The Germans knew there would be no buyers for stolen Jewish real estate. The BBC, which made no effort to warn Jews about their predicament, had broadcasted a warning that any real estate transfer would not be recognized after the liberation. (Indeed, after the war all real estate transactions were reevaluated by the courts, and the sale price readjusted or the property returned to the seller.) Salvator Kounio, in anticipation of the German looting of Jewish fortunes, sold his photography supply shop at 15 Venizelou Street to a Christian. The transfer was made in a legal way, but the date was altered to sometime before such sales became illegal. Someone betrayed him to the Germans, who arrested him together with his German-Jewish wife and two teenage children. They were transferred to the Hirsch camp and deported to Auschwitz. Among the thousands of deported Greek-Jewish families, they were the only family of which all members survived and were reunited after the war. Another family, the Salems, gave some Persian carpets to a Christian friend for safekeeping. The Germans arrested them; they too had been betrayed. While everyone was collecting their belongings for the long trip, Mrs. Salem took her jewelry box and slipped out into the street. She was understandably excited and afraid, and yet determined not to let the Germans steal everything she had. A young man was passing by. She ran to him and in a desperate, pleading voice, asked in Ladino, "Are you also a Jew?"

The man, Solomon Ouziel, taken by surprise and realizing the seriousness of the situation, replied, "Yes, what can I do for you?"

Mrs. Salem gave him the box and said, "Give this jewelry to my daughter, Lena Salem in Athens." Relieved by her desperate act, she returned home to her family and captors. These two families, Kounio and Salem, were the only wealthy Jews in the Hirsch camp when the deportations began. The remainder were the poorest in the city and the first to be deported.[71]

Important Conversation between Archbishop Damaskinos and Ambassador Günther Altenburg

The Jews of Thessaloniki sent heartbreaking appeals to Archbishop Damaskinos in Athens, pleading with him to intercede on their behalf. According to the biography of Damaskinos by Elias Venezis, the heroic archbishop met with Ambassador Günther Altenburg and asked him to stop the inhumane and anti-Christian measures. Altenburg replied that these measures could not be stopped and, on the contrary, *would expand to the rest of Greece* (emphasis by author). All Greek Jews would go to Poland, while Jews of other nationalities would go to their countries of origin. The archbishop asked, "Why would the Italian Jews go to Italy, the Spanish Jews to Spain, but the Greek Jews to Poland?"

Altenburg was uncomfortable with the question but replied, "They go to Poland to work."

The archbishop asked, "If they go to Poland to work, why do you send the women, the children, and the elderly?" The German representative replied, "Because it is cruel to separate the members of each family. They will live better if the entire family is deported."[72]

---

[71] Robert and Mimi Assael gave the stories of Salem to me.

[72] Elias Venezis, "Archbishop Damaskinos," *Chronika*, Athens, April 1982, chapter 34, 3.

I. Events – The German Zone of Occupation

The moment I read the words, "...these measures would expand to the rest of Greece," I felt as if I was witnessing a judge pronouncing a death sentence for all my relatives without the possibility of an appeal.

The First Transport

On Sunday, March 14, 1943, at 11:00 a.m., Rabbi Koretz, following German orders, went to the synagogue in the Baron Hirsch quarter and addressed the congregation. He announced their imminent deportation to Krakow. The people accepted the news with despair, tears, and prayers. The rabbi maintained his composure and tried to console them. He assured them that the great community of Krakow (not knowing it was already destroyed), "will look after our settlement there. Every one of us will find work according to his desire, ability, knowledge, and experience." Survivors later testified that documents granting land in the Ukraine were shown to the inmates of the Hirsch camp. The head of each family had to go to the bank and exchange Greek drachmas for Polish zlotys. Gold and precious items could not be transferred to Krakow; they had to be surrendered to the camp offices. Many threw their gold and jewelry down the toilets. The deportees in the first transports to Auschwitz were forced to send attractive postcards depicting a fictitious Waldsee to their relatives in Thessaloniki.[73]

On March 15, the entire Hirsch population was placed in railway cars. The Jewish police searched all the rooms to make sure no one was missed. Two thousand four hundred Jews were pushed and urged to hurry lest they miss the train. Sixty or seventy were forced into cars which normally held but forty. Mothers searched for their children—two, four, sometimes even eight. They counted them and tried to keep them close, their eyes filled with tears. The Germans treated everyone who was slow with bestiality. The sick, the insane, invalids from the Albanian war, orphans, old people—all of these ceased to be individual human beings and in a few minutes were reduced to a flock of creatures deprived of their human rights. The Hirsch

---

73 Molho, *In Memoriam*, 154.

quarter did not remain empty for long; it was quickly refilled with Jews rounded up from other neighborhoods. When these were deported, new groups of exiles replaced them.

A Jewish policeman, Mois Saltiel, a few days before his execution, described the incredible attitude of a German during the arrest of a Jewish family. Like a true barbarian, the soldier woke the children early in the morning and forced them to get ready. His ferocious manner suddenly disappeared when he saw a cage with a little canary. His voice became kind and sweet. "The poor canary will be left alone in this house," he said. He took the cage and went out into the street in search of a Christian house to shelter it. Then he returned to the Jewish roundup. A typical arrest was thus described:

> At 5:00 a.m. the neighborhood was surrounded by German soldiers, Greek and Jewish policemen. They knocked at the doors, checked the list of Jews, and compared it with the people they arrested. Anyone who was slow in getting out of the house received insults and blows. Children and the aged were placed in carriages while the others walked. As soon as they left the houses, German trucks entered the neighborhood and everything of value—furniture, rugs, paintings, linens, utensils, etc.—was loaded into them. Since the neighborhoods were not exclusively Jewish, the Christians observed the proceedings from their windows, balconies, or doorsteps. Some felt sorry for what they saw.[74]

Many other Christians, however, were glad for the opportunity to scavenge Jewish goods once the German looting ended. Others demonstrated their human compassion by saying, "Now the place is clean without them" or "The Germans did very well." Some passing Italian officers looked with contempt at their German comrades in arms but were unable to intervene in favor of the victims. Kind Christian civilians threw supplies and useful items to the deported Jews, who gratefully picked them up. Dimitrios Spiliakos and Peter Levi helped many individual Jews and also protested the anti-

---

[74] Matarasso, *And Yet Not All of Them Died,* 49. (Greek)

I. Events – The German Zone of Occupation

Jewish measures by going directly to the office of the Greek governor-general and German collaborator Simeonidis. They were joined in their endeavors on behalf of the Jews by their colleagues, attorneys Dimitris Dingas and Professor Vizoukidis. Simeonidis, the highest Greek official in Thessaloniki, told them, "We want to remove the thorns from your garden, and you protest?" These brave men went to Metropolitan Gennadios, to whom they submitted an appeal to help the Jews. This religious leader and brave humanitarian then visited Max Merten and pleaded in the name of Jesus Christ for "clemency and magnanimity" toward the Jews.

Archbishop Damaskinos. He issued a formal protest against the deportations of the Jews of Greece. (Source: Kessel archive via CC0)

Archbishop Damaskinos and the presidents of 42 Greek organizations, foundations and unions sent an appeal to the Greek prime minister protesting the violation of the Capitulation Agreement, which stipulated that all Greek citizens were to be treated equally, regardless of religion or race. They insisted that if an imaginary danger indeed threatened the army of occupation, then only young Jewish males should be sent to a specified area of Greece. The appeal ended with a threat against the Greek government of occupation: "The nation one day will examine the actions of its leaders and notice whether they failed to condemn the deportation of the Israelites."

It was not until 1988 that the well-known actor of the Greek National Theater, Theodoros Moridis, revealed the inside story of Archbishop Damaskinos's letter of protest:

> During the period of the German occupation, representatives of the various professions used to meet in secret in the offices of Archbishop Damaskinos in order to study the different problems the occupation presented. One day we were informed that George Politis's wife, a Jewish woman well known to us, asked to be present in our clandestine meeting. She came and pleaded with the archbishop and the representatives of the various organizations for assistance for her coreligionists, whom the Germans had begun to arrest. It was a heartbreaking presentation. As soon as she departed, we all decided to protest in writing. Our great poet, Angelos Sikelianos, offered to compose the statement, and a committee of three men, Angelos Sikelianos, George Karantzas, president of the newspaper editors, and I, representing the union of Greek actors, undertook the dangerous mission of delivering the protest to Prime Minister Logothetopoulos, who in turn would present it to the German commander. This was done in a couple of hours. The office of the prime minister was near the office of the archbishop. Our document was not just a written protest by Archbishop Damaskinos, it was a written protest of 42 deans and presidents of organizations who met under the chairmanship of Archbishop Damaskinos. It was a protest by the totality of citizens of Athens, perhaps the only one made in a German occupied territory of Europe, and this I believe has a unique and profound meaning.[75]

Many prominent Jews of Thessaloniki had moved to Athens between the start of the war and the period of the

---

[75] Theodoros Moridis, "The Inside Story of the Damaskinos Letter of Protest," *Kathimerini*, July 19, 1988; reprinted in *Chronika*, September 1988, 23.

I. Events – The German Zone of Occupation

deportations in Thessaloniki. They, together with Athenian Jews and Christians, tried to persuade the Greek government to try to prevent the deportations. They proposed the following different suggestions and fallback positions:

1. To consider the Jews as political prisoners and move them to Peloponnesus or to an island under Italian occupation.
2. To exile only persons between the ages of 18 and 45 who were capable of work.
3. To exile only men between the ages of 11 and 60, and allow women, children, and old people to remain in their homes or in an area occupied by the Italians.
4. To exile only the inhabitants of the poor working neighborhoods if the Germans considered these areas dangerous to their occupation forces.
5. If all the above suggestions were rejected, then place children below the age of ten under the protection of the International Red Cross. These could be placed with Christian families or with Jewish families possessing Italian or Spanish citizenship."[76]

Greek Prime Minister Logothetopoulos not only failed to protect his Jewish citizens, but, as he confessed to an important Greek political figure, he was in favor of the deportations because Thessaloniki and other Greek cities would then have plenty of vacant houses to shelter Christian refugees from the Bulgarian menace in Thrace and Macedonia. The suspicion that the Greek government was in favor of the deportations is supported by the fact that abandoned Jewish property was treated in the same way as that of enemy aliens residing in Greece. Also, abandoned Jewish property was put under the administration of a committee of refugees from the Bulgarian zone.

In order to prove to the Greek nation that this suspicion was not true, it was suggested to the Greek government that it demand an immediate suspension of the deportations or resign in protest. The appeal which offered this honorable alternative to the government was signed by the leaders of all the nation's

---

[76] Molho, *In Memoriam*, 134.

political parties. Logothetopoulos was forced to make a symbolic but meaningless gesture to save the Jews. He sent a confidential report to the German ambassador, Altenburg, dated March 18, 1943, in which he described the terrible events which had occurred in the Baron Hirsch camp as follows:

> According to the latest reports, the first transport of the Greek citizens forcibly removed from their native soil took place on Monday. They departed under truly dramatic circumstances and were led to an unknown destination. As I explained to you a few days ago, it is natural for the Greek people to be anxious about the fate of tens of thousands of law-abiding and peaceful compatriots, who until now have faithfully served their Greek homeland and shed their blood for it in the recent war period.[77]

This letter alone could not stop the Germans.

The Jewish population, which had trusted its religious and community leaders, realized its mistake. Many people openly accused Rabbi Koretz for his attitude, which had facilitated the application of anti-Jewish measures. They condemned their leaders for servility and more-than-necessary willingness to comply with the German orders, for failure to anticipate the German intentions, and for discouraging resistance and escape. On March 17, Rabbi Koretz spoke to a crowd of Jews who overflowed the synagogue of Monastirioton in hopes of hearing some message of salvation. He said, "The times are tragic and difficult. Have patience and courage." He continued by complimenting the rich who helped the poor. He commented on the good personal appearance of the people and the favorable impression they would make among the Jews who would welcome them in Poland. His audience shouted him down in their impatience. They called him a traitor and accused him of selling out to the Germans. He was forced to leave the synagogue protected by a cordon of Jewish police.

Declassified American documents reveal that the United States was promptly informed about the deportations by a

---

[77] Nora Levin, *The Holocaust*, 520.

I. Events – The German Zone of Occupation

secret agent: "The property of all Jews is being confiscated. They are being arrested and sent to Krakow via Gevgeli, irrespective of age and health. They are allowed to take 15 kilos of foodstuffs, but are not allowed to take any money." Agent "Z" reported that "all the property of the Jewish community of Thessaloniki is managed by the Bank of Thessaloniki, formerly a Jewish bank taken over by the Germans in 1941, and now subordinate to the Reichsbank."[78]

The EAM group of the University of Thessaloniki created a mechanism to direct Jewish students to partisan territories.[79] They also helped many families escape south to the Italian zone. The prewar Metaxas dictatorship had deprived and persecuted the community of leaders from the aggressive leftist Jewish organizations. These leaders later fell victim to the Germans, who showed great preference in executing Jews in their reprisals for partisan actions. Despite the fact that it took a long time for the Jews of Thessaloniki to realize they should not trust the Germans or their own leaders, it is estimated that approximately 3,400 people managed to escape. By that time, however, escape was fraught with danger.

Mois Saltiel, the Jewish policeman who told the story of the German who loved birds, conceived of a scheme which, if successful, would have enabled him to save all his relatives. He found a coffin and a pushcart. Eight or nine members of his family were dressed in black and carried their false Christian identity cards. They formed a funeral procession and attempted to leave the city. At one intersection, an inquisitive German guard realized the truth. The entire group was arrested, summarily tried, and executed.

Many rumors circulate in times of crisis. The latest rumor in Thessaloniki was that all old people belonging to prominent families would not be deported but remain in a home for the aged. Robert Assael, who did not believe there were any Jews in Krakow to welcome them, received this latest rumor with joy. His father, Mois Assael, aged 93, was a member of the Community Council of the city of Thessaloniki and a vice president of the Greek Red Cross. He definitely qualified to

---

78 National Archives, No. 758148, translated by myself from Greek.

79 Joseph Matsas, lecture in Greek. English version in *Journal of the Hellenic Diaspora*, Vol. 17.1 (1991), 55-58. Matsas was a partisan of ELAS.

stay in a home for the aged. Once he no longer felt obligated to stay with his elderly father, Assael decided that he was free to try to save himself and his wife Mimi. He contacted Emilio Neri and accepted his invitation to move into his beautiful home. The Assaels were not the first Jews Mr. Neri, a civilized and gallant man, helped. Rene Gatenio was already hiding in his house; he had hidden Dr. Siaki and his wife, daughter and mother-in-law in another house; and he had also sent the Abrabanel family to safety. At the same time, Mr. Neri was in the process of saving others. A Greek friend of Mr. Neri provided the Assaels with false identity cards in the names of George and Maria Komninos. In return, he was given some money and a wristwatch. While the Neris were out during the day, the three Jews stayed in their house with instructions not to open the door or answer the telephone unless the telephone rang and stopped twice. Then, on the third ring, they could answer, and it would be their friend Solomon Ouziel, the young man who had Mrs. Salem's jewels. Ouziel would help them eventually as he was an Italian citizen with freedom to move about the city. He went to Athens, where he delivered to Lena Salem her mother's jewelry.

Dr. Kuenka was an official of the Red Cross. He was granted certain privileges, such as living outside the ghetto, not wearing the Star of David, and owning a telephone. Many times he was observed talking with the German consul in Thessaloniki. The Germans decided to arrest him in total secrecy; agents of the SS intelligence service (SD) entered his house during the day and hid in the basement. After Dr. Kuenka and his wife secured the door with a heavy iron bar and went to sleep, the agents emerged from their hiding place and opened the door for the Germans waiting outside. They stormed the house and arrested the Kuenkas, who were transferred to the Hirsch camp and placed in isolation. On the day of the third transport, they were covered with a blanket and placed on the train at the last moment; neither the Jews nor the Jewish police recognized them. Dr. Kuenka's friends launched a wave of protests with the Germans. German cynicism knew no limits. An order issued on March 21, 1943, signed by Max Merten, ordered reprisals against the Jews because "the Jewish Doctor Kuenka escaped." Twenty-five Jewish hostages were arrested and the curfew hours increased.

I. Events – The German Zone of Occupation

On March 25, 1943, Dr. and Mrs. Kuenka arrived in Auschwitz.[80]

In mid-March, the German Organization Todt requested 3,000 workers to complete some military projects in Greece. Eichmann gave his permission to use 3,000 Jews from Thessaloniki. Rabbi Koretz believed that people could be saved by volunteering as workers. He may have suspected that conditions in Poland were not healthy for the deportees, and he thus urged men to volunteer for work in Greece (although it was well known by then how bad conditions were in the Greek labor camps). There were no volunteers. Koretz insisted that the Germans accept 15,000 workers instead of the 3,000 requested, but the Germans refused his offer. He went to suburb "151" and pleaded with the Jews to volunteer, promising on behalf of the Germans that their families would not be deported. The people no longer believed him, and they knew the value of German promises. Many escaped and joined the resistance in the mountains.

Weddings in Thessaloniki

The great majority of the Jews of Thessaloniki believed that, like their ancestors four and a half centuries before, they too were going into exile, this time to Poland. With the desire to continue life as usual, young people in love married. In the beginning, an average of ten weddings per day took place. Eventually, all suppressed feelings of affection found their expression, and the number of weddings reached 100 per day. All implied or given promises were fulfilled inside the camp. Rabbi Koretz encouraged these marriages. "The people show exemplary courage and fortitude," he said. "The number of weddings increase. Have confidence. We will reestablish our community in Krakow. God will help us."

---

80 Molho, *In Memoriam*, 148.

The Illusion of Safety

Soufli, Didimotihon, Nea Orestias, Naoussa, Langada, Katerini, Veria, Florina, Chania

In addition to the great Jewish community of Thessaloniki, there were a number of smaller Jewish communities within the German zone of occupation. Didimotihon with 900 people was the largest community, and Katerini with 33 was the smallest. It would have been extremely easy for these Jews to abandon their homes and find shelter in the villages of the surrounding countryside. Since many Jews were small merchants, artisans and peddlers, they were familiar with the areas around their city, and escape would have been easy. Instead, their losses amounted to sixty percent for Naoussa and up to 100 percent for Langada. The only exception was the community of 33 Jews in the small town of Katerini. While two were executed in Katerini and one in Thessaloniki, the remainder survived the war under circumstances unique in the history of the Holocaust:

> On March 29, 1943, Rabbi Koretz attempted in vain to contact by telephone the director of the Greek police in Katerini. He then sent a telegram and asked Police Chief Papageorgiou to arrest all the Jews and send them to Thessaloniki the next day. Papageorgiou invited some Jews to his office and showed them, under strict confidentiality, the telegram he had received. Then he told them he was going to delay his reply for three hours to give the prospective victims time to escape. Every Jew was informed. They collected some bare essentials and some food supplies, and within two hours they left the city of Katerini.[81]

In his book *In Memoriam*, Michael Molho gives credit to Mr. Papageorgiou, the Chief of the Police in Katerini, for the survival of the city's Jews.[82] "It is not so," I was told on April 25, 1998, when I was interrupted during my lecture in the Greek Orthodox church in Cincinnati, Ohio, by Mrs. Lena Iosafat and her son Matt of Katerini. I remember I was very

---

[81] Molho, Ibid., 141.
[82] Michael Molho, *In Memoriam*, 134.

surprised! I said, "Who are you? How do you know about Katerini?" They told me that a telegram requesting the arrest of the Jews was sent by Rabbi Koretz to the Police Chief Papageorgiou of Katerini. The telegraph operator who received it, whose name the mother and son did not remember, immediately contacted David Iosafat, husband of Lena, told him the contents, and promised to delay the delivery for a maximum of 24 hours, from 2 p.m. of the day that he received it.

David contacted the heads of the seven Jewish families of Katerini and prompted them to go to the mountains. Some were in favor to leave and others were against. After a secret vote, they decided to go. Two of Lena's cousins, Machel Amar and his brother, decided to remain in Katerini. The rest organized their departure with horse-drawn carriages. Machel was arrested. When his brother went to visit him in prison, he was also arrested. They were both deported. This indicates to me that the Greek police delivered Machal and his brother to the Germans. Only Machel survived and came back from the concentration camps. He emigrated to Israel after the war. Conclusion: The real hero of Katerini is an unknown telegraph operator.

If the life of even one Jew matters, then the chief of the police Mr. Papageorgiou and his policemen descend to nothing else but German collaborators.

The story continues:

> The escapees found shelter in nearby villages, and especially in Kalivia-Harathra, where Mayor Vassilios Vassiliadis, now a deputy in the Greek parliament, assisted them in finding accommodations in good houses. The Jewish women, dressed like villagers, would go to the city to find provisions. All the people recognized them, but none of these exceptional Greek Christians betrayed or blackmailed them. Many even donated food and medicine, and neighbors who held their furniture and other household goods for

safekeeping on the day of their departure returned them after the liberation.[83]

In March 1943, Max Merten instructed Rabbi Koretz to apply the Nuremberg Laws throughout the German zone. Koretz sent two employees of the Jewish community, Eliezer Mitrani and Raoul Bouncily, to Florina and Veria, where they executed their instructions with speed and discipline. Many rumors had reached Florina about the deportations from Thessaloniki. The president of the Jewish community of Florina, Jacob Kohen, and its rabbi, Mois Bivas, called Rabbi Koretz on March 17, 1943—two days after the first transport from Thessaloniki had departed. They asked him if anything bad was going to happen to the deportees. Rabbi Koretz assured them that all rumors were baseless and that there was no reason to worry. In another telephone discussion with Menahem Stroumtsa, the president of the Jewish community of Veria, Rabbi Koretz said: "According to our information, the first transports that left Thessaloniki arrived without mishap in Krakow. Our coreligionists there gave them a cordial welcome and tried to shelter them and help them organize their lives." This answer encouraged many Jews to remain in their homes rather than escape to the countryside. On April 30, 382 Jews were arrested in Florina and transferred to the Hirsch camp in Thessaloniki. On May 1, the Jews of Veria arrived in Thessaloniki after having been enclosed in their synagogue for three days. This group of 660 people included 386 Jews of Veria, 170 Jews of Thessaloniki who had gone to Veria to avoid hunger (the surrounding area was rich in agricultural products), and the remainder were refugees from the Bulgarian zone. On May 8, nine hundred seventy Jews from Didimotiho, 160 from Nea Orestias, and 32 from Soufli were transported to the Hirsch camp. The next day, early in the morning, all these people, together with more Jews from Thessaloniki, were deported. Among the Jews of Didimotiho, there were eight families (thirty people) who had Spanish nationality. Nothing could be done to prevent their deportation, and none returned from exile. Only 58 Jews from Florina escaped to find asylum in the surrounding villages.

---

83 Molho, Ibid., 141.

I. Events – The German Zone of Occupation

Following his phone call to Rabbi Koretz, Menahem Stroumtsa's suspicions were aroused, and he tried to persuade the people of his community to leave Veria and go into hiding. The great majority of the Jews of Veria preferred to stay in the city.

Meanwhile, in Thessaloniki, the roundup of Jews continued:

> The Germans would shout: "Is there anyone else left in the house? Bring everyone down without exception! Search everywhere—in the attics, in the yards, in the bathrooms!"
>
> One guard appeared on a balcony and said, "There is a seriously sick person here; he has pneumonia and is delirious. Should I bring him down?"
>
> A German replied, "Yes, idiot, bring him down immediately." After a few minutes we saw a man of about forty, pale and sick, coming slowly, supported by his wife and son . . . Their eyes expressed fear and anger . . . All this human mass moves slowly under pressure of force and threat of death. They say they will take them to Krakow in Poland. To do what? To use them in the munitions factories?
>
> But why then do they need the old people? The children? The sick? The weak? The mothers are the most anxious. They look with painful fondness at their children and shiver with the thought that even one of them might be lost.
>
> A poor uneducated woman thinks aloud: "Tell me, brother, do you suppose they collected us like this to execute us?" Nobody replies. Sixty or seventy people are pushed into a railway wagon. It is difficult to breathe the air that comes from the small, barred windows. Very little water is provided for the trip. People stumble, fall or retrieve items that fell from their hands.[84]

---

[84] Matarasso, ... *Kai omos oloi tous den pethanan, (...And Yet Not All of Them Died)*, 45.

Yomtov Yakouel, legal adviser of the community, escaped as did many Jewish police and others. A small, secret, underground business flourished. For a sum of 35 to forty gold sovereigns per person, false identity cards were made and people (villagers, boatmen, railway employees) who were willing to risk helping a Jew escape were supplied. Three young men were surrendered to the Germans by a boatman who took their money. The Germans executed them by firing squad inside the Hirsch camp. They forced all camp inmates to watch the execution and draw their own conclusions. At the last moment, their parents pleaded with the Germans to execute them in their place. This was rejected. Others had a similar fate: Ino Atas was executed in Thessaloniki on April 5, 1943, for attempting to escape. On the same day Alberto Benveniste, Tori Kuenka, and Maurice Errera were also executed.

The people continued to prepare themselves to face the rigors of the cold climate in Poland. They sold or gave whatever they could to Greek Christians in exchange for warm clothes, strong shoes, or knapsacks: a Singer sewing machine for a warm dress, a bed for boots. Except for the Jews already in the Hirsch camp, the others had the opportunity to buy things from Greek shops. They preferred, however, to make all their purchases through Christian friends because merchants increased prices enormously as soon as they realized a client was Jewish. Many people bought dollars, preferably in large denominations, thinking that it would be easy to transport and conceal them.

In April 1943, Greek Prime Minister Ioannis Rallis was persuaded by the Jews of Athens to go to Thessaloniki and attempt to stop the deportations. Rabbi Koretz, in the presence of the Greek Metropolitan, visited the prime minister and suggested that the remaining Jews be exiled to a Greek island instead of to Poland. This was the first time Rabbi Koretz acted as a leader of his people. The Germans promptly arrested him and his family and contained them in the Hirsch camp. Dieter Wisliceny's report of the incident, discovered after the war, is revealing:

> The arrested Rabbi Tzevi Koretz said the following during his interrogation about his discussion with Prime Minister Rallis. Rabbi Koretz was convinced

I. Events – The German Zone of Occupation

that the resettlement of the Jews would continue. He therefore decided to ask Greek officials to intervene. On April 7, 1943, he learned that Prime Minister Rallis would be in Thessaloniki on April 11.

He contacted Dr. Panos, who agreed to transmit his request to Governor-General Simeonides. On Saturday, April 11, 1943, Panos invited him to the Metropolitan's palace at 2:30 p.m. Koretz described the meeting as follows: when he saw the prime minister, he lost his composure and with tears in his eyes asked Rallis to intervene with the German authorities and prevent the liquidation of the 2000-year-old Jewish community of Thessaloniki. Rallis replied in an evasive, indifferent way. The event as told by Koretz could be true. Koretz was accused for meeting Rallis without the knowledge of the governor-general. He rejected this accusation, insisting that without the invitation of the governor-general he would never have seen the prime minister.

Another report describing the incident was sent to Ambassador Altenburg at the German embassy in Athens from Schoenberg:

The Metropolitan, who was present, escorted the rabbi out and told him, "You see, then, that the Premier can do nothing in this matter." The report continued: "The commanding officer has placed Rabbi Koretz and his family under house arrest. He is to be deported on one of the next transports and as a 'prominent Jew' will be held in Theresienstadt for possible exchange with appropriate German prisoners."[85]

None of the memoirs from Greek Jews matches in eloquence Consul Berry's report to his government in Washington:

Thousands of people, regardless of sex, age and family were crowded into the camp pell-mell, and

---

85 P. K. Enepekidis, *The Secret Archives of the SS*.

confined under conditions so terrible from the point of hygiene that they cannot possibly be described. Woe to anyone who dared make the slightest timid request. There were terrible scenes; mothers searched for their children, husbands for their wives. The unfortunate inmates of Baron Hirsch were not only obliged to endure great physical suffering, resulting from hunger, thirst and cold, but every evening at 10:00 they were forced under threat of death to dance and show every sign of gaiety, while the SS turned upon them the brilliant lights required for making films which would prove to the world how happy the Jews were to be under German protection.

As soon as freight cars were available, men, women and children were piled in . . . seventy to eighty in cars that were not large enough for more than thirty to forty people. The hygienic conditions of these cars were deplorable. There was no ventilation. Only one can of water was allowed, and another can was provided for personal necessities. No one was spared . . . not even women in childbirth, inmates of orphan asylums and old men's homes, or the insane. The last ones were deported like trapped beasts.

Wounded soldiers and veterans of the campaign in the Albanian mountains were taken, regardless of every effort to resist. The Greek authorities in Thessaloniki were unmoved by the measures the Germans took against the Jews. The newspaper *Nea Evropi* published anti-Semitic articles with the express purpose to arouse the Christians of Thessaloniki against the Jews. The sinister Papanaoum was the leader of this group of torturers. He and his associates amassed large fortunes from the confiscated Jewish property, and they didn't even attempt to hide the fact.[86]

Rabbi Koretz was replaced by Rabbi Chaim Habib, a truly holy man beloved by the people. He was soon enclosed in the Hirsch camp, where he was forced to sweep the streets. The

---

[86] National Archives, No. 013766, Source "Z," April 8,1943.

I. Events – The German Zone of Occupation

deportations continued in an orderly manner with practically no resistance from the Jews. One group of deportees was ordered to change its Greek drachmas to Polish zlotys. One night there was a great commotion in the camp. There had been a mistake; their destination was not Poland but rather Theresienstadt, where the zlotys would be worthless. They had to be exchanged for marks. The people pushed each other to make the exchange and never got to sleep. At 4:00 a.m. they had to prepare themselves for a trip where neither zlotys nor marks were of any value. 42,300 Jews were deported on board trains, from March 15 until May 9, 1943.

The seventeenth transport departed on July 1. The Germans spread a false rumor that the 820 people who boarded the train were going to receive better treatment than the previous groups. Most of these prisoners were members of the Community Council, their families, and those influential citizens who had carried out all Rabbi Koretz's orders. All were intelligent and honest, but they were too timid and lacked the courage to think for themselves in times of crisis. One of them told Dr. I. A. Matarasso: "You ask me why I work so diligently and how in these difficult moments I find the stamina to perform this work. I will tell you. I have one hope. Part of the community will remain in Thessaloniki to manage the real estate holdings." This was just another of the German ploys that kept their machine of destruction running.

By the end of July 1943, there were no more than 500 Jews in Thessaloniki. One had been brought back to Thessaloniki, as Consul Berry reported, because another Jew had given away his secret. "He was imprisoned and beaten up for several days until he finally confessed that, before he left, he had handed over for safekeeping to a certain Valera, a druggist, 700 gold sovereigns. He was then taken by two German officers who brought him back to Thessaloniki, together with a Jew who had given him away, to Valera, who was forced to admit to having the gold. The gold was then handed over and divided equally between the German officers."[87]

The special German SS units sent to Thessaloniki were very efficient. In the above report, Consul Berry also mentions how these Germans disposed of children who died of

---

87 National Archives, No. 33856.

suffocation in the death trains. "A German soldier, who arrived recently, said that on his way to Thessaloniki he had counted 18 dead children, aged from one to two years, who had been thrown out of the wagons at stations on the way to Poland. The German soldier said he was disgusted and sickened by the horrors he had seen."[88]

Even the Jewish traitors were not spared by the Germans. These traitors were Greek Jews who betrayed their coreligionists to the Germans. Leon Sion or Topouz, a brutal man with Herculean power, Jacques Alballa, a Spanish Jew, and Edgar Kounio, a 25-year-old Jew from Thessaloniki who distinguished himself by acts of sheer brutality, were deported to Bergen-Belsen near Hanover. The most sinister traitor, Vital Hasson, age 26, escaped at the last minute to Albania and took refuge in Italy.[89]

Many Jews from Thessaloniki maintained Spanish citizenship. They were invited to go to the Beth Saul synagogue to receive an important announcement. Some, mistrusting the Germans, stayed away. Most, however, believing they were to be "repatriated" to Spain, went. The Germans promptly surrounded the synagogue, arrested them, and transported them to the Hirsch camp. There they were forced to ask their families to join them, bringing all their valuables. The German foreign office offered two solutions to these Spanish citizens: repatriation to Franco's Spain or deportation. Edward Gasset, the Spanish charge d'affairs in Thessaloniki, had instructions to accept only fifty people. But there were 367 Jews with Spanish citizenship in German hands, and they were to become the subject of complicated negotiations between the two dictatorial regimes. By the end of July 1943, the only Jews left in the Baron Hirsch camp were those with Spanish citizenship, the remaining 120 "privileged" members of the community, some Jewish policemen, and Jews recently captured in their hideouts after they were betrayed by Christian traitors.

Wisliceny, in a cynical gesture, decided that only 74 of the 120 remaining community leaders were to be considered "privileged."[90] A secret list was prepared between July 30 and

---

88 National Archives, OSS 51060 report No. 107902, Source "Z."
89 Molho, *In Memoriam*. 128.
90 Ibid., 152.

I. Events – The German Zone of Occupation

August 1, 1943. Everyone tried to place his family on this list. On August 2, a special train transported the 74 "privileged" Greek Jews and the 367 Jews of Spanish nationality to Bergen-Belsen. One woman ill with typhus was placed in a separate railway car, together with a Jewish physician. The Spanish and "privileged" Jews traveled in less crowded conditions— only ten people per car, to a camp where the chances of survival were greater. (Originally Bergen-Belsen was a holding camp for Jews to be exchanged with German prisoners in Allied hands. In their section of Bergen-Belsen, old people and women with small children did not work, children were not separated from the parents, and luggage was not confiscated upon arrival.) The 46 community leaders who were dropped from the "privileged" group, together with the remaining captives, were sent to Auschwitz and possibly certain death. On August 7, 1943, some 1,800 slave laborers who had survived the horrible conditions of their work projects in Greece were returned to Thessaloniki. Emaciated, demoralized, and dressed in rags, they formed the nineteenth and last transport from Thessaloniki. It had taken just over four months to destroy one of the main cultural centers of Judaism.

The 1,000-mile trip to Auschwitz took seven to nine days. Rudolf Franz Hoss, the commandant of Auschwitz who supervised the extermination of three million people, told Wisliceny that the Jews from Thessaloniki were "all of such poor quality" that they had to be exterminated quickly.[91] For three weeks, they had nearly halted the deportations to Auschwitz due to the spotted typhus that they brought to the camp. After the departure of the last transport, 72 Jews remained in Thessaloniki. There were also several Jews, whose future was undecided, in the Pavlos Melas concentration camp. Another 15 Jews married to German, French, or Italian Christian women were tolerated, although their shops were confiscated and they were not allowed to work. Rumor had it that they were exempted from deportation because Max Merten was in love with one of the women. In the beginning of 1944, one of these women died in childbirth. Her husband was deported immediately, his house looted, his remaining

---

[91] Raul Hilberg, "Documents of Destruction; Alexandria document VII-173-B-16-14/26 Microfilm T175, Roll 409."

possessions confiscated. The child, an infant of eight days, remained "free" in Thessaloniki.

Many Greek traitors bought factories, shops and laboratories at unrealistically low prices. A traitor, Laskaris Papanaoum, who eventually escaped to Germany, "bought" all the leather shops. He had the knowledge and the ability to betray the hiding places of many Jewish fortunes to the Germans. The Jewish neighborhoods were left empty and deserted; looting was rampant. The Germans sold the Baron Hirsch neighborhood to the traitor Nikolaides, who demolished the buildings and sold the materials at great profit. The neighborhoods "151" and Kalamaria were sold to German collaborators and demolished. The beautiful synagogue, Beth Saul, was also destroyed. The only buildings that remained after the war were the synagogue and the insane asylum, which were used by the German transportation company Schenker.

The Franco government finally approved entry to Spain for the 367 Spanish Jews in Bergen-Belsen, but it asked the Germans "to transfer them in small groups of 25 in such a way that one group will be formed when the previous group has already entered Spain." Eberhard Von Thadden of the foreign ministry in Berlin objected to this plan because it would take a long time and present serious difficulties "in forming the necessary guard, etc."[92] Eichmann, on the other hand, was told to treat the Spanish Jews in such a way that, were they allowed to emigrate, they would not spread "undesirable atrocity propaganda." In August 1943, the Germans decided to treat them as "exchange Jews," and they were moved to the Bergen-Belsen "residence camp" to join the numerous Dutch Jews there. (The nephew of Leon Trotsky was perhaps the most important resident of that camp.) A few months later the Spanish envoy in Berlin informed the German foreign office that the Spanish government was prepared to repatriate all Spanish Jews in German-occupied territories. The Germans replied that only those who had not been "sent East" could be given to Spain.[93]

---

92 P. K. Enepekidis, Doc. CXI 4958, Nuremberg Trials.

93 P. K. Enepekidis, *Secret Archives of the SS*, Berlin Foreign History INL 11 No. 8 8/19/1943.

I. Events – The German Zone of Occupation

Those from Thessaloniki now in Bergen-Belsen fell into this category. On February 7, 1944, the first group left the camp, and a few days later others followed. The 365 Spanish Jews (two had died) remained in Barcelona until June 14, 1944. Then they were sent to Casablanca and, ultimately, to Palestine. In August 1943, six Jews from Thessaloniki with Spanish nationality, five members of Moissis Abraam Gattenio's family and Jacob Boton, were captured by the Germans while hiding in Italian-occupied Larissa. They were sent to Thessaloniki and interned in Pavlos Melas. The Spanish embassy in Athens appealed to Ambassador Altenburg for their release. On September 30, 1943, the Germans released the six Jews for transfer to Spain. On November 30, the six arrived in Athens without any belongings. On March 25, 1944, they were rearrested and interned in the Haidari concentration camp in Athens.[94]

The German Transport Ministry was obligated to pay the Greek State Railways for the transportation of the victims to their death. It was recommended that payment come from the confiscated Jewish assets. The military administration refused to pay the bill. Despite considerable correspondence between the parties, the bill was never paid.[95]

On September 6, 1944, the German evacuation of Thessaloniki became evident. Engineers began destroying fortifications and emptying their warehouses of munitions, food and clothing. Bridges and key installations were mined. They freed Italian and Yugoslav prisoners of war to the care of the Red Cross. Incredible as it might seem, there were still Jewish captives in prison: seven Greeks, one Yugoslav, an American and two Spanish families. They had been captured by the Greek Security Battalions after the last transport left on July 31. There was a gentleman's agreement between the Germans and these Greek traitors: gold and jewelry belonged to the Germans, and anything else was left for the Security Battalions. The promise of booty led these Greeks to hunt for Jews. The Jews in Pavlos Melas were too few to be sent to Poland, so the Germans decided to execute them.

---

94 P. K. Enepekidis, To Vima, article 8.
95 German Ministry for Transport 17TRA or 20, March 11, 1944.

The Illusion of Safety

Fofo Eskenazi, her son, and Susan Isaiah were liberated when friends bribed the Germans with fifty gold Napoleons. The remaining prisoners, except for Chaim Misrahi (who was saved by Red Cross officials at the last moment), were forced to undress for a search. Chaim Misrahi was a witness while Germans took their rings, watches, shoes and suits. The victims covered themselves and boarded the truck to a nearby field. It was 11:00 p.m. on September 8, 1944, when Misrahi and other Greek prisoners heard the machine gun fire. One of these victims was Rebecca Franko from Kastoria, a beautiful woman of 22 years old. She was about to give birth on the day the Jews of Kastoria were to be deported. A Red Cross representative pleaded with the Germans not to deport her with the others. The German commander allowed her to be transported to the local hospital, but her husband was deported. She gave birth to a daughter and remained in the hospital, forgotten, until September 1, when she was betrayed. Her daughter was given to a Christian family.

The long arm of the Gestapo reached even those who felt safe. The Italian consulate of Thessaloniki helped the Jewish families of Marko Mosseri, Fernandez, Valeri, Torres, and Daniel Modiano to escape to Italy. In September 1943, these families were living in a hotel by Lake Maggiore. Their fate was described by Susan Zuccotti:

> Fifty-five Germans invaded the shores of beautiful Lago Maggiore on the Swiss frontier. In Meina, a village on the lake between the more famous tourist towns of Arona and Stresa, 16 Jews from Greece took lodging in the Hotel Meina. Someone informed the Germans. On September 16, one week after the German occupation, the SS stormed the hotel. They seized a family of six from Thessaloniki, including the children ages 15, 12, and eight. They kept this family and ten other victims under guard for a week, apparently debating what to do with them. Finally, they shot each victim in the back of the neck and tossed the bodies into the lake. The SS auctioned the belongings of the victims in Meina's public square. The next morning most of the bodies rose to the surface. They were taken to the center of the lake and thrown

I. Events – The German Zone of Occupation

in again. After this, only one was ever recovered for a proper burial.[96]

Fifteen of the "privileged" Greeks died in Bergen-Belsen from typhus before or shortly after the liberation of the camp. Rabbi Koretz, who endured hard labor in Bergen-Belsen, was transferred to Theresienstadt where he caught typhus and died in the small town of Troebitz three months after the camp was liberated by the Russians.[97] In September 1945, when word reached Thessaloniki that this group had arrived in Siderokastro on its way home to Thessaloniki, the surviving remnant in Thessaloniki talked of lynching them. Several of the "privileged" Greeks had occupied important positions in Bergen-Belsen; Alballa was for a time the Lagerführer (camp leader). Dr. John Allalouf, an honest man and a great human being, saved many people and was given honorary Dutch citizenship by Queen Wilhelmina of Holland after the war. Dr. Allalouf and Dr. Leon Kuenka were both given the Legion of Honor by the French government for their work in the concentration camps. Bergen-Belsen was liberated on April 15, 1945. When the British entered the camp, they found 58,000 people starving and sick from the epidemics that raged there. In one day alone, the British counted 1,563 dead among the free inmates. Twenty thousand Jews were to lose their lives in the weeks following the liberation as a result of a typhus epidemic.[98]

---

96 Susan Zuccotti, *The Italians and the Holocaust*, 1987, 290.
97 Personal communication with Professor Yitzhak Kerem.
98 Sam Bloch, "Holocaust and Rebirth," xlvi.

Chapter Two

The Bulgarian Zone of Occupation

If God created the world, I would not like to be God.

— ARTHUR SCHOPENHAUER

The losses of the Greek Jewish population in the Bulgarian zone of occupation were as follows in the communities listed:

Communities	Population (prearrest)	Population (postwar)	Percentage of Loss	Date of Arrest
Alexandroupoli	140	4	97%	March 1943
Drama	1,200	39	97%	March 1943
Kavalla	2,100	42	98%	March 1943
Komotini	819	28	96%	March 1943
Serres	600	3	99%	March 1943
Xanthi	550	6	99%	March 1943

The Jews of Old Bulgaria were not deported despite strong German pressures. The Bulgarians resisted the Germans, in part because public opinion was against the deportation of Bulgarian Jews. Bulgaria was not an enthusiastic German ally, especially after it was evident that Germany was going to lose the war. In the cities of Kavalla, Serres and Drama, the Bulgarians asked the Jews to collaborate with them in their anti-Greek policies. The Greek Jews refused to cooperate. The Bulgarians became furious with the Jews and, with German encouragement, applied the Nuremberg laws; Jews were forced to wear the Star of David and were given special yellow passports which indicated their religion. They were forbidden to walk on the main streets of their own cities, engage in any commercial activity, or change their place of residence; their houses had to have an obvious sign, "Jewish Home," written in Bulgarian.[99] In June 1942, they were forbidden from acquiring Bulgarian citizenship. This made possible their future deportation.

In the summer of 1942, several hundred young Jews were mobilized in forced labor battalions. Those who survived returned in the autumn. In January 1943 groups of Jews from the occupied cities were dispatched into Bulgaria proper to work on road projects. Jewelry, gold and other valuables were confiscated and given over to the National Bank of Bulgaria. To save themselves, some Jews escaped to Thessaloniki and Veria in the German zone.[100]

In September 1942, German Foreign Minister Joachim von Ribbentrop ordered the deportation of Jews from various European countries; Bulgaria was among the first on the list mentioned. The Bulgarian government indicated its delight with the German plan; however, it felt that male Jews could not be spared from their road construction work due to labor shortages. When the Germans realized that Bulgaria was unwilling to deport its Jews, they asked for the "resettlement" of Jews from the newly annexed territories. The Bulgarian commissioner for Jewish affairs, Alexander Belev, agreed to German demands to deport the Jews of the newly acquired territories in Greece and Yugoslavia.[101] It is obvious that this compromise to sacrifice the Jews of Macedonia and Thrace was made in an effort to save the Bulgarian Jews.

Shortly before midnight on March 3, 1943, a Bulgarian national holiday, a terrible tragedy unfolded in the Jewish neighborhoods under Bulgarian occupation. It was a cold

---

99 Molho, *In Memoriam*, 244.

100 Joseph Nehama, *In Memoriam* (Thessaloniki: 1974), 131.

101 L. S. Stavrianos, *The Balkans* (New York: Simon and Schuster, 1968), 768.

I. Events – The Bulgarian Zone of Occupation

winter night with temperatures below freezing. Bulgarian soldiers forced the doors of Jewish houses, viciously pulled people from their beds, regardless of age or sex, and loaded them still in their pajamas into trucks. Over 4,221 people were simultaneously arrested in Kavalla, Serres, Drama, Alexandroupoli, Komotini and Xanthi. They took neither clothes nor food, and Christians were strictly forbidden to give them food.

The U.S. government was immediately informed about the plight of Jews in the Bulgarian zone via the OSS, which was alerted by Greek intelligence and another "reliable" source.[102] The U.S. naval attaché in Ankara informed Washington that "on March 4, 1943 at 1500 hours all the Jews of Alexandroupoli were arrested and sent off to an unknown destination. This report was confirmed by Agent Pherrai on March 13, 1943.[103] The most reliable and prompt source of information was sent by agent "Z" on March 5, the day after the arrest.[104]

The German consulate of Kavalla sent the following report to the German embassy in Sofia:

> ... the deportation proceeds without any difficulties. The only thing worth mentioning is the obvious compassion that the Greek people of Kavalla, Xanthi, etc., showed towards the departing Jews. They gave them gifts and bid them farewell in a disgustingly warm manner.
>
> Reliable German sources report that some Bulgarians, obviously influenced by the Communists, participated in this revolting spectacle. As for the Jews themselves, it is said that they accepted their deportation with, outwards at least, signs of indifference.[105]

---

[102] National Archives, OSS Confidential, No. 73800.

[103] National Archives, OSS Restricted, No. 10662, Naval Attaché Ankara (Source: Greek Intelligence).

[104] National Archives, OSS Secret, No. 39165.

[105] Hans Joachim Hoppe, "Greece and Its Neighbors," April 1984. Unpublished lecture described in *Chronika*, December 1990, 12.

In Kavalla, the prisoners remained without food for three days. On Sunday, March 7, they were moved to Drama and from there by train to Siderokastro. They continued on foot to Petritsi, where they boarded narrow-gauge Bulgarian trains to the tiny concentration camps of Simitli, Doubnitsa, Gourna, and Zoumaia. A few days later they were sent to Lorn Limina on the Danube, where they boarded barges to Vienna.[106] A non-Jewish nurse, Nadejda Vasileva, recorded the dramatic scenes at the Lorn Limina station. The deportees shouted from the closed cars in Bulgarian and Ladino: "Are there no humane people who will at least give us some water?" She attempted to give them water but the police interfered with the distribution of water.

New transports came the following day to Lorn Limina, and Nadejda Vasileva was given special permission to distribute water and food, with the help of gypsies, through the holes and windows of the cars. A railroad worker used a hose to give them some water. From a rear car, people shouted that there was no water or air. An old man had died and a woman had given birth. A nurse came to treat the sick inside, but was not allowed to do so. Vasileva followed the cars on foot to the Lorn Limina station. On the grounds of the harbor area were scraps from the salted fish given to those who were going to their deaths. Four vessels carrying 4,219 captives left Lorn Limina for Vienna. The guards were mainly Bulgarians; the Germans supervised the entire operation. The trip to Vienna lasted five to ten days. From Vienna the Jews were transported via Katowitz to Treblinka, where all were killed a few days later.[107] Only sixty Jews from the Bulgarian-occupied zone survived by going into hiding.

The Bulgarians looted the houses and shops of the deportees and sold at auction whatever they did not take. In the 1960s, when diplomatic relations were reestablished between Greece and Bulgaria, the Bulgarian government returned several trunks filled with items taken from the Greek Jews. In 1977 the Greek government delivered these to the Jewish community in Athens, which, in turn, entrusted the examination of these trunks to Dr. Daniel Hanan (Nicholas

---

106 Levin, *The Holocaust*, 558.
107 Morse, *While Six Million Died*, 295.

I. Events – The Bulgarian Zone of Occupation

"Nikos") Stavroulakis, an art historian. He was so deeply moved by the items (family pictures, wedding rings, family documents and other personal effects) that he proposed the establishment of a Holocaust museum in Athens. It was inaugurated that same year as the Jewish Museum of Greece.[108]

Anagnostopoulos remembers the tragedy of the Jews of Drama:

> There were about 1,200 Jews in Drama, living in harmony with the other citizens. Some of them were rich merchants, others were artisans, and many were poor workers. Soon they were forced to place the Star of David with the name of the head of the family written in Bulgarian on the front door of their houses. Another star was attached to their garments.
>
> The marked houses and people made the neighborhood appear as if it were quarantined! I remember a Jewish boy, very thin, very pale, selling some razor blades. His intelligent black eyes had an expression I will never forget. Every so often he looked at his star and, in the middle of this unjust persecution, you could sense that his soul was free, proud, erect.
>
> One day the Bulgarians arrested the entire community and placed them in a tobacco warehouse by the lake. In the morning, the women were allowed, under guard, to get water from the lake. I saw some of the women wearing ill-fitting men's trousers; these were very pretty girls who were trying to hide their beauty and pass unnoticed. In a few days we all knew they were taking them all away. The main street was filled with people. The tragic procession was escorted by heavily armed guards. The old people walked with difficulty. Some sick men and women were carried by those who were younger and stronger. Babies and

---

[108] *Chronika*, Athens, November 1983, 27; translated into Greek from the *Jewish Press*, August 12, 1983.

children were crying. Some tried to maintain their self-discipline, but most just stared ahead.

Suddenly I saw Mr. Jacob with his wife and five children. I told my mother, who was holding my hand: "Mr. Jacob, the repairman!" He was a middle-aged man, as poor as could be. Every spring he used to service our wood burner. He heard my voice, turned toward us and, moving his head politely, greeted us. We moved our hands, returning his greeting. He tried to smile, but his smile was only a bitter complaint, a big 'Why?' My mother said, "Patience, it will pass."

Soon some Christian boys, becoming more interested, began pushing the crowd to see better. I heard, "Here is the ice cream man. I see him!" He was 35 years old, dressed in white during the summer. He knew the names of all the boys and used to tell us jokes. Now he held his youngest boy in his arms. A seven or eight-year-old boy was walking next to him, holding him by his pants. Next to him was his wife, holding a baby in her arms and trying to hold back her tears. The boys started yelling, little realizing the magnitude of the tragedy: "Hi, ice cream man!" He looked as us with tears in his eyes and a very painful expression on his face. "Farewell," he said with great difficulty. "You will not eat my ice cream again." Seeing our friend crying, we started crying too, although we did not fully understand what he meant.

The last one in this procession was Samouyas, the "crazy man" of the city. He lived alone in a hovel of a room and he liked to tease people and be teased by them. The Bulgarians did not pay any attention to him. They did not know he was Jewish. But when Samouyas saw the great procession, he joined it at the end. The guards ordered him to leave but he would not. "I am a Jew too," he repeated many times. "Where all the Jidio (Jews in Ladino) go, I go too," and smiled with self-satisfaction at his many Christian "friends." At that moment the Jewish conscience of the scorned and

I. Events – The Bulgarian Zone of Occupation

mentally sick Samouyas rose proudly and made him join his people. None of them returned.[109]

In Bulgaria, the Jews were going to be deported just as they were deported from the Bulgarian zones of occupation in Greece and Yugoslavia. A Bulgarian member of parliament, Dmitar Peshev, had a very close friend who was Jewish. A man told him, "Do you know that your best friend is going to be killed?" That question forced him to think and take some action.

He persuaded other Parliamentarians as well as the Archbishop of Bulgaria to oppose the deportations. The Archbishop talked with King Boris and urged him not to obey the Germans. The 50,000 Jews of Bulgaria were not deported. Soon the Russians arrived and executed all the collaborators of the Germans, including the members of the Parliament, except the man who initiated the effort to save the Jews. (King Boris was honored as a Righteous Among the Nations. When Yad Vashem, discovered how badly he treated the Jews of Bulgaria and, especially, how brutal he was to the Jews of the Bulgarian zones of occupation in Greece and in Yugoslavia, the award was removed.)

---

109 Dion Anagnostopoulos, "The Final Solution," *Chronika*, April 1988, 7.

Chapter Three

The Italian Zone of Occupation

A great deal of intelligence can be invested in ignorance when the need for illusion is deep.

— SAUL BELLOW

The losses◊ of the Greek Jewish population in the Italian zone of occupation were as follows in the communities listed:

Communities	Population (prearrest)	Population (postwar)	Percentage of Loss	Date of Arrest
Agrinion*	40	38	0%	
Arta	384	60	84%	March 25, 1944
Athens**	3,500	4,930	-45%	March 25, 1944
Corfu	2,000	187	91%	June 9, 1944
Chalkis	325	170	48%	March 25, 1944
Ioannina***	1,850	163	91%	March 25, 1944
Karditsa****	150	?	?	
Kastoria	900	45	95%	March 25, 1944
Larissa	1,120	726	35%	March 25, 1944
Patras	299	209	33%	March 25, 1944
Preveza	250	15	94%	March 25, 1944
Rhodes-Kos	1,900	200	89%	July 20, 1944
Trikala	520	360	30%	March 25, 1944
Volos	872	645	26%	March 25, 1944
Zakynthos	275	275	0%	
Total	14,605	8,285	87%	

◊ Footnotes for the table are on the next page.

The Greek Jews who were fortunate enough to live in the Italian zone were treated by the Italian army in a most civilized manner. There was no discrimination against the Jews, and a sense of justice and chivalry prevailed. These Jews had a false sense of security, and it is possible that they did know they enjoyed more privileges and freedom than the Jews in Italy.

The latter, in spite of their small number (50,000), had contributed two prime ministers and a minister of defense to Italy. Fifty Jewish generals had served with distinction during World War I.[110] However, in 1938 the Fascist Grand Council approved Mussolini's "Aryan Manifesto," which revoked the symbiosis. King Victor Emmanuel countersigned these laws even as he expressed his sorrow for the Jews. "There are twenty thousand spineless people in Italy who are moved by the fate of the Jews," Mussolini commented. "I am one of them," the king replied. As a result of the new laws, over 1,000 Italian Jews were expelled from their professions and fired from

◊Chart Footnotes:
*Two women died of natural causes. No one was arrested.
**The losses from Athens are approximately one thousand. The increase after the war is due to the relocation of small-town Jews to the capital. There are approximately another 200 Jews in Athens who were not listed in the community register. It is estimated that 1,475 people returned from the concentration camps. The above statistics were issued by the Central Jewish Council of Greece (KIS). The total of 87% refers to all Greek Jewish losses.
*** There is some discrepancy with the numbers from Ioannina. According to Uncle Michael Matsas's research, which was the basis for the engraved marble plaques in Ioannina, in this ancient Jewish community of about 2,000 people, 1,960 were deported and 1,850 were killed.
****Professor Yitzchak Kerem discovered that Esther Shalom's aunt, of the Kalonymos family, was one of several Jews of Karditsa who did not manage to leave their homes in time and were arrested and deported by the Germans. Letter from Yitchak Kerem to author. When Italy capitulated, Karditsa remained free and unoccupied by the enemy for a while. Later, many Jews obeyed the German registration order but almost all went to the countryside prior to March 1944 – Personal correspondence from Joseph Matsas.

---

110 Michael Matsas, "Jewish Contributions to Civilization," *Jewish Review*, Athens, June/July 1966.

I. Events – Italian Zone of Occupation

government positions, and 95 university professors were dismissed. They were prohibited from attending public schools and universities or using public libraries. Jewish doctors could not treat Christian patients. Yet, thanks to General Carlo Geloso, commander of the Italian zone of occupied Greece, Greek Jews enjoyed the same civil rights as all Greek Christian citizens.

When the Germans entered Athens on April 27, 1941, the president of the Jewish community, Zaccaria Vital, and members of the Jewish council and other officials were arrested, interrogated at length, and then released. Rabbi Elia Barzilai was appointed president of the community but was not ratified as such by the Italians until September 1, 1941.

Moses Soriano, a Jew from Rhodes who had Italian citizenship and was a friend of Italian Ambassador Pellegrino Ghigi, acted as a liaison between the Jewish community and the Italians. To placate the Germans there was an initial inclination to agree to the imposition of the yellow badge for Greek Jews, but, because that requirement was degrading, the Italian ministry revoked the decision. The Greek government of General Georgios Tsolakoglou also proposed a racial decree with restrictions against the Jews, but the Italians did not approve it. On June 20 and on July 14, 1942, members of the pro-Nazi student organization Elliniki Socialistiki Patriotiki Organosis (ESPO, the Greek Socialist Organization) sacked the offices of the Jewish community and even took the membership lists. The same group planned to burn the synagogue on Melidoni Street. The Italians learned of their plan, and Colonel Luigi Mondini ordered carabinieri to guard the building. In September 1942, the ESPO offices, were demolished by PEAN, under the command and supervision of its leader Constantinos Perrikos, ex-officer of the Greek Air Force. Subsequently, Perrikos and most of the participating individuals were arrested and ultimately executed on February 4, 1943 by the Germans. The destruction of ESPO ended the general Nazi movement in Greece.[111]

---

[111] Contributed by George L. Paidas, recipient of an honorary diploma on the 50th anniversary of the demolition of ESPO by PEAN, given to him in gratitude, by EMEIC (Institute of Hellenic History). Letter and documents were sent to me by Mr. Paidas of Florida.

After the ESPO ransacking of the synagogue, the Jewish community formally dissolved itself, and a secret Jewish committee was formed in the autumn of 1942. Among its members were Moses Soriano, Jack Hanen, Albert Nahmias and Moses Levi. The committee kept in touch with Rabbi Barzilai and assisted Jewish refugees from the north, Jewish Palestinians of the British forces, and others who were being hunted by the Germans. General Geloso decided not to apply racist laws to the Jews under his jurisdiction because of his personal beliefs and also his friendship with Moses Soriano.[112]

Hundreds of Jewish families took refuge in Athens during the Greek-Italian war, for Athens had been declared an open city and hence was spared the aerial attacks targeting Thessaloniki, Patras, Ioannina and other cities. The Greek Jews trusted the Italians as human beings. They trusted even Mussolini. Perhaps some of them were aware of his colorful comment about the Germans: "Thirty centuries of history permit us to regard with supreme pity certain doctrines supported beyond the Alps by the descendants of people who did not know how to write and could not hand down documents recording their own lives at a time when Rome had Caesar, Virgil and Augustus."[113] Mussolini even successfully resisted German efforts to deliver German Jews who had found shelter in Italy to the SS.

In May 1942, the Italian police requested that all Jews in their zone register their names and addresses. They reassured the few who wondered why the Jews were singled out for such obvious discriminatory treatment: "As long as we are here, nothing will happen to you." The Italians did not comply in 1942 with the German request to deport the Jews in their military zones of occupation in southern France, Yugoslavia and Greece. When the Germans began the deportations in Thessaloniki, General Alexander Lohr solicited the aid of General Carlo Geloso to transfer the Jews from occupied Greece. Geloso replied that he could not participate in such an enterprise without orders from his government. The Germans

---

112 Joseph Lovinger, president of the Jewish Community of Athens. Letter to the author, March 16, 1989.

113 Susan Zuccotti, *The Italians and the Holocaust* (New York: Basic Books, 1987), 30.

I. Events – Italian Zone of Occupation

addressed a note to the Italian Minister of Interior, who in turn consulted with Geloso, who again refused to authorize deportations in his zone of occupation. His successor, General Domenico Tripiccione, was asked to assist in deporting the Greek Jews, but he too refused. Dieter Wisliceny was prevented from pursuing Jews who sought asylum in the Italian zone. The Italians even requested that he refrain from visiting their zone too often, and they hinted he might even be arrested by the Italian police.

On July 11, 1942, the same day the Jews of Thessaloniki were forcibly gathered in Eleftheria (Liberty) Square, the Germans were planning to "standardize in all of Greece" the anti-Jewish racial measures. In October 1942, Heinrich Himmler visited Mussolini and obtained his consent to expel the Jews from all occupied territories. Thus, when the Germans began the deportations from Thessaloniki, the Italians should not have been surprised. They were not confronted with a fait accompli, as General Geloso later stated.

On February 25, 1943, Joachim von Ribbentrop met with Mussolini in the Palazzo Venezia. By that time the Axis powers were losing North Africa, and Italy was about to be invaded. Ribbentrop demanded that the Jews of southern France be deported immediately, and he expressed outrage that Italy had accepted with gratitude a donation of three million francs from the Jews of Nice for relief to bombed-out civilians. Mussolini said, "My generals have a different mentality in these affairs," but promised to take care of the problem personally. He appointed General Guido Lospinos as Commissioner for Jewish Affairs, with a special police force under his command. After further discussions, the Italians finally conceded to the Germans that:

1. Jews holding Italian citizenship would be subject to the same treatment current in Italy.
2. Jews of Greek nationality would be arrested and interned in suitable camps on the Ionian islands or in Italy.
3. Jews who were citizens of friendly or neutral countries would be compelled to return to their countries.

In the meantime, German police in Athens interrogated many Jews about the cultural institutions of the community, about the assets of the Athenian Jews, and about their contacts with Jewish organizations abroad. The Greek police were ordered to make lists of all Jews in the city. The Gestapo used the same tactics in Athens that had proven effective in Thessaloniki. They also took approximately forty Jewish refugees from Central Europe who were in Athens and forced the Jewish community to give them financial assistance beyond their immediate needs. The Germans used them as informants on Jewish affairs.

The Italians, who did not like the German intervention in their zone, began to show more interest in Jewish affairs. During the deportations in the north, Italian Consul General Giuseppe Castrucci gave Italian naturalization papers to Jews; 550 Jews, mostly women, were rescued from the Hirsch camp in this way. They boarded an Italian troop train and were transported to temporary safety in Athens. Castrucci resisted German pressure by reminding the Germans that "Italy has special rights in Greece." Another 100 people were spirited to safety by the staff of the Italian consulate. Many of these refugees were sheltered by the Italians in Greek public schools, and the Italian army gave them provisions. Spanish Jews, realizing that the Franco regime was avoiding any concrete steps to save them from the clutches of the Germans, abandoned Thessaloniki while it was still possible and fled to Athens. All the newly arrived Jews graphically depicted the German terror in Macedonia. It is possible they offered advice to the Jews of Athens, who enjoyed their illusion of safety. But advice offered is not the same as advice heeded. Moses Soriano, who was the director of the Alhadef factory, with the assistance of General Geloso helped many Thessaloniki refugees hide in the Britannia factory. Soriano later escaped when the Germans searched for him.

Since the Italians issued so many "laissez-passers" to Jews, the Germans counteracted by demanding that these recipients not be allowed to enter the Italian zone but go to Italy. The Italians rejected these demands and even requested the return of all deported Italian Jews. Berlin replied that those who were mistakenly arrested would be released; the whereabouts of those "already sent to work in the eastern territories" would be investigated. When the Jews of Athens learned about the

I. Events – Italian Zone of Occupation

deportations in Thessaloniki, they panicked. On April 19, 1943, Moses Soriano advised Secretary Prato of the Italian embassy that, when circumstances so required, the Jews of the Italian zone would be "very pleased to be interned by the Italian authorities in Italian territory." A few days later, Ambassador Pellegrino Ghigi in Athens, reporting this panic, informed Rome that "a large number of them would welcome almost gratefully an order deporting them to Italy." Fortunately for the Jews of Greece, Rome did not approve this internment because of the "complex logistics of the operation."[114] The Italians had not yet acceded to the German demands before they were overwhelmed by the events of July 24, 1943, the Fascist Grand Council's overthrow of Mussolini, the Allied landings in southern Italy, and the decision of the new government under Marshal Pietro Badoglio to surrender on September 8, 1943.

Since the beginning of 1942, the Germans used special agents to locate the financial assets of the wealthy Jews in the Italian zone. A captured German agent confessed the following before he was executed by the XIII Division of ELAS in April 1944:

> My true name is Billy Horst, but I used at different times the following names: Fritz Kroujt as a German, Arnaout Groubaou as a Jew and George Karakajanis as a Greek physician... I am fluent in German, English, French, Greek, Italian and Dutch.
>
> In order to go to England, I was operated on so that anatomically I could present myself as a Jew. In England, I was recommended to the intelligence service as a Jew from Cologne and I was given different assignments. In 1935 I was sent to Athens as an agent of the British Intelligence Service. As a Jew and a British agent, I was able to travel and spy against England... After 1941 the Gestapo requested me to locate and point out Jewish-owned stores in Athens. This activity continued until I departed for my new assignment in your area at the end of 1943."[115]

---

114 Ibid., 17.
115 Kostas Triantafillidis, "My True Name Is Billy Horst," *Kathimerini*, Athens, May 10, 1976.

In September 1943, after the Italian capitulation and prior to the German takeover of Athens, the Italians destroyed the Jewish lists. On September 21, 1943, Rabbi Elia Barzilai received a telephone message from Dieter Wisliceny requesting his appearance. The rabbi immediately informed the Jewish Community Council, the Greek authorities and Archbishop Damaskinos. All the Jews were informed that the "war" against them had just begun. The rabbi then visited Wisliceny, who requested within two hours:

1. A list of all the Greek Jews of Athens with their addresses and occupations.
2. A list of all the Greek Jews of Thessaloniki who moved to Athens between 1940 and September 1943.
3. A list of all Jews of Italian nationality who arrived in Athens under Italian protection.
4. Separate lists of other Jews according to their nationalities.
5. A list of the Jews who helped refugees from Europe go to Palestine.
6. The formation of a "committee of elders" who would be entrusted with the affairs of the community.

Wisliceny ended the meeting with this threat: "Bad things will happen to all of you if you do not obey me to the letter." The OSS in Cairo informed Washington on September 22, 1943, that "the arrest of Jews in the Athens area had been ordered and has begun. Their property is being seized."[116]

Rabbi Barzilai convened a general meeting of the Athenian Jews at the Melidoni Street synagogue. A committee was selected and entrusted with the task of asking Archbishop Damaskinos, who was known for his noble sentiments toward the Jews, to intervene on their behalf. None of the participants in this meeting agreed to become a member of any committee whose purpose was to collaborate with the Germans. Instead, the committee, headed by the rabbi, visited the archbishop. He advised: "There is only one solution. Hide yourselves, disappear." The rabbi asked if the Jews could find refuge in the

---

116 National Archives, OSS No. A 15374 Report No. 7758.

I. Events – Italian Zone of Occupation

churches. "With pleasure," the brave archbishop replied. "Only you should not imagine that you would be safe inside the churches. They will arrest you without the slightest hesitation."

On September 22, 1943, Rabbi Barzilai and the committee visited Greek Prime Minister Rallis. Rallis attempted to calm the fears of the delegation and argued that the Jews of Macedonia and Thrace brought their destruction on themselves. Echoing German propaganda, he insisted that the Jews of Athens "were different." As the Greek prime minister, however, he wrote a second report on behalf of the Greek Jews which concluded:

> The Greek people have always regarded with strong sympathy their Jewish compatriots, and do so even today because the Greek Jews have always been a precious element of order and loyalty in the country. For all these reasons, it would be wise, in the event that it is not possible to revoke the decision, to make the restrictive measures here only such as are in force elsewhere, for example, in Hungary.[117]

The following day, the rabbi again saw Wisliceny. He told him he did not have any archives and that he had no people who would be able to find the information he was ordered to supply. Wisliceny became furious: "I need all the information I asked," he yelled. "I give you another forty-two hours. Take care of it or I will feel sorry for you!" Following this conversation, Wisliceny took a squad of SS and forcibly occupied the community offices. They found no lists.[118]

Baruch Schibi, the journalist and Zionist who failed in his attempt to go to the Middle East, became one of the EAM leaders in Athens. During these critical days, he closely watched these events:

> From the beginning I joined EAM. I was in charge of section 3A in the center of Athens. When Rabbi Barzilai announced in the synagogue that he had

---

117 Molho, *In Memoriam*, 105.
118 Ibid., 201.

received an order from the Gestapo to present within two days a list of the Jews of Athens and their addresses, I immediately met with my EAM colleagues, who at that time were all Christians, and I suggested that we should abduct the rabbi and send him to the mountains. In this way I wanted to give a message, "Disappear!", to all members of the Jewish community. At midnight, I met with the representative of the Central Committee of EAM.

He was a teacher, but I did not know his name since we all lived a clandestine existence. He declared that he was willing to share with me the responsibility for this enterprise. In the morning at 7:00 a.m., accompanied by the teacher and a member of my team, Athanasios Andronis, we visited Joseph Nehama, a member of the Jewish committee that followed the activities of Wisliceny. He was a historian and represented the upper class of Thessaloniki. He said that the idea was good. I asked him, "What should we do if the Rabbi refuses to follow us?" Nehama's reply is still present in my ears, although over 32 years have passed: "It would not be the end of the Jewish people if a rabbi were lost." This meant only one thing to me: kill the rabbi if he refuses to escape. We agreed that even if the Germans executed hostages in retaliation, our action was worth it. With my two comrades, we visited the rabbi. I kept guard outside while they went to talk to the rabbi inside his house. The rabbi asked for time to decide. At the same time, being afraid that any delay would make us lose the opportunity to abduct the rabbi, we asked Nikolaos Louvaris, a government official, to ask Archbishop Damaskinos to allow Rabbi Barzilai to go as a monk to a monastery. Damaskinos indeed sent a message to Barzilai and asked him to get ready to go to a monastery.

In the meantime, the resistance organization, with the journalist Costas Vidalis in charge of the operation, was ready, and so we preferred the solution of going to the mountains. Vidalis and I visited the rabbi's house again, and we decided on the details of "his departure," with which the rabbi and his family were more than willing to cooperate. Attorney Elias Kefalidis and

I. Events – Italian Zone of Occupation

Solomon Sasson were designated as the men who were to be in charge of the rabbi and take him temporarily to a house in the neighborhood of Dexameni. The rabbi, his wife and daughter were issued false identity papers. On Saturday, September 25, 1943, the small group went to Elefsina; from there they went to Galaxidi.

The ELAS regiment in Dervenohori gave them every possible assistance but could not find a strong enough mule which could support the rabbi, who was overweight. The partisans eventually produced Eda, an Italian mule captured in the battle of Roumeli. The rabbi's family departed two days later, escorted by a Jewish partisan named Maccabee. They eventually reached Karpenissi and the village Petrino, where the rabbi remained until the end of the war. The news of the rabbi's disappearance spread like wildfire. The Jews of Athens tried to find means to disperse themselves and hide.

My position as a leader of EAM gave me the possibility to ask members of the resistance in Athens to offer refuge to many Jews.[119]

Baruch Schibi became a true leader of his people. By acting in a preventive manner, he enabled many Jews to go into hiding without fear of breaking any law since there were no rules restricting Jewish movement before October 8, 1943. Equally important, those who assisted Jews in protecting their possessions, finding apartments in Athens, or going into the mountains, did so without violating any law. Thousands who were not brave or who did not have the proper connections saved their lives thanks to Baruch Schibi, the resistance organizations of EAM and ELAS, and the "resistance" actions of Damaskinos and individual Christians. Preventive action in this case proved to be more effective than audacity. Baruch Schibi earned the respect and affection of thousands. He took risks knowing the danger. His knowledge was translated into revolutionary behavior.

---

[119] Baruch Schibi, letter to the author, February 4, 1976.

The Illusion of Safety

One hundred and thirty-five Jews thought they could save themselves by converting. The priests accepted them with understanding and kindness following an order of Archbishop Damaskinos. The latter's personal archives reveal the measures he took to save as many Athenian Jews as possible. He called P. Haldezos, Director of the Administrative Services of Athens, to his office and told him:

> I made my sign of the cross; I talked with God and I decided to save as many Jewish souls as I can, even if I place myself in danger. I will baptize the Jews and you will give them certificates which will enable them to have identity cards proving that they are Greek Christians.[120]

The Catholic church in Italy also offered baptismal certificates. In order to make them more effective, they backdated them willingly. Yet few Italian Jews took advantage of the offer. Most of the converts were from mixed marriages. Conversion was a serious matter in Italy, and Jews preferred not to abandon their heritage. Many Catholic priests took advantage of the persecution of the Jews in order to gain converts, while other priests "refused to sanction conversions under false pretenses." Not so in Greece, where everyone knew that the conversions had nothing to do with religious beliefs. Damaskinos was a leader in a country where heads of the church traditionally lead the nation in times of peril. He had been exiled during the Metaxas dictatorship, and after the Second World War he became viceroy. Damaskinos was a Greek patriot. Hundreds of Jews were given false identity cards by the Greek police. Angelos Evert, commander of the Athens police, gave them to more than fifty Jewish families. Their new identity cards allowed them to hide in Athens and its suburbs. Haldezos and another colleague in the city hall provided 500 Athenian Jews with false certificates, which enabled them to obtain new identity cards. Hundreds of other Jews were able to obtain false identity cards through Dimitris

---

120 Elias Venezis, *To Vima*, Athens, 2/2/60.

I. Events – Italian Zone of Occupation

Vranopoulos, police chief of Piraeus, and Michael Glykas, Chief of the VI Department of the Athens police.[121]

Thousands of Jews, the great majority of the 8,000 the Germans did not capture, owe their lives to the resistance organizations of EAM-ELAS. They moved to the free countryside. Seven individuals found shelter in Epirus under the protection of the right-wing resistance organization EDES; they were treated well also. Without the resistance organizations the Jews would have been in great peril in the villages and in even worse danger in the cities. Although traitors in the cities were often stabbed to death by EAM, many Jews still were betrayed while in hiding.

Stroop's Order of October 7, 1943

On Thursday, October 7, and Friday, October 8, 1943, the eve of Yom Kippur, all morning and evening newspapers in Athens published an order signed by General Jurgen Stroop that all Jews present themselves at the synagogue for registration. The Germans appointed a committee presided over by Moissis Siakis to persuade the Jews to register, since in the two weeks following the order only 200 had obeyed. Very slowly, more and more Jews lost their fear of the Germans and registered until the number reached about 1,000; most of them were poor and not able to stop working and go into hiding.

The U.S. government was forewarned about the events that would occur in the Italian zone. Five months earlier, on May 11, Consul Burton Berry sent a confidential report:

> The Jews of Thessaloniki have already been deported to Poland where it is believed that their fate is a dark and terrible one. This informant says that when he was in Thessaloniki, he saw these people being herded like cattle into railway boxcars, preparing to leave for the north, and he gave other unsavory details about the frightful conditions under which they were forced to travel. He also reports that *a German Anti-Jewish*

---

121 Jacques Kostis, letter to the author, July 10, 1976.

Committee has arrived in Athens to mete out a similar fate to the Jews of Southern Greece [emphasis added].[122]

In most Greek cities, except Athens and Patras, the Jewish community usually voluntarily lived in their own quarters. They socialized among themselves, and few of them had close Christian friends. The Greek Jews, after living for centuries as a tolerated minority, were conditioned to adopt a second-class, submissive way of thinking. Their community leaders were usually elected on the basis of their wealth. They were conservative men who believed that everything was subject to negotiations. They believed they could "make a deal" with the Germans as they did with everybody else. They could not abandon their possessions and so thought that nobody else should "rock the boat" and escape their vigilance by leaving the city. They did everything in their power to stifle dissent. Their religious leaders were ineffectual. Rabbi Molho wrote, "Is not, perhaps, all this enormous destruction somehow the finger of God? It is known that in the last decades the Jews of Thessaloniki neglected their religious duties."[123]

The most important of all Greek Jewish leaders, Rabbi Koretz, believed that obeying German orders was the best way to save the Jews. But did he really have to do a better job than the Germans could have done themselves? Did he have to persuade the Jews of Florina and Veria to remain in their cities when it was extremely easy for them to go to the mountains? Did he have to ask the chief of police of Katerini to arrest the Jews of his city and send them to Thessaloniki? Had the role of Rabbi Koretz descended to that of an SS officer, who would normally have made a request like this?

When the German restrictive orders came, the Jews in most cities did not act like proud individuals but rather submitted as a group to the registration process. In Thessaloniki, those Jews who wished to save themselves from the degradation of deportation moved to the Italian zone of occupation, joined the resistance or went to the free territories. In Athens in September 1943, the Jews were given a fighting

---

122 National Archives No. 8 8.401/74, November 20, 1943.
123 Molho, *In Memoriam*, 202.

I. Events – Italian Zone of Occupation

chance thanks to resistance leaders like Archbishop Damaskinos, Chief of Police Angelos Evert and EAM leader Baruch Schibi.

In the literature, the Greek clergy is given the greatest credit for the survival of most of the Jews who were not captured. But if Archbishop Damaskinos helped save so many Jews, where were his counterparts—the bishops of Ioannina, Arta, Preveza, Veria, Corfu, Rhodes and Chania—whose Jewish populations were totally destroyed? Bishop Chrysostomos of Zakynthos, who acted in a heroic manner, is listed among the righteous, but his defiance of the Germans could not have saved a single Jew.

Bishop Gennadios of Thessaloniki is also listed among the Righteous Among the Nations. He pleaded with the Germans for "magnanimity and clemency," but no Jew was saved by him. The difference between the archbishop and the bishops was that Damaskinos acted as a resistance leader in a city where the population was practically in revolt against the Germans. It is true that Athens, an enlightened city with a miniscule Jewish population, did not have the level of anti-Semitism that existed in Thessaloniki and other provincial cities. But this did not make a drastic difference in the number of those saved. Even in Athens, where only a few thousand Jews were dispersed among one million people, many Jews were betrayed and captured. Perhaps a few more Jews could have been saved in Thessaloniki and other cities if the Christians there were less apathetic or hostile than they were in Athens. The fact remains that approximately 7,500 Jews, or 95 percent of those who were not captured, do not owe their lives to any specific benevolent Christian who hid them in their home. The Jews used their false identity cards, escaped to the Middle East, and, most of all, went to the free mountains. In the final analysis, the question as to whether Jews could have been saved in great numbers in any particular city did not depend as greatly as one might suppose on anti-Semitism, the quality of the Christians, or the assistance of the clergy. In Greece, two elements were of paramount importance: Jewish leadership, which failed miserably in Thessaloniki or Ioannina, and the assistance (or lack thereof) of the right and left resistance organizations.

In cities where the resistance organizations were strong, such as Athens, Trikala, Larissa, Volos, Patras and Agrinion, the great majority of the Jews were saved. In Ioannina, Arta and Preveza, the Jewish leaders were inept, and the deportations took place at a time when the resistance organizations of EDES and EAM were busy fighting each other in that area. They did not make any effort to save the Jews. The great majority of the Jews perished.

In the cities of Macedonia and Thrace, the Jewish leadership was bad, and the resistance organization of EAM was not as strong in March 1943 as it was in March 1944. Right-wing resistance did not exist. The number of German collaborators was great. Some of them had formed armed bands, which ELAS destroyed after the deportations. Worst of all, the Jews there were taken by total surprise, as in Poland.

On October 9, 1943, two days after General Stroop, known as the "Butcher of the Warsaw Ghetto," issued his order in Athens, the American diplomat Leland Harrison notified Washington, D.C. by telegram. Two weeks later, on October 22, Consul Berry forwarded the following "Regulations" to Washington, D.C.

REGULATIONS

1. All Jews subject to this order must immediately return to their permanent homes in which they were living on June 1, 1943.
2. Jews are forbidden to leave their permanent residence or to change their place of residence.
3. Jews in Athens and its environs are obliged to appear within five days at the Jewish Religious Center in Athens for registration. Those living outside Athens will report to the Greek mayor or to community officers.
4. Jews who do not observe these orders will be shot. Non-Jews who hide Jews, give them shelter, or help them to escape will be sent to labor camps or receive a more severe punishment.
5. Jews of foreign citizenship must report on October 18, 1943, at 9:00 a.m. to the Jewish Religious Center in Athens and there register a copy of their evidence of foreign citizenship. Outside Athens they are to report to the above-mentioned Greek authorities.

I. Events – Italian Zone of Occupation

6. The Jewish Religious Center in Athens is designated from this moment as the only representative of all Jewish interests in Greece. It must immediately form a council of elders and take up its duties. Further instructions will be given later.
7. After registration, every male Jew, fourteen years of age and over, must report every second day at the above-mentioned place.
8. Jews are forbidden to walk on the streets or in open places between the hours of 5:00 p.m. and 7:00 a.m.
9. The Greek police will be ordered to control the enforcement of the above order most severely, and immediately to arrest Jews or other persons who prevent its being executed.

All those are considered as Jews who have at least three grandparents of Jewish race, regardless of their religious affiliations.

Athens, October 3, 1943

>The Higher SS and
>Police Leader of
>Greece Stroop
>SS Brigade Leader and
>General Major of the
>Police[124]

Consul Berry reported further data:

> One must confess that the Athenians have shown a more humane attitude than the people of Thessaloniki and because of that there is reason to hope that a large part of the Jews can be saved from falling into German hands. There have been cases, however, in which in order to find a safe refuge, it was necessary to pay fifty or even one hundred English gold pounds to the person who gave him shelter.

---

[124] Berry, National Archives, No. 35522.

The EAM organization has recruited a large number of Jews who know English and has sent them to their headquarters in the mountains. Others, most of them young men, have joined the guerrillas. Others went to live in the region called "Free Greece." Others went to Euboea in order to escape by boat. The EAM, which has organized several groups, asked everyone in good circumstances to assure the support of two destitute Jews. The organization has distributed leaflets to the Athenians, asking them to give assistance. In the place of embarkation in Euboea, the guerrillas have permitted only Jews to depart, and it was only after taking an oath [that they were Jews] that the refugees were allowed to continue their journey.

EAM permitted only Jews to depart because boats in both the British-Greek and American services transport Jews only if there happen to be vacant places. A change of policy would facilitate the escape of Jews. The benevolent attitude towards the Jews on the part of EAM makes the task of rescuing Jews simply a question of organization and financial support.

During the five-day period specified by the German order, only fifty to sixty persons, chiefly those who found no place of refuge, registered. In view of this, the Germans prolonged the registration period to October 17, but there were some who registered on October 18 without being penalized.

The Germans gave to each one who registered a white card without photographs on which were written the name, address, and occupation together with a list of dates, indicating that the bearer should report every second day. In the case of an invalid, an exception was made, and he was told to register every fourth day. Those married to Christians received brown cards.

Until October 20, they had not pillaged any Jewish shops with the exception of the shop of Alhadef and that of Eliezer Solomon and a warehouse at 60 Kypseli Street. The furniture of several private houses has been removed. Houses of Jews, occupied by Christian friends who have declared that they have bought the property, have not been touched. The hidden Jews will

I. Events – Italian Zone of Occupation

suffer only if the Germans offer rewards to those who denounce them, as such a reward is a great temptation to people suffering from hunger.[125]

On October 18, 1943, the Spanish and the Argentinean Jews were requested to register at the community offices. The Spanish embassy protested vigorously: "Taking under consideration the friendly relations which exist between Spain and Germany, this Embassy cannot comprehend the reasons for which the Spanish citizens were subjected to a treatment less favorable than that which was given to citizens of other nations. The Spanish laws prohibit the mention of race on identity cards. For this reason, I am obliged to give new I.D.s to these Sephardim."[126]

There were 35 Argentinean Jews in Athens. Twenty of them obeyed the German order to register. Argentina's consul general in Athens, Juan Faguis, also protested:

> The Argentinean constitution does not make any distinction between race or religion. All Argentinean citizens are equal while the Argentinean authorities do not have the right to ask an Argentinean citizen what his religion is. The laws of Argentina forbid Argentinean citizens who live outside the country to belong to political parties, religious communities, etc. The tens of thousands of German citizens who live in Argentina enjoy complete freedom and have all rights without any restrictions in comparison to citizens of other countries.

The hint was well taken by the Germans. This vague threat of retaliation most probably saved the Argentinean Jews.

---

125 Berry, National Archives, 9-1483 October 22, 1943.
126 Enepekidis, op. cit.

The Illusion of Safety

Escape by Boats

In his book *Open the Gates,* Ehud Avriel notes a Mossad contribution to the rescue effort. (Mossad was a branch of the Haganah, the Jewish defense organization of Palestine.) Early in 1944, Agami, a Palestinian Jew and a Mossad agent, went to Izmir and met with Rafael Baki, a wealthy Jewish merchant who had a brother living in Athens. Baki used to send his brother medicines and food with the help of Greek fishermen who smuggled people and merchandise between Greece and Turkey. Agami contacted the leader of the fishermen, Thomas, who informed him that he was not actually a smuggler but rather a member of the EAM-ELAS resistance movement. Agami proposed to Thomas a cooperative agreement between the two resistance groups, Haganah and EAM. EAM was to help transfer Jews from occupied Greece to Turkey, while Haganah was to provide EAM with medicines, blankets, and uniforms or one gold sovereign per person. As Baki in Athens transported Jewish families to Euboea, Thomas and his small boats transferred them through treacherous mined and patrolled waters to Izmir. The Turks in turn helped these people go to a rest camp for transfer to Syria and eventually Palestine. The agreement between Agami and Thomas provided that only Jews were to be transferred in his boats. The British were constantly afraid that spies would infiltrate the Middle East, and the exclusive participation of Jews in the Thomas rescue effort was designed to eliminate the British objections. In addition, the British were not in favor of increasing Jewish immigration to Palestine. One day Agami was meeting with Thomas in Baki's living room, and Thomas told him that on the last trip he had included a non-Jewish patriot of Greece. He was positive that he was not a spy because he knew him well. His name was George Papandreou, the future prime minister of Greece. Agami accepted Thomas's statement and paid him the extra gold coin.[127]

The need to cross the Aegean was so great that hundreds of Jews, including a group of Spanish citizens who did not trust the Franco regime, faced terrible dangers by attempting the journey. They crossed on unreliable boats that they bought at

---

127 Ehud Avriel, *Open the Gates* (New York: Atheneum Press), 150.

I. Events – Italian Zone of Occupation

great prices and whose captains were often either crooks who stole their money or traitors who handed them over to the enemy. In one case, a dishonest man masqueraded himself as a priest to gain the confidence of a group of escapees. They gave him an enormous sum to rent a boat that was to meet them in a small port of Euboea. The boat never arrived, and the "priest" disappeared, leaving the people alone on a deserted coast infested with German patrols. Groups of British military, Jews, saboteurs, volunteers for the Allied forces, and others used this escape route. One boat was struck by a terrible storm and was unable to reach Turkey. It sought shelter in the German-occupied island of Chios. The Jews were arrested along with the rest of the passengers. Soon the Germans learned who the Jews were, but they did not have the means to deport them. They were kept in the local jail and freed only in October 1944 when the Germans abandoned the island.

A party of 26 Jews, including seven women and three children under nine years of age, arrived in Cheshme on March 2, 1944. Consul Berry interviewed four for his report:

> They left Athens in mid-December and went to Euboea by boat. After waiting there one-and-a-half months, they finally succeeded in obtaining transportation to Turkey and they left Euboea on February 28. Because of stormy weather, the boat was obliged to put in at Skyros for one night. The four members who were interviewed were Jacques H. Benrubi, a civil engineer and a Paris graduate; David J. Faraggi, director of the Austro-Hellenic Tobacco Company and Honorary Chancellor of the Austrian Consulate General in Thessaloniki; Moise Nachmias, director of an oil company; and Oscar Salem, director of the Salem Bank of Thessaloniki. They did not leave Greece because the situation changed, but because it was the consensus of opinion that the Jews of the Italian zone will soon be arrested. Even Salem, who is of Spanish nationality, feels that it is not safe to stay in Greece.
>
> Those who are hidden, if they do not stay with friends, pay a high price for their quarters. More and more Jews, because of poverty, are forced to register. No penalty is imposed for late registration and since

there was no persecution of those who had obeyed the order, gradually more and more Jews register. It is very expensive to remain in hiding. Recent changes in the system of having the registered Jews report have aroused some suspicion. Instead of being obliged to report every two days . . . each time the Jews report they are told when to return and are allowed a very short interval in which to appear, often not more than fifteen minutes. This means that all registered Jews of Athens are gathered periodically in one place, and it is feared that on one of these occasions the Germans will seize them. The fear is strengthened by the German insistence that the registered Jews persuade others to register.

The Christians of Thessaloniki had an unsympathetic and sometimes hostile attitude toward the Jews during the persecutions of 1943. Not so of the Christians of Athens for whom the refugees expressed their respect and admiration.

In other parts of Greece, like in Ioannina, the Jews do not wear the yellow star, they were not required to register, and they have to pay for a permit to leave the city. Otherwise, their daily life goes on much as usual. In Corfu there are also no reports of persecution.

There is no organization or underground movement for aiding the Jews of Greece. Those who leave the country do so upon their own initiative and through private channels. For the rich the undertaking is difficult and full of hardships. Some wealthy people pay for the expenses of poor ones. It is not easy even for rich Jews to obtain passage from Euboea to Turkey, because the English and American services can take only a limited number of Jews.

EAM maintains a consistently benevolent attitude toward Jews, often actually protecting them from open hostility on the part of the inhabitants of certain Albanian-speaking villages on Euboea, but it cannot give them food. A recent arrival reported that he lived on onions for six weeks and he was devoured by lice.

The Jews made the most urgent plea that the Allies and especially the United States of America should provide organized aid for escape from Greece,

I. Events – Italian Zone of Occupation

especially for the poor ones who are registered with the Germans. All Jews remaining in Greece, whom the Germans can find, only await the fate that befell the Jews of Thessaloniki in March 1943.[128]

The Greek-British Service operated small boats and encouraged the departure of selected groups, primarily those eligible for the Free Greek forces in the Middle East. This service occasionally caused complications for the Jewish escapees.

In December 1943, the escape movement came to a near complete stop when EAM, in control of the island of Euboea, seized two of the boats in the British-Greek Service and refused to allow departures except for Jews. Consequently, until January 1944 the British lost what had come to be their more or less regular service of crossing and recrossing the Aegean. EAM relented only when threatened by the British with a total stoppage of supplies. But even then EAM reserved the right to control all departures, with the understanding that army officers and men of military age, with the exception of naval and air force personnel, would not be allowed to leave. Boats approaching the Turkish coast ran the risk of being fired upon by Turkish guards, but this was probably unavoidable because of the impossibility of giving notice of arrival and the difficulties of establishing identity. In general, the Turkish attitude was gratifying.

If those who arrived in Izmir had funds, they rented rooms in hotels and pensions; the others were given shelter by the police for less than a week and then were transported to Syria. The Greek consulate in Izmir recorded that approximately 1,100 Jews reached Izmir before February 1944.[129]

According to the British and royal Greek view, EAM complicated the selection of the escapees by insisting "it is the patriotic duty of all army men and officers to stay in the country and fight the enemy." EAM did not encourage the departure of Christians over forty years of age, and the groups it allowed to cross did not include women and children, except for the Jews.

---

128 National Archives, No. 1746 (R-1618).
129 National Archives, Modern Military Section 868.4016/75.

The Illusion of Safety

People left Athens in groups of two or three; some by train and some by bus. All had permission by the police to leave Athens on some pretext or another in order to pass the German control. One of the groups spent a night in a village and was picked up the following night, as scheduled, by a small fishing boat with motor and sails. The captain drank for several hours with the German guards in a nearby port, and when he judged they were no longer awake for their duties, he sailed out of port.

Another EAM-sponsored group was organized in Athens and told that the organization in Euboea would have the necessary instructions. But the local EAM did not receive any notification. One of the group had to go back to Athens to arrange the matter. This group of fifty refugees had to walk for 12 hours to reach the ELAS headquarters of Euboea. Later the partisan leader informed them that they could return to the same fishing village, but because German troop movements were reported in the area, they had to follow a different, even longer route, requiring 14 hours of walking. Their despair was tempered by the fact that a couple of days later, in the fishing village, a member of the party arrived from Athens bringing the permit for their departure.

It is estimated that approximately 1,500 Jews found safety in the Middle East. Some went to Turkey by train, and they contacted the American consulate in Istanbul. On February 19, 1944, such a man met Consul Berry, who reported his story to Washington:

> My informant, a well-to-do Jewish rug merchant, left Athens February 8 and traveling by military train up to a point, then by the regular express, arrived in Istanbul, February 12. He said that all the homes and movable property of those who left were immediately confiscated and the Jewish shops were completely looted. Those Jews who reported to the authorities, as well as a number who were later betrayed by people who had given them refuge, have been assigned to work in the gunpowder factory at Haidari on the road to Eleusis. Jews of foreign nationality registered on October 18. The Spanish Jews, about 150 in number, who had escaped to Athens from Thessaloniki, are in a serious predicament. The Spanish government has refused to accept them on the grounds that they are

I. Events – Italian Zone of Occupation

Communists, and they are now making desperate efforts to obtain transit visas to Turkey in order to proceed to Palestine.

It was stated by the informant that immediately following the breaking off of diplomatic relations between Argentina and Germany, on the night of January 28, between 11:00 p.m. and 2:00 a.m., the SS arrested twenty Argentine subjects. Other Greek Jews fled to Italy, and some of them escaped to Switzerland, while others, including the Bomburg family which had connections with the Italian Legation in Athens, are reported to have been killed on the Italian-Swiss frontier.[130]

Belevy, a captured partisan, was tried by a German courtmartial. His trial took place in the literary club "Parnassos." He declared in front of the judges, "I am a Jew and I fought as a Jew and I will die as a Jew."[131]

The fear of betrayal was real because the Germans, aware of the existence of false identity cards, employed a new lethal weapon—the Jewish traitor who knew his prospective victims personally. The traitors offered "protection," or they blackmailed the people they discovered, and they delivered many into the hands of the Gestapo. The brothers Recanati, David Benejia, and Daniel Kohen (or Mihailidis) were the most important Jewish traitors.[132] Another group of traitors who could do for the Germans what the Germans were unable to do by themselves were Greeks of the security battalions and many ordinary Greek Christians. The last group would have been far more numerous if it were not for fear of retribution by EAM.

The peculiar accent of the Ladino-speaking Jews of Thessaloniki could be recognized only by traitors. The same would be true for the general appearance or physical characteristics of the Jews, which the Germans could not distinguish by themselves. People were stopped in the streets. If their Jewish identity were discovered, the German collaborators demanded money, gold, watches, or even shoes.

---

130 (R-2494) 3/18/1944.
131 "Les Juifs en Europe," Editions du Centre, 54.
132 Molho, *In Memoriam*, 182.

Many of the victims were delivered to the Germans anyway. Over 200 Jews were caught while they were "in hiding" and delivered to the Haidari concentration camp in Athens.

Among the German documents, there are many concerning the betrayal of Jews by different traitors who were motivated by a variety of reasons. For example, on August 31, 1943, a lady cautiously entered the German embassy in Athens and was admitted to the Office of the Counselor, Dr. Vogel. She made her deposition and departed. Dr. Vogel dictated to a tape recorder what the mysterious lady, a French woman married to a Greek, told him. She did not wish to reveal her name and requested to be called "Madame Rose." This is what she declared:

> At 10 Abramiotou Street (Monastiraki) telephone 34-104 there is an office which is directed by two Jews from Thessaloniki. Its secret mission is to supervise the transfer of Thessaloniki Jews to Palestine. The two owners of the office are Albert and Emmanuel. The last name of one is Kohen. Also with them is an English Jew, who, while he was in Poland or someplace else, served with the Gestapo as a German. He knows several languages perfectly. Two among the Jews who are going to be sent to Palestine within a few days sleep in the house of an old lady in Podonifti (Terma Patission, Nea Philadelphia). One of the Jews from Thessaloniki was baptized here and changed his name from Albert to Theodoros. He is married to my daughter.[133]

Madame Rose did not approve of this marriage because she did not like the groom from the beginning. She begged that her daughter be spared, being totally ignorant of her husband's activities. She stated that Theodoros or Albert (Kohen) listens to foreign broadcasts and always knows the latest news. Madame Rose learned all by eavesdropping on discussions that took place in the adjacent room: she knew a bit of Greek.

On December 20, 1943, the Germans arrested a group of Jews who were hiding in an apartment at 47 Kefallinias Street.

---

[133] Enepekidis, article 11.

I. Events – Italian Zone of Occupation

They were Alberto Gattenio, Levi Benojilio, and Zerman and Loucia Benojilio. Since they were Spanish citizens, the Spanish embassy protested. The Germans attempted to explain the reason for the arrest as follows: "They are Jews who traveled from Thessaloniki to Athens with forged identity cards which had Greek names. They were therefore arrested on the basis of proven crimes." The Spanish ambassador submitted many documents rejecting the accusations and demanding the release of his citizens. In April 1944, Ambassador Sebastian De Romera threatened the German ambassador that he would report this affair to Madrid. On May 30, 1944, they were released from the Haidari concentration camp.[134]

During these difficult times, the traitors were continuously active, as the following German document illustrates:

> On January 19, 1944, it was reported to the Germans that on 5 Sparta Street, Athens, and in the residence of the Greek, John Bouraki (a jeweler) there was hidden merchandise belonging to Jews which was given for safekeeping by the escaped Jew, Benahmia. Besides the above-mentioned fabrics, they said that in this same house there were watches and jewelry belonging to the Jew, Bourla.[135]

Bourakis was interrogated and confessed that he possessed merchandise belonging to the Jew, Benahmia, who had been in hiding for the last six months. In an attic, they found the merchandise, which they confiscated.

Patras

Something extraordinary happened in Patras. The hero responsible for the low number of losses (33%) was Mr. Wolfson, an interpreter for the German Commander of Patras. When Mr. Wolfson saw the order for the obligatory registration of the Jews, he immediately went to the shop of Isaak Matsas and told him about it. Matsas, who was the president of the

---

134 Enepekidis, article 11.
135 Enepekidis, article 19.

Jewish Community, then contacted all the heads of the Jewish families and asked them to meet him that evening in the synagogue. There, he told them that he has information that forces him to take his family to the mountains the following day. He advised all of them to do the same. All those who could afford to go to the mountains did so. Only the poor, who remained, obeyed the German orders after they were published in the Greek newspapers.

Mr. Wolfson was considered to be a half-Jew by the Germans. He was able to send his German Jewish father to the mountains. His mother was a German Christian. Thousands of German half-Jews served in the German armed forces in the first years of the war. In 1942, only one-quarter Jews, who had only one Jewish grandparent, served in the German forces until the end of the war. After the war, the parents of Mr. Wolfson went back to Germany, while their son remained in Patras as a businessman and a good friend of the Jews of Patras.[136]

(By the way, the German Jewish field marshal, Erhard Milch, served as second in command of the German Air Force, Lüftwaffe, under the command of Hermann Goring who famously declared, "I decide who is a Jew!")

The Theft of Jewish Wealth

In April 1979, a high Greek government official published, under an assumed name, previously unknown details about the German plunder of Jewish assets in Greece. The German military command issued a law stipulating that all Jewish assets in Greece belonged to the Greek state. Whoever informed the German authorities about hidden or undeclared Jewish assets was entitled to 20 percent of them. The remaining 80 percent belonged by law to the Greek state. It is obvious that the "law" and the "participation" of the Greek authorities was only a smokescreen covering the Germans' orgy of plunder and crime. The assets of the Jews were delivered by the SS officers to their departments. A large part, however, consisting especially of jewelry and other precious

---

[136] Personal communication by Joseph Yohanas, June 1976.

items, was kept for themselves, something which stimulated their appetite for "action." The case of the Jewish community of Rhodes represents a typical example.

After the fall of Italy, General Walter Schimana sent Anton Burger, Friedrich Linnemann, and other "specialists" to Rhodes on a special mission. They confiscated gold and jewelry and placed the loot in nine big boxes, which Burger transferred by plane to Athens. The biggest portion of this treasure, which was estimated at 300,000 gold sovereigns, was delivered to the German authorities, while the remainder was stolen by Burger and Linnemann. These two officers used a trusted intermediary who sold the gold and jewelry to two Athenian jewelers for 4,000 gold sovereigns, while the real market value was 15,000 gold sovereigns. General Schimana gained the most out of this "deal." Of the nine boxes, he sent only three to Vienna on board a special Lufthansa plane. The plane was shot down near Belgrade by Allied aircraft. Gold coins and jewelry fell over a wide area and were collected by surprised Yugoslavs. The remaining six boxes were divided among high German officials; Schimana's portion from Rhodes was eighty thousand to one hundred thousand gold sovereigns. This was revealed after the war by Arthur Zaits, head of the German Secret Service in Greece.

When in June 1941, the SS were sent to the Russian front, the German commander of Athens, Colonel Schubert, appointed Leopold Huger on behalf of the SS the "comptroller" of Jewish fortunes in Greece. Huger provoked the envy and jealousy of Chief of German Naval Intelligence Captain Neneke, who accused him of keeping most of the proceeds from the confiscation of Jewish assets for himself while very little was delivered to his superiors. One of the first and most important fortunes to attract Huger's interest was that of the Britannia Company. Huger sold its merchandise, consisting of woolen fabrics of great value, through intermediaries in the Athenian market. Huger and his collaborators gained enormous amounts of money.

Another German citizen, Pavlofsky, who was employed by a jewelry shop in Athens, was sent to Thessaloniki, where the SD section asked him to appraise the value of the precious stones that were confiscated from the Jews of Thessaloniki. The false or defective stones were sold in Germany. Zaits also revealed that in October 1943 the SS commander of

Thessaloniki sent three boxes of the jewelry of the Jews of Thessaloniki to Berlin by plane with a strong fighter escort. The boxes were insured for 600,000 gold sovereigns. When the Allies entered Germany in 1945, they discovered treasure of great value hidden in a salt mine by Himmler's service.

In February 1943, the Germans organized a special service under the name "3000," whose purpose was the infiltration of the Middle East by German agents. The officers of the "3000," at the beginning, financed their enterprise with Greek counterfeit currency, but later they discovered the Jews were a better source of funds. Arthur Zaits wrote:

> The people of "3000" were not in charge of the persecution of the Jews, but they started a systematic unofficial persecution because they found it very profitable. Many of those whom they arrested were taken to their lair on 8 Pamisou Street, where they took everything they had or extorted enormous amounts in order to let them go and live. Many Christians were victimized in the same fashion. In order to find more victims, the "3000" service organized escapes to the Middle East with Greek agents, employing its own boats. Cars of the service transferred its victims, consisting mostly of wealthy Jews, to a remote coast where a boat would take them for the trip to Turkey. Every passenger carried with him as much gold and precious items as possible. When many passengers were collected, the boat left Piraeus escorted by another armed vessel belonging to the service. The passengers boarded the boat, and they were on their way to Turkey when, at a prearranged point, the armed vessel fired once as a signal for the boat to stop for inspection. Since the official documents of the passengers were never in order, the boat was forced to return to Piraeus, where the passengers were taken on board trucks to the lair of 8 Pamisou Street for the "consequences." During one such "pirate mission," the armed boat was forced to exchange fire with an Allied

I. Events – Italian Zone of Occupation

submarine, which surfaced by accident in the waters of Kavo Doro.[137]

On November 25, 1943, the military governor of Greece issued an order confiscating all the assets of the Jews of Greek nationality who did not register with the authorities: "Assets are considered all items and rights representing monetary value, real estate, rents, farm income, corporate agreements, demands of every type, stocks and bonds. All confiscated assets will be given to the Greek state for management."[138]

Rabbi Barzilai went to the seat of the political committee of EAM and made an appeal, which was broadcast by the recently established radio station of the Resistance. The appeal was made to Jews in free countries, as well as to President Roosevelt, Prime Minister Churchill, and Rabbi Wise of New York. Parts of the appeal are as follows: "Appalling suffering is undergone by Greek Jewry. Unfortunately, Greek security battalions also participate in the execution of anti-Semitic measures. Few Jews have been saved, and they owe their safety to EAM/ELAS. I appeal for medicines, clothes, food. Signed, Grand Rabbi, Elia Barzilai."[139]

The British Foreign Office expressed its concern about this appeal, which the American agent "Z" also reported to Washington. The British embassy in Washington, D.C. sent a memorandum to George Warren of the United States State Department, which read in part: "The Senior British liaison officer at ELAS headquarters has interviewed the Chief Rabbi and has formed the opinion that the latter has no political feelings."[140]

John Pehle of the War Refugee Board did not trust the British. Commenting on a suggestion that the United States, Great Britain, and Greece should formulate a policy regarding the escape of Jews, he wrote: "We are inclined to believe that

---

[137] Sarantis Asteriadis, "The Hell of the Jews of Rhodes," *Chronika*, Athens 1979, 3.
[138] National Archives, letter of Special Attache Hirschmann to McKelley.
[139] National Archives, No. 2456-2828 (R-2445) File No. 820-02.
[140] Public Record Office London No. FO 371.

this suggested action would probably not be calculated to facilitate the rescue of Jews from Greece."[141]

As soon as the anti-Jewish measures were announced, the Turkish Consul General presented himself at the German embassy and clarified his views on the subject: "Turkish law forbids all Turkish citizens from registering themselves with foreign political organizations. On the other hand, the Turkish Consul said a registration of the Turkish community had already taken place and this included the Jews. As proof, the Turkish consul general showed us the enclosed list of seventy-one Turkish Jews, adding that he would be glad to provide more information for every single one of these Jews."[142] The Turkish consul general gave the impression that he protected many Turkish citizens. At the same time, he betrayed these same citizens to the Germans, facilitating their arrest on March 24, 1944.

Germany and Argentina broke diplomatic relations on January 28, 1944. The 19 Athenian Jews of Argentinean nationality were immediately arrested. Numerous Argentinean protests failed to release them until the Germans felt that "their release is desirable because we do not wish to give the government of Argentina an excuse to retaliate against the German citizens residing in its country."[143] These 19 Jews survived because of this perceived threat of retaliation against Germany.

On October 9, 1943, the Spanish embassy in Athens attempted to save nine Spanish Jews married to "Aryan" women from persecution. They were Manouel Boulis, Jacob Saporta, Marcel Kohen, Solomon Arditti, Salvator Hassia, Alberto de Magio, Alberto Gattenio, Solomon Biti and Francis Salem.[144] [Author's note: Since the German archives did not mention these men again, in June 1975 I inquired of the Jewish community of Athens whether these people survived the war. Yohana Vital, president of the community, informed me that all of them were alive and well!"][145]

---

141 National Archives, No. 2844 (R-2642).
142 Enepekidis, article 15.
143 Enepekidis, article 16.
144 Enepekidis, article 11.
145 Jewish Community of Athens, letter no. 354, 6/23/76.

I. Events – Italian Zone of Occupation

In the Greek Islands

Nearly four years after plans for the "Final Solution" went into effect, the 5,000 Jews of the Greek islands continued working and living in their familiar environment, waiting for the war to end. By March 1944, the Germans were in control only of the cities, while the countryside was in the hands of the partisans. In Rhodes and Kos, moreover, one could see and easily reach the Turkish coast. The Germans arrested island Jews on the following dates: Euboea— March 24, 1944; Chania, Crete—June 6, 1944; Corfu—June 9, 1944; and Rhodes-Kos— July 20, 1944. The Germans left Greece on October 12, 1944.

Euboea

Euboea is so large and so close to mainland Greece that few people think of it as an Aegean island. In Chalkis, its capital, 325 Jews were centered around its old synagogue. In October 1943, most of the island's Jews went to the villages of Euboea, which were in free territory. At least ten families escaped to Turkey on every kind of small craft, braving German patrols, mines, and bad weather. Ninety people registered with the Germans. Others, including the rabbi, remained hidden in the city. On the night of March 24, 1944, ninety people were arrested. Another 17 Jews who went to villages were captured during German search-and-destroy missions; they were deported to the camps. The handsome 25-year-old Simon Frankis was caught by the Germans and their collaborators; he was executed in the military barracks. A few months later, the rabbi, Moissis Douliski, and Mazalto and Froso Levi, who were in hiding, were betrayed and imprisoned. They were not deported. A few days before the liberation of the city, they were set free.

Corfu

On June 7, 1944, the Allies entered Rome. The Jews of Corfu believed that the war was practically over. The Germans thought otherwise. They placed posters all about the island ordering the Jews to return to their homes by June 8. At 5:00

a.m. on Friday, June 9, the Germans knocked at every Jewish door and ordered everyone, including the sick and the invalids, to go to the army square. By 6:00 a.m. the entire community was assembled in the square surrounded by German and Greek police. Suddenly air-raid sirens announced the approach of Allied planes. As the captives instinctively sought cover, the Germans fired in the air, forcing them to remain in place. As the planes flew over the city, a German officer assisted by an interpreter took the roll call, family by family. The captives were taken inside the neighboring old fortress, where all were forced to surrender their valuables: gold, jewelry, money, even scissors and shaving blades, and the keys to their homes, which the Germans looted and then sold what they did not want. The mayor of Corfu, a German-appointed collaborator, gave a speech to his municipal council: "Our great friends, the Germans, cleaned our island of the Jews."[146]

On June 11, they placed 300 women on barges pulled by motorboats. Midwives were allowed to accompany the deportees and assist the pregnant women. The barges arrived at the port of Igoumenitsa on the Greek mainland, where waiting trucks transported the women to Athens. On June 14, the male prisoners, along with the remaining women and children, were transported by barges pulled by a tugboat towards Lefkas. The Germans encountered numerous problems in this deportation. On May 15, 1944, Obersturmführer Anton Burger arrived in Corfu and contacted Emil Jaeger, commander of the island. The latter reported the following:

> On May 24, six barges were made ready for the future transfer of the captives. There was not enough "personnel" to proceed with the arrests. Burger obtained the assistance of the Feldgendarmerie and the Secret Police stationed in Ioannina. On May 30, Captain Magnus, Commander of the Navy in western Greece, placed at my and Burger's disposal (in spite of the enormous expense of 9,000 gallons of petrol), other

---

146 Gideon Hausner, *Justice in Jerusalem*, 128.

I. Events – Italian Zone of Occupation

barges for the transfer of 1,795 Jews from Corfu to Patras.

Dr. Miklos Nyiszli, who did autopsies in the Auschwitz concentration camp, related the arrival and fate of the Corfu deportees from the June 11 transport:

> Last night they burned the Greek Jews from the Mediterranean island of Corfu, one of the oldest communities of Europe. The victims were kept for twenty-seven days without food or water, first in launches, then in sealed cars. When they arrived at Auschwitz's loading platform, the doors were unlocked, but no one got out to line up for selection. Half of them were already dead and half in a coma. The entire convoy, without exception, was sent to number two crematorium.[147]

The Jews of Corfu might not have been deported if SS officials had heeded the conclusions of a "feasibility" study prepared by Colonel Jaeger:

> The tonnage of the regular vessels, which at present are at our disposal, is totally inadequate for the execution of the above order. Even the transfer of ten Englishmen required four days for their trip to Igoumenitsa where, it should be noticed, there were not any necessary vessels. The arrest of 2,000 Jews of Corfu would have met many great obstacles, and it could possibly seriously harm the defense of the island. [Note: The Allies spread the rumor of an impending invasion of Corfu, which prompted the Germans to keep their troops on constant alert.]
>
> 1. In case that additional vessels were available, they should first be used to transfer the Italians of Badoglio, who as former soldiers are much more dangerous than the Jews against whom, by the way, we never expressed any complaint.

---

147 Niklos Nyiszli, M.D., *Auschwitz* (Greenwich, CT: 1960), 83.

2. The Jews possess considerable gold reserves, jewelry, merchandise, etc. They are forewarned. Their contact with the crews of WU VII/999 would constitute great danger because the Jews would use bribery in order to be able to go to the mountains. It is suggested that the Jews should be arrested, have their homes closed, and keys delivered to the Greek authorities. Consequences: burglaries on the part of the Greek police, the population, and the soldiers.

3. Gold used for bribes would have corrupted our soldiers and German prestige, and this would only serve the enemy and the communists. On this last subject, the elections of the local Greek soviets in Corfu took place, unfortunately, without our knowledge. The communists received instructions in case of German withdrawal to move toward the city of Corfu.

4. Even if the necessary vessels were available, the action should be completed within a few days, and this is not possible since we lack both boats and reliable personnel.

5. Since the population is sympathetic toward the Jews, whom they consider as Greeks, we should anticipate perhaps a passive resistance on the part of the Greek crews of the boats.

6. A Red Cross vessel, which is still docked in Corfu's port would spread "atrocities" propaganda. Considering everything, the situation is certainly totally unsuitable for the time being.

Summary: Corfu is a military bastion. It is not possible that we should desire the deportation of the Jews because of the increase in the activities of guerrilla bands and loss of prestige in the eyes of the population. Certainly, the unavoidable barbarisms would only provoke distasteful repercussions. To all this it should be noted that we are not in a position to undertake this action speedily and painlessly.[148]

Colonel Jaeger, however, was not privy to Hitler's "Final Solution."

---

148 NOKW 1915, Nos. 3784/44 and 6493/44.

I. Events – Italian Zone of Occupation

Rhodes and Kos

On January 20, 1944, the Jews of Rhodes and Kos received the good news that King Victor Emmanuel III gave back to them and to all the Jews of Italy their civil rights, which they had lost under Mussolini. The Dodecanese were part of Italy, and therefore Italian law applied. The new liberties mesmerized the Jews and made them feel that they were not in danger.

In June 1944, Anton Burger and his assistants arrived in Rhodes to organize the deportation of the Jews. Their first step was to restrict the Jews to the locales of Trianda, Climaso and Villanuevo. Very few Jews thought of seeking refuge in the many villages of the island. One Jew, married to a Christian, went into hiding in the village of Monoloton. He was betrayed to the Germans and executed on the spot. The Germans used the services of the traitor Pepo (or Kosta) Recanati, who gained the confidence of the Jews by speaking with them in their Jewish-Levantine-Spanish dialect. On July 20, 1944, the Jews of Rhodes were arrested. A German soldier, Erwin Lenz, testified:

> I went to the city of Rhodes to see a dentist. I noticed hundreds of men, women and children standing and facing a wall in the blistering heat. Greek and Turkish civilians who offered them something to drink were kept away. I noticed they had very little luggage. I began talking to other German soldiers standing guard, and I was told that the Jews did not need any luggage since they would not live very long.[149]

The military commander of the Aegean, Lieutenant General Ulrich Kleimann, when informed that the deportation had aroused doubts and gossip among the soldiers, ordered all such discussions to stop. These were matters, he said, that soldiers "from their narrow point of view could not judge." The Germans confiscated everything of value from the deportees and looted their shops and houses for booty to send to

---

149 NOKW 1715, Deposition de Lenz, du 19-v-1947.

Germany. The deportees from Rhodes were later joined by the Jews arrested in Kos.

In June 1944, the German commander of Kos, Colonel Ruf, an anti-Nazi, contacted the Italian commander of the police, Dante Zucchelli, an anti-fascist and also an intelligence agent of the Allies. He posed the question: "In case the Jews of Kos are arrested, will there be an appropriate place to hold them?" The Italian replied: "We will find the proper place." Ruf obviously chose this way to warn the unsuspecting Jews of the storm about to hit them. Zucchelli immediately contacted Chaim Menasse, the president of the Jewish community, and suggested the Jews leave for nearby Turkey in order to save their lives. He was willing to issue false certificates of Turkish citizenship to save as many as possible.

Menasse agreed, but in a second meeting he told Zucchelli that the Germans were not going to take any measures against the Jews of Kos; he had been "assured by someone who knew the Germans well." Thus, the warning by the German and Italian officers was ignored. On Sunday, July 23, 1944, Colonel Ruf received the following order:

> The Commander of the Security Police of Greece intends to deport the Jews of Kos. The deportation should be carried out by the secret police, which should be assisted by the military command. All Jews, of every gender and age, have to be arrested and be ready for transportation by sea. They can carry with them blankets and food. All Jewish assets become the property of Italy. During the arrest, looting, maltreatment, and executions should be avoided. Every measure should be taken to ensure that the attitude of the Greek citizens will not be unfavorably influenced toward us. Jews of Turkish citizenship will not be arrested.

Colonel Ruf, on receiving the order for the arrests, conferred with his subordinates and Zucchelli, who later commented: "It was obvious that what Ruf did that day was against his will."

Zucchelli worked for two nights preparing false certificates in order to save more than the six people who were in fact Turkish citizens. When Zucchelli informed Major Mueller, who was in charge of the deportation, that there were many with Turkish citizenship, Mueller brought all the Jews to the courthouse and read a list of Jewish names. He began with the six known to be Turks. Then he read the names of those for whom Zucchelli had provided false certificates. Some girls protested: "Either all or none!" The German became angry and left the room saying: "Enough—the six people are free and they can leave. The rest remain here." By the way he handled the matter, it appears he knew who were Turks. This meeting sealed the fate of the Jews of Kos who, along with the Jews of Rhodes, were among the last to arrive in Auschwitz. (One man, Mois Menasse, somehow managed to escape when the group was in the outskirts of Athens.)

In Rhodes, on July 24, over 1,700 prisoners were placed on board two coal barges pulled by a motorboat. As they passed by Kos, the 94 arrested Jews from that island joined them. After an eight-day voyage they arrived in Piraeus.[150] Seven captives had died on board. An old woman who did not disembark quickly enough was executed. The martyrdom of the Jews of Rhodes began at the very moment they were loaded, already thirsty and hungry, into the hulls of the barges. Under the hot August sun, the dead remained with the living in the filthy atmosphere of the barges. Upon arrival in Athens, they were moved to Haidari, Hell's portal.

The Island of Zakynthos

It is assumed that the 275 Jews of Zakynthos were not arrested and deported by the Germans thanks to the efforts of Metropolitan Chrysostomos:

> When the Germans learned that Chrysostomos had studied in Munich and had met Hitler a long time ago, they treated him with respect. He took advantage of this respect for the sake of the people of Zakynthos. When the subject of the Jews arose, he and Mayor

---

150 According to Dante Zucchelli, Chief of the Italian Police, 94 Jews were arrested and not 120, which is the number mentioned in the Jewish Encyclopedia.

The Illusion of Safety

Loukas Karrer tried everything in order to save them. A telegram that he sent to Hitler became the lifesaver for the Jews. The reply was: "Let the Jews remain in Zakynthos under the personal responsibility of the Metropolitan and the mayor." That was all. The 275 Jews of Zakynthos were saved.

When the German commander of the island asked Karrer to bring him a list of the Jews of Zakynthos, the mayor offered an old gold ring to the German as a sign of hospitality and told him that the Jews are in the city catalogues together with every other citizen. He was not in a position to give him such a list. The following day the mayor, accompanied by Bishop Chrysostomos, visited the German and handed him a document. When he opened it, he saw there were only two names on it: the bishop's and the mayor's.[151]

Author's note: The Jews of Zakynthos were not arrested for the same reason that the Jews of Albania were not arrested. The Germans were simply forced to leave Greece and retreat from the Balkans to avoid a confrontation with the approaching Soviet Army before they had a chance to start the deportations.

I never believed that the Germans would have allowed the Jews of Zakynthos to survive, whereas they sent to the crematoria German Jewish invalids, recipients of the Iron Cross for gallantry during World War I. This is my opinion, since I know how my Albanian relatives survived and we know the tragic story of the deportation of the Jews of Corfu.

Cornelius Ryan, in his book, *The Last Battle* (Simon and Schuster, New York, 1966, pp. 43-44), writes the following: "Joachim Lipschitz . . . a half-Jew . . . in 1941, on the Eastern Front, had lost an arm. In April 1944, he had been marked for internment in a concentration camp. From that moment on, he had been in hiding [in the house of his fiancée] . . . The Gestapo planned to round up all those with even a drop of Jewish blood on May 19, 1945."

---

151 *To Vima*, 12/2/89, as reprinted in *Enimerotiko Deltio of the Jewish Community of Athens*, March 15, 1989.

I. Events – Italian Zone of Occupation

I hope that the above words of a prominent historian like Cornelius Ryan will put an end to the story of the telegram which was sent to Hitler and its reply which saved the Jews of Zakynthos or that the Albanian government was able to prevent the arrest and deportation of all the Jews, Albanian and foreign, residing in Albania. The reason I don't believe these stories is simple. In my opinion, no Greek or Albanian Jew deserved greater German respect than the patriotic invalid Joachim Lipschitz did, and it is obvious what the Germans planned to do to him, if only they had a little more time.

Lately, credit for the survival of the Jews of Zakynthos is given to the people of the island. The problem with this effort is that, if the Germans had attempted to arrest the 275 Jews of Zakynthos, they would have likely succeeded in capturing at least a few old, sick Jews or some invalids. But not even one Jew? Nobody ever accused the murderous Germans for incompetence.

On August 10, 1944, one month before the Germans were about to leave Greece, the U.S. government decided to make a symbolic gesture and try to help the rescue effort. I.A. Hirschman was requested to explore and expedite every possible means of expanding the program of rescue from Greece. MacFarland volunteered to open a separate base and telegraphed his superiors for their support and assistance. His superiors informed him that the Turkish Foreign Office should first approve the project. On September 9, 1944, the Turks authorized the establishment of an independent American base on the Turkish coast to be used exclusively for rescue operations of Greek refugees. Herbert Katzki, an American official, accompanied by Moshe Averbuch of the Palestine Rescue Committee, arrived at Izmir and contacted the Turkish secret police. They were informed that instructions from Ankara to authorize the opening of a base had not been received. There were instructions, however, to grant all facilities to refugees coming by sea from Greece. The Turkish official added: "The Germans had already evacuated the islands and they would soon abandon Greece."[152] It was too late to establish a base!

The Turkish Jews had been released on April 2, 1944, and they were repatriated to Turkey by train.

The last transport of Jewish deportees left Greece on August 3, 1944 for Auschwitz. They included the Jews of Rhodes and Kos who were arrested the previous week as well as many Jews who had been in hiding in Athens. Two days later, the Germans and their collaborators arrested 17 men and 13 women who were in hiding. They sent them to the Haidari concentration camp in Athens where they joined the other arrested Jews who possessed Argentinean, Iranian, and Spanish passports. On October 8, 1944, all the remaining Jews were released from captivity.

On October 12, 1944, the Germans left Athens. Roland Hampe, a German soldier, wrote: "We found the streets filled with a sea of humanity so dense that our car could only pick its way through with difficulty. I have never seen men in the grip of such joy and enthusiasm."[153]

---

152 Letter by Hirschman to John W. Pehle, executive director of the War Refugee Board, Treasury Building, Washington, DC, container No. 26.

153 Roland Hampe, *Die Rettung Athens*, Wiesbaden, Germany.

Part II

PERSONAL MEMOIRS

Chapter One

The German Zone of Occupation

He who accepts evil without protesting against it is really cooperating with it.

—HENRY DAVID THOREAU

The stories of the Greek Jews who were not captured by the Germans have one thing in common. The Greek Jews were totally unaware that by 1943 and 1944 the great majority of European Jews were already dead. They did not grasp the seriousness of their situation. The judgment, however, of more knowledgeable people was different. The resistance organization EAM issued a truly historic proclamation that was circulated in January 1943. A copy of this proclamation was discovered during a renovation of a shop on St. Markos Street in Athens in the 1980's. (It was inside an electric meter reader.) Now it is on display in the Jewish Museum of Greece, with this inscription: "The Central Jewish Council of Greece feels today a great obligation, even after the passage of so many years, to express to EAM its gratitude for this proclamation."

The proclamation states:

National Liberation Front (EAM)

For all the Greek people, brothers and sisters:

A new crime against our people is planned by the conqueror. We face a new demonstration of fascist brutality, which this time affects the Jewish members of the Greek people. The bloody conqueror prepares one of the most formidable and disgusting pogroms against the Greek Jews, like those which were organized in Germany and Poland. In Thessaloniki, thousands of innocent women and children are threatened with executions, mass slaughter, and concentration camps of the horrible Gestapo. The common thieves and murderers of the "New Order" in Europe are thirsty for blood and new victims. This new crime is not directed only against the Jews, but against the Greek people, because the Greek Jews are a part of our people, because their fate is connected with the fate of the entire Greek people.

The heroic war in Albania is a very recent event in which Jewish boys, with the same patriotic self-sacrifice, offered their blood in the struggle against fascism and the salvation of our country. Those who died in the Albanian front, were wounded, or are invalids are not few. Many Jews from the beginning of our struggle fight together with the Greek people for the liberation of our country. Therefore, when the conqueror attacks the Jews, it attacks the heroic liberation struggle of our people. The pogrom against the Jews attempts to attack the spirit of defiance of our entire people, which has become for the enemy a true nightmare now that he is collapsing under the blows of our allies on the Eastern front and in Italy. For this reason, EAM invites the people of Athens and all Greeks and every Christian to help in the salvation of the Jews, with mass protests, committees, and general mobilizations in order to prevent the horrible pogrom, which is in its planning stage. Let's give shelter and hiding places to every fugitive Jew.

II. Personal Memoirs – The German Zone of Occupation

DOWN with every pogrom against the Jews.
DEATH to the conqueror and every active traitor.
LONG LIVE the National Liberation Front (EAM).

Athens - January 22,1943
The EAM of Roumeli, Thessaly, Epirus, Thrace,
Macedonia, Ionian-Dodecanese Aegean Islands, Crete,
Peloponnesus and Jews.[154]

The First Escapees

Among those who followed the retreat of the British troops in 1941 was Mentes Besantsi, a Zionist leader. He was twice elected a member of the Greek parliament and wrote powerful anti-Nazi articles in the French language daily *Independent*. The Germans captured him during a raid on the village in Crete where he was hiding. Another Jew from Thessaloniki, Zak Ventura, a journalist and member of the Greek parliament, was arrested under similar circumstances on Crete. They were both transferred first to Larissa, where they were imprisoned, and later to Thessaloniki. For a while they were freed under the obligation to present themselves daily to the German police. In March 1943, they were arrested and deported to Auschwitz. They did not return. The fact that journalists and cosmopolitan men such as the late Mentes Besantsi and Zak Ventura did not flee from Thessaloniki when they were released is a good indication of how effective the German propaganda machine was in persuading the Jews that they had nothing to fear as long as they obeyed orders. Another journalist, Baruch Schibi, who attempted to get out of Greece, was more fortunate. This is his story:

> When it became obvious that the Germans intended to attack Greece, I had no doubts, neither about the prospect of Germany winning a war with Greece nor about the German intentions toward the Jews. I left Thessaloniki because I was sure that I was to be among the first Jews arrested. My plan was to go to the Middle

---

154 *Chronika*, November 1989, 12.

The Illusion of Safety

East. I managed to find my way to the island of Crete. An Allied convoy was ready to depart for Egypt and I was to board a ship when I saw the Germans arriving. It was too late to leave Greece. I decided to return to the Greek mainland while the battle for Crete continued in all its ferocity. Small fishing boats took me from one small island to the other. In Athens, the Gestapo was already looking for me on the basis of instructions they received from the German occupation authorities of Thessaloniki, but they were not able to discover my hideout. From that very first moment I joined the resistance organization, which ultimately became known as EAM.[155]

Something Inevitable

S. Perahia of Thessaloniki was convinced that once Greece was occupied by the Germans, the racial Nuremberg laws would be applied against the Jews sooner or later. As soon as Thessaloniki was occupied, he devoted all his energies to save his family well before the inevitable persecution. His immediate family consisted of his wife and three children, ages twelve, seven and one. They also had a young maid named Bourla from the Jewish orphanage of Thessaloniki. Mr. Perahia relates:

> My first move was to leave Thessaloniki and move to Athens, which was under Italian occupation. During 1942, this trip was extremely easy. When the persecution began in Thessaloniki, a rumor circulated to the effect that all Jews who went to Athens from Thessaloniki would be forced to return there. I applied to the City Hall of Thessaloniki requesting permission to move officially to the city of Athens. Permission was granted, but I started developing another fear. I was worried about the possibility that the Italians might apply their version of racial laws in the territories

---

[155] "The First Escapees," by Baruch Schibi, in Miriam Novitch, *Le Passage des Barbares* (Nice), 13; translated from French by the author.

attention, yet I decided that I had to take the chance. Among the many relatives I had, I was the only one who felt this way. I had to struggle with my father, my two sisters and especially my husband, who believed they would all come back from Krakow. When I realized they were all trying to prevent me from leaving, I knew I would never, with my own hands, deliver my four-year-old son to the mercy of the Germans. I declared to them, "You can do whatever you think is right; as for me, I will take my son and leave." Only then did they decide to follow my example. My brother, Mentech Nachmias, who lived in Athens, paid a respectable amount of money to a Greek railway mechanic who helped us move from Thessaloniki to Athens. This frightening journey lasted seven days and nights instead of the usual ten to 12 hours. My father, Jacob Nachmias, fell seriously ill during the trip, which was a veritable ordeal until we arrived in Platamona, where the Italian zone of occupation began. In Athens, we lived like free people until October 1943, when we had to go into hiding. A basement became our hideout. Friends had a great deal of difficulty providing us with the bare necessities. After six months of misery, we decided to make another dash for freedom. We went to the island of Euboea, where a fishing vessel took us to Turkey. The Joint Distribution Committee helped us move to Aleppo, Syria, and from there to Gaza in Palestine.[157]

The Slave Laborers

Leon Levy escaped from a forced labor camp. He recounts:

On the morning of March 24, 1943, our neighborhood was surrounded by Germans and Jewish civilian guards who ordered every man between 16 and sixty years of age to come out of their houses, each

---

[157] "From Thessaloniki to Palestine," L. Sasson. Letter to the author, translated from French by Leon Matsas.

bringing with him one blanket, a plate, a spoon and a fork. Over 1,000 men were collected, and after standing for three to four hours in a square we were led on foot to the enclosed camp of Baron Hirsch near the railway station. We waited there for a week. Then we were loaded into cattle railway cars and were transported like animals to Thebes. There we had to work very hard constructing a railway station and a railway line. Our daily food consisted of a tasteless bean soup without fat. The first days we did not even have drinking water. We had to drink water from the train engine, although we knew it was dirty. In the same forced labor camp, there were Russians, partisans, free workers and others. One day a young Jewish boy escaped, and the Germans decided to execute 200 of us in retaliation but didn't. While I was there, 25 other prisoners escaped. There were free workers in the camp who came and went through the main entrance upon showing the guards their special identity cards. I arranged with one of the free workers to find an identity card and clothes for me and meet me at 1:00 p.m. in a secluded spot. I went to the right spot at the right time, but nobody was there. I entered a nearby construction site hoping that he might be there. At this point a German saw me. He ordered me to pass the barbed wire fence and get out of the camp. I refused because his gun was pointed at me and I thought he would shoot as soon as I touched the fence. But he insisted and I had no choice but obey. I crossed the fence and for some unexplainable reason he did not shoot but ordered me to walk 300 yards and present myself at the main entrance. While I was walking toward the gate, he followed me with his gun trained on me. When I was around twenty yards from the entrance, I decided to walk in a different direction. I was actually escaping, and I was afraid that at any moment a bullet was about to hit me in the back. [Author's note: I suggested to Leon Levy that the German soldier was probably a good man who forced him at gunpoint to escape. Otherwise, why didn't he shoot him or sound the alarm? Levy did not reply to my letter.]

II. Personal Memoirs – The German Zone of Occupation

I walked fast, in spite of the tremendous heat. It was July, and I wore many layers of clothes. I walked for six hours. I stopped to drink from a small stream when out of nowhere a man called me. You can imagine my anxiety. The man was a free worker from Thebes from whom I bought raisins, oil, and other items. He took me to his mother-in-law's house, which was not too far away. There they wanted me to stay for the night. I refused to sleep in their house because I was filled with lice. We discussed the possible ways of going to Athens. They found a guide who took me through the hills to Dervenohori. There I met a few black marketeers who also wanted to go to Athens. One of them made a deal with a German truck driver to give him 5,000 drachmas for every passenger he would transport to Athens.

In Athens, I lived with my brother, Sava Levi, until October 1943. By then I knew that my wife and children had been arrested by the Germans and sent to an unknown destination. I was determined never to allow myself to be captured alive again. My brother and others were shocked by my appearance when they first saw me. After I told them about my lice, hunger, and other experiences, they agreed that it would be a big mistake to trust the Germans and follow their orders. My brother's family, together with almost fifty other friends and relatives, moved to the free village of Ougra near Thebes. I wrote to my parents in Ioannina: "The sickness that afflicted our family recently is so serious that it is going to spread to Ioannina, too. You should start taking the appropriate medicines as soon as possible." Unfortunately, they did not leave; they were arrested on March 25, 1944.

I wanted to go to the Middle East. I contacted someone who could offer me transportation, and he asked for 3,000,000 drachmas. I did not have such a large amount. Since I was a customs official, I contacted my union, and my colleagues decided on the same day to give me the money I needed to escape. I again contacted the person I mentioned before. We agreed where and when he would meet me, but he never showed up. I went to meet the others in Ougra.

Since the village did not have a teacher, I taught elementary school until the time of liberation.[158]

Would You Like to Be Saved?

One morning Dimitris Zanas woke up because there was a great deal of noise in the street. He and his friend went to the balcony and saw a group of Jewish families about to walk to a collection point. They noticed two pretty girls. "What a pity to let these girls go!" Dimitris said. They both put their overcoats over their pajamas and ran into the street. They walked beside the girls. One was Dorin Adritti, and the other was Medi Florentin, whose sister Fani was an ELAS partisan. Medi could have left with her sister, but she preferred to go where her parents went. Dimitris asked Medi, "Do you want to be saved?" Medi turned and asked her mother and uncle who were walking next to her. They both replied "Yes." Dimitris took Medi away without being noticed or stopped by anyone. The same thing happened with his friend and Dorin. (Medi was taken to a farm near Genitsa where she met and fell in love with Stratos Paraskevaidis, whom she eventually married. Dorin also survived the war.)[159]

The Two Prisoners

Robert and Mimi Assael continued hiding in the comfortable surroundings of Emilio Neri's house. Rene Gatenio had already been sent to Athens. Whenever they asked Neri to arrange their departure, he replied, "You are safe here. I have to help others who are in danger. You will leave later." The day finally arrived.

On August 3 at 11:00 p.m., two *carabinieri* (Italian military policemen) arrived at the house. The Assaels thanked their benefactors and placed themselves at the disposal of the

---

158 "The Slave Laborers," Leon Levy, letter to the author 10/10/75.
159 Would You Like to Be Saved?" story told to me by Mimi Assael October 12, 1975.

II. Personal Memoirs – The German Zone of Occupation

policemen. They were supposed to be prisoners of the Italian court in Athens. All necessary papers were prepared by the Italian consulate. They went to the same railway station where all transports began. The train, known as Tradotta, was filled with Italian soldiers, some of whom politely gave a seat to Mimi Assael and some other women. The trip was a pleasant one. The Italian soldiers sang many Neapolitan songs. Near Thermopylae a large bridge had been blown up by the partisans. All men had to walk a distance of approximately two kilometers to go to the other bank and to another waiting train.

Robert Assael and another Jewish friend of Emilio Neri, a Mr. Frances, walked this distance escorted by the guards who had their visas. Mimi Assael and the other women were taken by a car over a makeshift road. The Italian commander on the opposite riverbank was very skeptical when he was told that a woman (Mimi Assael) did not have a pass *(passa Lassare)*. She claimed to be a prisoner, and yet she was not guarded. Mimi Assael told him, "Please don't mix up the Germans into this." He understood and dropped the subject. They boarded the new train and arrived uneventfully in Athens. They found shelter in the house of Martha Matkovidi, where they stayed after they thanked the *carabinieri* and gave them a gift. (The Jewish members of EAM had a list of those who volunteered to hide Jews in their homes.) The next day the two Italians came back and told them, "Last night we went to the hotel where the *carabinieri* stay in Athens, and they did not let us sleep there because we told them that the purpose of our trip was the transfer of prisoners. When we could not say what we did with the prisoners, they threw us out, and we had to sleep in the park." Assael gave them money, and they went away happy.

The Assaels requested another hiding place. They were accepted in the house of Panteli and Mariana Mantzorou of Agiou Meletiou Street. They were members of the resistance who were proud that they had protected two British soldiers, two communists, and, finally, two Jews. The Assaels counted 358 days of living indoors in that small, pretty house. They taught French to the two sons and daughter of their hosts and managed to read all the books they had in their library.[160]

---

160 "The Two Prisoners," story told to me by Robert and Mimi Assael, October 12, 1975.

Princess Alice Saved Her Friends

Princess Alice and her father King George I of Greece were close friends with the family of Chaim Kohen of Thessaloniki. Chaim Kohen was a former member of the Greek parliament and, before the war, the royal family used to visit the Kohen family frequently in their villa.

In 1943, Princess Alice lived alone in a royal building in Psyhiko, a suburb of Athens. Prince Philip, her son, who eventually married Queen Elizabeth II, was in England. Their friend, Mrs. Kohen, now widowed, lived in Thessaloniki with her daughter Tilda. Of the four Kohen sons, Jack, Elias and Alfred had managed to escape to Egypt.

When Princess Alice learned that the Germans were going to deport the Jews of Thessaloniki, she sent a message to Mrs. Kohen, who was then in Athens, and offered the Kohen family asylum in her home. This was a very dangerous proposition for the Princess. Tilda arrived first and entered the house, then the mother and finally her fourth son Mihalis. They occupied a two-room apartment in the third floor of the building. Princess Alice told her servants that Mrs. Kohen was an old governess of her children.

Princess Alice died in 1969 and was buried in Windsor Castle. In 1988, her remains were transferred to Jerusalem to fulfill her wish to be buried next to her aunt Elizabeth, a cousin of the last Tzar of Russia. She was named Righteous Among the Nations by Yad Vashem for saving the Kohen family in 1994.[161]

The Chambermaid

Dr. Martin Luther, head of the Jewish Department of the German Ministry of Interior, complained to Foreign Minister Joachim von Ribbentrop that the events of July 12, 1942, in Thessaloniki, organized by German Max Merten and Governor-General Vasilis Simeonides, the Greek collaborator, incited many wealthy Jews from Thessaloniki to leave the city and find refuge in the Italian zone of occupation. Among those

---

161 *Chronika*, Volume 134, December 1994, page 7.

II. Personal Memoirs – The German Zone of Occupation

who left Thessaloniki then were Ida Angel and her husband and two sons.

Ida relates:

> Living conditions in Athens were not good, but at least until September 1943 there was no difference between Jews and Christians. In September, the Germans could be seen everywhere. For security reasons, we were dispersed. My son and I found one hiding place, and my husband and other son found another. One day my landlord asked us to leave immediately. He most probably suspected our true identity in spite of our false papers. I found another shelter in the house of one of the secretaries of the Spanish embassy. My official position was that of a chambermaid. He agreed to guard my secret provided I pay the rent on his apartment and perform the duties of a maid for his family. The secretary entertained lavishly, and, in my capacity as a maid, I had the pleasure to serve the clique of Greek collaborators and even some white Russian emigres!
>
> One morning four SS men, accompanied by an interpreter, entered the apartment. My son and I were arrested and transferred to the basement of the Gestapo on Merlin Street. "Where is your husband?" they yelled. I was interrogated in the typical Gestapo fashion. When one torturer became tired, the other replaced him, while a radio played a gay melody. One of the SS gave me a glass of water, hoping I would talk. "Your son will be treated the same way," they said as they pushed me and my nine-year-old son into the humid cell. The next day we were sent to Haidari. There I met many Jews of Greek, Italian, Spanish, and Portuguese nationality. One kind woman gave me a robe because mine was stained with blood. The Jewish prisoners received smaller rations than the Christians, who used to tell us, "You might be taken to another camp, while we might be executed."
>
> I was sent to Auschwitz together with my son, who was taken away from me as soon as we arrived. I was led with other prisoners to the camp. On the way I noticed the tall chimneys in the distance. I asked the

The Illusion of Safety

SS soldier who accompanied us what they were. "Garbage is burned there," he replied. I survived Auschwitz. The hope of finding my husband and other son kept me alive. On the day of the liberation, I was in a coma, and a French nurse saved me.

For months I was between life and death. When I finally arrived in Athens, what happiness! I was reunited with my husband and son, whose hiding place was not discovered. The memory of my younger son will always remain with me.[162]

On May 26, 1944, the Spanish consul sent the German ambassador the following letter:

> The General Consulate of Spain has the honor to bring to your attention that the German police found the Greek Jews, Ida Angel and her eight-year-old son, hidden in the house of Mr. Eugene Pahlevsky, who is an employee of the Consulate. They also found in the same place the Greek Jews, Ino and Daniel Gattenio.

The General Consulate of Spain expressed its great sorrow for the mistake made by Mr. Pahlevsky:

> We express our feelings of humiliation and surprise, since we never suspected that he would be able to do what he did. The Ministry of Foreign Affairs will be informed about this affair, and until its decision arrives Mr. Pahlevsky will be temporarily relieved of his duties.[163]

---

[162] "The Chambermaid," Ida Angel, in Miriam Novitch, *Les Passage des Barbares*, 98.

[163] P. K. Enepekidis, *The Secret Archives of the SS*, Article No. 9.

II. Personal Memoirs – The German Zone of Occupation

You Are Born Alone — You Die Alone

Yacov Assael recounts:

It became obvious to me that the Germans did not consider us equal to the Greek Christians when we were singled out for the infamous gathering in Plateia Eleftherias (Liberty Square). Hundreds of Greek Christians stood around watching, and I knew many of them. It was extremely embarrassing to me to have people who had known me as a human being only a few hours before watch me in this subhuman condition to which I had fallen. I realized how weak we were. We were thousands of Jews surrounded by about 100 Germans. We did not have any power. They had it all. Afterward we felt embarrassed looking at the Greek Christians, and they felt embarrassed looking at us because they were unable to help us in our misfortune. When it was rumored that we were to be resettled in Poland, people started providing themselves with warm clothing to face the cold climate there.

One day I was at my friend's house. His name was David Souleme. A Christian fellow came from Athens, where one of the Souleme brothers lived, and said he was able to get one person out of Thessaloniki. He was sent by Yacov Souleme of Athens expressly for this purpose. In the room there were, besides me, two Souleme brothers, a married sister, a younger sister, the fiancée of one brother, and their mother. A great discussion started. One brother insisted that the other should escape to freedom. Because they could not come to an agreement, they asked their mother to decide. The mother ran to the kitchen crying. The older brother persuaded the younger to leave. Before his departure, the older brother realized this might be the last time they would see each other. He showed his brother David the place he intended to hide their money and jewelry if necessary.

I believe that, in order to survive, you have to think about yourself first and then about others. I thought that a person is born alone and dies alone. In my case,

The Illusion of Safety

I remember I always thought about my own escape, and so I looked out for myself. My girlfriend, a Christian, was happy that I decided to escape, and she obtained a false identity card for me issued by the Greek police. Friends of mine asked me to join the Jewish police. The Germans said that the policemen and their families would be the last to be resettled in Poland. I refused to be a German collaborator. My big problem was the compromise my conscience had to make in abandoning my old father and sick brother. One night as we were sitting around and listening to music, my girlfriend came and told us that her father, who was a baker, received orders to bake extra bread for the following day because many Jews would be deported. When my father heard that, he told me that I should leave immediately, and he gave me almost all the money and jewelry he had. As for himself and my brother, he said, they did not need anything. What mattered most to him was to see me leave the city safely. Many parents did not act like my father. They did not allow their children to escape. Parents of a friend of mine told him that, if he left, they would take drugs and kill themselves. He did not escape to safety, and they all perished in Poland.

I started my trip early in the morning. At the bus station, I was met by my girlfriend and a man who helped in my escape. This man gave me a letter of recommendation for his brother-in-law, who lived in the village of Kailaria. In this letter he said that I was interested in buying milk because I was in the cheese business. He signed the letter with a fictitious name. He was certain that the brother-in-law would surely recognize his handwriting. In case his letter fell into the hands of the Germans, he would not be in trouble. In Kailaria, when I gave his brother-in-law the letter, he recognized the handwriting. I told him who I really was, and both he and his wife became frightened although they promised to help me. Their house was located opposite the local German army's headquarters. My hosts told me to act like a cheese merchant and to go to the coffee house and talk to the people until the right person was found who could lead me through difficult trails to the Italian zone of occupation.

After a couple of days, I started my journey with two black marketeers, who together with three donkeys were going south. One night I caught them searching my belongings. I woke up, but I did not say anything. When we approached the border, I found out that a soccer game was in progress between teams that belonged to towns located on either side of the border. As soon as the game was over, I joined the people who were returning to their town in the Italian zone. I thought how easy it was to find safety and how many people could have done just what I did.

In Larissa, I was afraid to go to a hotel and stayed instead with a Jewish family that offered me hospitality. Thanks to a hotel owner who had connections with the police, I obtained a new false identity card in a fictitious name of a Christian from Larissa. In this way I severed all my ties with Thessaloniki. The hotel owner to whom I gave a gold Napoleon as a souvenir made arrangements for my trip to Athens on board a crowded bus. Some of the passengers escaping Thessaloniki were Jews like me, but we did not speak to each other.

I heard that Jews and other people crossed the Aegean and went to Turkey. My friend Souleme and I decided to go to the island of Euboea. We took with us several empty oil cans so that we would look like black-market merchants. When we got to the island, we found a captain who was willing to take us in his boat. The boat could hold thirty people, and the total price for the crossing was 100 gold sovereigns. We were ten people on the island, and we needed another twenty in order to raise the necessary money. Back in Athens, we tried to find others who were willing to participate in our adventure. People were hesitant, because they did not know whether the boat was seaworthy or whether the captain would turn them over to the Gestapo.

I realized that in order to get people to risk their lives I had to resort to lies.

Yacov Souleme went again to the rich man Raoul, who had refused to join us a few days before, and told him we were ready to leave and that, to be fair to him, we wanted him to know about it.

The bluff was successful. Raoul and four members of his family wanted to come and, in addition, he asked if he could bring along another family of two parents and four little girls.

We were now 25 people. The captain made his final preparations when a few military people joined our party. They had rifles with them, something which could endanger our lives if the Germans captured us, but we had no choice. The journey was quite uneventful, except when we sighted a German patrol boat which did not stop us. Within 20 hours we were on Turkish soil. We were taken to Smyrna and from there to Aleppo by train. The British questioned every one of us to make sure we were not spies. From Smyrna we were taken to Gaza in Palestine. Friends of mine from Tel Aviv asked me to leave the camp and go with them. They explained that the Jews were the ones who had power there and that nobody could touch me. I jumped over the barbed-wire fence of the British camp one night. A truck driven by my friends was waiting for me. I was taken to Tel Aviv to the club Kadima, a place frequented by Jews from Thessaloniki. At one time, I did not feel at all as if I were part of the Jewish people. In Tel Aviv, I felt that I indeed belonged to it. David Souleme and his Athenian brother Yacov now live in Israel. No one else in the family survived.[164]

Eighteen Months Indoors

Chaim Pardo of Thessaloniki, his wife Eugenia, and their three children, ages 13, nine, and four, were forced to move to one of the "ghettos" established by the Germans in Thessaloniki. In April 1943, the Pardos had the good fortune to have a trusted friend. Dr. George Karakotsou, at the height of the persecution of the Jews, invited the Pardo family to go into

---

164 "You Are Born Alone—You Die Alone," Yacov Assael (Yad Vashem, Jerusalem, Israel), tr. from Hebrew by Avi Richter.

II. Personal Memoirs – The German Zone of Occupation

hiding in his house, where he lived with his wife Phaedra, his four-year-old son, and a maid. Pardo's daughter Rosa remembers:

> The Karakotsou family had a friend who was an officer in the German army. He was an Austrian, and we knew only his first name, Walter. He knew that a Jewish family was hidden in Dr. Karakotsou's house. Any time our neighborhood was going to be surrounded and the houses searched by the Germans and their Greek collaborators, Walter, who was in a position to know about it, would warn our host, and we would get ready to hide in the specially made closets. Fortunately, they never came to search specifically for us.
>
> From the window of the Karakotsou's house on Tsimiski Street, we saw the long columns of Jewish men, women, and children who were taken on foot to the Baron Hirsch camp. From there the trains took them straight to Auschwitz.
>
> The house on Tsimiski Street was just a few blocks from our own house. The neighbors, as we found out after the war, were not aware of our presence there. My father was included among the 100 Jews whose names were given by Rabbi Koretz to the Germans, who threatened to execute one of them for each Thessaloniki Jew who attempted to escape. My father never left the house during our 18 months of hiding. The rest of us used to get out at night, exercising great caution. The Germans could not possibly suspect that a Jewish family would hide right in the center of Thessaloniki. We found out later that our family happened to be the only one to do so.[165]

[Author's note: It is known that seventy Jews were hiding in Thessaloniki. One source said they belonged to five families. Another source said they were Jewish men married to Christian women or Christian men married to Jewish women.]

---

165 "Eighteen Months Indoors," letter from Rosa Pardo Asser to me, April 8, 1989.

On April 8, 1989, Mrs. Rosa Pardo Asser wrote to me describing the totally exceptional story of the survival of her family in Thessaloniki.

In 1997, in the United States Holocaust Memorial Museum (USHMM) in Washington, DC, I proposed that Dr. George Karakotsos and his wife Phaedra should be honored as Righteous Among the Nations.

Somehow Rosa was told about my proposal. She, again in a letter, reminded me politely that only those who survived have the right to propose to Yad Vashem to honor their saviors.

On February 9, 2000, Rosa sent me her very well written book *548 Days with Another Name* (in Greek). When I read page 70, I understood why it took over 50 years before the Karakotsos family was honored. In the meantime, all the members of that family died.

I understand Rosa, and I like her very much. She is kind, forgiving, and generous.

The time came to honor the Karakotsos family. On August 12, 2001, Yad Vashem recognized George and Phedra Karakotsos as Righteous Among the Nations.

Rosa wrote in her book (my translation to English from Greek), "Before the Germans were about to leave, in one room the adults had long discussions. A lawyer, Mr. Argyropoulos was coming and going. Eventually, we learned that our father transferred to Karakotsos our four apartments on Edmon Rostan Street. After the Germans left, and we went out from our hideout, we were very poor and very happy."

Sarina Saltiel-Venezia, in the following story, tells us what happened when the Germans realized that the Pardo family escaped.

The Betrayal

Sarina Saltiel-Venezia had two sons. Her husband was an Italian citizen. This is her story:

> On February 25, 1943, the Jews were interned in quarters reserved specifically for them. My house was already located in one of these quarters, and therefore we did not have to relocate. They assigned two families to our home, Pardo and Carasso. The Germans had a

II. Personal Memoirs – The German Zone of Occupation

list of affluent members of the community. These persons formed a group of hostages. If one of these people escaped, special measures were taken against all the others and even against the people in whose houses these persons lived. One day my guests disappeared. I knew they were looking to join the partisans. It did not take long before I was asked by the Germans to give the addresses of the fugitives. I said nothing. To punish me, they sent me to the Baron Hirsch camp. "You are going to leave with the next convoy," they told me. I submitted an application to the Italian consul, begging him to grant me Italian citizenship since my husband was Italian. I waited for the consulate's reply, and my two sons and I tried to hide every time there was a transport from the camp. The transports toward Poland continued throughout the months of March and April 1943. Even now I wonder how we believed that we were going to go to Poland and live a peaceful existence there! They deported even the aged and insane. Yet nobody associated Poland with death. My dear brother-in-law, Mordo, whose wife was expecting a child, told me: "It is better to leave early because perhaps we will have better accommodations. Also, my wife might give birth to a baby before we leave and traveling would be more difficult then."

In the camp, we were forced to change our drachmas for Polish zlotys. They were payable in a bank in Krakow, and that made us believe we were going to Krakow. It became known after the war that on March 13, 1943 (that is, two days before the departure of the first convoy from Thessaloniki), the liquidation of the Jewish ghetto of Krakow was completed.

In the Baron Hirsch camp, I witnessed two executions. The first took place on April 5, 1943. In the presence of all the inmates, they executed three young men who attempted to join the partisans. They were Ino Atas, Tori Cuenca, and Maurice Errera. The second execution involved Alberto Benveniste and Nissim Kamhi. One day a German arrived and read a list of people who were considered Italians. Many of the people listed had already been deported. My name was announced, but not those of my children. I refused to leave without them. People advised me to plead with the Italians. I met Captain [Lucillo] Merci, who listened to my appeal and extricated my two sons from the camp. On July 14, 1943, the Italians formed a convoy of approximately 300 people who were taken to Athens. They treated us very well.

On September 8, 1943, our little interlude ended. Many Jews who were saved by the Italians in Thessaloniki were captured by the Germans in Athens on March 25, 1944. A man from the Resistance assisted a group of us to find temporary shelter until the right moment arrived to go to the mountains. A Greek woman was in charge of bringing food to our hiding place. One day the woman arrived accompanied by a man in civilian clothes. "He is a police agent," she said. "He told me that you are Jews, but you can buy his silence." We understood. We gave him everything we had. Many among us departed immediately. Our Resistance contact arrived, and we told him our adventure. "She will pay dearly for this one day," he said. He found another hiding place for us in the house of a very good family. Since we did not have any more money, my son, accompanied by our landlord's son, sold cigarettes in the streets. We remained in that house until the end. Our former companions were not as fortunate as we were. Their new hiding place was discovered. Jack and Valentine Chaoui, Julia Barreau and her husband Angele, Henri Barzilai, the five members of the Benveniste family, the Canons, and the Bolton family were arrested and deported to Auschwitz.[166]

---

166 "The Betrayal," Miriam Novitch, *Le Passage Des Barbares*, 1982, 44.

II. Personal Memoirs – The German Zone of Occupation

The Last Will

Sarina Frances relates:

The Jews of Spanish nationality did not have to live in ghettos or wear the yellow star. My brother, however, was a Greek national, and he occupied a house in the elegant neighborhood of Quais, which was declared "Aryan." When he was expelled from there, he came to live with us. In the meantime, my husband became seriously ill, and I wanted to transfer him to a hospital. Jews were not allowed to use an ambulance unless the Gestapo gave them special permission. Believing that my passport gave me a measure of protection, I went with my son to the luxurious villa at 42 Vellisariou Street, which was the Gestapo headquarters. The two officers Wisliceny and Brunner were there. Their ferocious dogs chased us away. My brother was arrested and sent to the Baron Hirsch camp. Before leaving he gave me an envelope, which I put in a drawer. I found it again after the war, and I realized that this was the last will and testament of my brother. As far as we know, he is the only Jew who, before leaving for Poland, wrote his last will.

I remember the day of his departure. Since I did not wear a yellow star, I had the right to take the bus. I went to the door of the camp and saw the column of deportees. I ran alongside my brother and held his hand. I must have looked very upset, because the deportees tried to console me with "courage, we'll come back." They honestly believed that they were going to Krakow in Poland. On July 28, 1943, they ordered all Spaniards to present themselves at the Beth Saoul synagogue. A Jewish policeman came to tell me that we had to move to the Baron Hirsch camp. "In order to go where?" I asked him. "To Poland, like all of us," he replied. I ran to the convent of the Sisters of Saint Vincent de Paul. I gave them my family jewelry and told them, "If I don't return within ten years, you can keep these for your charities." In all haste, I collected some clothes, placed my poor husband in a wheelchair, and joined my coreligionists at the Baron Hirsch camp.

We went to Bergen-Belsen, and after six months of deprivations we were sent via Spain to Morocco. After the war I returned to Thessaloniki. I love this city. My husband died a little while after our return. The good nuns returned my jewelry. We started life again, but every street empty of Jews. Every Jewish holiday, every encounter with other Jews in Thessaloniki reminds me of the past. I can't find solace near the tombs of my ancestors. Even the cemetery is destroyed.[167]

A Difficult Choice

Moshe Nachmias, his wife, children, mother, and widowed sister with her three children, all from Thessaloniki, were taken by the Germans to the Baron Hirsch camp. There they waited to be "transported" out of the country.

At this time, the legal adviser of the Italian consulate discovered that Italian women who lost their citizenship when they married Greeks could regain their Italian citizenship by filing for a divorce. Once they again became Italian citizens, their husbands and children also became free. All the women who filed for divorce were kept in the Baron Hirsch camp. Mrs. Nachmias was among them, and she and the children were released. Moshe Nachmias was put in a morally terrible position. He had to choose between his wife and children or his mother and sister and her children.

After a great deal of soul-searching, Nachmias decided to stay in Greece with his wife and children rather than follow his mother and sister to Poland. With the assistance of the Italian consulate, he joined a group of thirty men - husbands and relatives of Italian women. They were released on July 8, 1943.

The Jews were forced to pay the Germans for their stay at the Hirsch camp prior to their departure for Athens. In Athens, Moshe Nachmias and his family received assistance from the Italian consulate until the Germans took over. At that time, he was provided, like most other Athenian Jews, with false

---

[167] "The Last Will," Miriam Novitch, *Le Passage Des Barbares*, 1982, 43.

identity papers and found a hiding place in the house of an elderly couple in the neighborhood of Lykabettos.

For a long time, Moshe Nachmias contemplated taking the great risk of going by boat to Turkey. He was finally convinced to do so when his nine-year-old son told him, "Let's take this chance, Father; maybe we'll become free." From this moment on, the Nachmias family went through a nightmare of events on land and sea. They followed the usual escape route to Euboea, where they had to wait for three months for their voyage to Turkey to begin. At one point, a shepherd helped them hide during a German raid, and he provided them with food and other supplies. They made it to Turkey, hungry and frightened, but alive.

In March 1944, they finally arrived in Palestine, where they settled. At the time this interview was taken in 1962, Nachmias was one of the managers of Discount Bank in Tel Aviv.[168]

Philip Friedman in his book, *European Resistance Movements,* wrote:

> Whereas most other nations have legacies of heroism in which heroism meant physical and military prowess, in the case of Orthodox Jewry the concept of heroism is interwoven with the idea of spiritual courage, of sacrifice for the sake of religion known in Hebrew as "Kiddush Hashem" (sanctification of God's name). This was the main form of resistance carried out by the Orthodox Jews. It was a resistance stemming from religious inspiration, and contained a deeply rooted ancestral heritage epitomized by the saying, "Not by force but by the strength of the spirit." The Orthodox Jew did not believe that it was possible or even desirable to resist the Nazis in any way.[169]

The following story related by Sarina Azaria of Veria gives an example of this religious point of view.

---

[168] "A Difficult Choice," translated from Hebrew by Ari Richter, Yad Vashem, catalog No. 932483.

[169] Philip Friedman, "Jewish Resistance to Nazism 1939-1945," *European Resistance Movements*, London: Pergamon Press, 1960, 201.

Sarina narrates:

When it became known that the Jews were about to be deported, I told my husband, "We are not going to Poland."

"We have to go," he replied. "It is shameful not to have the courage to share the fate of all the people of Israel. I swore in the synagogue to go with the others on God's way for his Kiddush Hashem."

"But you have young children," I told him. "God does not wish our destruction." I would not have been able to persuade him if it were not for a message that the mayor sent, advising him to leave as soon as possible. I told my daughter, "We will leave from the back door, and you will stay in the house so nobody will understand that we left. You will join us in two days." At midnight we left together with my two sons, one of whom died for Israel during the War of Independence. We took off our yellow stars as soon as we found ourselves in free territory on the foot of Mount Pierion. My daughter joined us in two days in the village where we stayed for the duration of the war.

When my husband became seriously ill and I was afraid he might not live, I decided to go to Veria in search of medicines. I was dressed like a villager, and I went to the house of my neighbor in Veria. "Mrs. Sarina," she told me, "you know they arrested all the Jews and your house is occupied!" It was dark, and I went to our doctor's house. They did not want to let me in. I begged them, and finally they gave me medicine. I left the city immediately and did not return until Veria was free again.[170]

---

170 Sarina Azaria was interviewed by Miriam Novitch in 1958. The Azaria couple was murdered by burglars a few months later.

II. Personal Memoirs – The German Zone of Occupation

A Committee Arrives

Nissim Alkalay of Didimotiho remembers:

Our community was composed mainly of artisans and workers. There were also some rich businessmen and some doctors and lawyers. I was the principal of the Jewish school. When the persecutions commenced in Thessaloniki, we prayed in our synagogue for the storm to spare us. On March 4, 1943, I was in my school when a friend arrived to tell me about a "committee" which came to the city with the intention to deport the Jews. The committee ordered the Jews to assemble in the synagogue to receive a special communication. "Let's leave," I told my cousin. "All this is the prelude of something bad!" We left the city and joined the partisans in the mountains. The people went to the synagogue, and when it was filled, the police encircled the building. Nobody was allowed to exit. They remained enclosed in the synagogue for two days before their train was ready. They were moved by the way the Christian citizens of our city tried to help them. They brought food and water in spite of the constant danger of being shot by the Germans. A well- known lawyer offered unsuccessfully to adopt two small Jewish girls.

On March 8, all those arrested were sent to Thessaloniki and from there to Poland. Eight families of Spanish nationality were also arrested and deported. When the war ended, out of 900 people, there were only three people left: myself and two Miskatel brothers. There had been great families here, who were highly esteemed; they all disappeared without a trace, and nobody was left to mourn them or recite the sacred Kaddish (the prayer for the dead).[171]

---

171 A Committee Arrives," Nissim Alcalay, letter to the author 1975.

Crete

Although Crete was part of the German zone of occupation, the Jews of this island were left undisturbed in their isolation until May 1944. It is possible that the lack of transportation was responsible for this delay, but in the end the Jewish population was almost totally destroyed. All those who were arrested perished.

Jacob Elhai of Baltimore relates:

> I was born in Iraklion, Crete, in 1914. For economic reasons I moved to Athens in 1940, and this saved my life. After Crete was occupied by the Germans, a fuel depot in Iraklion was blown up by saboteurs. The Germans wanted to execute hostages, and the Greek police volunteered to provide the Germans with Jews who were in the city. Three Jewish men were arrested and executed. They were my relatives: Abraam Elhai, Mosse Elhai, and Elia Sabator.
>
> The few remaining Jews went to Chania, which had a Jewish community of 350 people. In Chania, there were two synagogues, a community school, and two rabbis, Rabbi Evlagon and Rabbi Osmo. From Athens, where I was, I sent letters to my relatives telling them, "We are sick here. There is danger for you to become sick, too. Take the necessary measures to protect yourselves." They did not believe they were in danger and remained where they were until the day the Germans decided to arrest them on May 21, 1944. The Germans surrounded the neighborhood where all the Jews lived and asked Rabbi Osmo to show them each Jewish house. The rabbi did what he was ordered to do, and in a few hours all the Jews of Chania were arrested except for three people who happened to live outside the predominantly Jewish section of the city. Informed about what was happening, they escaped arrest and went into hiding.[172]

---

172 Jacob Elhai. Interview by me on October 12, 1975.

II. Personal Memoirs – The German Zone of Occupation

The United States was promptly informed about what happened in Crete, as the following document demonstrates:

May 25, 1944

All the Jews of Chania have been arrested and their possessions plundered. They were taken to prison with a change of clothing and six days food. A number of beggars were collected under German orders to plunder the Jews' possessions while propaganda pictures of the popular anti-Semitic agitation were taken. After this the beggars were driven off and the Germans seized their plunder.[173]

Jacob Elhai continued:

From Chania they moved everyone to Iraklion, where many Cretans offered to help the young escape. They refused because the Germans threatened to execute the remaining captives if there were any escape attempts. Eventually the cargo vessel *SS Tanais* arrived, and the Germans placed 350 Jews, 400 Greek hostages and 300 Italian soldiers who were prisoners of the Germans in its hold. The date was June 6, 1944. The destination of the boat was Piraeus. When they reached the Greek island of Santorini, the Germans who guarded the vessel disembarked after they made sure that all doors from which the captives could possibly exit were hermetically shut and nailed. The Greek crew of the boat received orders to continue on their trip to Piraeus. Once the ship was on the open sea, an explosion took place, and the *SS Tanais* instantly sank with all hands on board, with the exception of one engineer who swam to shore. The British admiralty declared there were no submarines operating in that area and that the boat was not torpedoed. It seems the Germans disembarked after they placed a time bomb on board. This is how I lost my parents, my sister

---

[173] Secret OSS L37591, May 25, 1944.

Rachel with her husband Marko Hanen and their six children, my brothers Isaak and Albert with their wives and five children, and my three young sisters, Sara, Chrysoula, and Rebecca.

There are other versions to the story of the *SS Tanais*.

The Mystery of the Fate of Cretan Jewry: Three Views

Thrasyboulos Spandidakis relates that 350 Jews of Hania, 48 Christians who took part in anti-German actions, and 112 Italian soldiers who refused to fight on the side of the Germans were placed on board the steamship *SS Tanais*. While the vessel was near Santorini, it was spotted by Allied planes which did not attack it because Allied headquarters in the Middle East was notified by radio of its human cargo by intelligence officers on the island. Other German vessels in the same area were sunk on the same day. Walter, the German naval commander in Iraklion, having been informed of the sinking of the German vessels in the Aegean, sent an order by radio for the guards on board the *SS Tanais* to set time bombs and abandon ship. Thus 510 souls tragically died trapped in the hold of the boat.[174]

Professor Shlomo Carmiel of the University of Tel Aviv spent four summers in Crete and throughout Europe researching the fate of the *SS Tanais*. Though it is believed that 350 Jews had been arrested on May 30, 1944, and were later placed on board the vessel; all subsequent trace of them was lost. Dr. Carmiel studied files and interviewed older Cretans, former German officers and soldiers, former British secret agents, and Cretan resistance fighters. His conclusion is that the Jews were actually arrested on May 20; this correction provided the key to the mystery of their fate. They were not deported as were other European Jews. Rather, they were executed in reprisal for the assistance they gave to the British

---

174 "Another version of the tragedy in the Aegean," by Thrasyboulos Spandidakis, Chronika, June 1988, 8.

II. Personal Memoirs – The German Zone of Occupation

Secret Service, which planned to abduct General Kraipe, the commander of German forces on Crete. After their execution, Dr. Carmiel believes their corpses were loaded aboard a ship the Germans later sank in order to destroy every evidence of their crime.[175]

Nikos Sgourakis of Iraklion, Crete, remembers the events of that period:

> On May 31, 1944, a German convoy of five or six vessels was attacked by American planes. Two vessels were sunk as they approached the port of Iraklion, and the remaining were destroyed inside the port, with the exception of one vessel on top of which the Germans raised enormous balloons in an attempt to protect it from further attack.
>
> The Jews who were arrested in Chania were transferred to Iraklion on board sixty lorries, together with other Greeks, and were enclosed in the Venetian castle Makasi. Representatives of the Red Cross were the only ones allowed to visit the prisoners and to provide food for them. In the afternoon of May 31, 1944, my father Minas was visited by an old man, Kapetanaki, who gave him a message from Biro, a German woman who lived in our city for many years and who now worked for the German commander. The message was to "inform the British not to sink the vessel, which will transfer the prisoners to Piraeus, and the Germans will release the Greeks (the 48 persons who took part in anti-German actions) upon the safe arrival of the vessel." The message was delivered to Petrakogiorgis, the Resistance leader who maintained radio contact with the Allies.
>
> In the afternoon of the following day, I met our family friend, Gianni Toutongaki, a bank employee, who appeared very excited. I asked him whether he was excited because of the air raid of the previous day. He replied, "What air raid? This did not frighten me so much as when a few minutes ago I saw the Jews being

---

[175] "New Research About the Fate of the Jews of Crete," Marcel Yoel, *Chronika*, March 1985, 5. Reprinted from *Jewish Chronicle*, 11/16/84.

brought to the port. I saw Mr. Koen (a distinguished citizen) and went to greet him. A German grabbed me by the neck and stuck his gun to my head." He then described the embarkation of the prisoners on board the vessel under strict security measures by exclusively German military police and not ordinary soldiers. In a few days, a prostitute revealed that a German officer who was on board the vessel returned and told her that the boat was sunk by a British submarine. He and many other Germans survived while all the others drowned.[176]

It seems that the Germans would not possibly sink their own last surviving vessel from that fateful convoy. They wanted the British to know about its cargo in order to protect the boat from Allied attack as it returned to its base. This eyewitness account, which became known in April 1990, is perhaps the most accurate one. Nobody found the Greek engineer who, according to Elhai, survived the sinking of *SS Tanais*. Regardless of who sank the boat, it is clear that the arrested Jews perished with the sinking of the vessel.

Up to the time of the publication of my original book in 1997, there were many theories as to what happened to the 343 Jews of Chania. The most believable one was that the boat *SS Tanais*, which was transporting them, was sunk by a British submarine. Eventually, the British Admiralty admitted that this was the truth.

Jacob Elhai of Iraklion continues with his story:

> With my wife Clare and daughter Elvera, I went to Athens, where I owned a barbershop in Thission. When Italy surrendered, I went to the Greek police station, where I told them I was a Jew and that I needed false identity cards for my family. They gave them to us, as they did for any Jew who asked. A friend of mine, Michael Prionistis, told me to go to Piraeus, find John Houstoulakis, and tell him that I asked him to help

---

[176] Nikos Sgourakis. "The Destruction of the Jews of Crete," *Chronika*, April 1990, 6.

you. I met John and explained to him that I was a Jew from Crete and that I wanted to go into hiding. He became very excited when he heard that I was a Cretan, since he was also born in Crete. He traveled with me to Peloponnesus by train. On the isthmus bridge control point, a Greek policeman suspected me because I did not have a travel permit. My friend and other passengers intervened and, possibly, bribed him; he let me pass. We went to Klenis, Corinthias, which was a village of 700 people. A job was found for me there on a farm. I guarded the crops. I was instructed to tell my host not that I was a Jew, but that I had killed a German and for that reason I went into hiding. I did that, but eventually I found out that everyone knew the truth. Since there was need for a barber, I opened a small barbershop. I was paid in foodstuffs and was able to bring my wife and daughter to live with me. After a while I felt that this village did not offer enough security for us, and we moved to the village Hiliomidi, where again I opened a barbershop. Every time the Germans raided the area, most men abandoned the village, and I used to go with them into the surrounding mountains. One time we were notified about the impending German arrival; practically every man left the village, but I felt tired of running and decided to stay home. The Germans collected everybody in a small square and the officer in charge started inspecting the multitude. He observed me and singled me out. "Why didn't you leave like the other men?" he asked.

I replied, "I did not think it was necessary to leave."

"Aren't you afraid of us?"

"No, why should I be afraid? I did not do anything against you."

"What is your job?"

"I am a barber."

"Give me a haircut then. I need one," he told me. So, I took him to the barbershop, which was close by, and I cut his hair. He had beautiful blonde hair. He caressed my little daughter who was there, and he told me that he never had as good a haircut as the one I gave him. He promised to send me a can of meat, and he kept his promise. Two or three months later, the news arrived that the Germans blew up the bridge on the isthmus of Corinth. I told my wife then, "We survived! The war is over!"

The City of Veria. After 2,000 Years, the Jewish Community no Longer Exists

Dr. Joseph (Iosif) Stroumtsa narrates:

On the eve of the Second World War, the city of Veria had 20,000 people. The Jewish community numbered close to 600 people. It had existed in Veria for 2,000 years. Most of them lived in the Jewish quarter built around a small courtyard that had only two entrances. In addition to the houses, there was a small synagogue and an elementary school. Although it was a ghetto, it had been free for many decades. Life in the city was peaceful, and the Jews lived in harmony with their Christian neighbors.

The first disturbing news came from Germany. It trickled in slowly from a faraway place. I was then 13 years old, an adult according to the Jewish tradition. We became very alarmed when first the Italians, in October 1940, and then the Germans attacked Greece in April 1941. This attack marked the beginning of the long night of occupation for all the inhabitants of Veria. But for most Jews the night would never be followed by the dawn.

The persecution of the Jews started as soon as the Germans entered the city. At first the measures taken by the Germans were mild but caused suspicions such as the expropriation of merchandise from the stores and the expropriation of furniture from homes, especially of radios. Another example of blackmail occurred one night when the Germans demanded that my father, as the president of the community, pay the bill at a restaurant where the Germans were having a party. Later on, they ordered us to wear the yellow star. I remember my twelve and thirteen-year-old friends wore the star with pride. We never tried to hide our

Jewish identity. Besides, we lived in a small city where we all knew each other.

In the summer of 1942, we heard the news from Thessaloniki (Salonica) of the humiliation of the Jews on Eleftheria (Liberty) Square and the creation of Jewish forced labor battalions. Towards the end of that year and the beginning of the next, we heard plans of the eminent relocation of the Jews to Poland in order to work in military factories. There was no mention of concentration camps. The news struck the alarm. We were seized by incredible fear.

Endless discussions started everywhere as to what to do. At home, in the synagogue, throughout the community, the main topic was the frightening dilemma: should we follow the road of exile, which unfortunately many considered as "God's road" (Camino del Dio), or should we flee to the nearby mountains, Vermio and Pieria, that were defended by the partisans of ELAS? Both solutions were fraught with dangers. The first one had the danger of uncertainty about the real intentions of the Germans. The second carried the danger of arrest and execution by the Germans, as their orders threatened, because the partisans did not have a firm hold of the surrounding areas.

The vast majority of the Jews of Veria consisted of poor laborers, artisans and merchants. A few young men had joined the partisans in the mountains, but most of them had stayed in the city to be with their families who were getting ready to depart for the big adventure. Of course, if they knew what was happening in the concentration camps, such a dilemma would not exist. All the Jews of Veria would have been able to go to the mountains and save themselves.

We tried very hard to gather more information. The leadership of the Jewish community of Thessaloniki, especially the chief Rabbi Dr. Tzevi Koretz, reassured us that there was no reason to panic. In a telephone communication with the president of the Jewish community of Veria, Menachem Stroumtsa, Rabbi Koretz informed him that the three million Jews of Poland were going to provide housing for the Greek

Jews when they arrived to Poland and also provide them with jobs. He asked him to make sure that all the Jews of Veria obey the orders of the Germans in order to avoid any punishment. They should also obtain Polish money and bring with them gold and jewelry to have in case of need. People listened to all of this with disbelief because they knew that Rabbi Koretz had been appointed to the position of chief Rabbi by the Germans after his imprisonment in Germany and his mysterious release.

The other source of information was the radio. Every night we would take it out of a secret place, the box where we stored coal, and with fear in our hearts we listened to the BBC broadcasts in Greek. We never heard a word of what was going on in the German death camps, information that would have solved our terrible dilemma. We now know that the Allies already knew what was going on since the middle of 1942. Why did the Allies with their silence help the Germans in their well-hidden trap of misinformation that led the Jews to inaction? That is the big why!

Finally, what led us to take the final decision was the urging of the chief of police of Veria, Georgios Stavridis. [177] In a conversation with my father, he insisted that what was happening was a bad sign. He did not trust at all the reassurances of the Germans. He urgently advised my family to go to the mountains. He said to my father, "Listen to my advice and stop thinking about it." When asked what to advise the other members of the community, being the president, he said, "Nothing. Whatever you tell them, they will object and they might even make you change your decision. But whatever you do, they will follow you." He also gave us and many others forged IDs. Thus, Joseph Stroumtsa became Petros Stavridis.

We prepared our departure in great secrecy. One day in March 1943 after sundown, but before the curfew, when public movement was forbidden, we left

---

[177] Georgios Stavridis was posthumously awarded as Righteous Among the Nations in 2015 by Yad Vashem of Jerusalem.

II. Personal Memoirs – The German Zone of Occupation

through the rear door of our house and climbed over the stone wall. We spent the night in the house of a Christian friend, Menelaos Papathemos, who rented rooms. Before sunrise we loaded our belongings and food provisions onto mules. We put our 85-year-old grandmother on a mule and moved towards the village of Sykia on Mt. Pieria. We took great precautions out of fear that we might be recognized by collaborators of the Germans. We reached the Aliakmona River which we had to cross. But the bridge had been blown up by the British as they were retreating. We were able to get across thanks to a primitive flat rowboat. It was a large platform that we were able to move by pulling a rope between the two banks of the river. Our grandmother on top of the mule did not realize that we had put her on a platform that was floating on the water and insisted that it was a miracle. She believed that the waters parted so we could get across like our ancestors with Moses crossed the Red Sea!

After a ten-hour hike without any incident, we reached Sykia, a village with about 40 houses. The village priest, Nestoras Karamitsos, took us under his care. He had a strong personality and was the undisputed leader not only of the people of Sykia but also of the surrounding villages. Thanks to Papa-Nestora (Father-Nestora) and even more thanks to the partisans of ELAS we finally felt somewhat safe.

We spent 15 months in the village. Throughout this period, the Germans along with their Greek collaborators made several military incursions into our area that forced us to hide in the forest under wretched conditions. I remember one time when we stayed in temporary huts made of straw for a week while the snow was piling up all around us as it reached 50-60 centimeters. Time passed by fast and we kept getting good news – the armistice of Italy, the invasion of Normandy, the victories of the Russians on the eastern front etc. The hope that our suffering would soon come to an end filled our hearts and enabled us to tolerate all the hardships.

However, the worst adventure occurred when even the German soldiers became aware that they were going to lose and that the end of the war was approaching. On June 1944, during one of the last attacks against the partisans, a villager that brought us food in the forest, came with some Germans and showed them our hiding place. As we learned later, this happened after someone else betrayed us to the Germans and after the villager was tortured by them. This is how they arrested 50 members of our group. These were Jews that little by little had followed us when our escape became known.

They took us behind the village of Sykia where all the houses of the village had been set on fire. The scene was appalling. They ordered us to walk among the burning houses. The Germans were beating us to walk faster while their vicious dogs attacked whoever they thought got out of line. They separated the men and the older boys (I was then 15 years old) and placed us in front of the wall of the church and aimed their guns towards us giving us the impression that they were going to shoot us. The women and children who were watching the scene started to scream and cry along with the rest of the villagers who were there, and kept begging the Germans to let us go. I said to my father, "Baba (Dad), they are going to kill us." "What can we do, my son?" he replied.

The Germans confronting the scene changed their minds and ordered us to continue our march in the same brutal way as before in the direction of the village Pallatitsa, a distance of about 4-5 kilometers from Sykia. There, inside a building that looked like a prison, they started to interrogate us systematically in the usual way, by beating their victims. At the beginning they tried to extract information from the young ones about the location of the headquarters of the partisans, their number etc. Then they turned their attention to more practical matters. They collected our gold, gold coins, jewelry, men's clothing, which they needed to avoid arrest by the Allies in the near future. Three or four days later the Germans left after they turned us to their Greek collaborators whose behavior was relatively good. Besides, they were preparing their alibi in anticipation of the accusations of collaboration with the enemy.

After they transported us to many other villages, we ended up in the village Koukos in Pieria in the area of Katerini, where the headquarters of the organized group of collaborators were located. While we were in the village, the partisans attacked the stronghold of these traitors. We were in danger of been hit by friendly fire. The most tragic thing of all, as we learned later, was that among the partisans that made the attack was Mendes Samouel Daniel. He was in charge of the partisan mortar and his parents were in the village. The partisans were not able to crush the traitors. (Their leader Kiabazak had once met Hitler. We do not know what happened to him. Mendes Samouel Daniel immigrated to Israel where he became an officer in the Israeli army.)

Of those who fled to the mountains, 150 people, all of them survived except for three who were arrested and executed. Of those who were deported by the Germans, 450 people, no one returned. We learned that in early April a special unit of Germans and Jewish policemen arrived from Thessaloniki. They shut all the Jews in the synagogue. Two or three days later the Jews formed a tragic procession. Loaded with their belongings and wearing the star of David, they marched through the main street of the city's market place and headed to the railroad station. On the sidewalks a lot of people watched in silence. Some of them whispered a few words of consolation, wishing them a quick return. Unfortunately, this wish did not materialize for any of them. After a brief stop in Thessaloniki, they were led to the death camps where they left their bodies in the frozen earth of Northern Europe. We waited impatiently the return of our relatives and friends for days, weeks, months, but no one showed up. From those that returned in Thessaloniki, we learned the unbelievable and appalling truth of the crimes that took place in the death camps. We learned of the murder of millions of our coreligionists whose only crime was that they were Jews.

We desperately tried to revitalize our community. The only Rabbi that had remained was Hanania Sabetai Azaria. At the beginning, every religious service we attended ended in mourning. The words of the prayers came out of our mouths with sobs. We looked at the empty seats where our relatives and friends used to sit. The seats were waiting in vain the return of Simon, of Yeouda, or of Moiz. It was so sad. The seats remained forever empty. Those who survived could not bear anymore to live in a place where everything reminded them of their loved ones and their unjust loss. Some immigrated to Israel, others moved to cities where they had a few relatives, and others went abroad. But they all left Veria.

So, after 2,000 years, the Jewish community of Veria disappeared. Like ghosts of the past, five or six Jews still wander in the growing former Jewish neighborhood, and they think they can still hear Jewish children singing Ladino songs. (Now, in 2020, not even one Jew remains in Veria).[178]

In 2020, I read an account which mentions my friend Joseph (Iosif) Stroumtsa, and I would like to set the record straight. In the 2018 book, *Holocaust in Greece,* Giorgos Antoniou mentions the puzzling murder of Yaakov and Sarina Azaria that took place after the war in Veria. (See the story in my book on page 164.) The murder remains unsolved, but there were many theories. On page 135 of his book, Antoniou writes the following: "Iosif Stroumtsa recalls a second unlikely possibility - the involvement of Israel's Mossad." Mr. Antoniou knew that the Azarias had four children in Israel, one of whom fell heroically in the war of 1948. Because I thought that this "unlikely possibility" was inconceivable, I called the 91-year-old Dr. Stroumtsa in Thessaloniki to ask him. He told me that this possibility was not reported by him, but was invented by the Greek police.

---

178 Dr. Joseph Stroumtsa (dentist), personal correspondence with the author, 2020. Translated from Greek by Ninetta Feldman.

II. Personal Memoirs – The German Zone of Occupation

Agent G-4

Alberto Moses Minervo from Chania contacted the British intelligence service and volunteered his services in the struggle against the Germans. His code name was G-4. For a while he pretended to be a visitor in the village Babali to Hani, near Chania. He noticed that the Germans used trucks painted with the Red Cross sign in their transportation of troops and military supplies. This disguise protected them from Allied air attacks. Minervo sent a message to headquarters in Cairo, and the British air force attacked the "Red Cross" convoys, inflicting great losses on the German army. Another of Minervo's suggestions proved very useful in the movement of Allied agents and other people who had to go to Egypt. The Germans allowed the fishermen of Crete to fish at night as they had always done, on the condition that a German soldier would be on board the vessel and half of whatever was caught would be delivered to the Germans free of charge. Minervo recommended that the fishermen offer the soldier a good quantity of *tsilcoudia* (a powerful Cretan alcoholic beverage), so he would sleep at night. An agent or two came on board the boat and exchanged clothes with one or two men who went into the submarine. Since the fishing boat left the shores in the darkness of the evening and returned before sunrise, the German on board never knew that such an exchange of people took place. If he had checked the number of fishermen, the number was always correct.

Minervo realized the value of alcohol as a weapon. In the village Kounoupidiana on Crete, a brutal German sergeant terrorized the population. He used to go to a tavern with his motorcycle. Minervo suggested that the tavern owner throw cigarette ashes into his drink and mix it well. This produces a synergistic effect, intensifying the action of the alcohol. The hated sergeant had an accident on the way to his base. Before he died, he told his colleagues that he fell by himself; the Germans did not retaliate against the population.

In May 1943, Minervo and his wife Victoria settled in Athens. In October, they went into hiding. One day he was on board a gazozene bus the Germans had stopped at a roadblock. They asked all passengers to get out for an identity card check. Minervo, who had a false identity card he had bought on St. Dimitrios Street, was afraid to subject it to the scrutiny of the

The Illusion of Safety

German police. He remained in his seat, although everyone else got off the bus. A German sergeant walked to the open window next to which Minervo was seated and asked him angrily why he did not come out. Minervo waved his card with self-confidence and told the German, in a conspiratorial way, "emet," which in Hebrew means "truth." The sergeant thought that Minervo was a German agent and this was a sort of a coded signal. He left him alone muttering *"a-ja-gut."*[179]

Matika Taboch of Veria recounts her story:

> Sometime in April 1943, the president of our community addressed the heads of the Jewish families, who were asked to go to the synagogue. My father returned from this meeting looking very unhappy. Menachem Stroumtsa told them he had received instructions from Thessaloniki to prepare his community for resettlement in Poland. He told them what they should take with them and reassured them that the Jews of Poland would take care of all their needs.
>
> The following day my mother sent me with a chicken to the brother of Stroumtsa, who was a *shochet* (sacrificial butcher), and I found the house closed and nobody there. The same was true of Menachem Stroumtsa's house. His wholesale food products business was also closed. When my mother realized that the Stroumtsas were gone, she immediately contacted our neighbor, Dr. Vizeridis, who advised her to leave Veria and promised to keep any valuable items for her that she was willing to leave with him. In two days, our family left Veria and moved to the village Sykia, where we learned the Stroumtsa family had gone. Soon not only our family but another ten Jewish families from Veria arrived in the village of Sykia.
>
> It is possible that Greek traitors who were active in this area informed the Germans about the presence of so many Jews in one village. Soon the Germans and their collaborators arrived, and the Jewish families

---

179 Alberto Minervo. Letter to the author, December 26, 1975.

were captured. The Germans took with them only men over the age of 14 and left behind the women and children. They moved the men to the village of Knissia. The women and children, worried about the fate of the men instead of their own, followed the German column as best as they could with tears in their eyes. From there the tragic column moved to the village of Palatitsa, where the Germans put all the men, women and children in a stable where they conducted a thorough search of their Jewish captives. They confiscated every piece of jewelry or gold coins hidden in our garments.

Matika told me that she remembers that a big can was filled with gold and jewelry. As if this looting was not enough, the German officers noticed two beautiful young women. When Matika's mother understood what they were planning to do, she put one of them on the ground, covered her with a blanket and let some people sit on her. She was saved and is now living in Thessaloniki. The German officers took the other woman with them and raped her.

The next day Mrs. Taboch recognized among the Germans a Greek man who was dressed in a German uniform and pretended to speak German. He was a man she knew whose name was Panagiotis. Other traitors were similarly camouflaged as Germans. The next day the Germans released all their captives, including the woman who was raped, and left. It is obvious that they pocketed for themselves all the gold and jewelry, and this is the reason they did not transfer the Jews to Veria and beyond. The Jews remained free but destitute. They moved to the village of Meliki, where they tried to find work, and lived a miserable life.[180]

George Ioannou of Thessaloniki remembers:

One winter day we suddenly saw people in the street, each with a big yellow star on his coat in the

---

[180] Interview with Matika Tabock Matsas, July 10, 1989.

area of the heart. Thessaloniki was filled with moving yellow stars which could be seen from a great distance. Our classmate Berahias came to school wearing his star. The boys saw the comical aspects of it and started teasing him. Suddenly one of them made a paper cross, took some resin from the pine trees of the schoolyard and stuck it on the back of Berahia's overcoat. The poor boy was walking slowly with the star in front and the cross in back! He was a tall, very quiet boy. In a few days, he did not come to school any longer.

One morning there was a lot of commotion in our apartment building. The Jews who occupied some of the apartments were supposed to get ready to be taken by the Germans. They all came down the staircase and stayed in front of the door for inspection before they joined those who were already in the street surrounded by heavily armed Germans. The doors of the Jewish apartments remained open, and their Christian neighbors went inside to quickly grab whatever they could. There was great fear because the Germans threatened to kill anyone who looted Jewish property. By the time I came back from school, I realized that real looting was taking place. I saw people dragging trunks or sofas or drawers. Others carried heavy books. In our building, I entered a Jewish apartment. It had nothing inside except garbage on the floor and some torn books in the bathroom. The tiles of the fireplace had been removed by someone who was looking for treasure. There was one bed left, with some broken springs. On this bed, which my family took upstairs to our apartment, I slept until I grew up.

I remember the floor of the Jewish apartment. It was filled with the shells of sunflower seeds. For days and nights they waited, always dressed for the deportation order. They did not cook or sweep the floors anymore. None had the desire to escape, something which was relatively easy. Mrs. Kohen, the mother of Izo, was worried only about the fact that the Jews of Krakow, where they were supposed to be going, did not speak Spanish. "We will manage," she said, "like in the time of Ferdinand and Isabella."

II. Personal Memoirs – The German Zone of Occupation

After the columns of the deported Jews disappeared, I went to school. On the way Greek policemen stopped me. I showed them an ID and they let me go. In the school, everyone knew what happened, but I did not detect any special sorrow although we did have Jewish classmates. During a break some children sang the "Jewish Hymn," a teasing poem sung in broken Greek to a familiar tune. If these few boys seemed happy, so did many of the rich merchants, the traitors, and the admirers of the Third Reich.

In the afternoon, coming back home, I saw the looting continuing. There were no more Germans on the street, but there were Greek policemen. Occasionally I heard gunshots, and, because of that, the looters seemed scared and in a rush. In the Kohen apartment, even the doors were removed. Many schoolbooks were thrown into the bathtub. I took them with some satisfaction. I was very poor in books. Many had Izo's name on them.

My father was a train engineer, and we did not know where he was for many days. When he came back, he was very depressed. My mother and he were crying. He wanted to see my three-year-old brother. We woke him up and brought him to the kitchen. My father had driven a train filled with Jews all the way to Serbia. The Jews started dying in these wagons. The Germans stopped the train, and they filled their pockets with watches, jewelry, and gold coins, which they grabbed from the people who did not have any water or even enough air to breathe. From one wagon they took out a dead little boy and threw him in a ditch, without, of course, burying him. Perhaps he looked like my brother. My father went again on trips like this. He spoke with disgust about the horrible things he witnessed in that hell.[181]

Triumph of the Spirit is the title of a 1990 movie, based on the story of the Thessaloniki Jew Salamo Arouch, whose entire

---

[181] George Ioannou. Excerpt from "In Those Days," *Chronika*, September 1984, 73.

family perished in the German camps. His father, a Thessaloniki stevedore, taught him to box as a boy. Arouch at 17 was crowned light-middleweight champion of the Balkans, and he hoped to follow a successful career as a prizefighter. Instead, two years later, he found himself in Auschwitz. An SS officer, a passionate boxing buff, was known for staging bouts between prisoners. Arouch was forced to fight on the very first day of his arrival in the camp. From that day in the summer of 1943 until the evacuation of Auschwitz in January 1945, he won some 200 matches.

"We fought until one went down or they got sick of watching," says Arouch. "They would not leave until they saw blood." The winner won extra food rations and lighter work as compensation for the brutal fight schedule. "The loser would be badly weakened, and the weak were shot."[182] Arouch, a father of four and grandfather of 12, settled in Tel Aviv. He faces a lawsuit filed in Los Angeles by Jacques Razon of Holon, Israel, who claims that he was the boxer portrayed in the movie as the champion, rather than Arouch, who was one of the boxers who survived.[183]

---

182 "Boxer Salamo Arouch" by Susan Schindehette, *Parade Magazine*, March 1990.

183 "Triumph of the Spirit," Film, *The Jerusalem Post*, May 26, 1990, 12.

Chapter Two

The Bulgarian Zone of Occupation

If we knew they were going to kill us, we would not get into the trucks. We would have found our own way to die.

—STELLA SALTI ABRAAM[184]

The Friday Night Service

Albert Yahbes was walking on a street in Kavalla when, without any reason, a Bulgarian officer who was probably told that Albert was a Jew beat him up. "This event," Albert recalled, "influenced me to ask my mother to allow me to leave Kavalla and go away from the Bulgarian zone of occupation." He continues:

My mother had to sell her jewelry in order to bribe a Bulgarian officer, who gave me a pass permitting me to go by boat from Kavalla to Thessaloniki.

It was September 1941, and this was my first trip away from home. My mother's brother, Mr. Touron, lived in Larissa in the Italian zone of occupation, and I decided to go there. I learned that they were, however,

---

[184] Eftihia Nachman, *Yannina* (Athens: Talos Press, 1966), 155. (Translation from the Greek by the author.)

in Doganis because the air raids and an earthquake had made Larissa a very unpleasant city to live in. They were kind enough to accept me in their family, which consisted of my uncle, his wife, their son and their daughter Esther, who eventually became my wife. Time passed. When things became difficult for the Jews in northern Greece, my brother attempted to repeat my journey. He managed to reach Thessaloniki, but the roads were blocked and he was unable to continue his trip south. He was forced to return to Kavalla, where he was arrested and killed.

When 35 Germans were ambushed and killed near our village, my uncle, his son, and I spent the nights away from our home, except for Friday nights when we came to celebrate the arrival of the Sabbath. On one such night, the Germans encircled the village and arrested us. They took us to the schoolhouse, and we thought this was the end. The next day they pushed us toward the river where the 35 Germans had been killed, and we thought they were going to execute all 160 of us on the same spot. They lined us up a few times and pretended to get ready to machine gun all of us, but they always stopped at the last minute. They placed us on trucks and moved us to a concentration camp in Larissa. They beat and tortured us during interrogations to discover if any of the men had partisan connections. The Germans did not know that we were Jews, so we were treated like any other prisoners, and that was bad enough.

We were moved to the Pavlos Melas prison in Thessaloniki. Prisoners, sometimes 100-150 of them, were placed in an open railway car ahead of the engine to discourage the partisans from attacking the trains. Other prisoners were deported as slave laborers to Germany. One day I was in the prison yard with those who were about to be deported. The pharmacy, which I knew was directed by an Italian pharmacist, was nearby. I pretended I could not walk because of rheumatism and entered the pharmacy. Since I knew Italian fluently, I begged the Italian officer to help me. He asked me to remain there for a little while. In the meantime, a fascist Italian sergeant entered and asked me what I was doing there. The officer intervened and told him that I was a patient and belonged there, and that he should leave the office. He then sent me to a hospital for Italians and Greeks. I was still a prisoner, and the Germans came and checked every patient.

The Italian doctor liked me, and he told me what my symptoms were supposed to be to justify my claim that I could not stand on my feet. One day the German doctor recommended that radiographs be taken. I was afraid that if anyone saw me naked during the time they took the X-rays, my Jewish identity would be revealed. When they came the next day to take me to the X-ray room, they did not find me. I went into hiding inside the hospital, and to make sure that I would remain hospitalized, I even cut my hand deeply with a knife. In one week my hand was in pretty good shape, and the news announced that the Russians had occupied Romania and were entering Bulgaria. I was transferred from the hospital back to the prison of Pavlos Melas. There was no fear of deportation; nobody discovered my Jewish identity. An agreement was made between the Germans and ELAS. The Germans would not execute the prisoners and dynamite the place, and the partisans would not interfere with the German withdrawal from Greece. While the German evacuation proceeded uneventfully, I was released with all the other prisoners.

In Thessaloniki I found out that none of the Jews of Kavalla were left in that city. I decided to go back to Larissa. Since there were no trains or busses, I walked all the way there for a happy reunion with the Touron family. The father had been released earlier; he arrived in Thessaloniki on a train which was ambushed twice by partisans. My cousin was freed on the same day as I, but somehow, we missed each other.[185]

---

185 Yad Vashem Archives, Nos. 032990, 2650/56.

The Jewelry

Maurice Benveniste of Kavalla related:

The Jews registered with the authorities. Their radios were confiscated. Their jewelry and other valuables were deposited in boxes, carrying the name of the owner, at the Narodnaia Banka. The tragic thing is that the jewelry survived while its owners did not. On the night of March 3 or 4, 1943, the Jews were all arrested. Young people who were members of forced labor units saw the deportees arriving at the port of Lorn on the Danube. I was successful in leaving in time, and I arrived in Athens with my cousin and a young girl. People in Athens sheltered us, but we wanted to get as far away from the occupied areas as possible. With a small boat we reached the east coast of Euboea, and from there we continued our voyage through the Aegean to the coast of Turkey. We were 38 fugitives; 34 were Jews. Some of the very few Jews of the Bulgarian zone who were not arrested happened to be away from their homes on the night of the arrest for family or business reasons.

Juda Perahia tells his story:

When the Jews of Xanthi were arrested, I was gone on business to Gumulgina, and I was in Kavalla on the night the Jews were arrested there. I heard the loud voices of the Bulgarian police as they moved from house to house carrying their lanterns to light their way. I spent the night in a rooming house, which they did not disturb. How did I survive? I happened to be out of town. We were free to go any place we liked.[186]

---

[186] Miriam Novitch, *Le Passage des Barbares*, 24.

Chapter Three

The Italian Zone of Occupation

Stupid is the person who believes in his neighbor, good and loving as the neighbor may be. Stupid is the person who relies on "justice." Do not believe anyone, be always on guard. This is the only way of surviving in this wolfish battle of all against all.

—Vladimir Zabotinsky

A Village is Burning

Joseph Lovinger, president of the Jewish community of Greece, and his wife Berta tell their story:

> On Friday night, March 24, 1944, my wife and I were arrested by two Germans of the SD. We were taken to the synagogue, but we managed to escape.[187] We were hidden in different houses. On Sunday, April

---

[187] Lovinger's son told me, when I met him much later in the USA, that his parents were used as interpreters in the synagogue because they knew fluent German. A few hours after the arrest, they decided to escape. They went to the German guard at the entrance of the synagogue and told him, "We are tired. We are going to get a cup of coffee and will return." The German agreed; they left and did not return.

23, 1944, we were given shelter by Emmanuel Kothris, the former secretary of the Eleftherios Venizelos Youth Organization and, until 1981, president of the Foreign Committee of the Parliament.

At that time, we had identity cards in the names of Ioannis and Eleni Nikolaidi, which were given to us by the late Angelos Evert. After having given us all possible help, Kothris escorted us, at the risk of his life, through Aghia Paraskevi and Marathon to the small port of Aghia Marina and from there to Euboea. Sotiris Papastratis, who was in charge of the partisans helping people escape to Turkey, was waiting for us in the small port of Tsakkei. Papastratis took care of us in the best possible way. When a boat arrived, which operated in the illegal crossing of the Aegean, he ordered that, together with Hungarian Ambassador Laszlo Velica and his wife, who was Jewish, we be given priority in our transfer to Turkey.

In the Turkish barracks of Aleppo, we found dozens of Jewish families from Greece who had arrived the same way we did, from the port of Tsakkei. They spoke in glowing terms of Papastratis, whom they called either Sotiris or "the short guerrilla." A few days later, the Germans invaded the Tsakkei village and burned down all its houses.[188]

In 1988, the Central Board of the Jewish communities of Greece decided to honor the village of Tsakkei with a memorial plaque.

Among those who helped the Jewish people, even before the Second World War, was Dimitrios Vlastaris, a high official in the Greek Foreign Office from 1938-40. He understood well the Nazi threat. Many Jews from Austria, Germany, Czechoslovakia, and Hungary were given permission by Vlastaris to pass through Greece on the way to Palestine. In 1940, he permitted Jews from Germany to board ships in the port of Piraeus on their way to the United States. In this way, Vlastaris gave visas to thousands of Jewish refugees from

---

[188] "A Village Is Burned," letter by Joseph Lovinger to me, March 28, 1989.

Central Europe who passed through Greece by land or sea. The German embassy in Athens continually protested against Vlastaris, but he ignored all complaints. The British were also angry with him for facilitating the movement of immigrants to Palestine.

In 1940, after the fall of France, Jews who had valid U.S. visas were not able to go to Lisbon to board the vessels which would transfer them to the United States. Vlastaris, in agreement with Joseph Lovinger, issued visas by telegraph cable through still-neutral Greece, which enabled these people to go to Lisbon via Piraeus. Ylastaris assisted refugees from Central Europe who boarded ships like *Astir, Aglnios Nikolaos, Pacific,* and others on their way to safety from the ports of Piraeus, Lavrion, Kea, and Iraklion. He also allowed provisions to be given to the refugees, and, with his help, sick people were transferred to hospitals for proper medical attention. Money for this humanitarian work was supplied by the Joint Distribution Committee headed by Menahem Ussishkin, later chief of the Jewish Agency.[189]

The Greek Clergy and the Jews

In Holocaust literature, the Greek clergy is given great credit for saving individual rabbis and Jews. Yet the only rabbis who survived the war were Rabbi Barzilai of Athens, Rabbi Pessah and Rabbi Siakis of Volos, Rabbi Cassuto of Larissa, Rabbi Sasson of Trikala, and the rabbi of Karditsa. All of them lived in resistance-controlled areas. The rabbi of Chalkis was captured by the Germans, but he was released a few days before the Germans left. [Author's note: To make sure I would not omit honoring those clerics who assisted the Greek Jews, I wrote to my childhood friend, Bishop Efthymios Acheloou in Athens, asking him to appeal to all those who knew of any assistance given by priests to the Jews to tell their story. On March 21, 1988, Bishop Efthymios published such an appeal in one of the most respected Greek newspapers, *To Vima.* In response to this appeal, I have not received any story about any priest who gave asylum or otherwise saved a Greek

---

189 *Chronika,* February 1988, 14.

Jew. This does not mean that there might not have been such instances, but neither Yad Vashem nor the Jewish organizations of Greece know about it. Neither does Bishop Efthymios. Father Athanasios Armaos of the Catholic Church of Greece responded to the appeal of Bishop Efthymios and gave the following information. Sister Eleni, in cooperation with the International Red Cross, distributed food to Jews in hiding. Father Irinaios Typaldos was arrested by the Germans and taken to the Merlin Street Gestapo headquarters, where he was accused of aiding hidden Jews. In spite of their interrogations, the Germans were not able to prove anything, and they released him in a few days. Both Sister Eleni and Father Typaldos were honored by Yad Vashem as Righteous Among the Nations. Father Chrysostomos Vasiliou cooperated closely with Eleni Toumpakari in hiding Jewish children. Father Vasiliou became famous for assisting Greek officers to escape to the Middle East. He was betrayed for this activity and was executed together with ten officers and 61 other civilian men and women.[190] It has also been mentioned in Holocaust literature that Greek Christians lost their lives in their attempt to save Jews. However, Yad Vashem and the Central Board of the Jewish communities of Greece do not have any records of such cases.]

The one case where Greek Christians indeed lost their lives in saving Jews involved the eleven ELAS partisans who were killed in the battle of Karalaka; 242 Germans were killed while their Jewish captives from Larissa were liberated. The author asked Yad Vashem of Jerusalem to honor these men because their lives would not have been lost if the Germans did not go to arrest the handful of Jews who were camped near the partisan battalion. Yad Vashem replied that they only honor individuals and not soldiers. Other mistakes are found in the literature about the Holocaust in Greece. For example, contrary to what is written in some books, no Jewish partisans participated in the operation that destroyed the bridge at Gorgopotamos, and no Jewish partisans operated as independent units in the Greek Resistance.

---

190 Letter to the author by Father Athanasios Armaos, 5/28/89.

II. Personal Memoirs – The Italian Zone of Occupation

The Disabled Veteran

Benjamin Capon, a disabled veteran of the Albanian war, presented himself at the Greek Red Cross headquarters in Athens in March 1943 and made an interesting proposal, one which was accepted by its president, Alexandros Zanna.
Capon remembers:

> I proposed that the International Red Cross should supervise an exchange of disabled German war prisoners at the hands of the Allies for Greek Jewish war invalids who were to be deported from Greece. The place of this exchange could be Smyrna [Izmir] in neutral Turkey. My idea was accepted as a valid one, and a document was immediately sent to Red Cross officials in Thessaloniki, requesting them to present this proposal to the German authorities. I followed the development closely. Within a few days a letter was received from the Red Cross officers in Thessaloniki, which they allowed me to read. It described the inhumane way the German soldiers treated the disabled veterans during the deportations in Thessaloniki. It mentioned how their wheelchairs, canes and crutches, and even their artificial wooden arms and legs, were taken from them before they were loaded onto the "death trains." The exchange of disabled prisoners was nothing but a utopian dream.
> On October 8, 1943, a great number of public posters announced the order requesting the Jews to register. My parents Isaak and Dona Capon were among the first Jews to register themselves. They received catalog numbers 38 and 39. My sister Sara Rousso, with her son Emilio and her husband Isaak Samuel, were also registered. They felt that all law-abiding citizens should obey the regulations. In March 1944, they were all taken by the Germans. Dr. Leon Kohen, who survived captivity, told me how my brother-in-law Isaak Samuel Rousso participated in the Birkenau revolt in which he lost his life. My wife Mafalda and I were issued false identity cards by the Palio Psihiko police department, which also provided my sister Victoria and my brother-in-law Alberto

Minervo with new identities. Two police officers served as witnesses in accordance with the regulations then in effect. They were Lieutenant Panagiotis Maltezos (now Lieutenant-General, retired) and another brave police officer whose name, unfortunately, I do not remember.

Finding civilian witnesses during these critical times would have been very difficult for us. Armed with these lifesaving identity cards we placed ourselves and our children, Isaak-Robert and Dona-Lilian, under the protection of a humanitarian couple, Nikolaos and Antonia Panagiota from Zografou, Athens. They also saved Alberto and Victoria Minervo and their first cousin, Samouel Minervo, a disabled veteran of the Greek-Italian war, from Chania, Crete. With no ulterior economic motive, the Panagiota couple used all kinds of machinations to shelter us in different parts of Athens. Antonia was the best friend and classmate of my wife from the time they were high school students in Chania. In the beginning, we all lived together in Vrylissia, but later we were dispersed to other sections of the city and its suburbs. Another Christian family which helped us was that of George Markoulaki, a jeweler in Athens; they even offered to give us their identity cards, something we did not accept, knowing what a perilous thing it could be for them.

On June 15, 1944, the Germans blocked the suburb of Zografou and let the Greek collaborators in the security battalions arrest all men above the age of 15. I was with my brother-in-law Alberto in a big square with thousands of other men. Groups of people were led in front of the Greek officers who checked identity cards, while a sole German corporal and his German shepherd supervised the proceedings. When I saw the Greek colonel in charge of the search, I knew I was in danger. He had been my major when I was a soldier in the Greek army. He knew me very well as the "good Jewish soldier!" I told my brother-in-law to join a group which would pass inspection before my turn came, so at least he would be safe before the officer saw me. When my turn came, a captain would check my card and read my name aloud. A group of sergeants would then search some lists which identified Resistance

II. Personal Memoirs – The Italian Zone of Occupation

members and Jews, and if the name was not included, the suspect would pass in front of "my friend" Colonel Yiannis Plitzanopoulos, who was seated on a canvas armchair. He looked at the suspect and made the final decision as to whether the man was free to go. When I was about to approach the colonel, I let God decide my fate. At this point, a sergeant gave him a paper to read. The three or four people who were in front of me kept moving and so did I! By the time the officer looked again, I was a free man. [191] [Author's note: The Panagiota (also spelled Panayotos) family were recognized by Yad Vashem in 1990 as Righteous Among the Nations.]

In a Children's Hospital

Katy Torres relates her story:

Before the war, my parents brought me from Thessaloniki to the Asklipion Voulas Hospital in Athens because my leg was stricken with tuberculosis. I was five when the war started. I remember I was in bed when the radio blared out the news. When the Italians came, they sang songs and said how much they missed their families. Then the Germans came, strict and quite handsome. Sometime in 1943, a nurse came and told me that my father had come to see me. I felt so happy! Suddenly I saw an awful-looking man with white hair and worn-out clothes. I thought there must have been a mistake. This man was not my father. I remembered him as somewhat heavy with jet-black hair and very well-dressed. He kept saying that he was my father, but I did not believe him. After that, he kept coming every Sunday, which was the only day of the week we were given a small piece of meat with potatoes. We shared the meal.

---

191 "The Invalid Veteran," letter from Benjamin Capon to me, December 26, 1975.

The Illusion of Safety

I was told that my mother and sister were supposed to have taken the next train to Athens, but something had happened and they did not. My mother was so beautiful, so gentle, so lovable! How could anything bad happen to her? Sometimes the girls in the hospital asked me, "Do you believe in Christ?" or "Why don't you believe in Christ?" Who was Christ and what did he have to do with me? I did not know. But I had a feeling that Christ had something to do with why my father, hiding in attics at night, had to sell cigarettes in the streets of Athens, and why my mother and sister had disappeared.

One day, four trucks filled with Germans and Greek police came to the hospital grounds. They searched for communist documents and weapons. They lined up 24 men from the hospital personnel and declared they would be shot if anything was found during their inspection. What a search! They went through everything.

Suddenly a good-looking German officer came to my bed and spoke in perfect Greek. "Who gave you this?" he asked. He pointed at a Greek-issue military canteen standing on my night table. "My father," I said. "Where is your father?" I sensed trouble and became confused. "I don't know where he stays." "What is your father's name?" My father had given me strict instructions to give his Christian name, because he was baptized. "Michael Michaelopoulos," I said.

He glanced at my chart attached to the bed and he became furious when he read my obviously Sephardic name. "How come your name is Torres and his Michaelopoulos?" He drew his gun and placed it next to my head. The muzzle was a fraction of an inch from my temple. I don't know how long he kept the gun in that position, but it seemed to me that it lasted for an eternity. I became hysterical. The nurses, together with my doctor, rushed to me. The doctor spoke to the German in a quiet, confidential manner. The German removed his gun, wrote a few things in a notebook, and left. I later found out that my beloved doctor, [Dr. Andriopoulos], told the officer that I was a terminal case, and that the chances of my leaving the hospital

II. Personal Memoirs – The Italian Zone of Occupation

alive were practically nil. Twenty-five years later, on a trip from the United States to Greece, I tried to see my savior again, but nobody could locate him.

Many hours passed before the search of the hospital was completed. Nothing incriminating was found and the 24 men were released unharmed.

Time went by. My father came every Sunday. The war seemed endless. Suddenly the war was over. People were hugging and kissing. The excitement and happiness were beyond description. "What is it going to be like without war?" A new beginning!

And my mother? If only my mother would come back. Please dear God, bring my mother. Someone told me that if I prayed every night and asked God to bring my mother back, God would. I did every night and waited every day. She didn't come back. My father found out through the Red Cross that she was in a concentration camp with my sister. After that, nothing. After all these years, I still feel that my mother lives somewhere. Beautiful people don't die. They live forever.[192]

Katy Torres with her father. (Photo courtesy of Katy's son, Saul McCormack.)

---

[192] "In a Children's Hospital," letter from Katy Torres of Washington, D.C., to the author, October 10, 1975. The doctor's name was discovered after 1975 by Isaak Dostis.

The Illusion of Safety

In Hiding

Rahel Hatzopoulou went into hiding in the house of Kaiti Hatjaki in the suburb of Pangrati. Because of her false identity card, she was not forced to remain indoors all the time. She gave French lessons to students to make ends meet.

On March 24, 1944, while walking on Dipylou Street, Rahel was approached by someone who informed her about the arrests taking place at that very hour on Melidoni Street, where the synagogue was located. She felt anger, sorrow, hate, and fear as she walked home, taking a shortcut through the Royal Gardens. On the way she met two other Jews, Elia Siakki from Volos and Abram Tovil, to whom she told the terrible news. Rahel did not feel safe in Pangrati. She moved, with the help of George Tsoutsani, to another house in Kokkinia. Sabotage at a nearby ammunition dump forced her to move again. She describes:

> On Tuesday, June 1, 1944, I visited Kanten Kohen, wife of Semo, without knowing of course that the Gestapo was searching for him. A few minutes later, the Germans entered forcibly with their pistols trained on us. They were accompanied by an interpreter and the Jewish traitor, Pepo Recanati. The first words which came to my mind were "Shemah, Israel!" ("Hear 0 Israel"—the first words of a Jewish prayer.) They searched for Semo in vain. They asked Kanten to take with her whatever valuables she had. Recanati then turned his attention on me and asked what I was doing there. I told him a story—that my three brothers were killed by the communists in Chalkis and now I had to work as a cleaning woman to survive. He did not ask me for my identity card, since all the security people knew about the false identity cards the Jews possessed. However, he asked me about the church of the neighborhood. "If you mean the big one," I replied, "it is the church of St. Spyridonos, but if you mean the small one, it is the church of Palaiomerologiton," and I made the sign of the cross, showing also the cross I had attached to a necklace. It seems that these words were enough to persuade them that I was not Jewish. Yet they took me in their car with Kanten, and this worried

me very much. The car went first to the synagogue, but fortunately for me they did not ask me to enter the building. If I did, the people there would surely have recognized me, and that would have been my end. Many people knew me, for my brother Menachem, whom this same Recanati had hunted and arrested only a few days before, was a lay rabbi in the community of Ioannina.

From Melidoni Street, we went to the Gestapo headquarters on Merlin Street in Kolonaki, an address which will be remembered for a long time by those who were interrogated there. I was released outside this fear-inspiring building, while my friend Kanten Kohen was kept in custody, and that was the last time I saw her. I was about to have a nervous breakdown as I walked toward Ermou Street. There was the danger that I was being followed, but I had no choice but to take that chance. I went to the commercial district, where I borrowed money from Mr. Zambia, who was safekeeping my dowry and that of my sister, Rebecca. With great delay, I returned to the house of Kanten, where her family and neighbors were worried about her. I suggested that someone should bribe Recanati and obtain her release. I gave whatever precious items I had toward this purpose, and so did her husband. On Thursday a Christian friend found Recanati on Romvis Street. Nothing could be done. The Germans would not release her.

I had to change my hiding place again because a new feeling of insecurity overwhelmed me. This time my new angel was a widow, Glykeria Sardi, who had two children and lived in a one-room house with a packed earth floor. I stayed with her for two weeks, and then I moved to the house of Panagiotis Antoniadou on Diakou Street. This family gave me all their affection and care, in spite of the fact that their son Antonis had been executed with 20 other hostages in Tourkovounia only a few days before I arrived.

During all this time I had to take care of my sister-in-law Raymonda and her son, who were also in hiding. I had to sell parts of my dowry to provide them with the bare necessities of life. Because of these activities, I had to be on the streets of Athens more often than good judgment dictated. At the end of July 1944, I was walking on Nikis Street when two Christian traitors arrested me. I suspect they were the same who, at the beginning of the persecution, confiscated a great quantity of merchandise belonging to my family, and this is how they recognized me. We walked toward Ioulianou Street when I took the courage to tell them: "You have nothing to gain by betraying me to the Germans, especially now that the war is about to end. Where will you go once Germany is defeated?" It seems these words brought them to their senses. They let me go.[193]

In the Caves of Porto Rafti

In 1942, Leon Kohen was a 16-year-old who, with his friends, was active in the Resistance. They painted anti-German slogans on walls and distributed Resistance leaflets in Athens where he lived. Leon asked his father to take the family and go to the Middle East, but his request was ignored. The grandmother was too old and the daughters too young for such a trip. There was also the question as to what they would do with their material wealth. Leon's mother happened to be in Thessaloniki, where she was arrested by the Germans (she did not return from captivity). In October 1943, the family went into hiding.

Leon relates:

> My father, with my sister Lina, age six, found a place in Kato Patissia. My grandmother stayed with a family in Nea Philadelphia, while my sister Deniz, age 15, and I were sheltered by different families at different times. The great number of the people who participated in our personal rescue effort is indicative of the number of friends we had and also of the dangers involved.

---

[193] "In Hiding," Rahel Hatzopoulou, letter to the author October 10, 1975.

II. Personal Memoirs – The Italian Zone of Occupation

My classmate Zaglanis gave me a remote uninhabited cottage belonging to his family. I spent the winter of 1943-44 enclosed in this freezing room. During the day I was alone and remained indoors, but after sunset I went out, slightly disguised to avoid being recognized. I was in charge of providing food for my grandmother, father and sisters using our food ration coupons, which were entrusted to our friendly baker, Papamichael. At a time when people were dying of hunger, his assistance was of great value to us, and it was potentially very risky for him and his family. Similar heroic gestures were made toward me by the families of many of my classmates who knew where I was hiding. Every day one of them sent me a plate of food.

One time I returned to my hut after visiting my grandmother and found that thieves had entered my room and taken away my blankets, cot, clothes and everything else I had. A note left behind informed me that they would not betray me because they considered me a "patriot." I was frightened. In my despair I went to the house of Papamichael, where I met his cousin, Elpidoforos Petsalis, who, after listening to my story, placed his hand on my shoulder and said: "We don't know each other well but I feel obligated to help you. I am not rich, but if you want you can be my guest." I gladly accepted his hospitality and especially his friendship. He was not an especially courageous man, but he was a sensitive, refined individual with good manners and a good education. In the months I spent in his house, we endured hunger and German searches, but we never lost our spirit.

During one German search, my grandmother was arrested. We never saw her again. A few days later my father was betrayed. Seven Gestapo men captured him, right in front of my little sister Lina, who they did not know was Jewish and therefore left alone. This was the last time she ever saw our father. These terrible events made me remember my original plan of going to the Middle East. I decided to take Deniz along with me and entrust Lina to our friends. I established the proper contacts and then joined the people who waited for the boat in Porto Rafti.

For a whole month we lived in caves. We were hungry, thirsty and cold. Every day we were hoping to see our boat, but many times we saw only German patrols approaching. Everybody would rush to the caves and stay in them until the Germans left. One day the boat arrived, and we went on board. It was a very small vessel, and very crowded. As we were crossing the Aegean the boat developed mechanical problems, and we went to the island of Tinos for repairs. In a few days we were again at sea, approaching the Turkish coast near Cheshme. The Turks refused to allow us to disembark, and it took many bribes before we were able to change their minds. It was a dark night, and the sea was very rough. Enormous waves pushed our boat toward the rocks, and water started coming in. The lifeboat that was used to transfer the people from the vessel to the shore could hold no more than two passengers. There were about 100 of us. By the time the turn for the last ones came, the boat began to capsize. We had to swim to shore and, as a result, one man lost his life.

Our adventure continued as we were taken to Palestine, where my sister and I escaped from the camp in which the British kept us. I joined the Resistance and fought in the war of liberation. My sister Lina was sent to me in Israel by my surviving relatives. Allow me to finish with this sentence: I curse the German people and all who did not help us, although they were able. I will never forgive them.[194]

The Deal

Maurice Soriano of Rhodes relates:

In July 1944, the Germans issued their first anti-Jewish regulations prohibiting Jews from residing

---

[194] "In the Caves of Porto Rafti," Leon Kohen, letter to author 3/15/76.

II. Personal Memoirs – The Italian Zone of Occupation

beyond a radius of 3.3 miles from the center of the city. We realized that our situation was not good, and we wished that more young people had not asked for "parental consent" and, instead, fled with the Italian troops. Those who fled became partisans and survived. At 5:00 p.m. on July 19, 1944, a new order was issued. It requested all Jewish men, 16 years or older, to report to Gestapo headquarters by 8:00 a.m. the following day. The headquarters were located in the Hotel Soleil. They were supposed to have their identity and work cards with them. A group of Germans accompanied by an interpreter, Kosta Recanati, questioned us, examined us, took away our papers, and finally imprisoned us in the same building. I noticed that the interpreter spoke Ladino fluently. Since I was the director of the Jewish community, I asked him how he had learned this language so well. He said that he had Jewish friends who spoke Ladino. Since we had no proof that he was Jewish, we had to believe him, but I doubted that this was the truth.

We remained imprisoned without food or water until the following day. At 9:00 a.m. Recanati and the Germans arrived. The directors of the community, Franco R. Kohen and I, were given a new order: "Inform all families to report here by 4:00 p.m. tomorrow. They should have a few clothes, food for ten days, and all their gold, jewelry and valuables. You will be resettled in a neighboring island and you will live off your savings." The chairman of the community was given a car. He was accompanied by Recanati, and he notified all Jewish families.

Recanati said the following in Ladino: "My dear friends, it is for your own good, if you don't want to suffer, to take with you all your savings. Savings in money, jewelry and gold so you will not die of hunger. I don't want you to reproach me afterward for not having told you." I am sure that 90 percent of the people believed what he said. After all the families were locked in the same building, the chairman was ordered to hand over their valuables. The Germans threatened to shoot anybody who did not cooperate in giving away his possessions. Even wristwatches were taken away. By now our panic reached its zenith. I realized that our situation was horrible, and in my despair, I offered Recanati 100 gold sovereigns if he could help me escape. He asked my nationality. I told him I was Dodecanese, and my wife a Turkish citizen. This information pleased him, and he promised to do something for us. My wife and our two children were in a village where I had sent them, although I knew this was against German regulations. They had all our valuables with them. I wrote a message for my wife on six slips of paper, hoping that a passerby would find and deliver my communication. One of these papers reached my wife. In my message I instructed her to contact the Turkish consul and ask his help. This honorable Turk intervened immediately on behalf of the Turkish citizens and those who were married to them. In this way I was one of those liberated.

My elderly parents continued to be imprisoned by the Germans. I had freedom of movement but was obliged to report to the Gestapo daily. I met Recanati and promised to give him anything he asked for the liberation of my parents. Thanks to his intervention, my parents were attached to a group of Turkish citizens who were released. As I was taking them away from prison, Recanati walked over to me and told me, "Tonight at 9:00 p.m. I will see you at the Hotel Albergo delle Terme." I kept this appointment and gave him the bribe, which was wrapped in a handkerchief. In the meantime, my parents were denounced to the Germans as Dodecanese who did not have the right to be considered Turkish nationals. Only through the help of an Italian physician were my parents admitted to a hospital prior to our departure for Turkey. In spite of the money we paid, the boat was leaking and in danger of sinking. I had an unpleasant argument with the captain before he was persuaded to turn back for repairs. Eventually we safely sailed for Turkey, where we remained for the rest of the war.[195]

---

[195] "The Deal," Maurice Soriano, translated from Hebrew by Avi Richter, Yad Vashem, Deposition No. 1745167.

II. Personal Memoirs – The Italian Zone of Occupation

The Longest Summer

Almost none of Karditsa's 150 Jews were arrested, although many obeyed the German registration order. They all went to the countryside prior to March 1944.

Markos Ganis and his family lived in Karditsa for as long as they could remember. He maintained excellent relations with the villagers of the nearby mountains. Every year, for their summer vacation, the Ganis family used to go to the village of Sermeniko or Filacti or Neuropoulis. In the summer of 1943, in spite of the war, they went as usual for their customary vacation. Life in Karditsa was almost as normal as it was during peacetime. When Italy capitulated, Karditsa remained for a while a free and unoccupied city. The Germans, however, attacked Karditsa quite often from the air. In order to protect themselves from the German air raids, the Ganis family decided to spend the winter in Filacti. In this quite casual way, they neither registered with nor were arrested by the Germans. The whole family still remembers the kindness and politeness of the villagers and especially the assistance they gave when Marko Ganis' daughter-in-law gave birth without a physician or midwife. During the German search and destroy missions, which took place in August 1944, they spent many days in caves and inaccessible mountain hideouts away from the village. In October 1944, they returned to the city after the longest "summer vacation" in their memory.[196]

Two Playboys

Joseph Yohanas of Patras remembers how his family abandoned the city as soon as they were advised to do so and walked together with other fugitive Jews for over four hours before they reached the free village of Zoumbata.

Yohanas, who resided outside Baltimore, relates:

> Zoumbata was an ordinary village of Peloponnesus, located far from any roads accessible by automobiles.

---

196 "The Longest Summer," letter to the author from Joseph Matsas, 2/25/75.

In spite of this, we did not feel secure enough and moved to the remote mountain village of Myra. On the day of Yom Kippur in 1943, many Jews from nearby villages came to our house for the traditional service. Some walked ten hours to reach Myra. Whenever we were warned that German units were approaching the area, the men would leave and hide while the women, dressed in village clothes, stayed behind. In December 1943, during a German attack, we left the village and went to Mazi, where we found shelter in a church. We were nine Jewish men and a priest. It was snowing and terribly cold. The priest started a fire and used church furniture as firewood during the two days and nights we stayed there.

I was a young, adventurous man, and I went to Patras without identity papers four times. The last time I felt the urge for some excitement was in January 1944. I entered the city uneventfully and met my friends. We were enjoying ourselves when we were approached by a group of Greek soldiers who served in a security battalion. They asked us for identity papers. All my friends had proper cards; I was the only one who did not. The soldiers released them. They asked me to show them a nightclub and promised to let me go. They just wanted to have fun, and they did not suspect me of anything. I readily agreed and showed them whatever they wanted to see. At one point we were in the square of the Three Allies, in the center of the city, when we were approached by a group of Italian fascists in civilian clothes. They insulted our group by yelling *"poutana Grecque* [Greek whore]". In a few seconds a fistfight developed. I did not get a chance to get away. We were right in front of German naval headquarters and were surrounded immediately by German guards. They broke up the fight and released the members of the security battalion, who were in uniform. They asked the rest of us, *"Papier?"* The fascists showed their papers and were released. Then they asked to see my identity card. *"Papier nix,"* was my reply. I was immediately arrested and sent to prison. I was placed in an empty cell for a week without anybody paying any attention to me. Finally, a guard asked me if I wanted

II. Personal Memoirs – The Italian Zone of Occupation

to notify my family. I asked him to contact my girlfriend, who I knew was friendly with a young German lieutenant named Werner. In a few hours, the lieutenant came to the prison. He talked to the prison officials and guaranteed that I was not dangerous in any way. I was soon a free man again.

This experience petrified my family. However, it did not sufficiently impress my brother Zadik, who now lives in Israel. He was a young stallion who wanted to have fun regardless of what might happen to him. He entered the city without any trouble, but, in a few hours, someone betrayed him and he was arrested as a Jew by the Germans. Since the Jews who remained in Patras were still free, the Germans did not treat my brother badly. They simply put him in prison, where he remained forgotten for a month. By that time my mother, dressed as a villager, secretly entered the city and went to the house of a neighbor who owned a nightclub. He told my mother where my brother was. The news of his arrest had become widely known. The nightclub owner had connections with the Germans. My mother gave him 25 gold sovereigns and one diamond ring. With this amount he bribed someone and obtained the release of my brother. His intimate knowledge of the city, with its alleys and narrow streets, helped him. Soon he was back with us in the mountains. He had no more desire for "fun" until the end of the war.

On March 25, 1944, the Germans arrested the Jews who registered with them. There was one woman who would not have been arrested if it were not for her pregnancy. She was in the village with us. Her name was Ziona Rafael. She wanted to deliver her baby in a hospital. She did on March 18. Seven days later, mother and baby were both deported; someone must have informed the Germans that they were still in the hospital.

The war between ELAS and the Germans intensified. We had to abandon everything and run while the Germans were launching their search-and-destroy missions from all directions. We ate crabgrass and chick peas and spent a whole week in a cave. We moved to the village of Leontino, where the Greek Red Cross distributed some yellow soup. The villagers refused it because they thought someone had conspired to poison them. We ate as much soup as we could. In the same village, we found shelter in an abandoned house. Nobody wanted to sleep in it because they believed it was haunted. Eventually we returned to the village of Myra, where we stayed until the liberation. I am proud to say that Patras was the first liberated city in Greece, and that I was the first Jew who entered it. The half-Jewish German interpreter Wolfson, who told Isaak Matsas to leave the city, survived the war, and he is still in Patras working as a businessman. His father and mother went back to Germany.[197]

Watching and Waiting

The family of Samuel and Astro Alballa consisted of two grown children, Victoria and Pepo, who now live in Israel, and two youngsters, Toula, age 7, and Moissi, who was just two months old in October 1943. While most of the Jews of Patras went to the nearby mountain villages, the Alballa family remained in the city. They gave the Germans the address of their apartment, but they did not continue living in it. A friendly family let them stay in their home until the day it was rumored that the Germans were threatening to kill all those who sheltered Jews in their homes. Their hosts were very straightforward. They did not wish to take risks, and the Alballa family was asked to leave immediately.

The Alballas again resisted the temptation to return to their apartment, where all their furniture was stored, and preferred instead to live in a nearby small apartment which Samuel Alballa used for his business as a representative of different commercial companies. The apartment was situated on a street corner. On the morning of March 25, the family was awakened by a lot of commotion on the two streets below, where many other Jewish families lived. They saw German soldiers and the Greek police escorting their Jewish neighbors.

---

[197] "Two Playboys," interview with Joseph Yohanas, June 1976.

II. Personal Memoirs – The Italian Zone of Occupation

Astro Alballa remembers:

> We were watching them passing under our windows with tears in our eyes, and we prayed to the Almighty not to let them stop at our house. I had our baby in my arms and our little daughter next to me. My husband was almost in shock, thinking of what could actually happen to us at any second. We waited in silence, listening for the slightest noise that would mean the difference between slavery and freedom for us. We did not know then that a knock at our door could actually mean death rather than just slavery.
>
> Pretty soon no more Germans and their captives could be seen. We realized that they did not know where we were, and we made plans for our dash toward the mountains.
>
> In the streets below people were seen carrying whatever they could loot from Jewish homes. Some of the items we saw could even be ours, since, as we found out later, the Germans broke down the door of our apartment and left it at the mercy of looters. We got dressed in such a way that we could be taken for villagers, with kerchiefs and shirts without ties, and we left the city in groups of two.
>
> We all met at a prearranged point in a nearby free village. From there we rented a horse for myself and the baby while Toula was taken on the shoulders of one of the other adults. We felt happy and safe when we met partisans of ELAS for the first time. They helped us to find shelter in a village house near the top of a snow-covered mountain.
>
> When liberation came and we returned to our house, I met a woman there who had occupied the apartment, which was still filled with all our furniture, since only small items were carried away by the looters. I thanked the woman for keeping the furniture. She felt very bad that we had come back.[198]

---

[198] "Watching and Waiting," letter from Astro Alballa to the author, July 1976.

Innocent Brothers

Emmanuel Velellis of Patras tells his story:

As soon as the Italians surrendered, we realized we should be on the alert. We took the precaution of sleeping in Christian homes, and we dispersed our things and prepared to leave the city. When the president of the community sounded the alarm and told everybody to go into hiding, we were ready.

On the eve of Rosh Hashanah (I believe it was September 23, 1943), we loaded everything we could onto a horse-drawn carriage, which a friend took out of the city to a small village. My parents, my wife with our two daughters, age one and seven, and my three brothers Peppos, Vittorio, and Alberto, left the city on foot. They went to a village, where our supplies were waiting for us. A civilian bus took all of us to the end of its line, on the slopes of the mountains of Panahaikou, which one of my brothers was familiar with because he belonged to a mountain-climbing club. We loaded everything onto ten horses and went to a mountain village. This was the time of many German search-and-destroy missions. They raided our village three times. We had to abandon everything and go into hiding. The last time, they dynamited the houses. We had to move on. We found shelter in the village of Demestiha Kalavriton, which served as headquarters of the British intelligence service. My brother Alberto, who is now in Israel, and I found work as messengers for the British. They gave us food in exchange for our services. My wife had to feed a baby, and the food situation was very bad for everybody. She kept asking me to return to Patras, as did almost fifty other Jews, since the Germans did not disturb those who registered with them and remained in the city. They also did not punish those who initially left the city and later returned. My wife's arguments seemed persuasive, but I refused to listen to her. I told her, "If you want to go to the comforts of Patras, go." "Can I take the children with me?" "No! The children stay with me." That was the end of our discussion.

II. Personal Memoirs – The Italian Zone of Occupation

The leader of EAM-ELAS in the area was Captain Steriopoulos. He asked my brothers Peppos and Vittorio to work for the Resistance instead of the British. My brothers were satisfied with the way things were at the time and declined the offer. Even in this remote village, we were not immune from German raids. Any time the Germans approached, the British left and went to the next mountain. We followed them wherever they went. Very often planes came and made their parachute drops. The villagers were eager to help in collecting whatever was dropped, and they hoped that one of the barrels would split on impact and spill thousands of gold sovereigns all around!

One day my brothers Peppos and Vittorio were arrested by ELAS partisans. They were taken away, and only at the end of the war did we find out they were not alive any more. They were in an ELAS improvised detention camp with 82 other suspects and collaborators. This was at the time when Aris Velouhiotis and his guards, who wore black berets, preferred to deal their blows against the German collaborators instead of attacking the Germans, who were in the process of withdrawing. During a German raid in the direction of my brothers' detention center, the partisans, instead of moving the prisoners, preferred to eliminate them. All 84 of them were thrown into a well after each received a bullet in the back of the head. My two brothers, who saved themselves from the Germans, suffered this unjust fate at the hands of the people who were supposed to be our friends. By the time the war was over, we all were sick with malaria. This, however, did not stop us from walking over 12 hours to return to the free city of Patras.[199]

---

199 "Innocent Brothers," interview with Emmanuel Velellis, June 1976.

A Modern Job

The most tragic and yet noble figure of the Jewish community of Patras was a widow, Esther Yohana, who had four sons and five daughters. On October 28, 1940, the first day of the Greek-Italian war, enemy planes bombarded the port of Patras. There was little damage because the Italian planes flew at a high altitude. There were few dead, but among them was Peppos Yohana, a university student and Esther's son. When the Germans arrested the Jews, her second son, Yohanas Yohana, was taken away and never returned. Two of her beautiful daughters, Finetta and Cleio, were married on the island of Corfu to two brothers, my mother's first cousins. Cleio was married to Matathias Kohen; Finetta was married to Menahem Kohen. Most of the Jews of Corfu were transferred by the Germans to Patras, where they stayed for a few days in a building across the street from the German naval headquarters. A Greek member of the security battalions who had access to the building housing the Jewish captives recognized Cleio and Finetta and remembered that they were daughters of the late Rafael Yohana, who had been his benefactor. A sense of obligation to express his gratitude to their father overwhelmed him. He approached them and told them that he would enable them and their families to escape, although he could not help their elderly mother-in-law. It was a magnanimous offer that should have been gladly accepted.

It was June 12, 1944. Almost 5,000,000 European Jews were already dead. Cleio and Finetta refused the noble offer of this man because they did not want to leave their mother-in-law, Diamantoula Kohen, alone. She was then in her eighties. A few days later, in the concentration camp, Esther Yohana lost her two daughters and her grandchildren. Menahem and Matathias were selected to work, and their lives were spared momentarily. When they discovered what happened to their families, they committed suicide together by touching the electrified fence.[200]

---

[200] "A Modern Job," information given by Joseph Yohanas, June 1976.

II. Personal Memoirs – The Italian Zone of Occupation

*Finetta and Menachem Kohen of Corfu.
Both died in Auschwitz.*

In Corfu, another first cousin of my mother, Semos Kohen, brother of Menachem and Matathias, did not obey the German orders. Semos with his wife, three daughters, and a son left the city of Corfu and survived in the countryside of the island. Their son Zinos lived in California, and their daughter Dora married Salvator Bakolas, who was a chemistry student and became a partisan. He is depicted in a photo on page 351 in this book.

After March 25, 1944, there were no more Jews in Patras with the exception of the half-Jewish interpreter Wolfson and a Thessaloniki Jew, as disclosed in the following document sent by the German consul of Patras to his ambassador in Athens:

June 19, 1944

I was informed by a reliable source that in a house on 14 Dodonis Street a Jew from Thessaloniki lives. He is known at the present moment as Spiros Recanatis. In order to deceive the German authorities, he falsely assumed this Greek name. It depends on you to bring this to the attention of the German military authorities.

The diplomat Zeileissen wrote in pencil on the margin of the consular document: "SS Officer Honscheid was given the necessary information on this subject."[201]

Shemah

On March 25, 1944, my first cousin Sam Meyer woke up early as usual because he had to go to a village outside of Ioannina to purchase milk for his grandfather's store. He had two big milk cans attached with rope on the sides of his bicycle's front wheel and two cans tied on the sides of the back wheel. Finding shelter among his numerous friends, the shepherds and villagers of the free territories near Ioannina, would have been the easiest thing in the world for Sam or any other Jew. Yet, Sam believed he had no reason to hide. He was sure that the Jews of Ioannina would not be deported like those of Thessaloniki. As he moved out of his street and into the Kourmanio Square, he saw people reading some wall posters. Sam stopped to see what the poster said. "Whoever is engaged in looting will be punished with death." He asked someone to explain to him what this German threat meant. "Today, they arrest the Jews," the man said. "Anyone caught looting their houses and shops will be killed."

Sam immediately returned home, where he talked with his [also my] grandparents, Sarina and Naoum Matsas, and his mother Rosina, who had just woken up. They went into the street and heard people crying or yelling. Some neighbors said, "They will deport us to Germany." Within an hour, at 8:00 a.m., the German authorities informed them that all the Jews should go to Mavili Square by Lake Pamvotis, with the exception of the Jews who lived within the great walls of the old city. Their concentration point was the castle square. Every family was entitled to bring along 30-40 kilos of clothes, food,

---

201 P. K. Enepekidis, "The Last Jew," *To Vima*, August 1966.

and valuables. By 10:00 a.m. everyone was at these points, and at 11:00 a.m. the great convoy began its fateful voyage.

In every truck was one German guard; yet in Perama, when the cars stopped briefly, Eliasaf Matsas, age 17, got off the truck. He pretended he was moving some sheep from the road. The shepherd understood and together with Eliasaf directed the sheep toward a nearby hill. [Eliasaf joined the partisans and fought heroically in many battles.]

The weather was unusually cold, and in Katara the snow was one meter deep. The convoy with the deportees from Ioannina arrived in Larissa on the morning of March 26, 1944, after a slow, arduous trip. In Larissa, the captives were placed in a large building surrounded by a yard and wire fence. The building used to belong to the Greek army. The Jews who were captured in Trikala, Larissa, and Volos were also there. For three days, no provisions for food were made, and people had to subsist on whatever food they brought with them.

In the camp at Larissa, the prisoners were ordered to deliver their gold and jewelry to the Germans. A line was formed by the household heads, who placed into a large bag, guarded by a German, what represented many years of work and privations, many hopes and dreams. The German held a rubber club and hit whomever he wished among those who gave their fortunes. Many people threw their valuables into the toilets rather than go on line. One rich man, Moussoulia Eliezer, offered his gold to a poor relative of his. The poor man became furious: "You give it to me now?" he yelled. "When I was in real need and I asked you to lend me five gold sovereigns, you refused. Go by yourself and give it to the Germans."

Simon Nachman, a survivor, related that Dr. Koffinas met there, for the first time after his release from prison, Sabetai Kabeli, the man he entrusted with the message smuggled out of prison in a loaf of bread, in spite of the danger involved. "Why are the young people here?" he asked. "Didn't you get the message?" "I did," a hesitant voice replied, "but I thought we should obey the orders and nothing would happen." Dr. Koffinas finally said to him, "The crime is upon your head." Dr. Koffinas died in Auschwitz. His daughter lives in Sweden. The message was given on March 17, 1944. That was eight days prior to the arrest of the Jewish community on March 25, 1944.

After three days, the Greek Red Cross brought food and cooking utensils to the camp. Sam Meyer volunteered to be an assistant to his uncle, Yeshua Matsas, who accepted to be in charge of all the cooking.

Sam relates:

> I became a cook for two reasons. First, because someone had to do this job and, second, because this work would enable me to be out of the main building and I could possibly find the opportunity to escape. On the sixth day of our life in captivity, a group of Greek citizens received permission, I don't know how, to visit us. When they were leaving, six young men, who erased the word "Jew" from their identity cards, intermingled with the group of visitors and were able to escape from the camp. They were Moissis Miyonis, Jacob Gerson, Abraam Svolis, Sam Kohen, Michael Kohen, and Yeshua Matsas, brother of Eliasaf, who escaped at Perama. [They all became ELAS partisans and survived the war unharmed, in spite of the great number of battles in which they fought.] I observed the whole scene, and I saw the boys escaping. I could not find a moment of peace after that. Another young man, Minas Hatzopoulos, was hidden in a Red Cross car. He was covered with blankets and empty bags while two girls preoccupied the German guards with small talk. The car left the camp with Minas inside. He also became a partisan like the others.
>
> On that day, we were a little late in our distribution of food, and it started getting dark before we were finished. I told my mother, my uncle, and my grandfather that I would like to escape, and they all agreed that I should if the opportunity arose. In the yard, I saw that the German guard was talking with some girls who, as I found out much later, were begging him to let them escape. He was asking them to give him gold sovereigns, but at that time all the gold was already taken and nothing was left. I noticed that the fence was destroyed at one point and that it would be easy to escape from there. I told my childhood friend Solomon Matsas about it. Carrying some cooking utensils, we went near the fence, pretending we were

somehow working as cooks. We saw that the guard was still talking with the girls. It was almost dark. I showed my friend the point where the fence was destroyed. Outside there was a water spigot. "Let's have an excuse. We'll say that we wanted to clean these dishes at the water spigot, if they see us," I said. At this point, Solomon jumped the fence and disappeared into the darkness. I hated myself for being so indecisive. I again saw the guard talking with the girls. I was so excited that I felt as if my blood was boiling. The words "Solomon is free, and I am still a prisoner" were pounding my brain. I passed the fence and ran into the darkness until I reached the railway line.

A Greek railway worker with a lantern was there. He asked me where I was going since the 7:30 p.m. curfew was about to start. I told him the truth, adding, "I am now in your hands. If you want, you can betray me to the Germans, or you can hide me until tomorrow." He was a good man and hid me in a warehouse behind some old desks and chairs. In the morning I went away. In a few minutes, I met a man who carried milk containers. I became friendly with him after I introduced myself as a colleague, and he directed me toward Loutro-Douvlatani, a village where I met many Jewish families from Larissa. I told them that I wanted to become a partisan, and they sent me on a three-day hike to the mountains of Thessaly, to the village Nevrovounista, the base of the first ELAS division. I was told they would not accept me since I was not "organized" when I was in the city. My other alternative was work, and I found a job as a cheesemaker. After a while, I met three shepherds who, in the summer, intended to move their flocks to Kalavrites, located near Ioannina. They promised to take me with them. When the time came for our move, they gave me a shepherd's stick and a woolen overcoat with a hood, and we hiked for nine days over the mountains with hundreds of sheep ahead of us. Near Aspropotamo, an ELAS partisan called Kalampaka met us and started asking me different questions about the sheep and our destination. He realized that I knew little about sheep. "You look suspicious to me," he said.

"Come to see my captain." I told the captain the story of my escape, but he did not believe me. He wrote an accusation stating that I was a spy attempting to pass from ELAS territory to EDES territory. The penalty for this was death. I was transferred under guard to regimental headquarters in Portouli, where I was again interrogated by the partisans. I told them the whole truth and, with pain in my heart, I began thinking how unjust it would be if I were executed by the people I loved, whose ideals I shared. In spite of all my efforts to persuade them that I was not a spy, it was obvious they did not believe me. At this point, a partisan approached me and said, "We Christians, when we are going to sleep, we make the sign of the cross or say a prayer. What do the Jews do?" "They also say a prayer," I said, "the Shemah." "Can you recite it?" "Yes, I can. Shemah Yisrael Adonai..."and I recited the prayer. He held me in his arms, unable to hold back his tears. "Don't be afraid," he said. "I believe you. I am also a Jew." We embraced each other and cried, not only for the fact that my life was saved from an unjust end, but also for the unjust fate that befell our people. The next day I found a job in a primitive sawmill, using the water of a stream for power. The family who operated it needed an extra hand because the father and one brother had been killed by the Germans during a recent raid. On two more occasions while I was there, the Germans arrived unexpectedly, and, both times, I ran out of the house toward the forest at the very last minute as German scouts fired at me. I heard bullets whistling, but fortunately none hit me. I remained in this place for four months. As soon as I heard that the Germans had left Ioannina, I immediately started a two-day hike over mountain trails and reentered the city. Ioannina's population was happy and joyful. A holiday atmosphere prevailed as a result of the liberation. To me, the city looked like a desert. Out of 1,850 Jews, I found only one family of four people left. People surrounded me and looked at me as if I were unusual. They asked me questions which I was not able to answer.

Three men who escaped from the camp in Larissa. Left to right: Jacob Gerson, Sam Meyer and Solomon Matsas. (family photo)

In a few days, all those who were partisans arrived. Others who were in hiding came back too. We had a difficult time finding a room in our own homes. All the houses were already occupied by people who resented our demand to be given a room. All Jewish shops were empty of merchandise, as the Germans had transferred everything of value into a large warehouse. The Jewish partisans volunteered to guard it to prevent looting at night. They hoped that this fortune would enable survivors and those who were expected to return from German captivity to start their lives again. The communist leadership of ELAS had other plans in mind. They distributed merchandise worth no more than thirty gold sovereigns to every Jew present in Ioannina. The remaining 99 percent of the great wealth the Germans had no opportunity to transfer to Germany was transported by ELAS to Albania, and it helped to finance their military attempt to take over

Greece during the civil war, which began just two months after the liberation.[202]

A German Jewish man told me that it has been estimated that one third of the cost of the second world war to Germany was provided by assets confiscated or looted from the Jews of Europe, including the gold teeth of those they killed.

Dr. Koffinas died upon arrival in Auschwitz. His daughter survived and settled in Sweden. During a vacation in Sweden, I contacted her. I wondered how she came to be in Sweden.

Perhaps she was there because of an agreement Himmler made? When he understood that Germany was losing the war, Heinrich Himmler, the notorious head of the SS, ordered his subordinates to release from the camps 600 Jewish girls who were accepted by the Swedish Red Cross. Maybe he thought that this noble gesture would save his life. It did not. He was hanged after the Nuremberg trials.

Plunder in Ioannina

After the Germans had transferred all merchandise from the numerous Jewish shops to a big warehouse, they formed a committee of prominent Christians who passed by every house, searching for precious items: silverware, furs, jewelry, etc. Some members of the committee decided to plunder for themselves rather than for the Germans. They opened holes in the pockets of their overcoats so that the items thrown into them would pass into the lining of the coats. Notorious for this was the Averof Street pastry shop owner Zogos, whose lining broke because of the heavy weight, and whose stolen items fell onto the floor in front of many people. The Germans threatened to punish severely anyone who was caught looting, but this did not stop the vultures who are always present in any catastrophe. Simon Nachman's many sewing machines were taken from his house over the tiled roofs of the neighboring houses. A barber who stole only one mirror was not as lucky as

---

202 "Shemah," letter by Sam Meyer to author, July 1975.

II. Personal Memoirs – The Italian Zone of Occupation

the influential or big thieves: he was caught by a German and shot on the spot.[203]

The mayor of the city, Demetrios Vlahlides, persuaded the German commander to give him the Holy Books (Sefer Torahs) of the synagogues for the city museum. The mayor returned the Holy Books to the community after the war. The big synagogue on Max Nordau Street (now renamed Josef Eliya Street) was transformed by the Germans into a stable for their horses.

Some religious items were used by people who had no concept of what their real purpose was. My mother, Esther Matsas, saw velvet bags for prayer books used as confetti containers during the Mardi Gras parties. Nobody knew what happened to the great number of religious books, candelabra, silver oil lamps, silver pointers, velvet covers for the arks, menorahs, megillahs, etc. They most probably were taken to Prague, Czechoslovakia, where a beautiful complex consisting of six synagogues and the old overcrowded cemetery of the Prague ghetto was designated by the Germans as the museum of an "extinct people," a euphemism for the Jewish people. The Germans collected a myriad of precious and beautiful religious items and books there from thousands of obliterated communities and desecrated synagogues.

Among the secret documents from the OSS (American archives) is document No. 824333, containing information related to Ioannina's Jews, which was dispatched to the OSS by Agent "Z" operating in Greece:

> The following are translations from the morning newspaper *Ipeirotikos Kyrix* [*Epirus Herald*], May 27, 1944, published in Ioannina [in an article entitled] "Jewish Property": More than two months have elapsed since the Jews were removed from Ioannina. Since that time committees upon committees have been formed, meetings upon meetings have occurred. Various rumors are heard. Also plans are formulated, but Jewish property dwindles since there is no final decision. We do not know whether this situation will continue for long. However, one thing is certain: if this situation is protracted for long, there will probably be

---

203 Interview with my cousin, Naoum Matsas, October 1975.

nothing left to distribute. It is accordingly necessary that the commission stop the discussions and proceed to the distribution of the existing property without formalities and legal proceedings in order to avoid complaints and to stop criticism and the many aspersions which are being cast upon the authorities of movable property, the preservation of which is utterly impossible.[204]

While the Greek report dealt with the looted fortune of the Jews, a German report dealt with the Jews themselves. This is the way the "action" in Ioannina is presented in German documents:

> On March 25, 1944, the transportation of Ioannina's Jews took place under the command of Lieutenant Colonel Hafranek of the police. He received the cooperation of the army, the secret military police (SMP- Ioannina branch 621) and the collaboration of the Greek police (*horofilaki*) ... At 3:00 a.m. on March 25, infantry units surrounded the ghettos.
> At 5:00 a.m. the leader of the Jewish community was informed that all Jews with all the members of their families were to present themselves within three hours at two prearranged concentration points. As far as luggage is concerned, each family was allowed to take with them 50 kg. Members of the Greek *horofilaki* and security police and members of the Jewish council communicated with the Jews. Simultaneously, it became known that any Jew who did not present himself to the concentration points by 8:00 a.m. would be shot. By 7:45 a.m. the whole ghetto was evacuated, and the Jews were at the collection points. Strong patrols of the German security police supervised the evacuation of the ghettos. Posters, printed in Greek, were placed on the walls of most houses, threatening any looters with immediate execution. The action took place uneventfully. At around 8:00 a.m., the transportation began. The trucks were already near

---

[204] National Archives, OSS No. 824333.

II. Personal Memoirs – The Italian Zone of Occupation

the concentration points. The loading was done under the supervision of the military police, and the responsibility for the counting and receiving of the Jews was entrusted with the assistant driver. By 10:00 a.m., the loading of all the Jews was completed, and the eighty-truck convoy started its movement toward Larissa. The action should be considered as totally successful since it was possible to transfer 95 percent of the registered Jews. The cooperation of the services that took part in the action, including Greek police, was exemplary. The Greek population, which was in the meantime informed about what was taking place, was out in the streets of the city. With a secret joy one could see reflected on their faces, the people watched the exodus of the Jews from their city. In only rare instances was a Greek moved to say "goodbye" to a Jew by waving a hand. One could easily verify the fact that this race was equally distasteful to old and young alike. Compassion for their fate or even an unfavorable comment about this action was not observed even once. The deportation of the Jews, according to many reports we received, produced great satisfaction among the populace. With this action, the sympathy toward the Germans increased. Since the withheld objects and foodstuffs were given to the Greek authorities for inventory control and management, the barbs of EAM propaganda were thus removed.

As far as EDES circles are concerned, only full approval is heard. The opinion is expressed that a German observer should definitely be added to the committee that manages the Jewish assets in order to prevent disagreements and wrongdoing during the distribution. It is generally expected that the prices in the black market will fall since the majority of the wholesalers of agricultural products were Jews. During the last days, a noticeable calm could be seen in the marketplace, which proves that the influence of the few Jews here was, in spite of everything, of a decisive nature. On March 25, 1944, 1,725 members of the

Jewish race were deported. [Signed] Bergmayer, noncommissioned officer.[205]

Even this report underestimated the success of the German action. Only one family of four persons escaped arrest. The Greek police were helpful indeed! Yeshua and Eliasaf Matsas attempted to escape, but the Greek police forced them to return to the collection area. [Author's note: This report, in its bureaucratic simplicity, explains why I grew up without my lovely, hardworking grandparents, without my many honest and decent uncles and aunts, and without my fun-loving cousins and friends. They were all included in this procession of 1,725 Jews of Ioannina, the city where I was born.]

A Jew or a Communist

Albertos Negrin contributed his story to the author:

In September 1943, the Negrin family of Ioannina was very fortunate. Two or three rooms of their big house were occupied by Father Athanasios, a high local official of the Greek Orthodox Church. He advised the Negrin family to go to the nearby villages, and he promised to help them find quarters there.

The usual discussions took place with Albertos's parents insisting that the Germans were not going to harm old people. Eventually Albertos and his aunt, Hanoula Eliya, mother of the late poet Yosef Eliya, decided to go into hiding in Athens. Father Athanasios requested from his friends at the police department the issuance of false identity papers for Albertos and his aunt. The gold and jewelry his family had was placed

---

[205] During the Nuremberg trials, the subject of the persecution of the Greek Jews was often mentioned. The official documents, however, reported at the trial are still classified. The Institute fur Zeitgeschichte of Munich has photocopies and microfilms of some of the documents, and Professor P. K. Enepekidis had the opportunity to study them. The following document, dated 3/27/44, deals with the transportation of Ioannina's Jews: "Secret Military Police" (GEP-621 Stationed at headquarters of XXXI Mountain Artillery). *To Vima*, August 1966.

in a hiding place on the side of a well they had in the basement of their old house. Albertos and his aunt went to Athens, where they hid themselves in two different houses.

In June 1944, sabotage took place in the suburb of Kallithea, where Albertos was living, and the Germans surrounded the area. Very early in the morning Albertos and the others were awakened by heavy pounding and knocking on the front door. When they opened the door, they saw a German soldier, a Greek soldier from the security battalions, and a man in civilian clothes. They told them that all men age 16 to fifty had to present themselves in the nearby football field within two hours. Kostas and Albertos got dressed and went to the field, where they found an estimated 10,000 men from the area. German soldiers, Greek police and Greek security battalion personnel were everywhere, while four German tanks took positions on the four corners of the field. After waiting for two hours, they were all placed in formation. An informer, wearing a hood over his head with only two openings for his eyes, inspected the people and, every so often, he pointed with his finger at different persons, whom the soldiers took away immediately. Everyone knew that these people were betrayed Resistance sympathizers, and that they would be executed in retaliation for the sabotage.

Albertos felt real panic. He knew that he looked guilty! A Greek officer was passing near him and, in despair, Albertos decided to take a chance. He asked for permission to talk to him, and he explained that he was a Jew who had no connections with the Resistance or the communists. He asked for help. The officer appreciated his sincere approach, and his face showed some hints of kindness. He said something to a Greek security man who came and, grabbing Albertos, yelled the insult "dirty communist" at him and pushed him violently to a remote area of the field. He left him there after he told him to sit quietly and look depressed. After a half-hour a Greek policeman arrived. He took Albertos in the usual brutal fashion and pushed him toward the exit of the soccer field. The German guards asked why this suspect was leaving like this. The policeman explained that his prisoner was a communist who promised to denounce his other comrades. The Germans let him pass. As soon as they were away from the area, and out of sight of everybody, the Greek policeman asked Albertos to pay him for the "service" he rendered to him. Albertos handed over all the paper money he had, but the policeman was not satisfied. He asked Albertos to give him the gold ring he was wearing, and he added, "Give me whatever else you have so I don't have to search you." He gave the policeman a gold sovereign he had, and he was allowed to leave. A truck was passing from Faliro. He flagged it down, climbed up, and left Kallithea.

Albertos went to the house of another friend, Vaios Nikolopoulos, who was a government employee in charge of salt production in Anavissos. He sent Albertos there as a worker. In February 1945, Albertos returned to Ioannina. His parents, who believed that the Germans would not bother the elderly, were already dead. Father Athanasios was far better informed about current events affecting the Jews than the Jews themselves. He acted as a great human being and Albertos remembers him with respect and affection.

Because the Negrin house remained occupied by Father Athanasios until the end of the war, it was not looted or vandalized. It was not excavated by treasure hunters either, and so Albertos found the hidden gold of his family intact. He did not have to sell his house for a nominal sum as did other survivors. The gold was safe in the well, and that helped Albertos start a new life. He found a nice girl, Nina, who had survived German captivity, and they were married. Nina gave birth to his first son Elia. Life was good to them again. The Second World War, however, had not yet ended for Albertos. The Greek civil war began raging in December 1944. The communists were close to Ioannina. Many men, including Albertos, were drafted as members of a civilian guard. One night forty of these men were guarding the water pumping station outside of Ioannina. They were surrounded by communist insurgents and captured, then taken as prisoners to Albania. Albertos was finally able to return to his family after eight years of captivity.[206]

Swimming to Freedom

Isaak Koulias relates:

After the Italians capitulated, I felt that the situation was going to become worse, and so I left Volos. I went to Athens, where I stayed until the time many Jews in hiding were betrayed and arrested by the Germans. Others were constantly being blackmailed by people who knew their true identity. I visited a friend of mine, Efthimio Bardi, who had a shop on Aiolou Street. I asked him to find a hiding place for me outside the city.

He recommended the village of Petromagoula near Livadia where a friend of his, Eustathios Klevinos, a kind and honest man, accepted me as his guest and gave me shelter. A few weeks later, the partisans attacked the Germans near Petromagoula. In a few hours hundreds of German soldiers surrounded the village and ordered everyone into the main square. They arrested all the young men, including me, and loaded us on six or seven trucks, which formed a convoy and took off for an unknown destination. A few miles out of the village the trucks stopped for some reason, and I managed to escape. I decided to take a chance and hid behind a big tree. Nobody noticed me. I stayed there, immobile, until the convoy went on its way. I waited until darkness fell before I walked back to the village and the house of Klevinos, whose two sons had also been captured by the Germans and taken away. He was very glad to see me. I remember his exact words of welcome. "If I had seen my two sons coming back, I would not have been as happy as I am by seeing you;

---

206 Story told to the author by his cousin, Albertos Negrin.

you were placed in my care by a friend and I feel responsible for anything that happens to you."

I continued living in the village, but it was a life of continuous fear. The Germans came often and I had to hide. The hostages, I found out later, were taken to a forced labor camp, where they suffered for three months before they were released.

In the meantime, I decided to return to Athens, where I was sheltered in the house of Nikolaou Manessi on Eptanisou Street. There I came in contact with Ioanni Stabouli, the captain of a small boat. He was active in smuggling people to Turkey. I paid him the necessary amount of money and was told to go to the Keratea monastery, situated on the Aegean shore. There were already some people waiting for the boat when I got there. Every day a few more people came with the same little suitcases and the same conspiratorial look on their faces. One day passed after the other, while nobody received any information explaining the boat's delay. At the end of two weeks of waiting there were more than 100 men, women and children eager for a passage to freedom. To make matters worse, a German unit came to an area close by the monastery to conduct amphibious exercises. Many people became afraid and decided to return to Athens. A British officer near me, whose name was Tom, told me that he was going to stay there and wait. I made up my mind to stay also. I had no place to return to. The small boat eventually arrived and, under cover of darkness, people began going on board. We were 100 on board a small vessel whose maximum capacity was no more than fifty. The captain was afraid his vessel would capsize. He was a very shrewd man—he sabotaged his engine and then declared the boat was unable to move before it could be repaired, and nobody had the parts needed to make the repairs. At least fifty heartbroken passengers returned to Athens the following morning.

A group of Jews from Ioannina were waiting, too. They were Sion Bakolas, John and Leon Kabeli and their sister Emily. The captain had official papers issued by the Germans permitting him to sail to the

II. Personal Memoirs – The Italian Zone of Occupation

island of Chios to bring cargo from that island to Piraeus. He went to the nearby German camp and asked the officer in charge to help him with his disabled boat. A German engineer was promptly dispatched, and in an hour the engine was fixed. In the evening the 50 or so passengers who had remained reboarded the vessel, which in a few minutes was on its way. There were twenty Jews, mainly families, the British officer, and men who wanted to join the Greek army in Egypt. Among them was a Greek officer who had been seriously wounded three times while fighting on the Albanian front. The voyage was uneventful until we approached the island of Andros. A terrible storm forced us to go to a small, secluded harbor. We ran out of all provisions except sugar. The captain moved us to a remote village on the island of Tinos, where he went ashore and bartered with the villagers: sugar for food.

We were close to Turkish Karakolia when the captain stopped and placed the women and children in a rowboat, which with difficulty reached the Turkish shore. Soon Turkish border police arrived, and the man in charge said, "We take a great risk allowing you to come. Don't do it during the day. Wait until dark." He forced the men to return to the boat and wait. When darkness fell, the rowboat started moving people to shore. In the meantime, another storm began to batter our boat. The engine stopped. To prevent losing control of the vessel, they dropped anchor. The storm was so great that the chain broke and the boat floated away from Turkish territorial waters and toward a Greek island. The rowboat was unable to return. We were 13 men on board the drifting vessel. The captain had gone to shore, and only one sailor was with us. At this point the Greek officer told us, "After the capitulation I became a partisan. The Germans captured me and condemned me to death. I escaped. I won't go back to Greece." After saying that, he jumped overboard and started swimming to shore. We all followed him. The night was dark, but our people had started a fire and we swam in that direction. After what seemed to be an eternity, I reached land, totally exhausted. Pretty soon we realized that one was missing. It was the officer who actually saved us with his valiant example. We spent the night on the rocks near the fire, together with the other passengers and Turkish soldiers. Meanwhile, the Greek vice-consul of Smyrna [Izmir] arrived with food and clothing. I lost everything I had, including my money, but I was a free man.

The date was March 24, 1944. On this day the Germans arrested the Jews of Athens. In the morning we searched for the body of the officer. We found it and were present at his funeral. Then we were moved by train to Halepi in Syria and from there to a camp in Gaza, Palestine. I continued on to Jerusalem, where I was sheltered in a Greek Orthodox monastery. The monks assumed that, since I was Greek, I was also a Christian. I had no place to go and was afraid the monks would ask me to leave if they knew I was Jewish. I decided not to talk at all about religion.

The Greek consular office of Jerusalem issued me a passport, which enabled me to move freely about Palestine. When World II ended, I was in Tel Aviv. I returned to Greece, where I had met my wife Perla Mordo, from Corfu. She was not as lucky as I. She had been captured by the Germans, and she is a concentration camp survivor.[207]

The Traitor

My brother Moissis Kamontos and I went to a village called Dentina, located in the mountains of Karditsa. Our parents were very old. We decided to spare them the discomfort of living in the mountains during the coming winter and provided them with a maid to help them with the housework. My brother returned to Trikala later to see how our parents were, while I remained in the village. In Trikala, he visited the National Bank, where he had been employed. His director and colleagues persuaded him to come back. The Germans had noticed that a great number of Jews

---

207 "Swimming to Freedom," interview with author 11/12/75.

II. Personal Memoirs – The Italian Zone of Occupation

had left the city. In order to persuade them to return, they started treating the remaining Jews with kindness and respect. They told them it was not necessary for old people and small children to suffer in the cold mountains, since they did not intend to harm the Jews in any way. Many Jews believed the Germans and returned to their homes. My brother, instead of returning to the village as he promised, remained in the city. Every day he sent me letters, explaining to me how good things were, while I sent letters in which I implied as clearly as censorship allowed that he should not trust anybody and should bring the family to the village. After months of fruitless correspondence, I realized I could not remain in the village by myself while my family remained in the city. I had no choice but to return to them.

All our provisions were loaded onto two mules, and a villager and I walked for 12 hours to arrive in Karditsa. There I was told that on the morning of that very day the Jews had been arrested. That date was March 25, 1944. I felt sick. I disguised myself as a village woman. I wore a black kerchief and dark glasses, and I boarded the train for the one-hour ride to Trikala. It was a holiday. The streets of Trikkala were deserted. In the central square, I saw five people who were hanged. As I found out later, they were Christian hostages who were executed in retaliation for sabotage.

To go to my home, I had to pass through several main streets. I was constantly afraid that the Germans would arrest me. I knocked at the door of my house. My brother had accepted as guests the family of his colleague, Tsovaridis of Kalambaka, a city which had been burned in retaliation for acts of sabotage. The Tsovaridis family answered the door. They refused to let me in because they recognized me and were afraid to give shelter to a Jewess. It was getting dark, and curfew time was approaching.

I knocked at a neighbor's door and asked her to allow me to spend the night there, promising her that I would leave in the morning. She took me in with pleasure. She described to me how all the Jews had been arrested, including my family: "When the Germans surrounded the Jewish neighborhood, your parents and brother were asleep and did not notice what was taking place. A woman from Kalambaka, Mrs. Tsovaridis, who lived in the house, woke them up and told them they were about to be arrested. Your brother Moissis was in his pajamas; he was still sleepy and dizzy from the sudden calamity. He did not know where to go. Our backyard is separated by a short wall from your backyard. He climbed it easily and asked us to give him asylum. We hid him in our house."

"When your brother's guest and colleague Tsovaridis learned about it, he threatened to betray us to the Germans for sheltering Jews. This threat forced us to tell your brother, 'We are sorry, Mr. Kamontos, we won't be able to hide you because he will betray us to the Germans.'"

My brother returned to his home and ran up and down like a possessed man. He remembered that there was a hidden entrance to the attic. Trembling with fear, he climbed up and remained immobile. When the Germans entered the house, they asked for my brother, according to their lists of the Jews. Tsovaridis pointed out to them my brother's hiding place. They ordered him to come down while they fired at the ceiling. When he came down, they hit him so hard that he lost consciousness. They dragged him to the waiting trucks, which were already overfilled. To speed up the loading, they threw small children like watermelons on top of the mass of innocent captives. The mothers were crying, seeing their children treated this way.

The following morning, I had to suppress my feelings of sorrow and allow my instinct for survival to take over. Disguised as best as I could, I walked through the well-known streets of my city, hoping that nobody would recognize me and betray me. I went straight to the station without looking at the faces of the people who passed by, and I took the train to Karditsa, using my police identity card at the checkpoints. From there I went back to the village where I spent the rest of the war. I found out later that my elderly mother died on the way to Poland, and that

II. Personal Memoirs – The Italian Zone of Occupation

my father died as soon as he arrived at his final destination. My brother died a few weeks before liberation.[208]

Tsovaridis, who betrayed his colleague, was never punished for his crime.

Other Trikala Jews, such as Chaim Atoun and his family, were already in hiding in free territory. On March 24, Chaim Atoun's wife became seriously ill. Since there was no physician or medicines in the village, Chaim Atoun left his son Jacob in the village and, accompanied by his daughter, took his wife to the city. They could not possibly have selected a worse time. All three were taken by the Germans. Young Jacob Atoun remained the only survivor of the family. A few years later he married Havoula Tovil, the only remaining survivor of the Chaim Tovil family, also of Trikala. Their daughter, Dr. Esther Atoun, interviewed Havoula, who gave the following account of how she escaped arrest and deportation:

> It was early in the morning of March 25, 1944.
>
> It was snowing. Since the night before, people were not allowed to circulate in the streets. A loud knocking at the door of our neighbor's house woke us up.
>
> We went to the window and through the sheer curtain saw the terrifying sight of German soldiers pushing our Jewish neighbors into a military truck.
>
> We realized that the next house they were going to visit was ours. We started preparing whatever we were going to take with us. All of a sudden, something inside me revolted. "I will not come with you," I told my parents. "I will climb over the part of the wall which is collapsed near the laundry room and go to hide in the Kariofilis house next door. They are Christians, and the Germans are not going to search there." My parents begged me to stay with them. In spite of all their appeals, I quietly ran through our backyard to the house next door. They were kind people and took me inside, gave me a nightgown and an icebag, and put me

---

[208] "The Traitor," letter from Rachel Alkalai of Tel Aviv to author, 9/18/75.

in bed so that I could pretend I was sick in the event the Germans checked their house too. I went to a front window and carefully looked at the street. With tears in my eyes, I saw for the last time an old man, my father, climbing with great difficulty into a truck.[209]

The Indentured Servant

The eight members of the Levi family were in a mountain village until the end of September 1943. The elderly Abraham Levi became sick, and for his sake the whole family returned to their home in Trikala. Eight days after their return to the city, the Germans demanded from the rabbi a list of all the Jews in Trikala. The rabbi was threatened with execution if he did not cooperate. He informed all the Jews of the city to present themselves at the synagogue and register as the Germans demanded. Four members of the Levi family went to register themselves, while the other four left the city and went to the nearby free village of Neohori, where they agreed the remaining members of the family would come as soon as their father was well.

In March, the Germans went to the Levi house to arrest them. Eleonora ("Lola") was not there, although she was registered in the German catalogues. Her sister Louisa was arrested, together with her father. Marina and 16-year-old Solomon were in the house, but they were able to persuade the Germans that they were not members of the Levi family, but in reality, belonged to a Christian family whose house was destroyed by fire. The Germans did not arrest them. Marina and Solomon immediately went to Neohori, where the rest of the family lived. They told them the bad news, and the reaction of sorrow, indignation, and hate they all felt was similar to that which filled the hearts of countless Jews who in the relative safety of hiding places learned that their worst fears had come true.

Eleonora, overwhelmed by the news and ignoring all danger, decided to go immediately into the city to try to save her father and sister if she could. She dressed like a village

---

209 Letter from Esther Atoun to author, 7/5/75.

II. Personal Memoirs – The Italian Zone of Occupation

woman and entered the city uneventfully. The person she contacted was a German interpreter who was the mayor's daughter and a personal friend of Eleonora. She expressed her amazement to see Eleonora in the city and asked her to leave immediately. By the time she had arrived in Trikala, the arrested Jews were no longer in the city but had been transferred to a camp in Larissa. Eleonora wanted to follow them to Larissa, although she did not have a plan or the means to free her relatives. She was merely in a state of despair that ignored all logic or instinct of self-preservation. The interpreter calmly persuaded her to accept reality as it was and try to save herself. Eleonora returned to Neohori and, from there, with the help of the resistance organization EAM, moved to the safety of Aspropotamos, a more remote mountain village.

Her brother Solomon and her sister Kaity became ELAS partisans, while she, her brother Zack, and her sister Marina went to the village of Moutsara, where one sister taught in the local elementary school while the other worked as a seamstress. Another sister, Nina, together with her husband and son, found shelter in a neighboring village. Life in the mountains was not bad. The Germans had already completed their search-and-destroy raids, and they never came back. Whatever unpleasant situations Eleonora faced were due only to greed or the immorality of the villagers.

One time, Eleonora went to Mouzaki, which was a four-hour hike away. There she was supposed to receive a sewing machine friends had brought for them from the city. Their friends left the machine in a villager's house; all he had to do was to allow the owner to pick it up. He did not. He asked Eleonora to work in his fields like an indentured servant under the threat of denouncing her to the Germans who had a post near the village. She worked in his field for a week. On the eighth day, an acquaintance of Eleonora came to the village and was shocked to hear what his relatives were doing. He forced them to let the girl take her sewing machine and go. Another time Eleonora accompanied her sick sister, who was suffering from typhus, to a partisan hospital. On the way there, in a totally deserted area, a young villager attempted to rape her. She told him that if he touched her, she would report him to the partisans, and that they would find him no matter where he went. The penalty would be execution. The villager was well aware of the strict application of the partisans' law. He apologized and let the girls go.[210] [After the war, Eleonora married my uncle Michael of Ioannina.]

When Jews from Thessaloniki passed through Larissa on their way to safety, Abraam Negris, president of the Jewish community, was able to assist them thanks to Colonel Theodoros Tsipas, a police commander who offered to help the persecuted Jews. A police lieutenant used to visit Negris' shop daily to receive photographs of Thessaloniki escapees who needed false identity cards, or Larissa Jews, who had begun preparing themselves for worse days to come. The lieutenant would return the following day with identity cards carrying Christian names. Many Jews who escaped from Thessaloniki disguised as railway workers were the recipients of these cards.

Although Larissa was in the Italian zone of occupation, German troops were stationed in the city. These consisted of a battalion of engineers and the Gestapo group of the railway station. The Germans had taken over the best houses, and they systematically looted them. Beds, chairs, sewing machines, etc., were sent to Germany.

In June 1943, the Germans started "requesting" specific items, which Negris had to deliver within 24 hours. The usual threat was "execution by firing squad for sabotage." It should be noted that these looters were ordinary Germans from the battalion of engineers and not the dreaded SS. When the Jewish houses were depleted of all desirable items, Negris and his assistants then resorted to collecting money with which they bought whatever the Germans requested. Jews who were able to afford it left the city and went to Athens. The majority of the Jewish population remained in Larissa either because of poverty or because they believed the promises of both the Germans and the Italians that nobody would disturb them anymore.

The Jews who went to the free countryside enjoyed total freedom and, according to Negris, all the fugitives who lived in the villages of Mt. Kissavos assembled in the village of Agia to celebrate the high holy day of Yom Kippur in October 1943. Their living conditions were not good at all, in spite of the help they received from the villagers and the Resistance.

---

210 "The Indentured Servant," interview with Lola Levi Matsas, 6/1/75.

II. Personal Memoirs – The Italian Zone of Occupation

Negris formed a committee of Jews and visited the Allied mission of Kissavo, in the village of Polidentri, and pleaded for financial assistance. The leader of the mission promised to contact the Jewish Relief Committee of New York. In a few days, the Allied officer replied that no help was forthcoming because of the "great amount of paperwork these organizations requested."

The Germans were of course aware that most Larissa Jews had escaped, and they attempted to persuade them to return to the city. They knew that the president of the community, Negris, and Rabbi Abraam Sasson were in Megalovriso Agias. The Germans sent a message through the prefect, asking the Jewish leaders to return to Larissa. They promised that not only would nothing happen to them, but that the German administration would assist the community in rebuilding the synagogue and the Jewish school. The leaders of the Jewish community not only ignored the German message, but they advised their people to go higher in the mountains. Some did not listen. They missed the comfort of their homes. They returned to the city, where they lived peacefully, unmolested by the Germans who requested them only to attend roll call regularly. This was an insignificant burden, and the Jews who remained in the city did not mind it.

At 5:00 a.m. on March 24, 1944, assisted by their collaborators, the Germans moved into the empty streets of the city and surrounded the Jewish neighborhood. In one hour, their black trucks were filled with 220 Jewish men, women and children. The deportees were transferred to the military camp of Larissa, where they were soon joined by the captives of other cities. Only 12 people survived their captivity.[211]

The Distribution of Loot

Israel Yahbes, an Argentinian citizen residing in Thessaloniki, was allowed by the Germans to go to Athens in

---

[211] "The Story of a Community President." Most of the material related to Larissa was taken from 30 articles written by E. Kalogiannis and published by the newspaper, *Eleftheria Larissis,* from 4/18/61 to 5/24/61. Negris sent me all the historic material he had in his personal archives.

July 1943. His shop at 18 St. Mina Street, containing furniture and merchandise, was officially given to a Christian tailor named Karmenidis. The Argentinian general consul attempted to protect Yahbes's assets and appealed to the "noble kindness" of his German counterpart in Thessaloniki. The German consul and Max Merten eventully replied. A French translation of this document survived the war.

> [Y]our shop was placed at the disposal of Gregorio Karmenidis on the basis of No. 1176/31 8/43, order of military inspector Mr. Kuhn. Your shop was given away by a committee composed of N. Bourderi, N. Gousiou and Andrea Mantalaki, expert appraisers who were appointed for this purpose by the Chamber of Commerce on Sept. 10. The delivery was done after the lock of the shop was broken.[212]

This is the way many Greek Christians enriched themselves, thanks to the destruction of the Jews. The unofficial way of taking advantage of the deportations was to plunder homes and shops or search for hidden treasure. After the war thousands of Jewish buildings were sold for a very small fraction of their value.

New Controversy

The Jewish community of Volos lost 26 percent of its members; this is the best record of all Greek cities with Jewish communities numbering more than 150 people. Who should be given credit for this victory? Rabbi Pessah or others? The truth is, as David Levi of Volos, a member of the community council in 1943, recalls:

> In preparation for the expected German persecution, the community archives were given to a Christian friend who returned them after the war.

---

[212] "The Distribution of Loot," P. K. Enepekidis, *To Vima*, August 1966, article 15.

II. Personal Memoirs – The Italian Zone of Occupation

Two days before the publication of the German order, Rabbi Pessah was ordered to go to the German commander. By mistake, or on purpose, the rabbi went to the mayor's office, where he was not received because he arrived during the afternoon siesta period. The Germans used their interpreter Traousmouj to find Jewish names from the lists of the electric company of Volos.

Leon Samouilidis and I were alerted by friends who worked in the German headquarters. Many Jews had already rented houses in villages controlled by EAM-ELAS.

After we informed all the Jews who were in their shops and advised them to leave the city, I visited Rabbi Pessah and advised him not to go to the German offices, but to abandon his house immediately and not sleep there that night. Instead, he should come in contact with Bishop Ioakim Alexopoulos and ask him to help the Jews. I also gave him money. [Author's note: The Bishop gave Rabbi Pessah a letter "asking everyone to help this old man." Rabbi Pessah and his family went to the mountains.]

The following morning, while I was leaving with my family, I passed by the street of the rabbi's house. A friend of mine, Bebos, told me that the previous night the Germans had entered the house, messed up everything and arrested a Christian whom the rabbi left in his house. [213]

Since publications in Greek and English describe Rabbi Pessah as "an octogenarian who led partisans or fought the Germans, gun in hand," it is important to emphasize that the rabbi had absolutely nothing to do with any form of armed resistance against the Germans. David, Rabbi Pessah's son, informed me that his father had discussions with the German commander, Metropolitan Ioakim Alexopoulos, the prefect, the mayor, and Red Cross officials. Moissis Sakis, a specialist in agriculture who was a leader of ETA *(Epimelitia tou Andarti—*

---

[213] Letter by David Levi to author, 10/2/78.

Guerrilla Commisariat) -ELAS in Thessaly and whose brother Leon heroically fell as a partisan of ELAS, protested strongly when I published the story of the Jews of Volos as it was told by David Pessah in the *Washington Jewish Week*.

This is Moissis Sakis's story:

> In September 1943, the Germans requested from the Volos city hall, in secret, a list of the Jewish families and their addresses. Employees who were members of EAM informed the Jews of the area about it. The Jews, aware of what happened in Thessaloniki, left their shops and homes in the hands of Christian friends and, with the assistance of EAM members, were provided with false identity cards stamped with a good imitation of the stamp of the German command of Volos. Many Jews rented houses in villages in ELAS-controlled territory. Approximately 75 percent of the Jewish population of Volos went to the mountains and avoided capture.
>
> Most of those who remained in the city were either indecisive or poor and did not have any means necessary for their escape to the countryside.[214]

The Retaliation

Nissim Batis, a wealthy merchant of Ioannina, was accused by the Italians of contributing money to the Resistance.

He was arrested, but when Italy capitulated, he was released, only to be betrayed and arrested again by the Germans. He was tortured in the basement of Zosimea School in Ioannina and then transferred to Thessaloniki.

In the beginning of August 1943, a German soldier was killed near the city of Florina. The German method of retaliation was known. Twenty Greeks had to be killed for each German. On the morning of August 9, 1943, 15 Greek citizens, including Nissim Batis and Aaron Levi, were hanged. Every

---

214 Letter by Moissis Sakis to author, 8/28/77.

II. Personal Memoirs – The Italian Zone of Occupation

year on August 9, the memory of the 15 martyrs is honored in Kladorahi of Florina, where a monument now stands on the spot where the victims were buried.

Isaak Batis, a pharmacist from Jerusalem, Israel, and son of Nissim Batis, tried in vain for years to find where his father was buried. In February 1985, while on a bus from Thessaloniki to Florina, he discussed his story with a Mr. Rizos, who was seated next to him. Rizos knew every detail of the execution and the annual memorial service. In a few hours, the Israeli pharmacist was in front of the monument honoring his father. His forty-year search had ended.[215]

Brief Stories

The history of the Greek Jews during the Second World War consists of thousands of stories—some well-known, others never told. Since it is impossible to include in this book all the stories I collected, some of them are presented here in a condensed form, while their original, detailed accounts and other stories and correspondence are safely kept by the Museum of Jewish Heritage - A Living Memorial to the Holocaust in New York City.

Many Jews wished they had the foresight to leave Europe and fight against the Germans. There were at least four Jews from Greece who fought the Germans in Africa. They were Jacob Alkalai, Elie Modiano, Hugo Bensousan, and Major Leon Dostis.

Jacob Alkalai was my mother's first cousin. Their great-grandfather, Moshe Alkalai, was the honorary French consul of Ioannina and, because of this, Jacob was able to claim French citizenship. Jacob fought with the forces of General Charles de Gaulle in the tank corps as a noncommissioned officer in North Africa and Europe. After the war, he immigrated to Israel.

Elie Modiano crossed the Aegean and went to Egypt, where he joined the Greek Royal Air Force. Hugo Bensousan joined the Greek Brigade in Egypt and fought in El-Alamein.[216]

---

[215] Isaak Batis, *Chronika,* January 1989, 22.
[216] Willis, Yolanda, *A Hidden Child in Greece,* 2017, 105.

Leon Dostis, a graduate of the Military Academy of Athens, fought on the Albanian Front as an infantry officer. He was awarded honors for his valor. During the invasion of Greece by the Italians, he was captured and was being transferred by ship to Italy with the other Greek prisoners of war. This Italian vessel was sunk by a British submarine, and he was among the few survivors. Later, he was captured again, this time by the Germans, who allowed the prisoners to return to Greece. The Germans did not know that he was Jewish. He managed to go to Egypt and join the Greek Brigade with the British Army under General Montgomery and fought against the Germans in El-Alamein. He returned to Greece as a captain. In Greece, he joined the Greek Armor Corp and was promoted to major. Leon immigrated to Israel and served in the Israeli army.

In general, Greece supported the Arab states until 1990 when Greece exchanged ambassadors with Israel for the first time. However, during the Six Day War in 1967 between Israel and its Arab neighbors, the Greek people were jubilant with the Israeli victory. They believed that the military genius behind the victory was a Greek man. They thought that it had to be Leon Dostis because he was the only one they knew who had graduated from a military academy and fought in two wars reaching the rank of major. They still do not know a fact that I learned only recently from my Israeli friend, that this Greek illusion was not true. Leon Dostis had nothing to do with the Six Day War. He served in the Israeli army as a researcher for new weapons.

Some Jews survived in Greece almost by accident. In Athens on March 24, 1944, Chaim Chaim and Abraam Dentes went to the community offices on Melidoni Street as early as they could to be first in line to get the Passover sugar and flour that was to be distributed that day. The offices were not yet open, and they decided to go to a nearby *taverna* for a glass or two of wine. They stayed longer than they intended, and by the time they left to return to the community offices, they saw many heavily armed German soldiers and many trucks blocking the streets leading to the synagogue and the community building. They suspected that something sinister

II. Personal Memoirs – The Italian Zone of Occupation

was going on. Without attracting attention, they slowly went away to take their families into hiding.[217]

Another example is Manoah, a Jewish professional musician who was employed by the military orchestra of Athens. He spent the war years as a member of the Greek units under the leadership of General Jürgen Stroop.[218] Stroop was the same German commander who suppressed the uprising and destroyed the Warsaw ghetto in 1943.

Some Jews died by accident. Albert Talbi left his hiding place on June 1, 1944. He was seeking medicine for his seven-year-old daughter who was seriously ill. He was betrayed and captured.[219]

Archbishop Damaskinos tried to save a woman. In a letter dated April 5, 1944, to von Gravenitz, an official of the German embassy, he wrote the following in an effort to save Edith Dimaki:

> Miss Edith Dimaki married on January 15, 1942, to Ioannis Dimaki according to certificate #2361 issued by the office of the Archbishop of Athens. The wedding took place in accordance with the Greek Orthodox rites. Since the German representative assured His Eminence that mixed marriages are exempt, the Archbishop believes that an error took place in this case. [220]

A note in the German archives reads: "Archbishop's secretary was informed by telephone that this is the family of Admiral Dimaki, who is active in Egypt as an exile"; therefore, "special treatment is unavoidable." Edith Dimaki, although a Jewess of Spanish origin and a Greek national, was deported.

---

[217] "A Glass of Wine," letter to the author by Jacques Kostis, 10/2/75.
[218] "The Musician," letter to the author by Jacques Kostis, 12/26/75.
[219] "The Traitor," Molho, *In Memoriam*, 326.
[220] "A Letter from Damaskinos," *To Vima*, August 1966.

The Grandmother and a Consul

The Italian general consul in Athens, S. Zitelli, attempted to prevent the deportation of a Jewish boy, Jacob Julius Gani, son of Matilda Alberitsi Barbiano, who was Italian. Jacob was baptized, but the Germans knew that the boy was also circumcised. S. Zitelli wrote in his appeal: "The fact is that the boy was young when he was entrusted to the care of his grandmother, who was Jewish. She, without the knowledge of the parents, had him circumcised. This is not strong enough reason to eliminate the value of his baptism. It simply explains how the grandmother attempted to introduce the boy to the Jewish religion." A notation written in the document indicates that Jacob Julius Gani was deported and did not survive.[221]

The only Jewish people who remained in Ioannina after March 25, 1944, were four women who had married Christians a few years before and had adopted Christianity. They were not arrested.

Others wanted to be arrested. On March 26 or 27, the two brothers Yesoua and Moshe Eliasaf Matsas returned to Ioannina. They dealt in milk products and wines. Because of their business they had to travel often out of the city and into the surrounding free countryside. They happened to be in one of the villages where they heard about the arrest of the Jews. They were worried about what the Germans would do to their families in their absence. They returned to the city and surrendered to the Germans. They never saw their families again, for which they so needlessly sacrificed their lives.[222]

Some were saved because they were not "free." Isaak Vrahoritis was a private in a Greek military unit on the Greek-Albanian frontier. On October 28, 1940, the Italian army attacked Greece. His unit was surrounded by superior Italian forces, and everyone was taken prisoner. Vrahoritis was transferred to Italy and was held in a prisoner-of-war camp. Nobody noticed the fact that he was a Jew. The union of war prisoners recorded cases of 61 Greek-Jewish soldiers who were

---

[221] "The Grandmother," *To Vima*, August 1966.
[222] "The Value of Freedom," interview with Eftihia Alkalai, June 1976.

II. Personal Memoirs – The Italian Zone of Occupation

captured by the Italian army on the Albanian front during the war between Italy and Greece.[223]

Moissis Batinos committed a crime for which a German military tribunal condemned him to prison for many years. This happened during the occupation, but before the arrest and deportation of the Jews. He remained in prison, forgotten and undisturbed, until the Germans left Greece and all the prisoners were released.[224]

Wealth and "Angels"

Wealth and "angels" saved people. Joseph Samuel from Volos, a very wealthy man, went to Athens with his wife, children and mother-in-law: there they received false identity cards. One day they were recognized. The blackmail commenced. Every day individuals presented themselves to him and extracted their ransoms. "You are a Jew. You are rich. Give us money or we will turn you over to the Gestapo." His wife suggested, "Let's go to a place very close to the Germans. We will look less suspicious there." We found an apartment building near the German headquarters and installed ourselves in a comfortably furnished apartment. We acquired the necessary provisions, and we stayed in this exclusive neighborhood until the end of the war. We fortunately possessed enormous savings.[225]

On March 25, in the city of Ioannina and away from the predominantly Jewish neighborhoods, the family of Isaak Vehoropoulos got up as usual in the morning. A neighbor came and with great excitement told them, "The Jews are arrested. Leave the house at once." Isaak, his wife Emilia, and their two daughters Jeanette and Toula abandoned everything and started running. They soon realized they did not know where to go. A man saw them, stopped them and said, "Don't run. Follow me at a distance. I will take you out of the city." They followed him until he stopped at one point and told them, "Now you are in free territory." The partisans of EDES protected and

---

223 Story told by Joseph Matsas, 1976.
224 Ibid., 1976.
225 "If I Were a Rich Man," Novitch, *Les Passage* op. cit., 92.

helped the Vehoropoulos family until the war ended. When they returned to Ioannina after the war, they searched for the man who had led them to freedom. They questioned many people. Nobody ever heard of him. Emilia Vehoropoulou, who is very religious, remains convinced that he was an "angel" sent by God.[226]

A Moving Story of Survival – The Frizis Family

As told to me by Iakovos, son of Colonel Frizis:

In Athens, an order was given for the Jews to register at the offices of the Jewish community. I went there with my mother and my two sisters. There were many desks with government employees, and people were lined up according to their last names. We went to the line for names beginning with the letter F. After my mother told the official our name, he asked, "Are you related to Colonel Frizis?" My mother said, "He was my husband." The man immediately got up, stood at attention, and with great emotion in his expression and in his voice he said, "I served under Colonel Frizis in the war. He was like a father to us. I cannot write your names in these German lists. Leave immediately!"

We went home and, before entering our house, we discussed what happened with our next-door neighbor Mr. Vogiatzis. He said, "If you are not registered, the Germans will not come here to look for you. In case they do, do not open the door. Go up to your terrace, jump the little wall that separates our terraces, and come down to my house." He was a good man. The Germans never came looking for us.

The Jews of Albania

Many Jews of Ioannina went to cities like Argyrocastro, Valona (Vlore), and Delvino as peddlers or small businessmen.

---

[226] "The Angel," letter to the author by Emilia Vehoropoulou, 7/8/76.

II. Personal Memoirs – The Italian Zone of Occupation

They settled there and, as the years passed, became prosperous. Albania and Ioannina were part of the Ottoman empire. Albania declared independence in 1912 and Ioannina became part of Greece in 1913.

In the 1930's, with the rise of Hitler, when it was still possible to flee, hundreds of German and Austrian Jews were welcomed by King Zog of Albania while other countries had closed their borders to them. Albania was initially occupied by the Italians in 1939 and then by the Germans in 1943. King Zog left Albania just before the Italian occupation.

My cousin, Menachem Solomoni, who came to New York from Albania in 1991, told me that the Germans did not ask the Jews of Albania to register with them. Registration was the first step leading to arrest and deportation. Also, my first cousin Pepos Kohen, from Albania, told me that the large Jewish shops in Valona remained open throughout the time that the Germans occupied the city.

By 1941, the Jewish community of Albania numbered about 150 people. My grandparents and my uncle, Semos Kohen, had fabric shops in Delvino and Agioi Saranda (Saranda).

A leader of the Albanian resistance movement, led by Enver Hoxha, asked Semos Kohen if he would sell on credit materials to clothe the partisans. His reply was, "Take anything you need." They took whatever they wanted and gave him a receipt.

For some unknown reason, in 1943, the Germans looted my uncle Semo's shop in Agioi Saranda but not my Grandfather's shop in Delvino. Semos Kohen and his family moved to a village controlled by the resistance. One day he was visited by Dr. Melios, a physician of the partisans, who was married to Victoria, the daughter of Menachem Yomtov. He told Semos, "I heard some resistance leaders talking about you. They said you gave them a lot of merchandise; however, you accepted a receipt from them. Now that the British gave them gold sovereigns, they will pay you. My advice to you is not to accept the gold."

In a few days a partisan came to the village and gave Semos a quantity of gold. He accepted it, but the next day he went to the nearby headquarters of the partisans and met the leaders to whom he returned the money, saying, "We have a common enemy. I can't fight the Germans as you do, but I can help with money."[227]

One day, the Germans came to the village. Someone betrayed them as being Jews, and a German sergeant placed my uncle Semos and his family in front of a wall and was ready to execute them. My uncle asked to see his commander. The commander arrived and asked my uncle in French, "Are you here because you are Jews?" My uncle said, "No. We are here because of my wife's health." He then produced a doctor's certificate. The German officer said, "We don't have any orders to do anything to you," and signaled to the family to leave the wall. The sergeant said to them, "No boom, boom."

As the Russian army was advancing through the Balkans, the German army withdrew from Albania. After the communist takeover of Albania, a distant relative of my uncle told the communists that my uncle had a big quantity of gold hidden. Uncle Semos was then arrested and forced to show them where he had hidden it. The gold was turned over to the communists and the family was given a receipt. They became penniless, but the receipt remains in the family.

None of the Jews of Albania were arrested by the Germans. Perhaps they were lucky, like the Jews of Zakynthos.

My grandparents, Joseph and Gracia Kohen remained in their house in Delvino with the Germans, who used it as their army headquarters. As the Germans were preparing to withdraw, they blew up their headquarters and destroyed my grandparents' home and shop.

After the war, my grandparents died. They were extremely poor. My uncle Semos was also very poor and died at the age of 56.

In 1991, with the collapse of communism, all the Jews of Albania left the country. The vast majority immigrated to Israel, and our relatives were sponsored by their American family members to immigrate to the United States. Aunt Julie, wife of my mother's brother Semos, her three children, their spouses and her grandchildren, a total of 33 people were settled in New York as refugees. Four more Albanians, relatives of a spouse, came with the group. They were assisted by the HIAS and the Sisterhood of Kehila Kedosha Jannina organizations.

---

[227] "The Jews of Albania," story told by Pepos Kohen, July 1993.

II. Personal Memoirs – The Italian Zone of Occupation

My grandmother Gracia Kohen lived in Delvino, Albania.

Uncle Semos Kohen, Aunt Julie and two of their children.

My maternal grandfather Joseph Kohen in Delvino, Albania, in front of his house which served as German headquarters. The building was blown up and burned by the Germans prior to their departure.

Chapter Four

Memoirs of Camp Survivors

Each individual is co-responsible for every wrong, every injustice and every crime committed in his presence or with his knowledge ... if he fails to do whatever he can to prevent it, he too is guilty.

—HANNAH ARENDT[228]

Chaim Bensousan, a salesman from Thessaloniki, kept a diary, which he gave to Dr. Leon Kuenka. Kuenka was an inmate of Auschwitz at that time. Some excerpts read as follows:

> We have already been on the train for 24 hours. We are now crossing the valleys of Yugoslavia. It is terrible to describe exactly what I feel, surrounded on all sides by my coreligionists. Surely it is yet too early to be aware of what can possibly happen to us during this trip or later, when we arrive at the place where they will dump us as useless objects. In spite of my thoughts, I try to instill courage in my wife and my little daughter. The crying of women and children can be heard. Sometimes even men whose nerves are weak

---

228 David Joroff, "Dark and Perverse," *Jerusalem Post*, 3/12/83.

start crying, and that is very cruel and painful to both contemplate and observe.

... Whenever I can, I write my thoughts in this notebook without being able to remember the dates.

I believe we have been traveling for five or six days. The car generates a formidable odor. We are forced to use this space, which is very small for all of us, even for our bodily needs. Last night a woman died of asphyxiation. It has already been 15 hours, and we have not been able to inform anyone to remove her...

As the days pass, the situation becomes more desperate. The old man Naoum, who owned a small leather shop on Tsimiski Street, is always seated close to me. He continuously cries and asks me, "What do they want us for? What can they do with me, an old man? Can I work at this age?" He says these words and cries like a little child. His crying is desperate and, as it is heard, spreads sorrow and pain.[229]

A Family Reunion

Isaak Tivoli, a Thessaloniki pharmacist, moved with his family to Athens. There he was arrested by the Germans, while his family continued to remain in hiding. He was transferred to Auschwitz, where he became a member of the "'Commando-Canada," the group of prisoners who "welcomed" the newcomers at the railway station.

One day, when a transport arrived from Greece, Tivoli was surprised to hear a familiar voice calling "Daddy" as soon as the door of a railway car was opened. He saw his two children, accompanied by his wife and mother. The situation was desperate. His supervisor, the "Lagerführer," who saw him embrace his wife, promised not to send her with the trucks; his sons would live, too. They were 18 and twenty years old, and they would become workers in the "lager." As for his elderly mother, there was no hope; Tivoli himself accompanied her to the trucks. He managed to maintain his composure while he built up her morale with false hopes. The next day Tivoli met

---

229 "Death Train," Matarasso, "... Kai omos oloi tous den pethanan," 65.

II. Memoirs of Camp Survivors

Dr. Albert Menasse and told him the story. As Menasse worked in the area where the women prisoners were kept, he tried to find out how Tivoli's wife was. He learned that the Lagerfuhrer kept his word and saved Mrs. Tivoli, but the next day the camp physician considered her too old (40 years) and reversed the decision.[230]

Dr. Albert Menasse's Story

Dr. Albert Menasse describes his experiences:

In 1942, I was a happy husband and father. My daughter, age 16, was about to graduate from both high school and the academy of music. She wished to enter medical school. I was a physician who after twenty years of practice had developed a good reputation in my city. After a hard day at the hospital, I loved to return home to my family and my music.

I spent two years as a German prisoner under the worst possible conditions, and many times I wondered what I did to deserve to lose the people I loved. My only crime was that I happened to be born a Jew. Neither my twenty years of service as a physician nor my service in the Greek army as a medical officer could erase this "crime" of being a Jew.

On June 8, 1943, at 6:00 a.m. the train stops. From our one and only barred window, the word Auschwitz can be seen. The door of our railway car opens, and people in striped suits order us to disembark. We sink into the muddy ground and try to collect our luggage and the members of our families. German soldiers guard us while machineguns cover the area. The word *schnell* (fast) is heard continuously. A Red Cross car parked at a distance is the only reassuring sign in all this pandemonium. We are 880 people, and we are forced to march in front of two officers. We are divided into four groups. The group of the old people and that of the mothers, sick children and obviously pregnant

---

230 Molho, *In Memoriam,* 152.

women are entitled to continue the trip on board the trucks. The others, able-bodied young men and women, have to go on foot under a torrential rain.

In the general confusion I do not see my wife and daughter. I am among a group of 300 men. All our luggage has been left on the train. After a painful march we enter the camp, which is surrounded with electrified fences. We see hundreds of emaciated people, dressed in rags, and working under brutal supervisors. I suddenly hear my name, and with surprise I see my nephew Solomon Mano who, with a dozen men, is actually harnessed to a cart filled with garbage. People extend their hands asking for cigarettes and, especially, food. We feel that a terrible drama must be unfolding in this place. I recognize someone else. He is Leon Yahiel, who was deported before us. He acts as an interpreter and says: "Prisoners, you are now in a death camp. Your wives and children, as I now speak to you, are already dead. The buildings that you see in the distance are not factories. You are all alone. You have to work under terrible conditions, and each of you should try to do whatever he can to last as long as possible."

A group of *Schreibers* arrives; they search everyone and remove jewelry, watches, pictures, whatever we have. I ask permission to keep my medical degree from the University of Toulouse and my first flute prize from the music academy of the same city. The German officer replies, "These diplomas are too pretty for a dirty Jew. Besides," he adds with an ironic smile, "you are not going to need them anymore." In a few hours, I am dressed in a striped suit, my head is shaved, my arm is marked with the number 124454, and I am indistinguishable from all other prisoners over which any German or other functionary of the camp has the right of life and death. A prisoner with an armband with a harp drawn on it comes into my barracks to find me. My nephew had told him that I play the flute. He examines me and promotes me to the position of musician of Birkenau. This title immediately gives me both the respect and envy of my comrades.

II. Memoirs of Camp Survivors

The following Sunday our orchestra gives a concert in the women's camp. There I see my daughter who, with signals, indicates to me that she too would be a privileged prisoner by joining the women's orchestra.

In Auschwitz, there were prisoners from so many countries that the camp was a veritable tower of Babel. The prisoners created their own dialect, which included words taken from all the languages of the world. A Greek word became very successful— *klepsi-klepsi,* for stealing. The Greek Jews used this word not because they were prone to stealing, but, on the contrary, they themselves were often victims of theft. Since they were unable to speak German, if they wanted to protest against the thief, they would use the word *klepsi.*

On October 22, 1943, a group of Italian Jews arrived in Birkenau. Among the newcomers was an American Jewish woman. She was ordered to get undressed in front of the German officer Schelinger.

The woman refused and grabbed his pistol. She killed him and another SS soldier before she too was killed.

My daughter Lillian was like everybody else, afraid of the dreadful selections during which anyone who was not considered fit was sent to the gas chamber. In October, Lillian sent me a message of despair. "Dear Daddy, I am afraid I will not see you or mother again. Send me your blessings." On October 22, 1943, while I played my flute with the camp orchestra as usual, we saw many trucks filled with girls. They had been selected. Lillian was among them.

Alexander Donat in his book *The Holocaust Kingdom* witnessed Greek women "going to the gas."[231] Donat describes:

They had been brought to Auschwitz only weeks before, slender, black-eyed Salomes, homesick for their sunny land and huddled together against the sleet and cold of the northern October. They sang a sentimental song called "Mama," whose melody made me weep. In a few

---

231 Aleander Donat, *The Holocaust Kingdom*, Talman Co., 1978.

weeks Auschwitz had withered those exotic flowers, their fiery eyes had become dull in sunken sockets empty and dead. Emaciated, dirty, repulsive, those Greek women could barely drag themselves around. Once so shapely, they now had legs like sticks and their breasts hung like buoys. Their complexions, made velvet smooth by the southern sun, were now covered with horrible abscesses, vermin bites, and the marks of scabies incessantly scratched. They stank of gangrene, dysentery, unwashed sweat, and wretchedness. When they went to their deaths, they sang the *"Hatikvah,"* that song of undying hope, the song of old people which has always carried the vision of Zion in its heart. Since then, every time I hear *"Hatikvah"* I always see them, the dregs of human misery, and I know that through mankind flows a stream of eternity greater and more powerful than individual deaths.

"Selections" took place preferably on Christian and Jewish holidays. Dr. Menasse continues his narrative:

> On February 3, I saw my number among the "selected" ones. All of a sudden, I had an inspiration.
> "I am a doctor," I protested. It worked. "We still need doctors," was the reply. For the time being, I had saved my life.
> One day my group was asked to harness ourselves to our carriage and transfer twenty Hungarian girls. The fate of all those who were led to their deaths left the other prisoners indifferent. They themselves were not sure whether they would see the next sunrise. A young girl who was on the carriage dared to speak to me in French in spite of the fact that many Germans guarded us closely with their guns turned on us. I was silent but overwhelmed by sorrow. "It is useless to feel so much pity," she told me. "We know that you take us to our deaths. Yet, as you can see, I remain calm. Tell me, sir," she added after a small pause, "don't I remind you of Marie Antoinette as she was led to the guillotine?" These were her last words. In a few minutes, we were asked to transfer their clothes to the hospital.

II. Memoirs of Camp Survivors

The prisoners were totally unaware of what was to take place once the trucks transferred them from the train to their final destination. One hot day in the summer, there was a little delay in the death process. A group of women and children had to wait their turn. There was a small lake in front of the "factory." Many children got undressed and went swimming. The women sat on the ground and ate the food they had with them. In a few minutes, a German appeared and said *"fertig"* (ready). The women and children entered the building without suspecting they would never get out again.

On Sundays the camp took a holiday appearance. The musicians dressed in their white uniforms with red stripes and gave concerts. Many excellent musicians gave solo recitals. There were soccer games between the teams of the different barracks. A swimming pool could be used by those who wished to swim. There was even boxing for those who liked the sport. The sound of music was often drowned by the noise of the trains arriving with their pitiful cargo. The prisoners saw with callousness the columns of the new arrivals. In 1944 the Jewish New Year was celebrated in the best possible way by the Commando-Canada. (This was the most privileged group of workers.) They were in charge of sorting out the things the deportees had left behind. A secret agreement existed between the German guards and the prisoners. Any valuable item found was given to the Germans; whatever could be eaten or pieces of clothing were taken by the prisoners.

The chief of Commando-Canada was the guest of honor. On a makeshift stage, artists sang and danced, and magicians performed tricks. At the same time the dreadful selections were taking place. In October 1944 the Russians approached Birkenau and the Germans started the evacuation of the camp, more through the chimneys than through forced marches and trains.

The members of the orchestra, like everyone else, heard the continuous, alarming rumors, and they did not know whether they would survive the repeated selections. In the music room a sort of religious communion took place among those whose common object of worship was art. They played for the first time a string quartet composed by the leader of their orchestra. During noon of the same day, the German physician did the members of the orchestra a favor. He considered them all fit for transportation. The train continued moving for two days. When it stopped, we were in Berlin. Allied planes were bombarding it. Amidst the tremendous noise from the exploding bombs, which could have destroyed our train, we were not afraid; we felt joy. We were placed in the great works of the Hankel airplanes in Oranienburg. Allied bombing had reduced production to zero. After twenty days of continued air raids, my group of 1,000 men moved to Sachsenburg. The crazy German commander ordered us to walk for ten steps and then run for the next ten producing utter confusion and many blows from the guards.

In Sachsenburg I witnessed the most bizarre industrial experiment. I saw a group of approximately 200 prisoners marching in a circle for ten hours a day. It was calculated that they covered forty kilometers a day. They were supposed to do that for a period of four to six weeks so that the manufacturer could test the strength of his new synthetic rubber.

We continued our trip to Bavaria, where we worked in the construction of factories under terrible conditions. On January 1, 1945, I became very happy. I developed all the symptoms of pneumonia. This guaranteed my removal from the totally inhumane working conditions and provided salvation even by death, which by then I almost desired. I was admitted to the hospital, thanks to my contacts, where the living conditions, the food and the lice were the same as before, except there was no work. If I wanted to drink water, I had to go outside to get some snow. Death did not arrive, and I dreaded that in a few days I would have to go back to work. On January 28, 1945, my Parisian colleague Dr. Silvan Levi proposed to me to send me to Lager-Dachau VII as a Moslem prisoner, unable to work. I accepted the proposal, although it could have meant a death sentence. Over 600 sick prisoners, surrounded by guards and their dogs, had to walk in subfreezing weather the three kilometers separating the two camps. We passed from the German village of Cofferin, where the villagers looked at us with curiosity. We saw women going into the market and children going to school. Many prisoners cried with despair, remembering scenes of a normal life. In the new camp I met the familiar faces of many Jews from Thessaloniki, who I had thought were already dead. They told me that in June 1943 2,000 Greek Jews were sent to Warsaw to clean the remnants of the ghetto. There they found much gold and diamonds, which they gave to the Poles in exchange for food. That is how they survived. When the Russians advanced, they were transferred to Dachau.

In Lager VII, I was named a doctor of a block. This entitled me to a double ration of food. Although my fever came back, I did not say anything, and I continued performing my duties because I did not want to lose my privileged position. The patients died continuously since there were no medicines. When I was delirious from fever, my medics took advantage of it and ate my food. Barouch Saban, a Jew from Thessaloniki who was in charge of the block, saved my life.

Allied planes flew overhead by the hundreds, and we knew that liberation was approaching. Yet we were not sure that we would remain alive. While a loaf of bread used to be shared by four people, in April 1945 a loaf was shared by twelve prisoners. The soup was nothing but salt water with an occasional potato peel. I started eating the grass that grew around the buildings. This was pretty soon imitated by hundreds of prisoners. In Lager III, a case of cannibalism was announced. The prisoners lost all human compassion. They wished the death of their neighbor in order to eat his slice of bread.

When the Americans approached, the Germans set the wooden barracks on fire. My nephew Solomon Mano and I ran out of the camp and jumped into a ditch. A Hungarian girl already occupied it and, extraordinarily, she had three loaves of bread! We had to threaten her in order to get one of the loaves. After a glorious dinner we heard machinegun fire and bullets whistling over our heads. When I dared lift my head, I saw an American tank firing in the surrounding forest while Germans surrendered with their hands high in the air. Hundreds of prisoners rushed toward the Americans, who pleaded with us to let them do their job. In a few minutes the Germans were cleared and the Americans gave us chocolates, candy and beer. For the first time in two years, I spoke to a free man as an equal. Dr. Albert Menasse was reborn.[232]

A Successful Escape

In January 1945 the Allies were advancing on every front, and the Germans thought that the day of reckoning was approaching. In Birkenau an order was received to evacuate some of the camp inmates to the interior of Germany. Approximately 100 Germans ordered a group of over 5,000 prisoners to fall into line for a long march. Elias Matsas, who now lives in the Bronx, New York, was one of the prisoners. He recalls:

> The captives, hungry, poorly dressed, and wearing wooden shoes on injured feet, marched in formations of four, covered by guards armed with machine guns. The exhausting march covered a distance of fifty kilometers. Many people were unable to keep up. If anyone showed a sign of weakness or left his line, he was immediately shot. We reached a railway station and were placed in open railway cars. There were at least 120 people per car. It was cold, and everybody was shivering. It is difficult to estimate how many were lost during the march and how many continued to die on the train.
>
> After two hours or so the train stopped near a forest. It seems that the Russians had surrounded the general area, and the train could not go to Germany as

---

[232] "The Story of Inmate No. 124454," Dr. Albert Menasse, *Birkenau;* published in Greek by the Jewish Community of Thessaloniki, (Thessaloniki: Typo Ellinismou), 1974.

II. Memoirs of Camp Survivors

had been planned. I remember it was snowing. We were ordered to get off the train. Some of the prisoners noticed that the Germans had aimed some machineguns at the column of prisoners. All of a sudden, we heard machine gun fire. They started shooting at the beginning of the line of captives. Everybody started running toward the forest; the bullets dropped many as they tried to escape. Nobody really knows how many were hit and how many were saved. When the noise of the machine gun fire stopped, and we felt they were not chasing us anymore, we lay down in a deserted spot of the forest to catch our breath. Leon Batis from Athens, a Pole and I slept exactly where we were.

The next day we were lucky enough to find the way out of the forest and reach a Polish village, where they gave us food and treated us well. Batis was all right, but I suffered from frostbite and was hospitalized by the Russians. Another Greek Jew, Sam Ganis from Arta, was even more unlucky than I. He was lost in the forest and, by the time he found his way out, he suffered so much from frostbite that the Russians had to amputate one of his legs.[233]

The Death of a Hero

Alberto Moissi Errera fought in Albania, and he received a field commission for bravery. In September 1943, he went to the mountains and, later, on a Resistance mission in Athens. In March 1944, he was arrested by the Germans and transferred to Auschwitz.

One day a group of five Greek Jews, including Alberto Errera, Ougo Barouch Venezia, and Henri Nehama Kapon, went to the shores of the Vistula River, escorted by two SS soldiers, to empty a truck loaded with ashes. They were emptying ashes into the river when one of the Germans said ironically, "Faster, faster, don't make the ashes of your

---

[233] "A Successful Escape," telephone interview with Elias Matsas of New York, November 1975.

brothers wait. The waters of the Vistula will take them directly to Palestine!" Errera could not take it anymore. He raised his shovel and brought it down on the head of the German. He jumped on the other German and threw him into the water. Then he tried to escape by swimming. His cowardly comrades, instead of imitating his example, pulled one German out of the water, saving him from drowning, and bandaged the head of the other. Errera swam desperately to reach the opposite shore. One of the German soldiers grabbed his gun and started shooting at the escaping prisoner. Wounded, he hid in the bushes, but German dogs discovered him. He was captured, tortured in a terrible way, and finally burned alive.

Four hundred young Jews, former stevedores of Thessaloniki's port, were also very heroic. When they were ordered to work as Sonderkommandos in the crematoria they refused to cooperate. The Germans executed them all the same day. One hundred Athenian Jews refused to work in the crematoria in 1944, and they were all executed.[234]

An Act of Defiance

The author's uncle, Michael Naoum Matsas, was born in Ioannina in 1912. In the following story, he describes the last months of his life as a concentration camp inmate:

> The Germans were retreating on all fronts; yet their orders were to take us along with them. We moved on foot and on board open railway cattle cars, hungry, freezing and maltreated. The mortality rate among the prisoners was appalling. One Ioannina Jew named Belis was beaten to death because he attacked and injured a German soldier. Belis was about 28 years old, strong and handsome. He could easily have been a wrestler. He was not well educated. He spoke very little, and he was extremely kind.
>
> Very few Ioannina men were lost during the period of our detention at Wolfsberg, where a doctor from Ioannina worked as a physician in the hospital. When

---

234 "The Death of a Hero," Molho, op. cit., 266.

II. Memoirs of Camp Survivors

the Russians approached our area, we were moved to the interior of Germany, and this was when our losses became great. I don't think I will ever forget the four sons of Rabbi Michel Mouchon of Ioannina. All four were good-looking and kindhearted. We were being transported in openair coal train cars. We were not given any food. During that time, Dai and Benous, the second and fourth brother, passed away. A few days later a German physician "selected" the other two brothers, Eliasaf and Bello.

In April 1945, I was part of a transport of 2,000 prisoners enclosed in a camp called Efliger, located in northern Germany by the Baltic Sea. In this last camp were 25 Jewish men from Ioannina.

Among us was also a physician we all loved. [Author's note: He was Dr. Errikos Levis, father of Professor Alex Levis.] He had been with us since the day we were arrested in Ioannina. During all this time, an enormous time when you are a prisoner, he helped us all like a good brother and doctor. He had the qualities you rarely find among human beings. In this last camp a combination of evils conspired to put an end to our misery. Most of us were sick. In order to climb one step, I had to support myself by touching the wall. Our doctor became sick with uncontrollable diarrhea and high fever. Worse yet, he lost his mind. He did not want to eat anything, and he suffered from incontinence. He walked, but in a state of shock. There was no doubt that he would lose his life unless we helped him. We were all in terrible shape, and the natural state of life in a camp such as this was dominated by an extreme selfishness. Everyone tried to help himself as best he could; we expected death as something pleasant and unavoidable. Yet, in spite of everything, we were determined to help our doctor who, in the past, had assisted us above his ability and beyond any call of duty.

Our group decided that the ones considered to be the most suitable men to help our doctor were myself, because I had been a medic in the Greek army, and Sam Hatjopoulos who, although ill, still retained some physical strength. We did the best we could for him, and we were successful. This still gives us a great deal of inner satisfaction to this day. His health improved, and he again joined our group during the subsequent extraordinary events.

One day in May 1945 the well-known order, *Eintreten* (step in line), was given. We were aware of the fact that this would mean more suffering. One of our group, I think it was Sam Matsas, told us, "Listen, boys. We always obey their orders to the letter. Let's disobey them for once. We are lost either way. Let's hide in this attic." With that, he showed us an easily accessible place. We all agreed, except Simon Nachman, who did not join our revolt. While we hid in this attic, Simon went into the courtyard and joined the other prisoners.

Many months later, when we met Simon again in Greece, we learned that the prisoners, around 2,000 of them, were led into a small forest. The guards commenced firing at them. Simon was among the first to fall to the ground. He was not hit; he had just fainted and was soon covered by those who fell mortally wounded over him. The following day, he regained consciousness. He slowly extricated himself, realizing that he was the only man alive in that macabre forest. He painfully dragged his emaciated body toward the road. It did not take long before he heard the noise of a military convoy approaching. He was too weak to move away. With great difficulty, he reached to get the chocolates that were thrown to him. The trucks were filled with friendly Russian troops. The chocolates and the knowledge that he was free brought him back to health and life.

In the meantime, our group of 24 Greek Jews passed a night of fear and uncertainty. During the entire night we heard nothing but explosions. The Germans were blowing up war material and military installations. None of us slept during those critical hours. In the morning Sam Matsas was the first to emerge from our hiding place. With Solomon Mordechai and another man, we went down to where the Germans had been. They realized that the guards were gone. ("We ran to inform the others," Sam Matsas relates. "We yelled, 'Boys we are free!'") After the initial excitement subsided, we all ran to the kitchen in search of anything edible. This took place on the morning of May 1, 1945. In the afternoon the Russian troops arrived.

It is easy to understand how we felt. But the following day I became critically ill, and I was moved to a Russian military hospital. I remember very few things that happened there. After a long time, I woke up and realized that I was still in the hospital. Chaim Kambelis of Ioannina was next to me, and he told me that I was between life and death for fifty days. I knew that I had escaped death once more.[235]

The Jews of Preveza

On March 25, 1944, all but five of the 250 Jews of the city of Preveza were captured by the Germans. Out of 245 deportees, only ten women returned. All able-bodied men who could possibly have survived did not because they participated in the Sonderkommando revolt. In the following pages, several different accounts of the revolt are mentioned. None of them seem to agree with the others in terms of losses, dates, etc. This revolt is included in this story of the Jews of Preveza, in honor of the three brothers of Mrs. Rena Carasso of Randallstown, Maryland, who lost their lives during this uprising.

Rena Carasso relates her experience as a member of the Jewish community of Preveza in 1944:

> Sometime during the period of Italian occupation, we became afraid that the Italians were going to take anti-Jewish measures. My father (Solomon Ganis) and his family, and also the families of Daniel Zafou and Makis Solomon, went to the small, nearby city of Vonitsa. We stayed there for six months. During this period nobody disturbed the Jews of Preveza, so my

---

[235] "An Act of Defiance," letter from Michael Matsas (my uncle) to author, June 1976.

family and that of Daniel Zafou returned to the city. Makis Solomon and his parents decided to stay away from the city for as long as the war lasted, and this is why the Solomon family was the only Jewish family of Preveza that survived the war.

Two additional men of Preveza not captured by the Germans were the two Gani brothers, who were in a village outside of Preveza on the day of the arrest. They now live in Metulla, Israel. We in Preveza heard about the deportations in Thessaloniki, but we were naive. We did not know what had happened to the Jews once they were transferred outside of Greece, and we were under the false impression that the wealthy and numerous Jews from Thessaloniki had provoked German greed and hate. We were few and poor, and therefore we had nothing to worry about!

When the Germans ordered us to register with them and to report every Friday, we obeyed. My three brothers could have fled to the mountains. They decided against it because they did not want to leave behind their elderly parents and their two sisters. The Germans kept asking the Jewish community for merchandise and furniture. They occupied a room in our house, and many times they brought prostitutes to it. My parents had to send me and my sister to a friend's house every time this happened.

On March 25, 1944, at 3:00 a.m., we were awakened by a loud knocking at our door. We were told to get ready immediately for a trip. There was no electricity at this time of the night. We managed to light only one candle. We looked in the dark for some clothes to wear. We were so rushed that we were not able to take any food with us. The whole community was placed on board trucks. When my brother tried to help my father climb into the truck, a German soldier knocked him down with a blow. During our trip to Arta, I remembered that, although packed inside the truck, no one spoke to each other. We were all numbed by the experience of losing our freedom and our humanity so suddenly. Together with the Jews of Arta, we moved on to Agrinion. No provisions for food were made by the Germans, and upon arrival in Agrinion we were all

II. Memoirs of Camp Survivors

starving. My father gave a gold ring for a loaf of bread. But even our gold jewelry was gone when the Germans forced us to surrender every valuable thing we had to them.

From Agrinion we were moved to Patras, then to Athens, and there we were packed into the train for the trip to the Birkenau concentration camp. Upon arrival there, the thing I remember with the deepest emotion is my separation from my parents and my three brothers. We asked some soldiers where my parents were going, since they were placed in a truck. Their reply was, "Your parents can't walk so far, so they give them a ride. You will walk and meet them later on." One week later, I was working outside the camp for men; that is how I saw again, and for the last time, my brother Pepo. We were already so much transformed in appearance that we barely recognized each other. He and my other brothers Moise and Albert were sent to be Sonderkommandos. This was the group that worked in the crematoria. They had plenty of food, which they used to retrieve from the people who passed from their hands and who did not need it anymore. Many times, they sent us food packages with Leon Batis, who was working near where we were working. The Sonderkommandos were executed by the Germans every six months. One month before their expected execution the famous act of defiance took place.

There were 135 Greek Jews in the unit that consigned Jews to the crematoria. At the head of this unit were three former officers of the Greek army, Lieutenant Colonel Joseph Barouch, and two lieutenants, Joseph Levy and Maurice Aron. These men decided to dynamite the crematoria and end the Auschwitz exterminations. Detailed plans were made to carry out the action and, bit by bit, they managed to collect stores of dynamite and weapons from German warehouses. On the morning of October 7, [236] the Greek Jews, with the help of two units of French Jews and one of Hungarian Jews, blew up two of the four

---

236 Date correction by Professor Yitzhak Kerem.

crematoria at Auschwitz. They fought off the Germans for an hour and killed four German officers and 12 German soldiers, but all were shot down in the struggle.

I remember it was the second day of Succoth. (We had many Hungarian girls who were very religious. They had even managed to have religious books with them against all regulations, and they knew when we had holidays.) When we were ready to march to work, we heard shots being fired. They returned us back to the barracks while the fusillade intensified. This is the way my brothers died. All the men from Preveza who were selected for work were members of this Sonderkommando unit.

Not until the war ended and the Americans and Russians transferred us with trucks, was I separated from my sister Elli. We were on board different cars, and mine fell into a ditch. The others went on, leaving us behind. I was transferred to a different convalescent camp and was afraid that I would not be able to see Elli again, even if she were alive and well. Many people were trying to find their lost relatives. A girl approached me one day and told me that in a camp not too far away there was a girl who looked exactly like me . . . and her name was Elli. My joy could not be described. In our camp Jewish Yugoslav officers tried to help us. I asked one of them whose name was Alfred Melamed to go with his motorcycle to find Elli and bring her to me. He understood how much this meant to me; he went and brought her back.

Although we were liberated in May 1945, since we kept moving from camp to camp and city to city, it was not until September that we finally arrived in Athens. There was nobody to welcome us. We were sent to the Eighth High School on Aharnon Street, which was already filled to capacity with returning captives. We were not even allowed to enter the building. We spent our first night in our homeland on the pavement outside the high school. I was so heartbroken that I thought, "It would have been better if I did not come back!"

II. Memoirs of Camp Survivors

The next day we decided to take the streetcar and go to the center of Athens. The conductor asked us for the fare and only then we realized that we did not have any money. A strange woman who understood what was happening declared, "For all those who don't have money, I will pay their tickets." This was a welcome ray of sun: She showed us that all humane feelings were not lost in Greece.[237]

This story is important because it mentions the fact that three families left the city of Preveza and went into hiding because they did not want to submit to the Italian request for registration. There are no other people the author knows who, like Makis Solomon, did not trust the Italians and the Germans until the war was over. Makis Solomon was just an ordinary person. He was not rich, but he was very frugal and conservative. He had a lot of common sense, and perhaps this characteristic was needed for survival in Greece.

The Revolt

Joseph Barouch, an officer of the Greek army, was arrested by the Germans in Thessaloniki in the spring of 1943.[238] In the camp he worked as a Sonderkommando. When on June 30, 1944, he saw the bodies of his parents, who were captured in Corfu, and that of his friend, attorney Yiomtov Yakuel, he decided to organize the revolt. His Greek comrades were on his side. The majority of the other Jews who came from all the countries of Europe believed the revolt would be in vain. At this point, a group of 34 Russian Jews arrived who were ready for anything. With gold and jewelry in abundance for the Sonderkommandos, they bought dynamite and grenades. Kaminsky, a man with iron willpower, became the new leader. The Germans suspected something, and they tortured him to learn what was going on. He did not talk. They executed him. On October 7, 1944, a French Jewish Kapo arrived. He read a

---

237 "The Jews of Preveza," interview with Rena Carasso of Randallstown, MD, July 1976.

238 Date correction by Professor Yitzhak Kerem.

list of 100 Hungarians; they obediently followed his orders to march out. In a few minutes he came again and read a list of 100 Greeks. Jacob Broudo believed this meant only one thing: that the time for them to be executed had arrived. He yelled, "What are you going to do? The revolt will start." The Greeks refused to follow orders and ran in different directions. The Hungarians did the same. The French Jewish kapo and the German guard were killed. The prisoners tried to leave the building to get their ammunition, which was hidden in the yard. They hoped that the revolt would spread everywhere, but this was only a wishful illusion. The German troops arrived, reinforced by German common criminals to whom they distributed arms. In spite of all the fighting, one Greek Jew managed to escape. He was Isaak Venezia from Thessaloniki. He reached the area of Commando-Canada and hid himself there. He related the above account after the war ended.[239]

Solomon Benanton of Thessaloniki was a prisoner in Birkenau on October 7, 1944, when the Sonderkommando revolt took place. This is his eyewitness account:

> At 2:00 p.m. we heard gunshots and wild barking. This was followed by an explosion and a cloud of black smoke over the area of the crematorium. New louder explosions took place, and we were ordered into our barracks. We were not far from Lager D. We saw stretchers with wounded. Soon it was all quiet again. There were a number of rumors circulating among us. We learned the truth much later from those who survived. There were 1,000 prisoners, mostly French, Belgians and Italians. There were 200 Greeks and 15 non-Jewish Russians. For months they used gold to buy supplies. They established contact with the women who worked in the ammunition factory and with Polish partisans who were thirty kilometers away. Their plan was a reckless one beyond any logic.
>
> They had to dynamite and destroy the gas chambers, the ovens and the gigantic pits which served like open-air crematoria. They were supposed to disarm the SS guards in a wild, desperate attack. They

---

[239] "The Revolt," Molho, op. cit., 307.

had to move into the *Effecten Lager,* where countless barracks served as storage depots for whatever items the deportees possessed, then pass through the hospital to the laborers' camp. If everything went as planned, the mass exterminations would come to a halt, and the most audacious prisoners would free themselves and join the partisans. By the end of September, they were ready. Dynamite and hand grenades were stolen by the women who worked in the factory "Union" and given to them. Gasoline cans were hidden in strategic locations. Unexpected events forced them to start the revolt during the day rather than at night as planned. One of the Russian leaders, Melnikof, was attacked and beaten by a German. The revolt started while German reinforcements quickly surrounded the area. Among the five leaders, two were Greek Jews. They ignited the dynamite and they all perished in the explosion. When the burned bodies were collected it was discovered that many SS soldiers also died in the explosion. The commander of the camp prevented the execution of the survivors. "We don't have the time to create new work groups," he said. He believed that within a few weeks everyone would be executed anyhow. Many people owe their lives to this diabolic calculation of this arch-criminal.[240]

A Rare Case of Survival

Heintz Kounio was 15 years old when he and his family became part of the first transport that left the Hirsch camp of Thessaloniki for Auschwitz.

Heintz narrates:

In Auschwitz there were three thousand Greek prisoners at that time, and none of them knew German. This gave us the greatest opportunity. We were lucky because our family spoke German. My mother was born in the German-speaking area of Czechoslovakia.

---

240 *Israelitiko Vima,* Thessaloniki, 4/1/45.

My father knew German and we, as children, were taught both German and Greek at home. The Germans in the camp ordered our group, "Those who know German, come forward." Out of 3,000 people, only we four moved forward. Since there were no Germans or Poles who spoke Greek, the German commander was forced to accept my father and myself as interpreters in the men's camp and my mother and sister as interpreters in the women's camp. He instructed his subordinates not to give us any heavy work, so that we would always remain inside the camp and be found instantly when needed. This is how our family was saved. Perhaps we have the unique distinction of being the only family that returned from the camps intact.

From the first moment we understood that something terrible was taking place in the camp. From every transport of 2,000 to 3,000 people, 90 percent would be "selected," and nobody would hear of or see them anymore.

We arrived on March 20, 1943. After the selections, we marched from the train station to the camp.

It was almost midnight. They let us stand for the entire night in front of a building that looked like a bathhouse. There was steam coming out of it and we thought, dirty as we were, we needed a bath.

We edged closer to each other to feel a little warmer on that cold night. In the morning they asked us to undress and tie all our belongings into a bundle. Then we deposited items into three separate boxes: our jewelry and gold coins in the first box, our cigarettes and matches in the second, and all papers, certificates and identification cards in the third.

After we abandoned our bundle of belongings we were led to a barber, who shaved every area of the body. All these proceedings were followed by continuous beatings for no reason. After that we were ready for the "bath." The water was freezing, and nobody could stand it, but the Germans, with their big sticks, forced everyone to stand still. Then, suddenly, as if to satisfy their sadistic instincts, they turned on boiling water, which created sores on our hands, backs and legs. We cried and they laughed, making even more noise than we did. After this bath we were given some terrible uniforms and led to a barrack. At the entrance a very fat man was waiting with a cane. The first thing he did was to break the cane on the back of an unfortunate prisoner. We began to realize that none of us were going to get out of there alive, yet we kept hoping that things would get better.

The next step was registration in the camp records. We were given numbers, which were tattooed on our forearms with a needle and ink. We felt only a prick from the needle. At the beginning the food was tolerable. Finally, exhausted, we fell asleep in our bunk beds. In the morning we woke up and they started counting us. One man was missing. Those who were in charge of order in the barracks looked for him everywhere. They finally found him asleep. He was too tired to even hear the roll call. His punishment was swift. We witnessed our first execution.

My father and I were sent to a tailors' area. We knew nothing about tailoring, but we were going to learn. Our appearance was improved, thanks to the clothing we found there. A great deal of barter took place between those who were working in sorting out the belongings of newly arrived prisoners and other inmates or civilians who worked in the camps. Twenty cigarettes for one loaf of bread. One silk shirt for a half-kilo of margarine. All this was dangerous, but prisoners took their chances rather than die of starvation. If anyone was caught, he was either killed or his life was spared and his uniform marked with a red circle, indicating that he had "attempted to escape." Such inmates were beaten with the slightest provocation, and their life expectancy was short.

Every day new transports arrived. Only 10 percent of the new arrivals were selected to live. Since the number of inmates in the central camp was not supposed to exceed 17,000, they had to select for death a number of people who were not needed. Christians or Russians were not "selected" as long as there were Jews. On the roll call of these days, we remained silent, awaiting the outcome. If the roll call lasted longer than usual, then the voice of the camp commander would be heard: "All Jews should remain still. The Christians, Russians and gypsies should go inside the block." Cold sweat bathed us. We used to ask the man standing next to us if we looked thin and weak, because the thin and weak were always the ones who were sent to the crematoria.

Shivering, I waited to see if I would hear my number or that of my father's. We had to get undressed and pass in front of the medical officer of the camp. If he decided that a man was "useless," the officer in charge would mark his number in a notebook. This sudden decision would either make the prisoners sad and speechless or produce diarrhea. If that happened, the ever-present kapos would beat him mercilessly. Then everyone, those who would live and those who would die, returned to the block. Those who were selected to die were called Moslems. Some of them would fall on the electric fences to end their misery faster. Others hoped that some miracle would save them at the last minute. I personally survived seven selections. During the last one I was very weak and terribly afraid, but I never lost my faith that God would save me.

In almost two years of living in Auschwitz, only twice did I hear of what could be considered a prisoners' revolt. Both happened in the crematoria of Birkenau.

The first one took place in September 1943. The unknown heroine was an Italian Jewish woman. She refused to be totally undressed when she entered the baths. A German pushed her back, demanding that she get undressed. Then something unheard of happened. Instead of obeying the officer, she attacked, like a person who is very brave or who has lost her mind. She grabbed his gun and started shooting all the German officers and soldiers who were there. Other Italians took the guns of the fallen Germans, but they were soon surrounded by heavily armed guards. They were all condemned to death.

The second revolt took place in October 1944. This time the organizers were Greek Jews and some Russian soldiers. Four women who worked in the "Union" ammunition factory collected dynamite, which

II. Memoirs of Camp Survivors

they delivered to their friends who planned the revolt. They intended to burn crematoria No. 2 and No. 3 and then explode the dynamite which was stored in crematoria No. 4 and No. 5.

They were supposed to go to their assigned positions at exactly noon when the food was distributed. At that time the guards were in their dining hall. Most probably someone betrayed their plans. Only crematoria No. 2 and No. 3 were destroyed. German reinforcements arrived soon. The heroic inmates were in the building which they set on fire, while the Germans were outside surrounding the area with their machineguns. The two crematoria remained out of order for a long time. Approximately 1,250 Jewish men lost their lives in the revolt.

On May 2, 1945, the block leader collected his things in a suitcase and tried to leave quietly and join the retreating Germans. Some of the prisoners caught up with him and lynched him. Practically all the other kapos and block leaders paid with their lives. A gypsy kapo, responsible for the death of thousands of people, was thrown alive into an oven, which they lit just for him. The day of liberation by the Allies came on May 6, when the survivors cried from sorrow and happiness and made flags with their national colors.[241]

Soon the Kounio family was reunited and returned to Thessaloniki. They were the only family to do so among the more than a million Jewish families who were deported to the camps. Kounio's description of the revolt proves once more that no matter how heroic the participants were, in this or in the Sobibor revolt, ultimately their action became only a symbolic and suicidal one.

The time to fight the Germans was before men, women and children were sent to the camps, when they were free in their own countries, before they and their families were registered and arrested.

---

241 N. Kondylakis, "Heintz Kounio," *Chronika*, Athens, April 1982, 11.

I Am a Pharmacist

Daniel Carasso of Randallstown, Maryland, relates:

I was in Birkenau in April 1943, and on my left arm the blue number 120812 was tattooed ... I was working hard with a pick when the order came that all health professionals should present themselves for a special inspection. My job as a civilian was that of a pharmacist's assistant. I had never gone to college. The working conditions were bad, and I realized that if I wanted to survive, I should grasp this opportunity which might never present itself again. I left my work and lined up together with 150 physicians, dentists, veterinarians, and pharmacists. My appearance and bearing helped me.

I stood at attention when an SS asked me, "Work?" "Pharmacist." "Which school?" "University of Athens." Out of 150 men, forty were selected for different posts in the hospital; the rest were sent back to forced labor. I was among the forty. We were bathed, given new clothes, and transferred to the hospital compound of Auschwitz. Doctors Errera, Samouilidis and Kuenka were with my group.

On the first day I was given the job of cleaning the floor and the windows. The next day I was appointed chief medic in Block 19, in charge of supplies and medicines. My boss was a Romanian SS man who, I realized, could be bought easily because he was greedy for gold or foreign currency. I started falsifying the records and indicated that my block had more patients than it actually did. In this way I received more bread and soup than I was supposed to. I was able to eat better, and I sold the leftovers for gold, which I gave to the SS man. He in turn cooperated with me. It was possible for me to distribute food to relatives and friends. Under the pretext that I was accompanying him, I was even able to go to the women's camp and distribute food to people I knew there. Zan Kuenka, the wife of Dr. Kuenka, even asked me for a tube of toothpaste—and believe it or not, I was able to provide it.

II. Memoirs of Camp Survivors

In the camp, there were free German civilians in different capacities. They had a lot of gold. I stole blankets and sheets from the hospital and gave them to the civilians in exchange for gold to buy other items or to bribe my Romanian SS soldier.

Eventually someone betrayed me. One day when a prisoner and I were returning with the food rations, we were stopped by the German guards. They checked my book with the number of patients I declared and counted the number of bread portions we received. There were twenty more than there should have been. One of them put my head between his legs while the other pulled my pants down. With a stick he hit me so hard that I had to go to the hospital and soak in a basin of water. This is how I lost my privileged job.

My new job was not bad if we consider the fact that survival was the main aim of all the captives in the camp. I became a Leichenkommando. A French Jew named Pierre and I had to collect the remains of all those who died in Block 19 and transfer them to a little room in which there were also two cots for us. We had a book in which we kept the serial numbers of the ten to twenty people who passed through our hands each day. From this room we loaded them into a van, which came for this purpose once a day. We used a great amount of lime as a disinfectant in our room. I managed to find a pair of pliers, with which we extracted gold teeth which we used to buy extra rations of food. Life continued like this in a world without any sensitivity or compassion. Whenever I heard that someone, friend or relative, died, I don't remember feeling any emotion. I only said, "Poor man! He did not make it either!"

On January 15, 1945, we were each given one loaf of bread and one package of margarine, and we started the "retreat." We moved from our camp to Mauthausen, to Melk, if I remember the names correctly. We ate grass and the bark of trees. I was so exhausted that I don't remember the moment of liberation by the American forces. I only remember that I woke up inside a hospital tent. I was given warm soup, and I slowly realized that I was still alive and somehow had managed to survive German captivity.[242]

With the Poles in the 1944 Uprising

Alberto Levi relates:

On April 9, 1943, our transport left Thessaloniki for Auschwitz. I was with my mother and my brother Dario. When we arrived and the first selection began, a friend of mine wanted to go by car rather than walk like we were supposed to. He pretended that something was wrong with his foot, and he was allowed to board a truck. That was the last time I saw him. In the camp proper, I was happy to see my friend Chaim Fayil, who had been deported in March. I instinctively started to greet him and leave my place in the marching column of newcomers, when he stopped me with a stern glance and one movement of his hand, placed momentarily like a knife on his throat. He made me realize that such a move could instantly be punished by death. As for himself, he was dressed in the striped uniform of the prisoners, and he was literally harnessed with others to a cart. Moments later we took a shower, and, in the process, we lost all our possessions, including the best and warmest clothing we had brought along to face the cold of Krakow. I was placed in Block 27 and shared my sleeping area with my brother Dario, my brother-in-law Alberto Nazari, and with Montagio and Samuel Florentin.

The conditions in the camp were of course horrible, but we all decided to do our best to survive in spite of everything. We tried to get organized with this aim in mind. My work commando was close to a group of women. I recognized a friend of mine, Rena Bebez, who, as if she read my thoughts, started singing a well-

---

[242] "The Pharmacist," Daniel Carasso, interview with author, August 1975.

known tune with words which told me that my wife Allegra was alive and well.

One day I had an adventure. I was a strong 25-year-old. There was a group of Greek women who were trying to move an overturned pushcart under the supervision of a woman kapo. I asked the kapo if I could help move this heavy load. She replied, "Move it by yourself. If you can't do it, I will kill you." I went under the cart; I said, "Shemah Israel" and moved it upright. The Greek women were very happy, especially when they recognized me as the husband of Allegra. The commotion attracted the attention of an SS sergeant, who came to see what was going on. "I will give you a prize for it," he said, drawing his pistol. In the meantime, a male kapo arrived, a well-known, sadistic gypsy. They both tried to hit me. The gypsy used his stick, which had a nail at its end. I was able to get the stick and run. The two men were laughing, and that's the reason I was not shot.

The next day there was a fire in the barracks. I was sent with some others to put it out. There was a pair of socks in the building, which I stole. I packaged them and sent them to my wife with Rena. During our captivity, I saw my wife only once, and even then, I was not able to speak to her. After the war, I found out that of all the deported couples from Greece, only five couples survived the miseries of our exile.

Sometime in 1943, approximately 1,200 able men were each given a loaf of bread and were transported to Warsaw. All the houses of the ghetto were burned, while the city around it was intact. From what we saw, we felt how brave our brothers were. Simon Siegel, a Polish Jew from France, told us the story of the ghetto uprising. Many of us wished we were with them. One day we found a girl. She was thin, blonde, and very pale. She was hiding. We gave her water and bread. The sun bothered her enormously. She went back to her subterranean hiding place.

My greatest hero is a Jew from Thessaloniki whose name was Saul Senior. He was a Zionist, and he asked us to go to Palestine if we survived. I say Kaddish for him every day. Senior saved my life when I had typhus and my weight was less than 43 kilos. He bribed the guard to make sure that I would not be "selected." He gave the guard a diamond ring while he kept bringing me and others bread and biscuits. Senior was very brave and intelligent. In the ruins of the Warsaw ghetto, which we were clearing, we found a lot of gold and jewelry. The area near the Judenrat building had most of it. People threw their valuables here and there before going to be interrogated. Many of us gave the gold and valuables we found to Senior because he knew how to use it properly on our behalf. He used to make exchanges with Poles. For something worth three zlotys, we had to pay ten to twenty. Senior tried to escape in order to tell the outside world what he knew. Giassa, a Polish girl, prepared false papers for him and was waiting with a taxi in the city. Senior was not successful in his escape. He was wounded in his legs and hospitalized. When he became well, the Germans hanged him. His last message to us was: "I am finished, but this does not mean you are finished. When freedom comes, go to Palestine."

One day the partisans shot and killed a brutal SS man named Alex. Alberto Geladi, Alberto Bubul and I were ordered to bury him. We opened a pit and threw Alex in with hate. A Wehrmacht officer saw me. He approached and asked us why we did that. I told him, "If I could kill him, I would do it. He treated everybody in an inhuman way." "Be careful," the officer said, "someone else could have seen you." We were surprised to see a good German.

The next day the partisans attacked the railway station where my brother Dario worked. They broke into the warehouse and captured tanks and trucks. When they came to free our camp, there was machine-gun fire, and some of us were hit. Dario was on a truck wearing a German uniform and his striped prisoner's hat for identification. I helped move the wounded to the partisan hospital. The doctors complained that they did not have any medicines and kept me with them when I told them I was a medical student. We were part of a Polish battalion at Deluga Street. Our partisans captured a German tank, and many people rushed to

II. Memoirs of Camp Survivors

examine it. I had a premonition that it was booby-trapped and asked my brother Dario not to go there. In a few minutes, the tank exploded and many people were killed. The Poles, including the partisans, were very anti-Semitic. We tried to protect ourselves. A Jewish girl who worked in the kitchen gave me twenty pieces of paper, which I distributed among the Jewish boys. When we showed her the paper, we got better food. From the original 1,200 Greeks, we were only 27 left alive by this time.

The Germans counterattacked. Everybody tried to run away. Yitzhak Arouch suggested that we should disperse. Morris Negrin, Chaim Saltiel, and Morris Bensoure, with Dario and myself, decided to follow the Poles since they knew where to go. At this point, Bensoure wanted to drink some water. As soon as he went out of the house, he was killed. The Germans were approaching as we ran away toward the Polish-held area. Many who were with us did not know the Polish password, and they were shot by the Polish partisans who mistook them for Germans. Our battalion was near a bombardment. Saltiel made a small barricade and improvised a Greek flag, which he placed on it. All Greeks were in this barricade.

One day a woman invited me to her house. She opened the door of a clothes closet, which was a hidden entrance to a bunker. I saw a table with candles and Hebrew words. She must have known that I was a Jew. "We are Jews," she said. "Tonight is the eve of Yom Kippur." I started to cry. She gave me food to eat, and I wanted to keep some for my brother. Ella Tiltigh—that was her name—noticed, and she insisted that I eat, that she was going to prepare a package for all the other Jews. Her brother-in-law Aaron Sakrevitz prepared a package and included many cigarettes in it.

An old man named Bemardi who was also in the bunker told me that the Germans were going to destroy all the revolutionaries when they attacked again and that we were invited to join them in the bunker. We refused and decided to fight or flee. The next day the Germans attacked. They arrested many people as we ran toward the villages. During the fighting we entered a bank and found a number of zlotys, which we took with us. In the villages, this money proved to be invaluable. We told a villager that we worked for the German construction company Todt, and he gave us turkey and vodka, for which we paid him. We heard the footsteps of many people on the second floor and asked who lived there. "A German patrol," he said, "They search during the day and relax at night." We did not want to hear any more. In the middle of the night, we ran away like thieves. In another village, a man told us, "If you have any money, I will let you sleep in my house." We preferred to sleep in the stable, as we were too dirty to stay in his house. We were relaxing when two unarmed men in German uniforms entered.

One told us he was a Polish partisan; the other was a German deserter. I proposed they come with us. We gave the Pole money to buy provisions for all of us. We pretended to be French workers. The German was afraid to be seen with us and ran away alone. In a village, seven kilometers from Graviech, we stayed in the house of Yan and Stephan Vosnia. They suspected we were Jews, and they wanted us to go away. In the meantime, the Russians arrived. There were Jewish officers who helped us. When we returned to Warsaw, I recognized the place where the cinema had been, and I realized that the home with the bunker and hidden Jews lay totally in ruins.

I thought the people were dead, and I cried. Later on, however, I met Aaron Sakrevitz, who told us they were all right. My brother and I started our long trip back home to Greece. We went to Tsernovitch, then to Minsk, and to many other cities. Someone told me that my wife did not make it. I felt very sad, and I said Kaddish for her. When I was back in Greece, I was in quarantine when a girl approached me and asked me why I looked so depressed. "What do you expect," I said, "I came back to nobody." "No," she said, "your wife is waiting for you." The next day we were reunited. Dario went to Palestine, where he fought in the War of Independence. Later on, Allegra and I joined him in Israel.

II. Memoirs of Camp Survivors

Other Greek Jews who went to clear the Warsaw ghetto in August 1943 and were able to return to Greece include the following: Isaak Arouch, Solomon Hayouel, and Albert Molho.[243]

A Story from Didimotiho

Nissim Behar of Didimotiho was in his shop, talking with a client, when he was told that the Germans had ordered all Jews to go to the synagogue. He asked his client, whom he had known for a long time, "Would you like to watch my shop for a half-hour, while I go to the synagogue to see what's going on?" "How could I know," Nissim Behar, now of Tel Aviv, continues, "that I would never again set foot into my shop, which was founded by my grandfather?"[244]

The Story of a Girl from Kastoria

Berry Nahmia was a beautiful 18-year-old when she was arrested by the Germans. This is her story:

> After a period of silence, which lasted for 38 years, I decided to write my story on November 7, 1985. All this time did not bring me the peace of mind which I so much deserved. One voice tells me not to touch this old wound which is ready to start bleeding again. The other voice insists that what happened should not be forgotten. It is our duty to future generations. For 38 years I did not talk about what happened, and I was not even able to write about it. I opened my heart only once. I told everything to my husband. Then I kept silent again, hoping that the passage of time would bring me forgetfulness and peace. But calm and peace have always been beyond my reach. For many of us who

---

[243] "With the Poles," Yad Vashem Catalog No. 032492 (tr. by Avi Richter).

[244] Nissim Behar's story, Yad Vashem Catalog No. 032690 (tr. by Avi Richter).

returned, life after the war has been more difficult than the Holocaust itself.

My family consisted of my parents and nine children. My father's name was Israel Cassuto. Our nine-day trip to Auschwitz was a horrible nightmare. Yet even this trip did not prepare me for what I endured there. As soon as we disembarked, Bertitse, an educated woman from Belgrade, offered to translate the instructions we were given. All of a sudden, I saw my 15-year-old brother, who obediently left his bag with all the other boys. "Alberto!" I yelled. "Keep your bag. Don't believe them." He looked at me but did not get a chance to say anything. The Germans pushed him, and I never saw him again. He was the only one among the members of my family who had a reasonable chance to survive.

When Bertitse finished, the German officer thanked her and asked her to join those who were going to walk to the camp. "No," she replied. "My children are in the trucks." "You will see them later," he said. "Please let me go with my children," she pleaded. "Go wherever you like," the officer responded. Bertitse joined her children in the truck.

One thing that I will never forget is the voice of an unknown Greek who worked as a Sonderkommando in crematorium No. 4, close to where I stayed. For a period of almost two months, every night he sang in a loud voice and like an old troubadour he told his story. His song went something like this:

> Girls—Greeks—who listen to me,
> I say everything by singing, so you will understand.
> Here the chimneys you see are the biggest factory of death.
> Thousands of Jews, old, young, children
> Fall into the arms of the flames.
> I know they will burn me too.
> After a while, I will not be around
> To describe what my tired eyes have seen.
> Do you hear me? Believe me.
> It's true, horrible, I live it every day.
> Girls—Greeks—I beg you,

II. Memoirs of Camp Survivors

If you get out of here alive,
Tell the entire world the story I sing to you.

Berry Cassuto Nahmia was the only member of her family who survived.[245]

The Auschwitz museum contains many documents related to the Greek Jews. There are railway tickets, lists of the different transports, and catalogues of the personal items of the prisoners. Many documents have German headings followed by translations in Greek. The dates correspond to the dates of the deportations from Greece, starting with March 16, 1943.

According to Molho, 45,659 Jews from the area of Thessaloniki were deported in 18 convoys. According to the accounts kept in Auschwitz, 19 convoys arrived from Thessaloniki carrying 48,874 people.

The exact number of Greek Jewish men and women who, upon arrival in the camp, were selected to work was 12,757, which represents 19.6 percent of the 65,000 Greek Jews who were deported.

The working conditions, the lack of food, the brutality of the system, the bad weather, the demoralization which came with the knowledge that all their relatives were lost, and the lack of rest and sleep devastated the ranks of those who were chosen to live. Out of 12,757 Greek Jews who were sent to "work" between March 20, 1943, and August 16, 1944, only 2,469 were still alive on September 2, 1944. This is 3.8 percent of the 65,000 people sent to the camp. On January 17, 1945, those who were still alive and able to walk were moved west. The remaining sick were left in the camp and were liberated by the Russians.

The number of people who returned to Greece after the liberation of the camps was smaller than 2,000.[246]

---

245 Letter to the author by Berry Cassuto Nahmia, Athens, Apr. 20, 1988.
246 Salvador Heintz Kounio, *Chronika*, Athens, April 1984, 9.

Chapter Five

Memoirs of Resistance Fighters

Only a lost people can lament so;
Smoke and ashes—this is its soul;
And its heart a desert wilderness
Without an ounce of anger or revenge.

Where is the fist that shall smite?
Where the thunderbolt to avenge?
To shake the world and rend the sky?
To overthrow my seat, my throne?

— CHAIM NACHMAN BIALIK[247]

Secrets have the explosive power of bombs. The Germans knew that well. This is the reason they confiscated radios, controlled the press, censored correspondence, and limited and controlled the movement of people in the occupied countries. They claimed great victories and kept silent about their defeats.

Naturally, the opponents of the Germans took exactly the opposite measures. They painted slogans on the walls at night. They printed illegal newspapers. They circulated mimeographed news bulletins. They dropped leaflets by plane. They operated radio stations and tried to prevent the Germans from

---

247 Chaim Nachman Bialik, from his poem "In the City of Slaughter."

confiscating all radios. They lifted the morale of the people and proved that the Germans could be beaten.

In Greece, the BBC was considered the best source of information, and most Greeks eagerly listened to its broadcasts. As far as the "Final Solution of the Jewish problem" is concerned, the Germans wanted to keep it secret from history itself. The German mania about secrecy was so great that they made many attempts to erase any evidence of mass graves and even any trace of a death camp like Sobibor in German-occupied Poland. The Germans were totally successful in keeping the Greek Jews in the dark about their plans to murder the entire Greek Jewish population. Not one Jew in Greece knew about the Holocaust prior to May 1945. This is a very important point to be understood. Only in this context of ignorance and illusion can the actions of the Greek Jews be explained.

In the following pages we pay homage to those Jews who fought against the enemy. They were very few. There could have been many more making a greater contribution to the Allied cause. Unfortunately, thousands of able-bodied veterans of the wars— in Albania in 1940, in Turkey in 1921—went with their families to their deaths. What a waste of manpower!

There are no more ferocious fighters than those who know that their enemy kills all prisoners. That was the case with the Jews who fell into German hands. A Greek Jewish fighter would have become even more ferocious if he knew that he had "no choice." His family's survival depended upon him. How different the outcome would have been if the Jews knew what would really happen to them if they continued their total compliance while the Germans were the masters of their cities.

In the Greek "free" areas, with its mountainous terrain, one can imagine tens of thousands of Jewish fighters who would have created impenetrable strongholds that the Germans would not have dared attack. Every Jew would have preferred to die in battle rather than in the gas chambers of the concentration camps. Even before the creation of ELAS, thousands of Jews who served in the Greek army could have created a self-defense force armed with knives. They could execute any Greek traitor who betrayed Jews to the Germans. Of course, all the above would have required the full cooperation of the British and the Americans instead of their silence. The Jews would have had to be told about the German

II. Memoirs of Resistance Fighters

plans long before their registration with the Germans and the Italians. Perhaps if this had occurred, there would not have been a Holocaust in Greece.

The Second World War began for the Greeks in October 1940. Out of 77,000 Greek Jews, around 4,000 fought on the front lines in Albania. They fought heroically, and their losses were heavy. Among those killed was Colonel Mordechai Frizis, whose troops helped stop the Italian advance into Greece. This was the first victory of the Allied armies in the Second World War. He fell on December 5, 1940, near Premeti, Albania, along with Second Lieutenant Yakoel Mois from Thessaloniki and Second Lieutenant Chaim Siakis from Larissa. Two hundred and sixty-eight Jewish soldiers and noncommissioned officers fell in combat or died as a result of their wounds. Hundreds more were wounded. There were 138 amputees whom the Germans assigned directly to the crematoria. According to Miriam Novitch of Kibbutz Lochamei Haghethaoth, their artificial limbs are kept in a corner of the Auschwitz museum.

In 1943, the resistance organization EAM pleaded with the Jews of Thessaloniki, asking them to not follow German orders and to leave the city. This was done with illegal newspapers and pamphlets, which also threatened traitors with severe punishment.

The EAM of the University of Thessaloniki created a system which directed Jewish students to partisan territories. Two hundred and fifty-two young Jews from Thessaloniki joined the partisan units which, at the beginning of 1943, faced great difficulties in the mountains of Pierion, Vermiou, and Pindou. In order to join ELAS, the young Jews had to traverse the plains of Thessaloniki, cross rivers and avoid the guards controlling the bridges. They walked at night in the fields, and during the day they hid in stables and ditches. Their escape coincided with German search-and-destroy missions. The Germans combed all the mountain passes. When the Jews from Thessaloniki met the partisan units, they were given guns. Some of the guns belonged to the Greek army, hidden by villagers after the Greek surrender. Other guns were given to the partisans by the British. Most Jews were veterans of the Albanian war, and they were immediately placed in fighting units. The rest received intensive training. All the partisan units received Jewish physicians and nurses. In one group of forty partisans, there were ten Jews. Tired and hungry, all the partisans sang inspiring songs of freedom.

After Italy's capitulation, the Germans occupied the Greek cities, while the Greek countryside remained free, thanks to ELAS and, to a small degree, to EDES, which liberated a great part of Epirus and Aitolo-Akarnania. In Athens 1,000 Jews participated in all activities, which prevented the mobilization of Greek men to serve under German command. The Jewish section of EAM coordinated the assistance (shelter, food, medical care and, especially, false identity cards) given to the fugitives from Thessaloniki. A weekly bulletin was issued with the signal: "Nobody should visit the German-controlled Community Center." EAM also, in pamphlets, encouraged Christians to help the persecuted Jews and to hide them. And EAM encouraged the formation of a committee of scientists, artisans, and workers who asked foreign embassies to intervene on behalf of the Jews.

Archbishop Damaskinos had tacit EAM support when he made his bold moves to save as many Jews as he could. With the assistance of EAM, hundreds of houses were found to shelter Athenian Jews when they had to abandon their homes, whose addresses were known to the Greek police. The Jews who took their families and went to the mountains did not remain idle there. They helped as couriers, nurses and teachers, and some performed secretarial duties. Artisans worked in tailoring and shoemaking; seamstresses made shirts from parachute material or made socks and hats; and young girls participated in cultural activities and theatrical performances or worked as teachers' aides.

The Jewish partisans, whose numbers surpassed 650, fought bravely and suffered many dead and wounded.[248] They were dispersed in all units of ELAS and could be found in every branch of the army. Most were in Thessaly and in central Greece. Some Jews, serving in the Greek army of the Resistance units, were captured and executed by the Germans. After the battle of Crete, the medical officer Salvator Sarfati died as a result of torture. In December 1941, three leaders of the labor movement of Thessaloniki were executed: David Samuel, David Tiano, and Alberto Carasso, whose son Markos

---

248 Joseph Matsas, letter to the author, Sept. 10, 1976.

distinguished himself as an officer of ELAS. Mois Carasso, brother of Alberto, was executed on May 1, 1944. In Drama the Bulgarians executed Alberto Kohen and David Mijan. Isaak Kohen from Volos was executed for act of sabotage and, in Athens, David Michael Kohen from Preveza was also executed.

The German military representative of Thessaloniki, Dr. Max Merten, during his trial in 1959, was considered responsible for the execution of six young Jews from Thessaloniki who were captured when they attempted to escape from the ghetto and join the partisans. Chaim Leon Levi from Ioannina was also executed for his resistance activities. In the town of Eretria in the island of Euboeas, Mordoch, one of the leaders of EAM, was executed, while the heroic teacher Moschovitz was executed (in Stropones, Euboeas) by the Greek collaborators of the Security Battalions. Roberto Mitrani, a medical student whose father was a professor, was arrested in Thessaloniki and sent to a slave labor camp in Thebes. He and other young men escaped and joined the partisans of Mt. Parnassos. He organized a primitive first aid station, but he also carried a gun as well as his medicines and fought in many battles. On January 5, 1944, his company fell into a German ambush near Ayia Triada, Kaloskopis. The area was white with snow. Roberto (or Hippocrates, as he was called), although wounded, continued to give first aid to his comrades. His commander, the popular leader Kalias, was also wounded. Roberto rushed to aid him. They were killed by machine gun bullets.

In a common grave, between Giona and Parnassos, rests the handsome hero Roberto, along with two other Jewish boys, David Russo from Athens and David Michael Kohen from Preveza, both 19 years old, and with them 27 other fallen partisans. Elias Nissim of Thessaloniki, although sick, took part in a mission near Grevena. He was wounded and transferred to the hospital of Pentalogos where he died.

A student, Stella Kohen, of the 50th regiment, fell on April 18, 1943, in the battle of Tahnitsas. The former partisan, Joseph Matsas, recalls other fallen heroes: Elias Alalouf fell in the area of Athens, Israel Sadicario from Volos and Abraam Joseph Bourla fell near Chalkis; Tselele Bourla from Serrai fell in Epirus; Savvas Pardo, his son Mois and Barron, factory workers from Kavalla, also fell in battle.

Casualties in the battle of Vermio were Niko Bourla of the 16th regiment in an ambush in Stavros Verias; Charles Carasso in Scalochori Kastorias; the female partisan Serror in Vermio; Molho in Halkidiki; and Frizis in Vermio.

From the Diary of a Jewish Partisan

Here is the diary entry of an unknown author:

May 6, 1944. At sunrise the night sentinels return to our little barn to enjoy the warmth of a good fire. Slowly we get up and talk about the unusually cold weather for this time of year. On May 1 snow fell and can still be seen in places where the sun did not yet melt it. We are at an elevation of 500 meters, and we represent an advanced post of our ELAS battalion on Mt. Olympus, which is stationed a few minutes march higher up.

I opened the door and the clean air rushed in to dispel the humidity that comes out of the wet overcoats and boots of the guards. Outside, I take a look and see only heavy fog, where I usually see the Larissa plateau. Behind me, on the contrary, Mt. Olympus, white with snow, is bathed in sunlight. The path that leads to the fields of Larissa is carved on the side of a cliff, on top of which we located our post. In the bottom of the canyon, some two kilometers from us, there is an opening with some barns which shelter Jewish families from Larissa. They escaped the fury of the Germans and live there hoping for a better tomorrow. We often go down there and they are very happy to see and talk with us. They feel that they are not alone in this corner of Olympus and have a sense of security, thanks to our nearby presence. Their women often wash our clothes and the young men organized a system of scouts which, night and day, bring us information that arrives with couriers from Larissa.

Every day the first thing I see is their camp and, today, fog covers the entire area; for some unknown reason I feel uneasy. I went to the spring nearby and the guard there commented about the bad weather

II. Memoirs of Resistance Fighters

down below. The cold water refreshed me and made me lose all bad thoughts and laziness. As I passed again next to the guard, a funny noise was heard. "Machine gun fire? Don't you think?" the guard says as he searches with his eyes the canyon below. For a second the fog is reduced and the guard looks with his binoculars and points out something. The fog retreated like the curtain of a stage in which a drama is about to unfold. The Jewish barns form the background of this first act.

In the square, at the opening of the canyon, I can see a great number of people with helmets and military uniforms moving right and left. They are Germans—a whole battalion of them. I shiver with the thought that my poor coreligionists, after all they suffered, fell again into the hands of the German beasts.

But all hope is not lost. I lower the binoculars which the guard gave me and I turned around to see him. Instead, I see all my comrades, ready with weapons in their hands. "Get your gun and kit fast," my captain tells me, "and give this note to the battalion commander." At the same time, he took the binoculars from my hands.

After running for ten minutes, I am in front of my major, to whom I gave the note and explained what I saw. He looks deeply into my eyes and, as if speaking to himself, says, "We have to save them." I returned immediately to my guard post, where I see the men forming a circle around a sweating and heart-poundingly tired civilian. I recognize him right away as one of the young Jewish men of the valley.

He describes how the Germans arrived at their encampment a little before sunrise, led by a civilian informer. They arrested the Jews in the barns and, after looting their belongings, were about to burn their shelter. A young man tried to inform us but the Germans fired and wounded him. This was the gunfire we heard earlier. Finally, a man managed to escape and came to tell us what happened. Agony is depicted on his face as he finishes his story while at the same time, feeling relief, he realizes from what he sees that there is hope for the people he left behind.

Three to four hours elapsed from the time we noticed the arrival of the Germans. During this period the main body of enemy troops remained in the encampment enjoying their victory. Three small groups of German soldiers exchanged fire with our advanced patrols on a front of two to three kilometers. During this time all our men from the battalion at Karyes arrived, around 150 men. Without wasting any time our forces were deployed on the cliffs surrounding the area of the barns. We occupied the high ground so fast that as soon as the order to open fire was given and the singing of our machineguns commenced, dozens of Germans fell dead and wounded. All conditions, from a military point of view, favored our ambush. Slowly and without reducing our heavy fire, we started descending, surrounding the Germans in a smaller circle. The Germans started to fire back, but we did not stop. We knew that our success depended on our speed of action. Our accurate fire brings down more Germans. Soon the enemy is seized by panic. They try to escape by running toward the opening of the canyon. I saw that the barns were on fire, and the question came to me, "Did the bastards kill the people?" This sad thought was in my mind when my captain ordered our squad to cover the entrance to the canyon and prevent the escape of any Germans. We ran, taking precautions, bent over; the German fire weakens. Some surrender, others try to hide, others abandon their guns and try to escape. We run, one behind the other, and fire our guns.

Suddenly I stop. Behind some bushes I see two or three girls and other civilians. There are tears in their eyes, which express gratitude as they see each partisan who passes in front of them ... I was sure that these few Jews had been saved, when something hit my left leg and my eyes could not see anymore. I fell down, losing consciousness. I was wounded.[249]

---

249 *Israelitiko Vima*, Thessaloniki, No. 25, May 17, 1946, author unknown. That a heroic young man with obvious intellectual abilities as a writer would describe this historic event anonymously is indicative of the

II. Memoirs of Resistance Fighters

One of the partisan leaders who participated in this battle on southern Mt. Olympus was Lieutenant Marco Alberto Carasso. Another partisan witness was Joseph Matsas.

Joseph narrates:

> Perhaps the greatest partisan victory of the Second World War took place in Karyes, on the southern slope of Mt. Olympus. The battle is known as the Battle of Karalaka. Five Jewish families of Larissa established their campsite in this location. They were betrayed, and an SS battalion surprised them early one morning. Albert Ovadias, Simon Levi and Jacob Magrissos tried to run and inform the partisans, but were gunned down and killed by the Germans.
>
> A fourth man, Elias Kohen, succeeded.
>
> Marco Carasso's platoon, together with other units, comprised a force of 150 who staged one of the most spectacular guerrilla operations of the Second World War. The Germans were encircled and ambushed from the sides of a canyon. German planes came to help, but the terrain of this gorge was such that they were ineffective. Some Germans managed to escape, but those who remained found a tragic end.
>
> One hundred and fifty Germans were killed, 78 were wounded and 14, including the German commander, became prisoners. Ten of the prisoners were executed because they attempted to disarm their guards. The remaining were also put to death. That is a total of 242 German dead.
>
> Partisan losses were eleven dead and ten wounded. In addition, three Jewish civilians were also killed. Immediately after the battle, a Jew named Ganis came and embraced us. "I have a son Marko who is seventeen," he said. "Take him with you, because you are the ones who saved our lives." Marko, a small boy, joined our unit and became our mascot.

---

situation in Greece almost two years after the Germans were defeated. If the German collaborators after the war knew who he was, he would be in serious trouble.

> We all loved him and tried to protect him in every battle. I loved him more than anyone else because for me he somehow became the symbol of our oppressed people.[250]

The personal historic archives of the president of the community of Larissa, Moissis Ezras, contain these additional details of the battle of Karalaka:

> There were some twenty Jews camping in Karyes. They belonged to the families of Marko Gani, Joseph Ovadias, Moissis Magrissos and Yehudah Kohen. Three young Jewish men were killed, while a fourth was wounded. Some Germans were so sure of themselves that they got undressed and went to bathe in a nearby stream. Antonis Angeloulis was the commander of the ELAS battalion which attacked the Germans. He was known as Vratsanos. During the battle the Germans forced the remaining young Jews to serve as stretcher bearers. Among the Germans who became prisoners was the battalion commander who, naked and on horseback, was led to the village of Karyes, where he was executed. Another German who was captured and executed was the son of a German General, who was the Aegean commander. The Germans offered to free 200 hostages kept in German prisons in exchange for his freedom. The message was received by ELAS too late. By that time all German prisoners were executed. The following day the Germans returned in force in the area to recover their dead.[251]

The battalion commander of ELAS, Antonis Angeloulis who was known by his Partisan name, Vratsanos, served as a second lieutenant in the Albanian front. From 1942 to 1944, he

---

[250] Interview with Joseph Matsas, April 10, 1976; also A. Angeloulis (commander of the partisan forces in the battle of Karalaka), "Vrondai O Olympus," 40-44.

[251] Xenophon Dassios, *Larissaiki Echo,* August 5, 1988; letter from Moissis Ezras to author, 4/12/84.

was a commander of saboteurs. As a young man, he learned from his father how to handle dynamite while they were working on roads in the mountains. He is credited for destroying 36 bridges and 20 trains with German troops. It is estimated that, thanks to his actions, 3,065 German officers and soldiers were killed or wounded.

He is considered as the greatest saboteur of the Second World War. He also wrote a book, "Vrontai o Olympos" "There is Thunder in Olympos." Harold Alexander, commander of the Allied Forces of the Mediterranean, honored him with the highest decoration.[252]

Saved by the Partisans

Rachel Kohen of Larissa recalls that when the news about the Jewish deportations from Thessaloniki arrived in the city, Rabbi Cassuto, truly a holy man, advised, "Don't let yourselves be taken by the Germans. Escape! Abandon Larissa!" In September 1943, the Germans occupied the city and ordered the rabbi to provide them with a list of the members of his community. The rabbi had no intention of cooperating with them and immediately went into hiding, first in the city, and later in the mountains. It is unfortunate that not all the Jews followed his example.

Rachel Kohen remembers:

> My father decided to leave. We all had false identity cards. We went to the village of Sikorion, near Mt. Ossa. The villagers knew who we were, but nobody would denounce us. They knew that the Resistance protected us and that any informer would be severely punished. There was very little food available in the village, and my father went once a week to Larissa to find provisions. The Germans, on the other hand,

---

[252] Letter to the author from Effie Papatheodorou, with website link https://ethniki-antistasi-dse.gr/antonis-aggeloulis.html from Harilaos Bougas, May 1, 2020.

raided the villages often and sometimes arrested and executed people on the spot.

One time they discovered eight Jews hiding in a village and executed them. We realized that we should go further away in the mountains. Many Jewish families were together. It was thought that this was not a good idea, and we were dispersed in many villages.

My family found shelter for a while in the stable of a peasant. Later on, we joined a group of twenty Jews near a camp of partisans at the foot of Mt. Olympus.

One day a German unit raided our area. They discovered our group, encircled the camp and captured us. Three of our men were gunned down. Our camp was looted and burned. They were about to transfer us down the mountain when the nearby alerted partisans attacked, killed many Germans and freed us while the rest of the German unit retreated in a disorderly manner.[253]

Beyond the Battle of Karalaka

During a dinner in 2012, I met Dr. Paul Levy, a consultant for the World Bank. He told me that he had a relative by the name Magrizos who was killed near Mount Olympus during WWII. He knew nothing else, not his first name, not how they were related, nor how he had died. The hostess Mrs. Nina Kaplanidis had my original book, *The Illusion of Safety*, which helped us in our search. Paul learned that his relative was his uncle Jacob (Iakov) Magrizos, son of Moyssis Magrizos from Larissa. Paul Levy has in his possession a photograph which was found in the pocket of his heroic uncle's shirt, perforated by one of the German bullets that killed him during the Battle of Karalaka on May 6, 1944. Magrizos' name is among the 14 names of the heroic fallen Greeks in a marble monument which commemorates the partisan victory in which 242 Germans were killed. Three of these 14 men were Jews.

On May 6, 1944, an SS battalion captured five Jewish families who established a camp on a southern slope of Mt.

---

253 "Saved by the Partisans," Eleftheria Larissis, 4/18/61.

II. Memoirs of Resistance Fighters

Olympus. Three Jewish men attempted to escape, and they were killed. A fourth man escaped and notified a unit of ELAS, which was under the leadership of Antonis Angeloulis. Angeloulis was known by his nom de guerre, Vratsanos. Some 150 partisans, including Jewish fighters like Lieutenant Marko Carasso and my cousin Joseph Matsas attacked the Germans. They killed 242 Germans and liberated the Jews. The commander of the Allied Forces in the Middle East sent a telegram to ELAS (No. 825/5/11/1944) with warm congratulations.

Alberto Levi of New York read the story of the battle of Karalaka in my book and went to Greece to visit the location of this great partisan victory. After a great deal of effort, he found it. He sent me photos of the monument which honors as "fighters of ELAS" the 11 partisans who fell in battle and the three Greek Jews who attempted to contact the partisans and were killed. The three names, Abram Ovadias, Iakov Magrizos, and Symeon Levis, are placed in alphabetical order among the heroes of ELAS.

I believed that these 11 partisans of ELAS deserved to be honored as "Righteous Among the Nations" and I proposed that to Yad Vashem in Jerusalem. Unfortunately, they said that soldiers cannot be so honored. The "Righteous" are people who risked their lives to save Jews. These partisans not only risked their lives but lost their lives, and they were volunteers like all Greek partisans.

Memorial to the Battle of Karalaka. (Photo courtesy of Alberto Levi.)

Too Many Traitors

Moissis Sakis of Volos, an agronomist, was in charge of ETA (provisions for the partisans) in the area of Velestinou-Piliou. He relates:

> My parents were hiding in a house in upper Volos on the day the Germans and Greek collaborators blocked the neighborhood, placed a machinegun right in front of their house, and searched for Jews and resistance sympathizers. The collaborators wore face masks, and the arrested people were sent to the "yellow warehouse." Many Jews were arrested, among them my cousin Nissos I. Kohen, who died in the camps. "It was a miracle," my father exclaimed when I finally saw him. "We were watching the Germans from our window shutters. They entered every single house except ours."
>
> My brother Leon, age 18, was an enthusiastic revolutionary. In October 1943 he became a partisan of the 24th regiment of ELAS Piliou. and although my duties kept me in the same general area our paths never crossed. On June 22, 1944, during a battle 14 kilometers from Larissa, Leon attempted to save a wounded partisan. He ignored all danger and was mortally wounded by German machinegun fire. In the summer of 1945, I tried to find his remains. I was told that all fallen partisans had been placed in a common grave in a central spot of the village Eleftheriou. After the liberation the tomb was destroyed and nothing remained.

As a leader of ETA, Sakis played an important role in providing supplies for the 54th regiment of ELAS, whose area of operations was very poor in agricultural products. ETA was responsible for collecting 10 percent of all produce and transferring it to mountain hideouts of ELAS. The Germans realized the importance of these activities and, with the assistance of Greek collaborators, used to block roads or villages in an attempt to intercept the mule convoys of ETA or capture those who collected the supplies.

In one such operation, Moissis was in the area of Gatjeas when he was informed that the Germans had blocked the

II. Memoirs of Resistance Fighters

entire area and were combing every house, looking for suspects. He ran to the friendly house of Anastasis Fiari, where the housewife told him that all men had abandoned the village and gone into hiding in the forest. She thought it would be better for him to stay in the house and pretend that he was a doctor, since her daughter happened to be sick and in bed. Sakis, who with his glasses and intellectual appearance could pass as a village doctor, promptly took his place next to his "patient." Soon a German entered the house and asked him for his papers. Moissis's identity card was in proper order; it had been issued by the German authorities of the same area. He made the German understand that the girl was sick with a contagious disease and the soldier left.

Among the "suspects" who were captured that day were the brothers Chaim and Valassi Kohen. The Germans used to bring their suspects to Volos, where a local Greek informer would point out who was a Jew and who was a communist. The Jews, including the Kohen brothers, were sent to Auschwitz; they did not return. The communists were kept in special camps in Greece, from where they were sent to the execution squads whenever the Germans had to retaliate for actions of the resistance.

Moissis Sakis continues his story:

> I moved from village to village, trying to supervise the collection of supplies and persuade affluent farmers to give their share. Of course, those who refused were forced to comply by members of the Communist Party and the local reserve ELAS units.
>
> I had to move constantly, and I usually spent no more than one night in any village. In committee meetings I often met another Jewish partisan, Theophilos Vitalis, who worked for EA (welfare department).
>
> In June 1944, realizing that we did not have enough produce, I proposed that all rations should be reduced, allowing, however, bigger rations for the fighting men of ELAS. The communist leader insisted that the bigger rations should be given to the members of the Communist Party. Because of my opposition, I was transferred the next day to the area of Pilion. I lost even my name "Prometheus." My new name was

"Farmer." I taught the villagers the latest methods in fertilization, irrigation, and how to fight diseases of plants and animals. I managed to improve their quality of life quite successfully, as I found out after the war when I returned to civilian life. [254]

Lieutenant Skoufas

Yohanas Hatjis, a modest and brave man, was born in Arta in 1916. During the Greek-Italian war, he fought as a sergeant with the VIII Division, which engaged in the most decisive battles of the war in the mountains of Albania. When he became a partisan, his abilities as a fighter and a leader of men quickly became known. ELAS sent him to school for reserve officers, from which he graduated as a second lieutenant. In September 1943 he was an officer of the 11/34 battalion of ELAS, which operated in Attica and Boeotia. His ability and self-sacrifice were admired by his comrades. Hatjis led most of the dangerous missions in his battalion and fought bravely in the battle of the "51st Kilometer" between Gravia and Amfissa.

On July 2, 1944, during one of the most important battles which the ELAS II Division fought against the Germans in Amfissa, Hatjis led his unit in the attack against the Germans, yelling, "Follow me" and "Forward, boys!" A bullet in the foot did not stop him. A second bullet hit him in the chest, wounding him mortally. Yohanas Hatjis, or "Skoufas" (a *nom de guerre* he selected, after the main square of his native city of Arta) was dead, and so was his Jewish community.[255]

On October 4, 1944, PEEA, the Political Committee of National Resistance, promoted Hatjis to the rank of first lieutenant for bravery beyond the call of duty. On the same day, PEEA promoted the fallen partisan Leon Sakis from an *andartes* to the rank of reserve sergeant major for valor beyond the call of duty.[256]

---

254 Too Many Traitors," letter from Moissis Sakis to author, 8/28/77.
255 "Lieutenant Skoufas," *Israelitiko Vima*, Thessaloniki, 1946.
256 *Acts and Decisions of PEEA* (Athens: Oikos, 1976), chapter 27.

II. Memoirs of Resistance Fighters

A Medical Officer's Story

Errikos Levis was a medical officer of the Greek army who served in the front lines of the Albanian campaign. In 1943, he served as a medical officer of the Greek police and the Department of Public Security in Athens. He recalls:

> When the Jews from Thessaloniki were deported, I thought it would be safer for my family to go to Ioannina, which was under the Italians. I obtained a transfer there easily and stayed in the house of my uncle, Dr. Nissim Levi. When a wedding was going to take place in Valona, Albania, and many relatives of the bride were going to go there for the ceremony, I advised my wife to go also and to take our son Alekos with her. She would be in good company and stay with our relative Isaak Yakouel.
>
> My intention behind all this was to be free to go to the mountains and join the resistance movement of EDES with General Zervas.
>
> In the meantime, together with some police officers and the commander of the Greek police of Ioannina, Major Makrinioti, we formed an espionage group in favor of the resistance. Since I spoke German, I was the "brain" of our unit.
>
> I noticed that the Italians were following my every move, and because of this I left Ioannina and went to meet Zervas in the mountains. I stayed with Zervas for just one day. He told me, "I have as many doctors as I need here, but spies like you I can't find easily." So, I returned to Ioannina.
>
> When Italy capitulated, the two Italian officers of the intelligence service of the Division whose headquarters were in Ioannina came to me and asked me to send them to Zervas. We dressed them as village women and gave them an escort to take them to the mountains. I did this with pleasure, but I wish I never had, as events proved later. Thanks to information that our group gave to Zervas and the British officers attached to him, sabotage operations against the Germans continued. The Germans in Ioannina kept requesting whatever they needed from the Jewish

community—furniture, household items, etc. The Jews gladly gave, having the illusion that if they gave them anything they wanted, the Germans would not bother them.

At 3:00 a.m. on a cold February morning in 1944, the German military police arrested me, Dr. Moises Koffinas, president of the Jewish community, and Semo Kohen, a wealthy merchant. They took us to the village of Strouni, where a small detachment seemed to be ready to execute us. I spoke to the German officer and told him, "Nothing will happen to Greece if you kill two doctors. But killing three people without a trial is a shame for Germany, which wants to impose a new order in Europe." Perhaps their "execution" routine was a trick because they took us to Gestapo headquarters on the island of Lake Pamvotis, where they interrogated us for three days. During my interrogation, I found out that the Italian officers whom I saved had delivered my file to the Germans before they came to me. The words "very dangerous" were written on my file!

We were moved to the basement of the Zosimea School, where the Germans imprisoned civilians who were given to the execution squads whenever a retaliation was needed in response to acts of sabotage. In Zosimea the situation was not bad for us, because I successfully treated a serious disease of the sergeant major who oversaw the prison.

On March 24 we were released, only to be recaptured hours later with the entire Jewish community of Ioannina. Of the three of us, only I returned. Koffinas and Semos Kohen died in Auschwitz. With those who remained alive, I was sent to Wolfsberg, where we built a camp for the Hungarian Jews. I worked as a physician of this section, while the kapos were Polish Jews. Until February 1945, I did not lose more than three Jews from Ioannina.

When the Russian troops approached our camp, which was located to the east of Breslau, they loaded us onto open wagons used for the transportation of coal and during a terrible snowstorm transferred us to Bergen-Belsen.

II. Memoirs of Resistance Fighters

Many died from cold and hunger in these few days of this trip. The Greeks and the Hungarians who survived were taken to the river Oder, in Stettin. Many more died there, but because the Russians were advancing, they took us to Bart on the Danish border. There on April 30, 1945, we were liberated, and the Germans, filled with panic, ran to save their lives.

For two days, the Russians looted the city and raped all the women, young and old. Almost all the young ones became pregnant. I was very ill, but the Russians made me well. Then with Michael Matsas [author's uncle], the two Matsas brothers who are in Israel, and Samuel Hatzopoulos and Kohen Fef, we managed to go to the British zone of Berlin with the help of a Russian, and, from there, with a British convoy, we reached Brussels. On August 23, 1945, we arrived by plane in Athens.

My concentration camp number is 289165, and it is fading with the passage of time. My wife and son remained in Valona, Albania, in her sister's house. A United Nations relief agency (UNNRA) operated in Albania, and one of its officers brought me into contact with my wife, who asked the British and American officials still present in Albania to help her return to Greece. They did, and in December 1945, I was reunited with my wife and son in Florina.[257]

Dr. Errikos Levis continued his illustrious career as a medical officer of the Greek army. His son was saved because he was sent to attend a wedding in Albania. In 1988, Dr. Errikos Levis, a retired colonel, was the recipient of the National Resistance Award of Greece.

Many years after the war, Dr. Levis's son, Alekos, immigrated to the United States and became a university professor. He is known as Alex, and we have remained friends.

In one of the parties in the professor's house, I was talking with Errikos who called out to another guest on the other side of the room. When he came over, Errikos said, "I want to introduce you to the son of Mr. Leon Matsas who offered you

---

257 Letter from Dr. Errikos Levis to author, March 29, 1989.

and your mother shelter in the basement of the National Bank of Greece in Agrinion in 1940." The gentleman introduced himself as the Ambassador of Greece in the United States. It's a small world after all.

Dr. Errikos Levis.
(Photo courtesy of his son
Dr. Alex Levis.)

I visited Dr. Alex Levis in 2019. He was a professor at George Mason University, teaching mechanical engineering. He served as Chief Scientist of the US Air Force at the Pentagon from 2001-2004, a three-star equivalent civilian member of the Air Force. He has over 300 research publications and is currently working as a scientific consultant. I am very proud of him.

Another man I am very proud of is Dr. Mimis Cohen, Professor and head of the department of plastic surgery in the medical school of the University of Illinois. He wrote books on plastic surgery, and he is internationally known. He is the son of Dr. Nissim Cohen, first cousin of my mother. During the Greek-Italian war of 1940-1941, Dr. Nissim Cohen was director of the second surgical hospital in the mountains of Albania.

On one occasion, Dr. Nissim Cohen and his orderly were in a Greek village, and they needed a place to stay for the night. His orderly, a street-wise young man, looked for the most impressive house and asked the owner for hospitality. The owner very nervously told him, "My wife is giving birth, the midwife does not know what she is doing, and you want to sleep here?" The orderly said, "My doctor is the best obstetrician of Athens." They were welcomed. Dr. Cohen who still remembered what he had learned as a medical student about

II. Memoirs of Resistance Fighters

delivering babies, had no choice. Two little girls were delivered, and the happy father gave to Dr. Cohen the honor of naming his daughters. The names are Eleftheria and Niki - Liberty and Victory.

Dr. Nissim Cohen.
(Photo courtesy of his son Dr. Mimis Cohen.)

With Gun in Hand

Joseph Jacob Salias from Volos was a pharmacist who owned an enterprise on Pavlos Melas Street, dealing in pharmaceuticals. In 1941, the Germans confiscated all his merchandise. He recalls:

> In July 1942, I happened to be in Thessaloniki and witnessed the barbarous events of July 11. I was deeply shocked and decided to join the partisans. I found a hiding place for my mother in a village. My sister, who was a Red Cross volunteer, became a partisan nurse. We joined the 54th ELAS regiment. There were other Jews there, and their numbers increased after the fall of Mussolini in September 1943. Our division fought in the Pilion Mountains and in Agrafa. We sabotaged the railroad line connecting Thessaloniki with Athens. This was a vital German supply line. Many Jews distinguished themselves. I remember the liaison

agent, Boby Samuel Kohen, who was only 14, and Leon and Eli Sakis, Yeshua and Menachem Kohen, Jack Nissan and others.[258]

The Deportation as Seen by a Communist Leader

In 1942, there were 150 Jews in Thessaloniki who were members of the Communist Party. In spite of a lack of leaders like Benarojia, the workers had an excellent reputation for never crossing picket lines or breaking a strike. Women tobacco factory workers were known for their aggressive participation in demonstrations.

The Communist Party attempted to persuade the Jews to react to the German measures with protests and demonstrations, a collective refusal to wear the yellow star, and the rejection of any offer to work as Jewish policemen. Unfortunately, all German regulations were accepted as the lesser of two evils. Later on, when the deportations started, although nobody knew their final destination, the Communist Party made the following proposals:

- Not to sell at very low prices any assets and furniture, but place them for safekeeping with members of the organization.
- Disperse Jews as individuals and families in different areas where they would be safe.
- Entrust all children to families located outside of Thessaloniki.

None of the above efforts were successful. We finally instructed their party organization to inquire how many members of the party wanted to go to the mountains as guerrillas. Approximately 75 to eighty persons declared their willingness to go. We divided them into three groups. One night the first group, accompanied by guides, began their march. They had covered a great distance until it somehow became known to the entire group that all the Jews had been collected

---

[258] "With Gun in Hand," Miriam Novitch, *Le Passage des Barbares*, (published by Nea Synora (A. Livani), 1985), 94.

in a camp surrounded by barbed wire near the railroad station. The column came to a virtual stop. They did not wait to think too much about it. They decided to go back to their people, declaring, "We know that nothing good will come of that, but we feel that our duty is to be with our families, no matter what happens to all of us." So, with the exception of five or six who did not have any family, all the rest returned to go inside the barbed wire camp. Did any of them escape death? Who knows?[259]

Who Was the Real Thief?

Saltiel Cattegno recounts:

I lived in Thessaloniki with my mother and brother. We were in the paper products wholesale business. To avoid German confiscation, we sold our store fictitiously to a Christian friend. We thought we could still be in business, operating from a back room of the store, serving some of our old customers. One day our friend did not allow us to enter "his" store anymore. To whom could we complain? One night I burglarized my own shop and stole enough merchandise so that I could become a street vendor.

In February 1943, my brother and I decided to escape from the ghetto, but how could we abandon our mother? Courageous neighbors of ours promised to take care of our mother, and so we began making plans. A friend promised to find Italian uniforms for us, but he was unsuccessful. We negotiated with a boatman who would take us to safety, but he demanded an exorbitant amount of money, and we were practically broke. Later we learned that this boatman pocketed the money and delivered his customers to the Germans.

Unfortunately, we thought too late about escape from Thessaloniki. The resistance movement in

---

[259] "The Deportations as Seen by a Communist Leader," Markos Vafiadis, *Apomnimonevmata* ("Diaries," Athens, 1985), 88-89.

Macedonia was starting to get organized around the time of the deportation. Finally, a friend, Raoul Frances, established contact with the resistance. We were now 15 young Jews eager to go. We agreed to meet in a valley far away from the city. One evening at 5:00 p.m. we left the ghetto, one after the other, and late at night we met at the designated point.

An old man, accompanied by a 12-year-old boy, waited for us. "We have a long way to go," the old man said. We marched during the entire night and crossed the Galikos river to avoid a nearby German patrol. We marched for four nights. During the day we hid in the bushes. Other men, including Jews, joined us as we were going on. Ultimately, we became 35 men. We had very little food and suffered terribly from thirst. Raoul Mano decided to enter a nearby village and buy four bottles of wine. After we drank the wine, we filled the bottles with water whenever we could. Finally, we arrived at the Paikos, where we found the partisan camp. Conditions were primitive and the supplies meager. Weapons were very few and very old. There were 300 guerrillas, among them 65 Jews. Suddenly we were told that the Germans were approaching. We started our retreat in very difficult terrain. We again lacked provisions, especially water. The Germans distributed leaflets promising amnesty to all partisans who would surrender to them. Some young men, totally exhausted from the retreat, allowed themselves to be captured. The Germans executed them.

Soon we saw our first modern weapons, parachuted to us by the British Royal Air Force. My brother, an accountant by profession, became responsible for the distribution of the arms. Every week new parachute drops were made by the British. We also received gold coins, which were used to buy provisions from the peasants. I joined a sabotage group. Our targets were railroads and bridges. The peasants helped us, and in spite of their poverty they refused payment for what they gave us. I remember that among the partisans two young Jewish men, Dick Benveniste and Jacques

Caton, were distinguished for their courage in combat.[260]

A Fallen Partisan

Samuel Askenazi was a sergeant with the Greek forces fighting on the Albanian frontier. He fought with such extraordinary bravery, especially in the battle of Klissouri, that he received a battlefield promotion to second lieutenant. He was also supposed to receive a decoration, but the intervening retreat and capitulation prevented that.

As soon as the Germans started their anti-Jewish measures, Askenazi went to the mountains and joined the partisans of ELAS. He became commander of the 10th company of the 54th regiment and took part in many battles. In Kakavo of Pilion, he fell during an attack on a German unit.[261]

Where Do You Go, Friend?

Armando Aaron, president of the Jewish community of Corfu in 1976, a well-educated, intelligent and dynamic man, relates:

In September 1943, Italy capitulated, but the Italian garrison of Corfu refused to surrender to the Germans. On the night of September 13 or 14, the Germans bombarded Corfu in force with high explosives and incendiary bombs. The Jewish neighborhood was one of those to receive the worse blows. Many houses were destroyed, including the synagogues Apuliano and Nuovo, which were burned to the ground. My 19-year-old brother David was one of the many victims of this merciless air raid. Another air raid victim was my close friend Solomon Hatjopoulos, whose wife Esther emigrated to the United States after the war. Once the Germans occupied Corfu, they

---

260 "Who Was the Real Thief?" Novitch, op. cit., 64, February 1959.
261 "A Fallen Partisan," *Israelitiko Vima*, 2/15/46.

terrorized the population into submission. Demobilized Italian soldiers warned many Jews to hide in the mountains (but nobody followed their advice).

The defeatist attitude of the community leaders did not help matters at all. Among the 2,000 members of our community, there were no more than fifty to sixty people who escaped arrest. If the arrest had taken place two or three days before the Normandy landings, rather than three days after D-Day, many more people would have tried to escape.

On June 9, 1944, almost no one believed that the Germans were going to deport us. My family and I were arrested under pitiful conditions. We were enclosed in the old fortress for five days. The attitude of the local Greek police was not that of Greek patriots, while the behavior of the Christian population in general was not one to be proud of. Our shops and houses were systematically looted, first by the Germans and later by the local population, who took over the buildings.

Our community went on its way toward Auschwitz without money, jewelry, soap or water. Only at the very last minute were local Red Cross officials able to give us some food. On our way to Lefkas many of the sick, the children and pregnant women succumbed to the unhealthy conditions to which they were subjected. In Lefkas we were placed in the square of the city, which is located by the sea. In spite of the terror the Germans inspired, the people of Lefkas tried to help us during the day we spent on their island. They gave us food and medicines in small quantities. They threw cigarettes to us. One priest approached a prisoner, Jules Yohana, and offered him a cigarette. A German guard who saw the gesture beat the priest unmercifully, and then asked our brother to kneel. The German took out his pistol and shot Yohana in the neck. I understood we were not simply being relocated to another city. Our personal hygiene had been neglected for so long that the situation was desperate. The Germans gave us permission to bathe in the sea. Two young men took advantage of this mass swimming, and they were able to swim underwater for a great distance and escape. One of them, Nissim Moustakis, is now in Israel. The

II. Memoirs of Resistance Fighters

other one, David Balestas, died in Athens a few years ago.

In Patras we were kept for a day, guarded by Greek soldiers who belonged to the Security Battalions. In the evening we were ordered into the street to get ready for departure. While I was in line, I saw a friend of mine from Corfu, who then lived in Patras. He happened to be passing by, and he also recognized me. The Greek guard gave us permission to speak to one another, and so I found myself standing a few centimeters away from my line. At this point the German guards arrived to take us away. My friend instantly disappeared. Within a few seconds I realized that the German guard who was standing next to me could kill me the same way Yohana had been killed, because I was not in line. Rather than subject my poor parents, who had already lost a son to a trauma like this, I preferred to move forward like a blind man, without knowing where I was going.

There was a barbershop nearby operated by a 16-year-old boy who had recently replaced his deceased father. He was outside his shop and observed our suffering. As I passed by, he approached me and in a kind voice asked, "Where do you go, friend? The Germans have blocked the whole area with traitors and police dogs. If they capture you, they will kill you and your relatives and possibly others among your coreligionists. All this because of you! Come into my shop. I will shave you, and you will wash yourself because you smell bad. Tonight, you can stay in my home. Tomorrow morning, I will show you the way to partisan territory. The only satisfaction I will have will be the knowledge that I saved a man from the German claws. I don't want anything else." I did exactly what he told me. This is how I escaped. It was against my will because I would have never left my parents and my two brothers on my own. I joined the partisan units of ELAS in Peloponnesus and took part in many attacks against the Germans. I maintained friendly relations with my savior, who continues working on St. Andreas Street in Patras. He is a humble man who has asked me never to give any publicity to his good deed. I have been respecting his wish for 32 years, and for this reason I don't mention my benefactor's name.[262] My parents and one of my brothers died in captivity. Markos, my other brother who was 19 survived the camps, but he was not lucky enough to return to Greece. In August 1945, while on his way home, he died in an automobile accident.[263]

When I visited Corfu in 1976, I went to the synagogue, which was well kept by an old man who had survived Auschwitz. This same day happened to be the Day of Remembrance for the Greek Jews who died during the Second World War, as well as the anniversary of the Jewish uprising in Warsaw. The local radio station broadcasted an eloquent speech written for the occasion by Armando Aaron, whose life had been shaken suddenly by the events of June 1944.

The Wounded Hero

Benjamin Negrin was one of the first men to become a partisan in Thessaly. His heroism and his leadership soon made him a platoon commander of the 1/38 regiment of ELAS.

When the Jews were deported in March 1944, he was in Mouzaki in Thessaly. In April, Negrin led his men against well-entrenched German troops. He was the first to pass the barbed wire and jump into the German trenches. He received seven wounds. The victorious guerrillas evacuated him to a mountain partisan hospital, where he could not wait until he recovered and returned to his unit. From then on he became known as the legendary "Maios" of his regiment. He survived the war, but the hardships of life in the mountains and especially his wounds soon exacted their toll. In autumn of 1945 Benjamin died following a minor illness.[264]

---

[262] Mark Mazower identifies George Mitsialis as the man who saved Armando Aaron. *Inside Hitler's Greece*, 1993, 255.

[263] "Where Do You Go, Friend?" letter from Armando Aaron to author, 6/10/76

[264] "The Wounded Hero," *Israelitiko Vima,* 2/15/46.

II. Memoirs of Resistance Fighters

The Saboteur

Jack Kostis was a law student and an aspiring novelist when the Germans occupied Athens. He became a member of the resistance organization Apollon, which was active in sabotage activities. He recalls:

> In Keratsini, we sank the German troop carrier B103. In front of the customs office in Piraeus, we sank the auxiliary vessel *Cyclops;* in another action, the *Ardenas,* which I remember had two chimneys, while another one was the *Orion,* a cargo vessel like the K273 which we also sunk. *Taxiarhis* was a tugboat we sent to the bottom. In the case of the *Santa Fe,* the saboteur was arrested when he placed the time bomb. He was executed. The second-in-command of our group, Nikos Adam, was also arrested and executed. I remained in my post as instructed and managed to save the remaining members of our organization from arrest. This insistence on saving others did not help me, however; soon the Germans arrived and arrested me. They took me to the Gestapo office in Piraeus, where I was severely beaten, but I managed to escape and go into hiding.

The Greek newpaper *Ta Nea* and the magazine *Romantzo* also praised the "assistance of a daring young Jewish man, Jacques Kostis" in the above sabotage operations.[265]

A Resistance Leader

Baruch Schibi, the journalist who became an EAM leader in Athens, played an important role in saving the majority of the Athenian Jews by removing Rabbi Elia Barzilai to the mountains. Twice, German agents discovered his Athens hideout and, under the pretense of searching, they ransacked

---

[265] "The Saboteur," *Ta Nea,* Athens, 6/25/46; *"Romantzo,"* Athens, 11/15/63; letter from Jacques Kostis to author, 6/10/76.

everything. This is how Schibi describes his activities as a partisan of ELAS:

> With the help of influential friends, I was able to force the suspension of the publication of an economic weekly journal which used to present anti-Semitic articles. I agreed with the general secretary of EAM, Hatzi, to produce a special edition of our clandestine newspaper, *Eleftheri Ellada,* on the occasion of the persecution of the Jews of Thessaloniki. Although all the material for this special issue was prepared, the project did not materialize because of the opposition of certain Athenian Jews, who were afraid the publication would attract and direct the German attention toward the Jewish community of Athens.
>
> In December 1943, I visited the newly appointed representatives of the Jewish community, and in the name of EAM I asked them to abandon their posts and disappear. They did not follow my advice.
>
> I continued my underground activities in Peloponnesus. In April 1944 the Germans sent six columns against us and surrounded us from all sides. I was in charge of intelligence and I joined in the preparation of the operational plans for the famous battle of Glogova, in which one German column composed of about 700 men was destroyed. Following this, the other columns were forced to retreat hastily in order to avoid becoming prisoners of the partisans.
>
> Many interesting events took place during that period. One of them is the following: It was February 1944. Everything was covered with snow. I was supposed to go from southern Mantinia to northern Mantinia on some business for the resistance. I was given an escort to accompany me from Nestani to another village nearby, where another escort would take me until I arrived in Lagadia, where the EAM Gortynia headquarters was located. The first escort was a Bulgarian—a former Bulgarian army sergeant who was taken prisoner by the English-French expeditionary forces during World War I. He was transferred to Peloponnesus 27 years before I met him. He was the only Bulgarian in southern Greece. His

religion was Greek Orthodox, and it was easy for him to marry a local girl. He was an official of the local church and possessed land and cows. He was a happy man.

On our way we came close to a water mill. My Bulgarian escort said something in Turkish to an old man who was there. I asked the old man in Turkish where he learned the language. "I am a Turk," he replied. "I lived in Monastiri. During World War I the city was evacuated. A Greek pharmacist who was my neighbor asked me to come to Greece. I have been in Peloponnesus ever since. Because of my Moslem religion, they did not give me a woman, and so I remained a bachelor." The Turk invited us inside the mill to warm ourselves. Inside the mill we met the owner, a young Greek. I realized how unusual it was to find four people with our diverse backgrounds in a primitive mill lost in a forest on a remote, snow-capped mountain: a Greek, a Turk, a Bulgarian and a Jew.[266]

A Partisan of EDES Treats Wounded Prisoners

Dr. Michel Negrin, my father's first cousin, remembers:

I graduated from the medical school of Athens just before the Greek-Italian war, and I served in the Greek Medical Corps until the time of the surrender. The winter of 1940-41 was marked by starvation for the population of Athens. I thought that the best way to avoid starvation was to go to a rich village which did not have a physician. Together with my widowed mother, Mazalto Negrin (sister-in-law of the author's grandmother Sarina), we left Athens. We went to the village of Agia, located four miles from the city Parga in Epirus.

I was a young, dedicated doctor, and it did not take long before I gained the respect and affection of the

---

[266] "A Resistance Leader," letter to the author from Baruch Schibi, 8/10/75.

The Illusion of Safety

population of the area. The villagers of Agia and other nearby villages were Christians who spoke Albanian. In the north there were villages like Peridica, Mararakia, etc., whose population was Moslem, also speaking Albanian. They were called *tsamides,* and they hated the Christians. They collaborated openly with the Germans, who armed them and used them as auxiliary units which terrorized the countryside. They burned and looted many Christian villages. Since I was the only physician of the area, I was called to treat the *tsamides* as well, and I saw patients in many of their villages, especially Peridica.

In October 1943, the Gestapo of Ioannina requested the Greek police of Parga to inform them as to whether there were any Jews residing in their jurisdiction and to report their names and addresses. The commander of the Greek police, in collusion with the mayor of Agia, gave a negative reply to the Germans. They were aware of the danger and the penalties that would be imposed on them in case the secret was exposed to the Germans. They felt that my presence as a doctor was indispensable, and they took their chances. I was told nothing, because they were afraid that I would leave if I knew about the German request. I continued treating patients, receiving my fees in agricultural produce then selling the products for gold sovereigns. The Greek occupation currency was totally useless by that time. But my success soon brought problems.

There were two priests in the village. One, Papa-Vangelis, was a kind man; the other, Papa-Kosmas, a mean and dishonest person. He knew I had gold, and he decided to blackmail me. One morning I was visited by his son, who was a known criminal on parole, and he told me that he had a letter in his possession incriminating me. If I did not want the Germans to see that letter, I should give him fifty gold sovereigns. I refused and informed the mayor of the village of the incident. The news of the attempted blackmail spread like wildfire. The reaction was swift and surprising. The people swore and cursed the priest and his family, and they threatened to burn his house if his son harmed me in any way. In addition, nobody continued

II. Memoirs of Resistance Fighters

to attend services at the church when Papa-Kosmas officiated. Armed villagers followed the son to prevent him from contacting the Germans, while another armed villager slept in our house to protect us at night. When I declared that for my safety and also for the safety of the village I should leave, pandemonium took place.

The enmity demonstrated against Papa-Kosmas can be described only in a theatrical scenario. The son was eventually executed by the partisans. The people unanimously insisted that I should stay and that nobody would dare disturb me.

Early in 1944, the Germans launched a search and destroy mission in our area. They were in hot pursuit of a large partisan unit, and I heard machinegun fire before I understood that the Germans were in the village.

My mother was afraid, and she cried as I was confronted by a German soldier who escorted me to his officer. There were many Germans and also many armed *tsamides,* who brought dozens of horses with them. They were sure the Germans were going to burn the village, and they were prepared for looting. The German commander interrogated the mayor of the village, who was pale and terrified. The mayor talked in Greek to a *tsami,* who translated in Italian to a German, who then spoke to his commanding officer. I summoned all my self-discipline and, with courage approached the German officer. I greeted him and asked him if he knew French. He did, and so I was immediately appointed as his interpreter. Up to that point, the *tsami* interpreter had accused the village of Agia of aiding the EDES partisans. He hoped the Germans would destroy the village in retaliation. I attempted to persuade the officer that the accusation was untrue. I won his sympathy, and he believed me when I declared it was not true that the partisans passed through the village the previous night. Actually, the partisans had been in the village the previous night, but I was not aware of it.

We went to the main square, where I saw all the men of the village had been placed in front of a heavy machinegun manned by German soldiers. The officer gave the order to release all the hostages. At that moment I knew I was the hero of the day. My happiness did not last long. I overheard a *tsami* collaborator speaking in Albanian: "Isn't the doctor a Jew?" he asked. I knew that the Germans had expelled the Jews of Germany and, I was in fear and agony during the remaining hours until the Germans left the village. Only then did the villagers express their appreciation for my intervention.

Since my mother and I were the only Jews in Agia, and in total isolation from the Jewish community of Ioannina or any other, I did not know about the German order commanding the registration of the Jews, or about any anti-Jewish German activities in Greece. I learned about the arrest and deportation of the Jews of Ioannina a long time after it took place. I was sitting in the coffee shop in the main square of the village when I overheard a stranger talking about the way the Jews had been arrested in Ioannina. He obviously did not know me and described in detail what took place. From the moment I heard the bad news, I was unable to enjoy a moment of peace. I did not feel insecure in the village, but I wanted to contribute to the fight against the Germans. The opportunity arrived in a few days. The partisans asked for volunteers, and I was among the first who joined them.

One battle I remember took place near Paramithia on the Menina position. After I finished my treatment of wounded partisans assigned to me, I treated ten wounded German prisoners. When they were able to travel, they were transferred to a remote harbor, where a British submarine approached and took them on board. I admit that, at that time, though my duty as a physician was to treat them and I did, my inner wish was to see them dead. My first instinctive thought was to poison them. Then I thought about letting them die from their wounds, which were serious. But I am glad now that my Hippocratic oath prevailed. In Menina a plaque commemorates this battle between the EDES partisans of General Zervas and the Germans. The scars of this battle are still evident in the buildings of the village today after 32 years.

My mother and I survived the war and the Holocaust; and now I am an ophthalmologist and a happy family man in Athens. My survival was purely accidental, and it was mainly due to the lack of food. As a Jew, I knew enough to be afraid of the Germans. I never heard of German death camps, however, until the war was over.[267]

The Two Davids

David Kohen, son of Michael, came from Preveza, and David Russo came from Athens. In September 1943, when whole caravans of Jews were sent by the resistance to "free Greece," two 19-year-olds, both named David, were among them. The headquarters of the Y/34 independent battalion of ELAS under Nikiforo Papazissi were in Koura of Attica. They joined this unit of ELAS, and it wasn't long before they saw action during the three-day battle of Dervenohori. From that time on they participated in many ambushes and attacks against the tyrants of their people.

They were volunteers for every hazardous mission. In the battles which took place in Sterea Hellas, they were in the company of Kallia. On January 5, 1944, they were in Agia Triada Koloskopis with thirty fighters. The Germans were waiting in their white camouflage capes. They ambushed the partisans. The two Davids and their comrades, after a brief skirmish, remained immobile on the white snow.[268]

A Partisan Leader

Lazarus Azaria, a specialist in agriculture, was employed in 1942-43 by the Bank of Agriculture in Karditsa, Thessaly. When the Germans commenced their anti-Jewish activities, he joined the local resistance branch of ETA. He improved ETA

---

267 "A Partisan of EDES," Dr. Michel Negrin, letter to author, 5/20/76.
268 "The Two Davids," Nora Levin, *The Holocaust,* 520

and made it an effective instrument for collecting and distributing needed provisions to the partisan units of ELAS. He was elevated to the post of chief of ETA in Thessaly and, in essence, of all Greece, since Thessaly is the greatest producer of agricultural goods in the country. Because of his activities on behalf of the resistance, he was called a "communist butcher" and was condemned to death by the Greek government immediately after the liberation of Greece.[269]

Fallen Resistance Fighters

Marco Alberto Carasso was born in Thessaloniki in 1922. When Greece was enslaved by the Germans, he did not accept defeat like so many men of his age. He was a student at the University of Thessaloniki majoring in physics and mathematics. Before too long, Marco became one of the resistance leaders among the university students. His father was executed in January 1943 while imprisoned in the Pavlos Melas prison. When a friend shook Marco's hand, expressing his sorrow over the loss of his father, Marco replied, "We are going to vindicate him." He kept his word.

In March 1943, Marco took part in the battle fought by the 16th regiment against the Italians and the *Comitatzides* (Greeks in the service of the Germans) near Kastoria. Marco fought so bravely and demonstrated such great leadership that he was sent to the officer's school of ELAS. After a few months he returned as a platoon leader. His men loved him. In the battle of Hassion he fought the Germans with passion, and, when the order for retreat was given, he was the last to withdraw. On May 6, 1944, Marco was one of the partisan leaders who defeated the SS battalion on the southern slope of Mt. Olympus, saving the Jews of Larissa there.

Marco showed the same bravery and determination in many other battles, and especially in the very important one of Palatitsia. During the month of June, battles for food were raging all over Thessaly. The Germans tried to prevent ELAS from collecting wheat, corn, etc. The partisans fought the Germans continuously while the villagers, under the protection

---

[269] "A Partisan Leader," letter to author from Moissis Sakis, 6/20/77.

II. Memoirs of Resistance Fighters

of the partisans, harvested their wheat. The battle which glorified Marco and placed his name among resistance heroes was the attack against a German train in Mouharem Han Edessa on July 23, 1944. Once the engine was blown up and the train stopped, Marco was the first to climb on board with gun in hand, shooting the Germans. In the hand-to-hand combat that followed, Marco fell dead. His whole battalion mourned the loss of a brave comrade and an avenger of his people.[270]

Elias Sam Nissim was a Greek soldier stationed on the Bulgarian frontier. In April 1941 he took part in the battles of Rupel against the invading Germans. When it became evident to him that the Germans did not have good intentions toward the Jews, he joined those who were fighting the occupier day and night. He became a partisan. Elias operated a mortar, and in the battles that took place in the Mt. Olympus area he was cited for gallantry. He fought bravely until his last shell. Sometime later, he took part in the battles near Grevena, although he was sick. He then was wounded and transferred to the partisan hospital in Pentalofo, where he died as a result of his injuries. His last words were: "Long live freedom! Death to fascism!"[271]

Abraam Joseph Bourla, a young man of 18 from Thessaloniki, was among the first who went to the mountains to form the resistance units. He bravely handled his heavy machine gun. In January 1944, during a battle against Germans, Bulgarians and Greek collaborators, he was wounded in his arm and leg. After four months he was ready to fight again. In September 1944, Bourla was part of an ELAS unit waiting to ambush a withdrawing German convoy on the road leading from Veria to Thessaloniki. The ambush location was betrayed to the Germans, who attacked the partisans with tanks and heavy weapons. Bourla fell next to his weapon. In front of him, many dead and wounded Germans lay on the ground as proof of Bourla's heroism and self-sacrifice.[272]

---

[270] "Fallen Resistance Fighters," *Israelitiko Vima,* 5/31/46.
[271] *Israelitiko Vima*, Thessaloniki, 8/3/46.
[272] *Israelitiko Vima*, Thessaloniki, 12/28/45.

Daniel Carasso of Randallstown, Maryland, relates:

Charles Carasso, age 22, was a sailor in the Greek navy. When the Greek armed forces were disbanded, he did not return home. He joined a resistance group. Between April 1941 and March 1943, he came only once to our Miaouli Street house in Thessaloniki. On that occasion he most probably came into the city for a clandestine mission. He came unannounced, late at night, and he slept in my bed while I slept on a sofa. Before sunrise he left without saying goodbye. I heard the noise of the door closing and I ran to the balcony. I saw Charles entering a civilian "gazozene" car (cars with a barrel in which logs were burned to produce energy), which came to pick him up. This was the last time I saw him. After the war, I met my brother's friend, Isaak Massot, who now lives in California and who served as a partisan with my brother in the same unit of ELAS. I asked him where my brother was, and in the beginning, he did not tell me the truth. Later he told me that Charles did not make it. Massot told me, "In 1944 a great battle took place between the Germans and our ELAS unit outside Larissa. Our unit was in the process of disengaging from the enemy and Charles, who handled a machinegun, was covering the withdrawal. He ferociously fought the attacking Germans, and he killed or wounded many Germans before an enemy soldier outflanked him and with a submachine volley hit his legs. He was captured and transferred to a German military hospital, where he was treated until he became well. That was one month after his rearguard action and arrest. He was condemned to death and hanged in the main square of Larissa."[273]

---

[273] Interview with Daniel Carasso, brother of Charles, October 1975.

II. Memoirs of Resistance Fighters

The Ambush

Ben Porath of Tel Aviv was a second lieutenant in the Greek army during the Greek-Italian war. After the armistice in April 1941, he returned to Thessaloniki, which was already occupied by the Germans. Prior to the promulgation of any anti-Jewish measures, the Germans, who already possessed lists of all Greek officers, arrested those of the Jewish faith and sent them to forced labor camps. Ben was not one of them. He explains:

> I was lucky to leave in time, and, with the help of my captain, I joined the resistance movement in Athens. Our group consisted of six men. One day while I was carrying 37 false identity cards for other people, I was followed by a German and a Greek collaborator. When we were in a narrow street, they ordered me, "Stop and put your hands up." Behind them were three Jewish resistance comrades of mine from Thessaloniki. They attacked them. I was free again. My two brothers and I decided to join the partisans in the mountains, and that is where we remained until the end of the war.[274]

A Stevedore Becomes a Partisan

David Aaron was born in Thessaloniki in 1915. His father was a stevedore in the port of Thessaloniki, and so was his grandfather. David was active in the Zionist movement, and when Italy attacked Greece he fought as a Greek soldier. When the Germans rounded him up with the other young Jews, he went into the truck on one side and climbed out the other. After this escape, he began to think of the future. He, with another five young Jews, found a contact man who promised to take them to a resistance unit. It did not take long before they realized he was actually going to surrender them to the Germans. They escaped and went into hiding in Thessaloniki.

One evening David met a man from Elassona who opened a loaf of bread that contained a booklet describing the aims of

---

[274] "The Ambush," Novitch, op. cit., 61.

ELAS. The following night David and his friends left Thessaloniki. Once they were out of the city, they removed their yellow stars and felt like free men again. They walked for three to four days before they reached a high mountain. In a cave there were partisans, with many young Jews from Thessaloniki among them. They were all exhausted from the long march but at the same time exhilarated by the experience. However, they did not have any time for relaxation. A message arrived informing the partisans that the Germans were coming. It was dark and rain was falling. The terrain was very difficult. Some partisans fell down a precipice and were killed. A 12-year-old boy guided them through the mountain trails to a dry riverbed and to safety. Fredzi's shoes were totally destroyed during the hike, and he had to use his pants to bandage his feet and thus improvise a new pair of shoes. One young boy named Moshe (who fell in Sinai in 1956) had come looking for his father, who was a partisan. In the meantime, he was assisting the doctor.

There were over 450 Jews from Thessaloniki in the ranks of ELAS. All partisans had pseudonyms. David's name was Keravnos, which means thunder. The partisans moved continuously while they ambushed the Germans whenever they could. For a period of three months David was attached to a British military mission where airplanes made regular parachute drops. In the middle of 1943, an Italian unit of 600 men attacked the partisans. Most of the Italians were captured, and, as prisoners, some of them helped David to store guns.

On another occasion a German raiding party attacked David's unit. There were 35 partisans, among them a brave young Jewish man called Carlo from Thessaloniki. Carlo had always said that he would fight until his last bullet and that with this last he would kill himself rather than fall into the hands of the Germans. In this battle Carlo did not hear the order to retreat nor see his comrades withdraw. He continued fighting until the Germans captured him. They moved him to the city of Kilkis. They tortured him and eventually tied him to the tail of a horse, which galloped until Carlo was dead.

David was at partisan headquarters when he heard that Lamia had been abandoned by the Germans. Greece was free! He decided to immigrate to Palestine and left on board *Haviva Raik,* named after the famed Palestinian parachutist. There

II. Memoirs of Resistance Fighters

David fought during the War of Independence in the ranks of the Irgun.[275]

Isaak Eliezer of Agrinion was active in EAM when, at the end of 1943, he was betrayed by a woman as the man responsible for food collection in the village of Kalyvia for the partisans. The Germans arrested him and transferred him to the prison of Agrinion, where they began to interrogate and torture him daily. Once the interrogation took place in the presence of the woman who had betrayed him. They used electricity and severe beatings as they asked him to name other members of EAM. He withstood all punishment without giving any names.

Apostolos Hatjopoulos, Isaak's friend, knowing that the Germans knew him only as Spiros Lazaridis, a Christian, approached Maria Dimadi, the interpreter for the German commander in Agrinion, and persuaded her to try to save him before the Germans found out his true identity. Maria, a true heroine of the resistance, was able to remove Isaak's file from the SS office and, since there was nothing on paper against him, persuaded the German commander to release him. After six months of imprisonment and torture, Eliezer was freed on April 12, 1944, thanks to Maria Dimadi. On that date almost all the Jews who were arrested on the Greek mainland on March 25 were already dead.[276]

Two Partisans in Love

Fani Florentin and Leon Matalon were deeply in love and engaged to be married. Leon decided to join the partisans of ELAS. He left for the mountains, but in three days he returned to Fani. "I can't live without you," he told her. They agreed to get married and then join the partisans together. The wedding took place in their house, and the following day they went to join ELAS. They suffered from hunger, lice, and bad weather while they were being chased by the Germans or ambushing them. Fani was the Red Cross nurse of her unit. During a

---

[275] "A Stevedore Becomes a Partisan," Yad Vashem, Oral History No. 03249, 1875/9.

[276] Philippas Geladopoulos, *Maria Dimadi* (Athens:Nestoras, 1982), p.83.

The Illusion of Safety

German raid she became sick with dysentery and could not be moved. Leon was allowed to stay with her while their unit was pursued up and down the mountains for 15 days. These two were left undisturbed in the village.

During another German raid, most of the unit managed to escape while Fani, a Christian girl and some men, including a Jew, went into hiding in the bushes. The Germans and their dogs searched all over. When one of the group sneezed, a German dog discovered them. The Jewish partisan took out his revolver and committed suicide, preferring to die rather than fall into the hands of the Germans. The others surrendered to the German soldiers. A Greek collaborator insisted that the two girls be hanged in the village square as an example to the people. The German commander overruled him and said, "I will take them to Thessaloniki, where they will be judged by a military tribunal." They were transferred to the prison of Pavlos Melas, where Fani was interrogated every day. She never disclosed the fact that she was a Jewess, nor did she give her real name and address. The interpreter was helpful and no harm was done to her. One day, when she was in the yard, someone called her by her real name. It was Jack, a Jewish prisoner, who used to be an employee of her father. She asked him not to tell anybody that she was Jewish. Jack was executed shortly before the liberation. Fani's female companion came a few days later to tell her the good news that her brother, who was a German collaborator, had obtained her release from prison. She came to tell her goodbye and ask if she wanted anything. Fani asked her to notify Dr. Doukidis, her father's friend who was also keeping their gold. Dr. Doukidis informed Stratos Paraskevaidis, her future brother-in-law (he married her sister Medi Florentin during the deportations in Thessaloniki). Stratos had connections and, with the gold sovereigns given him by Dr. Doukidis, bribed the Germans and freed Fani.

Meanwhile, back in the mountains, Fani's husband Leon was deeply depressed. It was believed that Fani had also committed suicide. The partisans, who knew how deeply Leon loved Fani, disarmed him and watched over him to prevent any foolish attempt at his life. When Thessaloniki became free, Leon entered the city and met Mr. Kohen, Fani's uncle, who told him the unbelievable news that his wife was alive and well, living in the Agia Triada neighborhood.[277]

The Prodigal Son

Samuel Kohen and his friend Abraam Svolis of Ioannina were a couple of young and adventurous 17-year-olds. It was October 1943. The arrival of the Germans and the boys' desire for some excitement made them go out of the city and try the new "sport" of being partisans. They took some necessary supplies with them and met Hrysafi, a partisan contact who led them to the headquarters of General Zervas, leader of EDES. Samuel remembers that while they waited for the company to return from their training exercises, they were offered lunch. It consisted of a watery soup flavored with oil and vinegar. They did not like its taste, so they opened their bag and took out some canned food to which they treated everybody present.

While they were enjoying their adventure, a prominent member of the Jewish community board, Sabetai Kabeli, was furious with the two young men who had not obeyed the German orders and in this way endangered the whole community. Kabeli spoke to Svolis's mother. She, just as easily as her son, left Ioannina and German-occupied territory and went to the mountains in search of her prodigal son. After a few days of moving from village to village and asking questions about where the partisans accepted new recruits, she confronted the two boys, who had just started preliminary training. She told them how the Germans were going to retaliate by killing members of their immediate families or of the community if they did not return immediately. She told them that their houses would be burned if they stayed with the partisans. The boys did not want to be responsible for such disasters. Their recruiting officer understood the situation and gave them permission to return to the city. Back in the city and the Jewish neighborhood, they discovered that everything Mrs. Svolis had said was totally false. The Germans never

---

[277] "Two Partisans in Love," story told to author by Mimi Assael, March 1976.

threatened any retaliation as a result of their departure, which was totally ignored even if noticed.

Three days later, Samuel Kohen and his friend Chaim Matsas left the city again and went to join the partisans. This second time they moved in the direction of Zitsa. They met left-wing partisans of ELAS who took them to the village of Korimadi. Within two days they were given weapons and swore allegiance to the aims of EAM-ELAS as regular fighters. They remained with their unit until the end of the war and participated in many battles against the Germans. Being a partisan did not mean fighting all the time. Samuel liked to play the bouzouki, and when he went to the mountains he took with him his favorite instrument. On many occasions he played it and sang, entertaining his companions around the campfire. Many times, after the Jews were arrested, he thought of the hundreds of young men and women who could have been free with him. If only the leaders of the Jewish community were better, or if only the Jews knew something of the German plans. He also thought of his friend Abraam Svolis, whose mother came to the mountains of Pindus searching for him with a false sense of maternal love. What he did not know until the end of the war was that Abraam, although arrested with his family, escaped from the Larissa camp and also joined the partisans.[278]

My Friend ... The Chief of Police

Joseph Matsas was a student of ancient and modern Greek literature at the University of Thessaloniki when the Germans started their anti-Jewish measures. He recalls:

> If I were asked what I remember most vividly from my last year of university studies, I would reply without any hesitation and use one word: hunger.
>
> This is the reason that, as soon as I graduated in February 1942, I tried to find work in a village. I was employed as a teacher in the village of Megali Vrissi of

---

[278] "The Prodigal Son," interview with my cousin, Naoum Matsas, Ioannina, October 1975.

II. Memoirs of Resistance Fighters

Kilkis. I taught there for a year. The people, mainly refugees from Turkey, who settled in 1921, liked me very much, and I could have remained there for the duration of the war. However, I had in the meantime become friendly with the high school teachers of nearby Kilkis and also with the chief of police. This bureaucrat, as soon as he received an order issued by the German authorities to arrest all the Jews who lived in the countryside and deliver them to the Gestapo, remembered me. He immediately asked the mayor of the community of Megali Vrissi to surrender me to him. The mayor happened to be in the city for business. I will never forget this good man. I lived in his house, and he wanted to protect me. He replied to the policeman with a great quickness of spirit, "Now you ask for him? He left some time ago. He went to meet his people in Thessaloniki."

The mayor returned from Kilkis in a great state of excitement. He told me about his discussion with the chief of police, and he made arrangements for my transfer to a neighboring village where I used to give private lessons to some high school students. I did not stay there, however, for more than a month, because the village was "visited" quite often by German patrols. The villagers were very friendly and sheltered the family of Abraam Levi from Thessaloniki for the duration of the war. The secret that this family was Jewish was kept by the villagers so well that I did not learn about it until after the liberation. The Levis also were unaware of the fact that I was a Jew, although we lived for a while in the same village and knew each other.

I decided to become a partisan in March 1943. My enlistment in the units of ELAS in the mountains of Paico, near Giannitsa, coincided with the spring search-and-destroy missions of the Germans. Our life was filled with adventure. We were forced to change our mountain hideaway every week. We suffered from hunger, cold, rain and uninterrupted forced marches at night. We were continuously pursued by German units. Many times, we marched barefoot, and we had to endure legions of lice. Our terrible ordeals were more than compensated for by our strong fighting spirit and a realization that we were free people who fought the enemy enslaving our countrymen. In the summer of 1943, we were organized in regular military units. Mine was the 16th regiment of ELAS, and we continuously battled against the Germans. My unit had many Jews who were injured or killed during these actions. Many fought bravely and they received citations for their valiant exploits.

I remember the great heroism of a Jewish girl, Matilda, who now lives in America. She was trained as a nurse. She was thin and of small stature. Everyone thought she could not possibly endure all our suffering. In spite of what everyone thought, she demonstrated a greater degree of endurance than her husband Leon, or any other partisan of our unit. During our forced marches, when we stopped to relax for ten minutes and we fell on the ground like corpses, Matilda ran from one end of the column to the other, offering her services to everyone who needed her. I personally owe my life to Matilda, because she cared for me and treated my foot, which became ankylosed after a prolonged march. In spite of all our difficult moments, we, the Jewish partisans who fought the enemy, had the enormous satisfaction of vindicating the unjust loss of our people, and during the period of occupation we were proud that we never surrendered or submitted to the will of the Germans. We preserved our bodies and souls, but we paid for them with great sacrifices. For me, the happiest day of my life as a partisan was one day in May 1944. We were near southern Mt. Olympus, and we planned a successful ambush of a German SS battalion. We killed many Germans, and the remaining ran for their lives, abandoning a group of Jewish families they had captured a few hours before.

During my life as a partisan, I enormously enjoyed getting mail with the "partisan mail service." I exchanged correspondence with Anna Gani from Karditsa. The letters were transferred from one mountaintop to the next, and they took a long time to find their destination, but in our case, a casual friendship developed into something stronger. We

II. Memoirs of Resistance Fighters

married after the war. I owe gratitude to the same service because it brought me the news that my brother Solomon had escaped from the camp in Larissa, and that he was alive and well.[279]

Many heroic Jewish partisans of ELAS received great honors as the following "Order of the Day" demonstrates:

> PEEA, the Political Committee of National Resistance, in its decision of October 4, 1944 (Chapter 26) promotes for bravery the following comrades, officers, noncommissioned officers, and *andartes* to the rank mentioned for each man because they died in combat, bravely fighting the enemy. They demonstrated superb fighting ability, excellent spirit, determination, leadership qualities and wonderful spirit of self-sacrifice beyond the call of duty. X division ... 2.) Second Lieutenant of infantry, Marko Carasso, to the rank of First Lieutenant, the following *andartes* . . . 17.) Ovadia Deno . . . 36.) Vital Beraha ... to the rank of Sergeant Major.[280]

The Waldheim Story

Yeshua Matsas of Ioannina relates:

> As soon as I realized that the Germans planned to exile us, my brother Eliasaf and I decided to escape.
>
> We made our first attempt when we tried to leave our neighborhood, rather than go to Molos, where all the Jews were supposed to be going. A Greek policeman who knew us forced us to change direction and go to Molos. When the truck convoy stopped in the village of Perama, we both got out of the truck and Eliasaf, with the assistance of a shepherd, was able to escape. I also

---

279 "My Friend ... the Chief of Police," letter from Joseph Matsas to author 1/10/76.
280 *Acts and Decisions of PEEA*, 21.

escaped, but my Aunt Sarina[281], who was in another truck, called me as I was passing nearby, and this was noticed by a German. I was soon followed by a German in a motorcycle, who ordered me to go back to the convoy.

In Katara there was deep snow, and the cars had a hard time climbing in spite of the chains on their tires. I again jumped and tried to escape. A German saw me and was ready to shoot me, but an Italian fascist saved my life by talking the German out of pulling the trigger. The German was not satisfied before he hit me on the head with the butt of his gun. The Italian again helped me by bandaging my wound. I still have a scar above my right eyebrow.

In the camp at Larissa, I was among those who were ordered to transport a basket of jewelry and gold coins collected by the Germans from our people. When I delivered the gold, the officer in charge, a tall, thin man, hit me on the head. When I stared at him for a few seconds, he hit me again. I knew that I would never forget his skinny face.

I offered to work as a cook because I believed that this would give me more mobility and also knowledge of what was going on around the camp. I saw two men, Moshe Katsapa and Jacob Gerson, leaving. That gave me an idea. I persuaded my cousin Mihalis Valais to come with me, and I told my father that we were going to go. He helped us erase the word Jude from our identity cards, using flour as an eraser. Valais and I waited until the guard was not a member of the SS but an ordinary soldier of the Wehrmacht. We decided to pass in front of him and, if he suspected us, to attack him and then escape. God protected us, and the guard did not stop us.

On the road we took, between wheat fields and the airfield, we saw four men walking ahead of us. They noticed us and were afraid of us, while we were also

---

281 Sarina was the author's grandmother. She acted as a midwife, delivering babies for free for very poor women in Ioannina. We are told that she delivered a baby on the moving train on the way to Auschwitz.

II. Memoirs of Resistance Fighters

afraid of them. Soon we realized that they were Moshe Katsapas, Svolis and two other friends of ours who escaped before we did.

We entered a village and, since I was a member of EAM, I asked who the representatives of the resistance were. The people did not trust us and sent us to the house of the priest, who gave us something to eat. He also gave us a guide to escort us to the next village. Eventually we established contact with ELAS, and we all became partisans of the 3/40 regiment. We participated in many battles. One ambush I remember vividly took place outside the village of Peta near Arta. The Germans lost 23 men. Since they started attacking us with their artillery, we could not accept any wounded Germans or take any prisoners. We killed them all.

After the war, as we had lost all our family, Eliasaf and I decided to go to Israel. We settled in the Negev, in Beersheva. One day I saw a wartime picture of Kurt Waldheim in a newspaper; he wanted to be president of Austria. I immediately recognized the man who hit me in the Larissa camp. For ten days newsmen and television and radio reporters besieged our house in Beersheva because of the profound interest that this revelation produced.

Michael Tal of Zurich, Switzerland, heard my story about Waldheim and invited me to his office. Reporters from *Voldwahen* interviewed and photographed me. They took me in their office where they showed me a lineup of the Second World War photographs of German officers. I positively identified Kurt Waldheim as the tall, thin, limping officer who came with a seaplane to Lake Pamvotis in Ioannina prior to our deportation, and who hit me twice when I delivered the gold in the Larissa camp. They asked me if I was willing to confront Waldheim in person. I agreed, for I was eager to see this man again. Waldheim refused to have such a meeting. They gave me tickets to go to the United States with Michael Tal to be interviewed by CBS. Tal had a heart attack the night before the meeting with CBS was supposed to take place, which was just one day before the Austrian presidential elections were scheduled. My interview with its incriminating evidence broadcast on that day was supposed to influence the outcome of the election in Austria. President or not, I am convinced that Waldheim is a Nazi war criminal who should be brought to justice. I will never forgive him.[282]

The Jews of Chalkis

Sotiris Papastratis relates:

As soon as German troops arrived in Chalkis, the committee of EAM issued a proclamation asking the people of Euboea to give every assistance to their Jewish compatriots. Representatives of EAM proposed to the Jewish community the immediate departure of all the Jews for the free territories of Euboea. The community agreed, and the exodus started. Police commander Economides and others helped by providing the Jews with false identity cards. Only 18 Jews out of 325 were arrested. Simon Frankis, a handsome 25-year-old, was executed, together with Christians.

Leon Amar and Abram Fornis became partisans of ELAS. Everyone remembers Sazika of EPON, with her songs. We all remember the Jewish teacher Menty Moschovitz. She was captured by Major Bayer, who was tried as a war criminal after the war. When the Germans discovered she was Jewish, they removed her clothes, brought her onto a balcony facing the main square, pushed a wooden post into her genital organs and threw her down from the balcony to the square. Unfortunately, Greek traitors participated in this brutal murder.

Bishop Gregorios protected the scrolls and other religious items which the rabbi entrusted to him.

EAM assisted not only the Jews of Chalkis, but all Jews who wanted to go to the Middle East. A

---

[282] Interview with Yeshua Matsas, July 10, 1989.

II. Memoirs of Resistance Fighters

Palestinian Jew sent us about 100 pairs of military boots. One of the escaping Jews boasted that he had 200 sets of German playing cards with him! He was going to sell them in Smyrna. He did not know that EAM-ELAS made any form of gambling illegal. We had to burn them while he begged us, "Keep them for the organization!"

Many of the arriving Jews were extremely pale from hiding indoors for so many months. Some were absolutely poor; others obviously wealthy. The danger was the same for all. While a group of very poor Jews was waiting for the boat, a group of rich Jews arrived. One of them, Benzonana, proposed that they depart first, so that he could hire a boat in Smyrna which would engage in the transportation of Jews only! I explained to him that we didn't have food for the people, while the rich could buy food from the neighboring villages. People would have to wait perhaps 15 days until the boat returned. He and the poor people had a meeting in which he proposed to give them 100 gold sovereigns, so that the rich could embark first. The poor people refused. The son of Benzonana held a second meeting in which he surprised everyone by offering 200 gold sovereigns for the right to embark first. The poor people distributed the coins among themselves and rushed to the villages to buy food.

The next day the boat arrived, and it was larger than expected. I proposed that both groups, all fifty people, go on board immediately. The captain did not even turn off the engine as people were getting on board. Benzonana stood and tried to stop the poor group from getting into the boat, demanding the return of the gold coins! His son was begging him to forget it. The captain screamed, "Either you get in or I leave empty!"

A Jewish couple were arguing and pushing each other. I was told they were the parents of a 12-year-old boy. They had sent him to the village Ahladeri, and he had not yet returned. One of them had to stay behind. The husband pushed the wife to go on board, and the wife insisted that the husband should leave. I told them

I would take care of the boy and send him with the next boat, and that both of them should go on board. They refused. I begged the captain to delay a little: perhaps the boy would show up. He said impossible, and the boat started to move. The husband literally threw his wife on the boat. She tried to jump in the water while others restrained her. The boat was still in the horizon when the boy with supplies came down the hill. Father and son embraced as we all cried. They left with the next mission.

A few days later, we had another group of twenty Jews. We were all hungry. A terrible rain and thunderstorm made life miserable. A thunderbolt fell nearby and killed some sheep. The shepherd cannot be consoled. The Jews beg me to ask him for two dead sheep. Among the Jews is a veterinarian from Drama. He assures me that there is no fear, the animals are edible, with the exception, perhaps, of the intestinal organs. The shepherd, still crying, gave us two sheep, one for the Jews and one for the partisans. Many of the Jews who were weak from starvation became sick after eating the roasted sheep. At this point word came that the Germans were coming. Only a few guards were left behind with orders to leave if the Germans approach. We froze all night in the mountains. The Germans moved in the direction of Kimi. We returned to the little port. In two days, the boat arrived[283]

Meyer Levis from Trikala was a specialist in agriculture. He fought as an officer of ELAS. Upon liberation, because of his activities during the war, he was fired from his position as an employee of the Department of Agriculture. During the Greek civil war of 1944-49, he was drafted as a reserve officer, but he refused to enlist and fight against his wartime comrades. He was arrested, and a military tribunal condemned him to death. He was executed on May 5, 1949, at the age of 31.

---

283 Sotiris Papastratis, "The Jews of Chalkis," *Chronika,* December 1981, 9.

II. Memoirs of Resistance Fighters

Yitzhak Persky, father of Israeli Prime Minister Shimon Perez, was serving in the British forces fighting in Tobruk where he was captured by the Germans. He was transferred to Greece and, after his successful escape to the mountains, joined the partisans of ELAS. He continued fighting the Germans until liberation. In September 1982, he died in Israel.[284]

Jewish Partisans Who Fought Under Colonel Nikiforos

Colonel Dimitrios Dimitriou, or Nikiforos, as he was known during the war, was the first Greek career officer, a graduate of the Military Academy of Athens, to go to the mountains as a partisan of ELAS in July 1942. He is a Christian who remembers his Jewish comrades. He also remembers, in his autobiography, the heroic Jewish colonel, Mordechai Frizis, who had been his commander in Albania in 1940:

> David Broudo and Robert Mitrani escaped, as I was told by the partisan physician Manoli Aruh, from a slave labor camp and joined us. Broudo, at a time when ETA was not well organized, undertook the very dangerous work of providing ELAS headquarters with supplies. This was more dangerous than fighting. He moved in all the areas of central and eastern Sterea Ellada, between the dense nets of Italian and German garrisons, in order to find and send supplies to our mountain hideouts. His courage, intelligence and resourcefulness made him dear to the partisans and the people. In order to carry out his mission, he, with indescribable courage, crossed the German lines many times and often participated in the battles we fought.
> In October 1945, I met David Broudo again. He was persecuted and in hiding with his brother. He immediately invited me to stay in their house. They were the only ones of their large family who survived. For as long as I stayed in Thessaloniki, David affectionately stood by me. Since I did not have any

---

[284] Moissis Sakis, "Jews in the National Resistance," *Chronika*, October 1982, 10.

contact with my family in Lamia for a long time, I asked David to help me. He promptly agreed to travel to Lamia and Athens. This cost him dearly. In Levadia someone recognized him. He was arrested and tried. David suffered in Greek prisons for ten years.

Robert Mitranis was a medical student. Since we did not have any physicians, we placed him in charge of medical services in our headquarters. When other physicians arrived, Robert became the doctor of the first battalion. His devotion to his *synagonistes-* partisans was legendary. He demonstrated great initiative in finding medicines and other supplies he needed for his work. Yet he fought bravely on the front lines in our battles against the enemy. He was a fearless fighter. If anyone called him, he would interrupt his fighting and rush to the aid of the wounded. When he was not busy, he used to study medical texts. On January 5, 1944, he was killed while pursuing the German forces which had raided Kaloskopi. Thirty of his comrades fell into a German ambush, and they were all killed in deep snow, which covered all traces of the ambushing enemy. All thirty are still buried in a common tomb in Agia Triada.

With Robert are buried two more Jewish partisans: David and Benjamin, whose last names I never knew. A monument has recently been erected in the locality of their death. Their names are inscribed on the marble column, together with those of their comrades.

Dr. Albertos Kohen, or Vladimir, joined my unit, the V/34 battalion, at the end of September 1943. Many other Jews came to the mountains at that time. He came with Dr. Manoli Aruh, and they both organized our medical service in a superb manner. In the battle of Arahova, we captured a great quantity of material, and also great tents, which were used to establish mobile hospitals. In the battle of Dervenohori and all other battles that took place later, Albertos Kohen offered his lifesaving services to all partisans who were wounded and who all remember him with affection.

In October 1945, I met him again in his native Kastoria. Our common friend, an attorney named Krikis, told him that I was passing through his city. We

II. Memoirs of Resistance Fighters

all three met secretly at night, because I was being pursued by the police. When I was leaving, he gave me a great number of gold Napoleons, which his family had placed in a hiding place in their house. The Germans had deported his entire family, and none of them returned.

Later we met again in Thessaloniki, where he worked as a physician. I remained hidden in this city until the end of 1945. During this period, my wife became seriously ill. Albertos supported me like a brother. Not only did he treat my wife, but he provided us with medicines and food.

The quality of Kohen's and Aruh's medical services was so good that our unit became famous. Manolis offered medical care not only to the partisans, but to the people as well. In addition, he fought bravely in many battles. In 1944 he became the physician of the II Division.

Louis Kohen, or Kronos, and his brother Yitzchak, who was 16 years old and known as Kronakos or Little Kronos, escaped arrest in Xanthi where they lost their family. Yitzchak bravely fought in all the battles. His brother Louis was placed in the supply section of our unit, and he demonstrated great bravery, devotion to duty and an ability to overcome all obstacles in order to keep our unit well supplied with everything we needed. On occasion, we were able to offer assistance to other battalions. Anytime I said, "Krone, do you have such and such items?" he would smile and reply, "We will do something about it!" And he did!

In addition, Kohen took part in battles as a fighting man. In our circumstances, even wounded partisans had to fight. He was also valuable to us in dealing with the British officers of the Allied mission, and also German and Italian prisoners, because of his politeness, noble character and knowledge of foreign languages. Every partisan of our area remembers Kronos, who was wounded in the battle of Kakoutes in September 1944.

Other heroic partisans who served in my unit were Moris Yesouroum, Moshe Yomtov (or Malagias) and Salvator Bakolas. Another Jewish fighter I want to mention is Maccabee, whose real name is Ido Simsi, which I learned only in 1987. He played a leading role in the headquarters of the II Division of ELAS. He was a brave and conscientious fighter of the resistance.[285]

Jews in the Resistance

Leon Bourla of Thessaloniki and his four children became partisans of ELAS. (Possibly a unique phenomenon in ELAS.) They were Yolanda, Dora, Charles (who was wounded) and Nikos, who was killed just before the war ended.

Sixteen Jews of Thessaloniki fell in combat as partisans of ELAS. They were:

Abraam Baron
Vital Beraha
Nikos Bourla
Charles Caras
Charles Carasso
Elias Kohen
Stella Kohen
Simon Fraggis
Frizis
Sabas Hasson
Moissis Hasson
Roberto Mitrani
Deno Ovadia
Flora Perahia
Erikos Pipano
Serror

After the end of the Second World War, many of the Jews who fought the Germans were persecuted by those who collaborated with the Germans and had positions of power in Greece. Five former partisans were executed by firing squad:

Samuel Dentis age 18 from Chania

---

[285] Colonel Dimitrios Dimitriou, Ret. "Jewish Participation in the National Resistance," *Chronika*, January 1989.

II. Memoirs of Resistance Fighters

Chrysoula Felous age 20 from Trikala
Savvas Issis age 26 from Arta
Meyer Levis age 31 from Trikala
Moissis Yesoulas age 26 from Volos

Five were condemned to death, but their sentences were not carried out:

William Azar from Volos, imprisoned in Aegina.
Rena Azouz from Volos. She was released and married Mario Benarojia of the United States.
Helen Beza from Thessaloniki, imprisoned in Thessaloniki.
Aaron Ganis from Volos, imprisoned in Averof.
Matika Kabeli from Trikala, imprisoned in Averof.
Lazaros Azarias, the partisan of ELAS and leader of the food provisions for the partisans, was condemned to death, but he escaped arrest and went to Israel where he became the director of TNUVA (a food processing company). [His brother became the Dean of the dental school in Thessaloniki. His name was Dr. Hanikos Azarias.]

Seven men and women were condemned to life in prison. They were:

Jacqueline Beza, wife of Mario Bener, from Kavalla
Menahem Bension from Kavalla
Alfred Beza from Thessaloniki
Monika Beza from Thessaloniki
Leon Kohen from Volos[286]
Salvator Kohen of Volos, now in Haifa, Israel
Samuel Kohen from Volos

Six former resistance fighters were condemned to up to 20 years in prison. They were:

Iakov Barzilai
Benjamin Benveniste

---

[286] Moissis Sakis, *Chronika,* April 1986, 12.

Morris Benroubi
David Broudo
Vital Dasa
Solomon Kapetas

Thirteen other Jews were exiled to the island of Makronisos:

Raoul Amosnino from Thessaloniki
Moissis Bourlas from Thessaloniki
Zaharias Kohen from Volos
Iosif DeCastro from Chania
lbert Franies from Larissa
Elias Kapetas from Trikala
Salvator Minervos from Chania
Yonas Mionis from Agrinion
David Moissis
Salvator Ovadias from Thessaloniki
Joseph Taraboulous
Albertos Yahon from Thessaloniki
Stella Yahon from Thessaloniki

In that difficult postwar period, Rabbi Harold Goldfarb, who was the director of the American Joint Distribution Committee, lived in Athens. He was extremely helpful in assisting these persecuted people with packages and whatever they needed. With the assistance of a prominent Jewish lawyer, measures were taken to persuade the Greek government to release these Jewish prisoners. It was emphasized that if they did not go to the mountains, they would have been killed by the Germans. Five of them refused to sign declarations of remorse, denouncing EAM-ELAS; consequently, they had to serve their sentences.

A solution was found, however, and these five prisoners agreed to renounce their Greek citizenship and immigrate to Israel. In this way all 32 prisoners were released, and five of them went to Israel. They were Salvator Kohen, Menahem Bension, Helen Beza, Salvator Minervo, and Yonas Mionis.[287]

---

287 Moissis Sakis, *Chronika*, April 1986, 13.

II. Memoirs of Resistance Fighters

After the Second World War, Greece was the only European country where those who fought the Germans were executed, imprisoned, exiled, or fired from their jobs, while those who collaborated with the Germans, instead of being punished for their treason, became members of the new ruling class.

For me, the question remains: How could the Holocaust have happened? One response is given by Judy Montagu:

> The Holocaust was just the latest in a long chain of Jewish suffering and death resulting from persecutions stretching back through the centuries in so many places where Jews have tried to live their lives in peace. One book that brought this grim reality home is called *The Foot of Pride*. In it, English clergyman Malcolm V. Hay chronicles 1,900 years of almost unrelenting Christian demonization of Jews. It is heartbreaking to read about the careful tending of the toxic soil in which the seeds of genocide developed.[288]

The same question is answered by Professor Daniel Goldhagen, in his book *Hitler's Willing Executioners*:

> [The answer can be found] in widespread, profound, and virulent anti-Semitism based on the traditional religious enmity to Jews. The German Protestant and Catholic churches, their bishops, and their theologians watched the suffering that the Germans inflicted on the Jews in silence.[289]

For many centuries, the church taught hatred toward the Jews. In 1543, the great German theologian, Martin Luther gave this advice: "Set fire to their synagogues, confiscate their assets, give them tools and let them earn their bread with the sweat of their brow. [And] if any Christian shows pity for a Jew, he will burn in Hell!"

---

[288] Judy Montagu, "Where God Stood in the Shoah," *The International Jerusalem Post*, April 15, 2010, p 12.

[289] Daniel Jonah Goldhagen, *Hitler's Willing Executioners: Ordinary Germans and the Holocaust*, 1997.

I told this to two brothers, German Jews who survived three years of German concentration camps. They both exclaimed, "This is exactly what they did to us!"

This kind of teaching paved the road to the Holocaust. Hitler took advantage of this pre-existing anti-Semitism. Early in his career, Hitler wrote, "Anti-Semitism is a useful expedient. It is the most powerful weapon in my propaganda and of deadly efficiency."

In 1965, with the Second Vatican Council, which was initiated by Pope John XXIII, two key points were made:

1. What happened in His (Christ's) passion cannot be charged against all Jews, without distinction, then alive, nor against Jews today.

2. Although the Church is the new people of God, the Jews should not be represented as rejected by God or accursed, as if this followed from the Holy Scriptures. [290]

Unfortunately, this sentiment came much too late for the Jewish victims of the Holocaust.

In 2000, Pope Paul II said, "We cannot possibly not recognize the betrayal of the Gospels which brothers of ours committed especially in the second millennium."

Regarding the responses of the Christian clergy during the Second World War, the churches of Europe remained impotent and so did most of the churches of the United States of America. Pope Pius XII not only remained silent, but in the book, *The Battle for Rome*, he is presented as a "moral coward with deep fascist tendencies. In spite of his white robes, he had a black soul."[291] This man may soon become a saint by the Catholic Church! We await judgement of him until the secret Vatican archives are explored and evaluated. Unfortunately, this has been delayed because of the coronavirus pandemic in

---

290 http://w2.vatican.va/archive/hist_councils/ii_vatican_council/documents/vat-ii_decl_19651028_nostra-aetate_en.html

291 Robert Katz, *The Battle for Rome: The Germans, the Allies, the Partisans, and the Pope, September 1943-June 1944,* Deckle Edge, 2003.

II. Memoirs of Resistance Fighters

2020.[292] In the book *Hitler's Pope*, John Cornwell describes that Pope Pius XII gave his message of indifference not only by his silence, but also especially by his "Reichskonkordat" of 1933.[293] This was a treaty between the Holy See and Hitler's German Reich, which insured that the Nazis would rise unopposed to power. This treaty, by Hitler's own admission, sealed the fate of the Jews in Europe.

---

[292] https://www.washingtonpost.com/history/2020/04/29/vatican-pope-pius-records-holocaust/
[293] John Cornwell, *Hitler's Pope: The Secret History of Pius XII,* 2008.

Jewish ELAS partisans David Brudo and Loui Koen pose in front of a German aircraft shot down by partisan ground fire in Lokrida, Greece. September 1944. (© Collection of the Jewish Museum of Greece.)

Napoleon Zervas (center with beard), leader of the military wing of the EDES resistance group, with fellow officers. (Source: Revizionist via CC BY-SA 3.0.)

II. Memoirs of Resistance Fighters

The journalist Baruch Schibi, Resistance leader (EAM-ELAS) who organized the escape of Rabbi Barzilai to the mountains. (© Collection of the Jewish Museum of Greece.)

Joseph Matsas, ELAS partisan. (© Collection of the Jewish Museum of Greece.)

Dr. Manolis Arouh, as partisan doctor, 1944. (© Collection of the Jewish Museum of Greece.)

Loui Koen ("Kapetan Kronos"), ELAS officer. (© Collection of the Jewish Museum of Greece.)

My cousin, Eliasaf Matsas, was the first to escape captivity after the roundup and join the partisans of ELAS. (Family photo.)

Albertos Amon and Pepos Koen, Jewish partisans of ELAS.
(© Collection of the Jewish Museum of Greece.)

Allegra Felous-Kapeta, was a partisan with EAM during WWII. (© Collection of the Jewish Museum of Greece.)

Dr. Lazaros Eliezer of Arta. Partisan doctor of the right-wing forces of General Zervas of EDES. (© Collection of the Jewish Museum of Greece.)

II. Memoirs of Resistance Fighters

Salvator Bakolas, partisan of ELAS. He was a chemistry student at the University of Athens. Second from right. (© Collection of the Jewish Museum of Greece.)

Dr. Moissis Yessurum (1) and, next to him, Salvator Bakolas (2) are Greek-Jewish partisans of ELAS in 1943. Lakis Santas (3) with Manolis Glezos (not pictured) brought down the German flag in 1941 in a daring rock climbing of Acropolis. (© Collection of the Jewish Museum of Greece.)

Part III

AUTHOR'S MEMOIRS

The Author's Memoirs

Self-sufficiency is the greatest of all riches... the greatest fruit of self-sufficiency is freedom.

—Epicurus

I was born in 1930 in Ioannina, a picturesque city located on the shores of beautiful Lake Pamvotis, famous for its lovely island where colorful fishermen live. Ioannina's landscape is dominated by an impressive walled city and the Aslan Pasha mosque. The Jewish community of Ioannina lived in and around the walled city of Ali Pasha, in almost exclusively Jewish neighborhoods.

My mother's and especially my father's family were numerous, generous and very hospitable. My paternal grandfather, his brothers, and many of their children engaged in the production of cheese and wine, as their ancestors had done for many generations, in this same city. My grandfather, who was born in 1860, loved his work and was known for his philanthropic nature, both in the community and in the villages that provided him with milk and grapes.

He was a personal friend of Bishop Spyridon, who eventually became the archbishop of Greece. One time, Bishop Spyridon had to use his influence to get Grandfather out of prison. At a time when there was democracy in Greece, Grandfather found a pretty royal emblem on the street. He pinned it on his lapel, so he would give it to one of his children. A policeman arrested him, took him to the police basement, and attempted to beat Grandfather with a belt. Grandfather was proud and strong. He grabbed the belt and beat up the policeman, who was soon screaming for help. At the age of 83 and on the way to Auschwitz, my grandfather said, "If I knew all this, I would have killed many of them with my bare hands."

Many villagers owed their prosperity to my grandfather, who used to buy flocks of sheep for them. By selling

The Illusion of Safety

Grandfather the milk they produced, their interest-free loans were soon amortized.

My father related to us the following colorful story about his father, my grandfather Naoum:

It was the year 1911, and Ioannina was still occupied by the Ottoman Turks. A wealthy and influential Turkish official, landlord of the island, had repeatedly invited my Grandfather Naoum to join him for an outing on the lake. My grandfather was very busy turning milk into cheese and kept declining his invitations. When Naoum realized that the man had become angry and felt insulted, Grandfather told him, "If you bring a boat in front of my shop, I will come." A few days later, to the whole town's surprise, everyone gathered all along the way to see a sailboat, with its sails raised, on top of a wagon drawn by horses moving up the main street of Ioannina and stopping in front of Grandfather's shop. Grandfather took one of his eight children with him for this memorable weekend on the island. The nine-year-old child was my father - this was his first vacation.

My father chose to be different from his brothers and became an employee of the National Bank of Greece. Until the age of five, I felt very comfortable in this Jewish environment, surrounded by my very affectionate relatives. I was not aware that there were others different from us or who would consider us different from themselves. I am convinced now that my immediate family's chances of survival would have been very small if we had remained in Ioannina, where 91 percent of the Jews were lost.

We did not remain in Ioannina or Arta or Preveza because of my father's proud and independent spirit, which antagonized the established order in the bank and in the Jewish community. In Ioannina, he felt ashamed that there were 12 old Jewish beggars. He campaigned for the establishment of a home for the aged. The wealthy people of the community were indifferent and resented my father's interference. The main contributor was a man who had lived in the United States for a few years. He lived frugally and saved his money. His job consisted of collecting worms, which he sold to fishermen. The home for the aged was named "Yeshua v Rachel," after him and his wife. There were no more Jewish beggars in Ioannina.

The services in the synagogue were not orderly, and the Christians used to describe any disorder in a public gathering

III. Author's Memoirs

as *"havra* of Jews." Father became instrumental in establishing a choir in the synagogue. He also persuaded the community leaders to sponsor a promising poor Jewish boy, Joseph Matsas, to finish the university and ultimately become a rabbi. The rabbis of Ioannina were not university or even high school graduates. (However, because of the war, Joseph became a partisan of ELAS instead of going to a rabbinical school after his graduation from the University of Thessaloniki.) In the bank, Father discovered an employee who was an embezzler. Father ignored all threats and reported him to the administration. The provincial atmosphere of Ioannina could not tolerate an idealistic Don Quixote like my father. The embezzler was not punished. Instead, the bank transferred my father to the nearby city of Arta.

The 2000-year-old Jewish community of Arta had a Jewish elementary school, which I entered at the age of six, one year earlier than I was supposed to. This happened totally by accident. The children I played with were one year older than me. When they started going to school, they simply took me with them. My parents did not object. Neither did the teacher. When my father went to enroll me officially the following year, he thought that I was going to be a first-grade student. To his surprise the teacher said, "He was my best student. He will be a second-grade student."

All the elementary schools of the city participated in a parade on March 25, a national holiday. Our school arrived early at the staging area and, to my surprise, I saw that other schools, which arrived after we did, started marching while we were kept waiting. My sense of justice was strong even then, for although I was the youngest child in my class, I went to our teacher and asked, "Why don't we move, instead of allowing the others to go ahead of us?" The teacher, who was a Christian, replied, "We are the Jewish school, and we have to wait until every other school passes." This was the first time in my life I felt humiliated. I sensed that something was wrong. I was a member of a "different" group of people who were perceived as inferior. I could not accept an inferior status for myself.

In 1937, I had my first great vacation with my grandparents Gracia and Joseph Kohen from Delvino, Albania and my mother. We met in Ioannina. We went by airplane from Ioannina to Athens. We vacationed in Athens and Loutraki. We returned by boat through the Isthmus of Corinth to Preveza.

In Preveza, we separated. My grandparents went to Ioannina and from there to Albania, and my mother and I went to Arta. The following year, 1938, we went with my father, my mother, and my sister Ninetta to Albania for three days. This was the last time I saw my grandparents.

During the German occupation of Albania, the largest part of my grandparents' house was used as the German headquarters, and my grandparents remained in their home unharmed. As the Germans were leaving Albania, they blew up and burned their house and shop in order to destroy their important documents. Then the Communists, who took over the country, confiscated all the assets that they had. My grandparents lived for the rest of their lives in horrible poverty, and we were unable to see them ever again because of the travel restrictions of the Iron Curtain.

At some time in 1938, Rabbi Kuenka from Thessaloniki became the new rabbi and Hebrew teacher of Arta. Within a few weeks, the community leaders decided they did not like his "voice" or the way he conducted the religious services. They wanted him to leave, in spite of his contract, and they did not pay him his meager salary on time. One day he came to our home and asked my father to accept some of his precious books in exchange for a little money. Father had to fight the unjust, wealthy community leaders. He was successful. They, however, as good customers of the bank, protested his meddling in the affairs of the community.

In 1939, my father was transferred to the city of Preveza. It was a port city, and I enjoyed the arrival and departure of the big vessels. I again became a student of the Jewish school adjacent to the synagogue. The front door of the synagogue was usually closed, and many times during services, which I attended regularly, Christian boys knocked loudly while the congregants continued their prayers as if nothing had happened. It took me a long time to realize that these Jews had great dignity and did not suffer the identity crisis of those who wanted to be accepted as both Greeks and Jews like I did.

Our school had two teachers. One taught us the typical Greek curriculum. The other, Rabbi Elia, taught us Hebrew and Jewish philosophy. I asked him once, "If God is good and omnipotent, why does he allow poverty, disease and injustice to thrive?" He did not reply. Instead, he had a talk with my father, who was persuaded that I needed special instruction.

III. Author's Memoirs

For as long as we remained in Preveza, Rabbi Elia became our Sunday dinner guest. He liked lamb with rice, and this was what we had every Sunday.

Scholarly discussions followed the dinner. The rabbi tried to convince me that there was a divine purpose and plan behind everything. He was sure that "even a leaf does not move without God's will" and that "God is thinking even of an ant." In less than three years' time, Rabbi Elia and his entire family were taken by the Germans.

For many years, I was afraid of dogs. This fear started in Preveza. I had to pass a street where a boy my age used to set his ugly dog after me. One day I met this boy in the port without his dog. For the first and last time in my life, I beat up someone. His father was nearby, and he chased me for two blocks along the fashionable promenade of Preveza until he caught me. Fortunately, there were some Jewish stevedores there who saved me. The boy and his dog did not bother me again.

I regret that I never discussed with my father his experiences in Preveza. It is too late to do so now. He died in November 1991 at the age of 89. His motto was, "The trees die standing." There is no doubt that he must have antagonized someone in Preveza, because in March 1940 he was transferred to the city of Agrinion. If we had not left Preveza, we would have shared the fate of this unfortunate community, whose losses were 94 percent. Thanks to pure luck, we ended up in Agrinion.

Agrinion's original name was Vrahori, which is possibly derived from the word Evraeohori (Jewish village). Before the Greek War of Independence in 1821, Agrinion had about 200 Jewish families. Most of these families were massacred by the Greeks during their revolt against the Turks. The few who survived this Greek Christian sense of justice either fled or converted to Christianity.

For example, a Jewish family that fled Vrahori or Agrinion is the Vrahoritis family of Ioannina. A family that converted to Christianity is the family of Papagiannis, Director of the National Bank Greece in Agrinion.

I learned about the massacre of the Jews when I was a high school student in Agrinion. One day, our teacher, Panos Papachristos, took our class out of the city and told us about what happened in 1821 and how the 200 Jewish families of

Agrinion were massacred. He took us to the countryside to teach this lesson because it was not part of the official curriculum. It was rumored that the teacher's ancestors may have been one of those families who converted to Christianity in 1821.

[Author's note: A Greek Christian physician once asked me to give him information about the Greek Jews. He wanted to write a historical novel about his great-great-grandmother who was a little Jewish girl when she was saved from death in 1821.

It is obvious that there were good people in 1821, just like the "Righteous Among the Nations" of the Second World War. For instance, those who saved the Papachristou family or the ancestor of the physician. One of the Greek leaders, Kanellos Deligiannis, was remarkable. He saved 12 Jews from the massacre of the prosperous Jewish community of Tripolitsa. He kept them hidden in his house for three years and, only in 1824, he secretly moved them to the island of Zakynthos, which was under Italian rule at that time.]

In 1940, there were forty Jews in Agrinion, out of a population of 30,000. There were only two Jewish students, my classmate Lazaros Mionis and I, among the 1,000 students of our high school. Lazaros and I were members of EON (National Youth Organization) and proudly wore its uniform. Much later, I learned that Jews were not permitted to join this fascist organization, and to this day I am grateful to the officials of Agrinion who either did not know this rule or chose to disregard it.

On October 28, 1940, I went to school as usual. The classes were assembled in the yard. A student recited the prayer, and the choir sang a hymn. At this point the principal, Mr. Pantazis, used to make some eloquent remarks before each teacher marched his class into the building. On this morning he announced that the war had started, the school would become a hospital, and we would not have classes until arrangements were made to transform the school into a tobacco warehouse. He sounded sad, but his 1,000 students were delirious with joy and patriotic enthusiasm.

We went down the main street yelling rhythmically, "We will win!"

It did not take long before the ambulances started arriving, filled with wounded soldiers. At night we were sleeping with our clothes on, ready to run to the air raid shelters at a

III. Author's Memoirs

moment's notice. The newspapers kept informing us of a "strategic retreat" until the day the Greek army stopped the enemy advance and pushed the Italian troops back.

It was rumored that *enas Hythreos* colonel stopped them! Eventually we learned that the rumor started as *enas Evreos*, that is, a Jewish colonel; but it became *Hythreos* colonel, or a colonel from the island of Hydra, because nobody could believe that the gallant officer Mordechai Frizis was a Jew!

In October 1940, Benito Mussolini hoped to conquer Greece quickly. Initially, the large Italian army overpowered the Greek army at the Albanian border, forcing the Greek army to retreat. At this critical moment, Frizis implemented his plan to expel the enemy, which he had developed prior to the war and which had been previously approved by the Greek Chief of Staff General Papagos. Frizis and his troops prevented the Italian Julia Division from encircling the 8th Greek Division and stopped the retreat of the Greek army. He counterattacked and liberated the Greek city of Konitsa and entered Italian occupied Albania. This was the first Allied victory of the Second World War.

Because of Frizis' victory, the Greek army regained its confidence and enthusiasm and chased the Italians deep into Albania - occupying one third of the country and remaining there until April 1941. Colonel Frizis led valiantly and courageously but was later killed in battle on December 5, 1940, while encouraging his troops from atop his horse. At that time, Prime Minister Metaxas and the heads of the armed forces sent their deepest condolences to the Frizis family and honored him for his bravery. In addition, busts of Frizis were placed in the War Museum of Kalpaki and in Chalkis, the town where he was born.

In October 1940, Adolf Hitler decided to attack Russia.[294] Mussolini attacked Greece on October 28, 1940. It is hard to believe that this was just a coincidence.

Greece's victory against Italy had enormous consequences for the outcome of the Second World War in the European theater and, indirectly, led to the defeat of Germany.

This is because, while Greece was still free and while the British had an important Mediterranean base on the Island of

---

294 Ladislas Farago, *Patton*, Dell Publishing, 1963, 640.

Crete and expeditionary forces stationed on the Greek mainland, the Germans could not turn their backs on Greece and begin their assault on Russia.

With the Greek-Italian war unsuccessful, the Germans invaded Greece on April 6, 1941. They later attacked Crete in a famous parachute drop, in which 5,000 elite German paratroopers were killed. Ultimately, they were able to conquer all of Greece.

In the meantime, a Russian spy discovered that the Japanese army was issuing summer uniforms to the Japanese soldiers. Because of this, he suspected that Japan was not going to attack Russia as was presumed but was going to attack the Allied forces in the South Pacific. He recommended that some Russian troops be withdrawn from the Japanese front and be transferred to Moscow. Stalin reassigned the great General Georgy Zhukov from Leningrad to Moscow to defend the capital.

Once Greece was conquered, the Germans began their delayed attack on Russia on June 22, 1941. This delay was significant for the outcome of the war. It was the beginning of the end for Germany in WWII. Confident of victory, Hitler announced his *final* drive against Moscow. In response, the Russians countered with a desperate defense. The Russian *Red Star* reported, "The very existence of the Soviet State is in danger. Every man of the Red Army must stand firm and fight to the last drop of blood." [295]

While the battle for Moscow was raging, Turkey, an ally of Germany during WWI, was watching and anxiously waiting. If the Germans captured Moscow and knocked Russia out of the war, the three million strong Turkish army would have joined the Germans. Such an alliance would surely have led to a German victory in Europe. The Ottoman Empire would have likely been reestablished and Greece would have been part of Turkey once more. Israel would not have been born.

Fortunately, this did not happen. By the time the Germans arrived in front of Moscow, it was winter and the German soldiers were still dressed in summer uniforms in the subfreezing weather. Wealthy German women donated their fur coats to warm their freezing children and grandchildren on

---

295 Werth, Alexander, *Russia at War*, Discus Books, 231.

III. Author's Memoirs

the Eastern front. But it was too late. The German army had to fight not only the Russians already there but also the newly arrived fresh Siberian troops who came from the Japanese border. The Russian counter-offensive was successful, ultimately marking a turning point in favor of the Allies in the war in Europe.

Because of Colonel Frizis' counter-attack and Greece's occupation of one third of Albania. Germany spent precious time to conquer Greece, thus, delaying its attack on Russia and putting Russia at a military advantage.

Supporting this idea, during the Nuremberg Trials after World War II, German Field Marshal Wilhelm Keitel said, "*The unbelievable strong resistance of the Greeks delayed by two or more vital months the German attack against Russia. If we did not have this long delay, the outcome of the war would have been different in the Eastern Front and in the war in general, and others would have been accused and occupying this seat as defendants today.*"[296] (In my opinion, he implied that the Allied generals would be tried as war criminals.) In addition, the Greek historian Anastopoulos, in his book *History of the Greek Nation*, writes, "Frizis executed a defensive maneuver and then a tremendous counterattack, without which the victory of 1940 would not have been realized." Another Greek historian, Simopoulos wrote in his book, *The Italian Division Julia in Pindos*, "The honor of the most glorious victory, which basically put an end not only to the battle of Pindos and Smolika, but along the entire front, belongs to the military tactics of Colonel Frizis."[297,298]

When I read these statements, one from an enemy general and the others from two historians, my admiration for Colonel Frizis rose to astronomical heights. They emphasize and

---

296 Willis, Yolanda, *A Hidden Child in Greece*, 2017, 16.
297 Haralampos Roupas, *EAM-Antistasi*, March 2002, 8.
298 In Greece, the two historians Anastopoulos and Simopoulos accused the Greek governments of the previous sixty years for religious discrimination. I also accuse some of these governments of religious discrimination since my three cousins, who are about 20 years younger than I (two architects and one engineer), served in the Greek army as soldiers although they wanted to serve as officers like all their Christian male classmates. I don't know how many other Greek Jews experienced the same fate.

The Illusion of Safety

describe the instinctive, military initiative put forth by Frizis on the front line. I am reminded of two lines of Chaim Nachman Bialik's famous poem, "Where is the fist that shall smite? Where the thunderbolt to avenge?" Frizis became the fist and the thunderbolt that helped defeat mighty Germany.

This is a unique case in history. The chief of staff of the German army attributes the defeat of Germany to the delay produced by the Greek army. The Greek historians credit this delay to Colonel Frizis. The unbelievable conclusion is that Frizis is elevated after his heroic death to the status of a mythical Greek hero and a great hero of the Second World War.

Greece was extremely proud of its victory in Albania and its contribution in the Allied victory of the Second World War. Colonel Mordechai Frizis was acknowledged as a heroic officer only by a few people every year on the October 28 Greek national holiday (which celebrates the Greek refusal to the Italian ultimatum of 1940). Due to anti-Semitism, the Greek governments did not officially honor him from 1945 until 2002.

For fifty years, my friend, Iakovos Frizis, engaged in a campaign to persuade the governments to honor his father. He

Memorial to Colonel Mordechai Frizis in Chalkis - initiated and fundraised by Greek-American Stefanos Becharas. (Photo courtesy of Marcia Ikonomopoulos.)

I am with Iakovos Frizis in Patras, Greece. 1954.

III. Author's Memoirs

published 100 articles and obtained 30 interviews. In 2002, a member of the Greek Parliament, Fotis Kouvelis, helped to make this possible. Colonel Frizis' remains were located in Albania and returned to Greece where they were reburied with great honors in the new Jewish cemetery of Thessaloniki. Streets were named for him in Athens and other cities and a statue of Frizis on horseback was erected in the city of Chalkis where he was born.

Everybody should be proud of Mordechai Frizis. May his memory last forever.

My family had its first contact with the Frizis family in 1940. During the early phase of the Greek-Italian war, when the Greek army was in retreat and the Italian army was advancing toward Ioannina, an order was given to evacuate the families of the Greek officers who were in Ioannina and send them to Athens. The plan of the evacuation of the families was very poorly organized, in terms of transportation and lodgings. The first stop from Ioannina to Athens was Agrinion. There were no hotel rooms available in Agrinion. So, three families of Greek officers who were evacuated were directed to contact my father, who was working for the National Bank of Greece in Agrinion, and ask him to find a place where they could stay for a few days.

My father offered the family of Colonel Frizis to stay in our apartment. The family consisted of Mrs. Frizis, two daughters and a son, Iacovos, whom I met again in 1954 when I was a dental officer in Patras while examining new recruits. My father arranged for the two other families to stay in the basement of the bank, which was also a bomb shelter. They were the wife of Dr. Errikos Levis, Jeannette, their son, Alekos (Alex), and the wife of a military dentist with her infant son.

A few weeks later, Frizis' orderly Moshe Matsas arrived in Agrinion. Moshe, was passing through Agrinion while transferring the belongings of the late Colonel Frizis to Athens. Moshe was deeply saddened and so were we, because, just a few weeks earlier, Mrs. Frizis and her three children had stayed in our house for a few days, and we got a chance to know and love them.

A few months after the Italian invasion, my father was mobilized into active military service. We moved to Ioannina to stay with my mother's sister, Eftyhia, while my father was in the army. Eftyhia's husband Nissim Samuel was a dentist serving with the Greek army in Albania. Every day and night we had to run to the air raid shelters within the thick fortress walls surrounding the old city.

In April 1941, the Germans attacked, and soon our victory turned into defeat. The Germans were soon followed by the Italians in Ioannina. Everybody had hoped that we would be under German occupation because, ironically, everyone believed that the Germans were more civilized than the Italians. Thousands and thousands of Greek soldiers were returning from the front on foot. Mother and I spent many hours every day in front of a relative's shop on Anexartisias Street, hoping to see my father among the retreating troops.

One day it was rumored that the Germans were about to enter the city. We gave up looking for Father, and we did not know what had happened to him. The Germans entered Ioannina in gray armored cars. Their uniforms and helmets were impressive, and they did not bother anybody.

In a few days my father arrived. He told us that he was so tired from walking that he eventually was the only soldier on the road between the advancing Germans and the retreating Greeks. Since he knew that the Greek army surrendered and saw that the German cars had plenty of space, he thought of hitchhiking. Totally exhausted, he extended his right arm in the typical way a Greek would to ask for a ride. His movement resembled a Nazi salute. Some Germans responded by greeting him the same way. They must have thought that he was a Nazi sympathizer. He could have gotten a bullet instead!

Soon he came to the spot where some weeks before he had stopped for a little rest on the way to the front. At that time Father, who was overweight, carried a lot of extra clothing, cookies and other food that Mother had given him, plus a large book. He had gotten rid of this extra load and now he saw, by the side of the road, that everything had been picked up, with the exception of the big book. The book, *English Without a Teacher,* was all muddy. People had stepped on it. Some pages were torn. He picked it up and continued on his way home. Father eventually cleaned and repaired this book. In 1953, when I was drafted into the army, I decided to learn English in my spare time. I took this book with me and started to learn English. This historic book now occupies a place of honor in my library.

III. Author's Memoirs

A few days later my parents, my three-year-old sister Ninetta, and I boarded a bus to return to Agrinion. The bus did not have any seats. All civilian buses had been converted to ambulances, replacing the seats with stretchers. The enterprising driver of such an ambulance got rid of the stretchers and sold tickets to people like us who wanted to travel. I did not know then that I had seen our many relatives in Ioannina for the last time.

The trip to Agrinion was not uneventful. The bus broke down in the middle of nowhere, and the driver, who had pocketed the money from the tickets he sold, abandoned his thirty or so passengers and disappeared. We were left without food or water somewhere in the mountains. At night we saw a big column of cars approaching. It was the occupying Italian army. In our desperation, my mother remembered the Italian she had learned while studying in a Catholic boarding school on the island of Corfu. She yelled, "Aspeta, Signore!" and she virtually stopped the invading army in its tracks. The entire Italian convoy was stopped for as far as the eye could see. Both soldiers and officers were greatly surprised to see a vivacious and beautiful young woman (my mother was then 34) in the Greek mountains in the middle of the night, speaking Italian.

An Italian officer asked my mother what was her name? When my mother said Mrs. Matsa, he expressed great surprise and immediately radioed his commander who was camped for the night a few miles back. The commander ordered him to facilitate the movement of the bus passengers to the city of Agrinion and bring my family to him.

In a few minutes, the passengers with their luggage were placed by two's or four's in the Italian trucks which advanced towards Agrinion. Finally, a Greek policeman declared that he wanted to be with my father. The very polite Italian officer gave all of us small pieces of cheese in plastic wrapping. We were very hungry. Then he arranged for a car to take my family and the policeman to his commander, General Mazza. He told us goodbye, and he joined his convoy. (The General's name was pronounced the same way as my family name. In Greek the ending for a man's name ends in "s" but the same name for a woman does not. The General had the same name as ours and both my father and the Italian officer believed that we were related!)

This story reminds me to describe a little of my family's history. My father's family came to Greece in the early 1500's when the Jews were expelled from Apulia, Italy. Many Jewish families who remained in Italy had converted to Christianity. [299] My father was a student at the Alliance Israelite Universelle. This was a Jewish school founded by a French agency where instruction was given in Greek, Hebrew, and French. While attending this school, my father, whose given name was Judah, spelled his name as Judah Mazza- using the Italian spelling. Much later, when he entered the Greek public high school, he changed his name to Leon Matsas (Leon for "Lion of Judah"). My maternal grandfather, Joseph Kohen, was born in Ioannina. As a young man during the time of the Ottoman Empire, he went to the nearby city of Delvino, which later became part of Albania. He started his own business as a fabric merchant. My grandparents, Gracia and Joseph Kohen, had three daughters, Annetta, Esther and Eftyhia and one son Semos. Their son Semos studied in Naples, Italy, and returned to his father's business in Delvino. My mother, Esther, and her two sisters, Annetta and Eftyhia were married in Ioannina. Tragically, her two sisters and their families were taken by the Germans in 1944.

Esther and Eftyhia were students in a Greek private school in Delvino. A prominent Greek lady told the director of the Greek school that she did not want her daughters to go to the same school with Jewish girls. She asked him to tell the Jewish girls the next day to go home and to never come back to the school. My grandfather, who was a very proud and wealthy man, asked some of his friends where did the rich Greek families send their daughters to school? The answer was that they send them to a Catholic convent school on the island of Corfu. Therefore, he sent his daughters to Catholic school in Corfu where the instruction there was in Greek, Italian, and French. This is how my mother learned how to speak Italian and French.

---

[299] By the time of the First World War, there were fifty Jewish Generals in the Italian army.

III. Author's Memoirs

My grandparents Naoum and Sarina Matsas (seated) with their children in Ioannina, 1920. [Standing from left to right: Eliasaf, Leon (author's father), Raphael, Rosina, Yeshua, Elias and Michael. Seated in front: Rebecca.] This photo was found in the street after their house was looted during WW2. Elias died before the war from illness. Michael survived Auschwitz. Rebecca was living in Egypt during the war and then moved to Paris in the 1950's. Leon survived in the free mountains. All the others were murdered by the Germans.

The Illusion of Safety

I am with my Grandparents from Albania, my mother and cousin Cleio Yohana Kohen from Corfu. Loutraki, Greece, 1937. Cleio died in Auschwitz.

The Jewish home for the aged in Ioannina, 1930's. All its residents died in the gas chambers of Auschwitz. (Family photo collection.)

III. Author's Memoirs

My family in 1945.

My first cousin Sam Meyer.

My uncle Michael Matsas after surviving Auschwitz.

My uncle Eliasaf Matsas in the Greek army. He died in Auschwitz.

My favorite aunt Emilia and uncle Eliasaf. Both were killed by the Germans.

My aunt Annetta. She was killed by the Germans.

My aunt and uncle, Eftyhia and Dr. Nissim Samuel, were killed by the Germans.

III. Author's Memoirs

Yeshua Matsas, my cousin, surrendered to the Germans to be with his family "in exile." He died in Auschwitz.

Leon Matsas, my father, in the Greek army, about 1920.

Now, back to my story with the Italian convoy in the mountains. The Italian commander, General Mazza, and my parents spoke in French. The commander was very cordial, and they all felt as if they were distant relatives. He told my father, "I will do anything for you." My father explained to him that he did not want to enter Agrinion on board an enemy car. After all, he worked at the National Bank of Greece. The commander said, "I understand". My father asked for us and the policeman to go back to the little town of Amfilochia.

My father thanked the commander for his kindness and on board a very nice car, we went to Amfilochia. There we found a civilian transport (small truck) with which we went to Agrinion.

The Italian troops were extremely civilized. They did not confiscate anything, and they did not execute any hostages or burn any villages in our area, even when Italian soldiers were killed by the resistance fighters.

As far as the Greek Jews were concerned, General Geloso, the commander of the Italian Zone of Occupation in Greece, had the right not to apply to the Greek Jews the strict fascist anti-Jewish regulations to which the Italian Jews were subjected. We were totally free, as all the Greek Christians were. By the way, a beautiful movie *The Gardens of Finzi-Continis* illustrates the treatment of the Italian Jews.

The great famine during the winter of 1941 made life miserable for the people of Athens, while we in Agrinion had plenty of food. Life was so quiet and peaceful that we were hardly affected by the war that was devastating the world around us.

School went on as usual, and I enjoyed the friendship of my classmates Kostas, with whom I played soccer, and Efthymios, who taught me how to ride a bicycle. Kostas Triantafilidis became a high school principal, and Efthymios eventually became an important bishop of the Greek Orthodox church and a prolific writer. Everyone knew I was Jewish, but nobody ever said anything against the Jews in my presence.

We have always loved the city of Agrinion and the surrounding villages. My mother, my sister, and I made a donation to our city of Agrinion in memory of my late father Leon Matsas in 1994. My friend Bishop Efthymios Acheloou recommended we give it to the cultural museum of the city. They accepted it, like "manna from heaven." People who remembered my father and our family expressed their love for all of us.

In 1942, a new mathematics teacher arrived and, one day, for no apparent reason, he began giving our class a passionate anti-Semitic lecture. For the first time I heard so many terrible accusations against my people, the Jews, that I started crying, while he continued the attack. My class of 100 boys remained silent, and only he and I could be heard for a long time until the bell rang for recess. A few days later, a jubilant boy met me in the street and told me our teacher was an informer and that he had been stabbed to death by men of the resistance the night before. His blood could be seen on the street in front of the post office. I immediately went to see the coagulated blood and felt

III. Author's Memoirs

not only joy for what had happened to my enemy, but I also wished I had had the guts to have been his executioner.

At that moment I arrived in the twentieth century. My education continued to improve, as I became a voracious reader of my father's extensive library and did not miss a single movie that was being shown in the local cinema. Movies became my window through which I saw the world and its history: *Les Miserables, Ben Hur, Emile Zola, Juarez, The Good Earth,* etc. Every movie was preceded by newsreels depicting great German victories in Africa and Russia. I must have witnessed the sinking of every American boat that went down in the Atlantic. I was devastated.

The newspapers, operating under strict censorship, were of no help at all. Our only reliable source of information came every day when my father returned from the bank and removed one shoe, always the same one, because he was a punctilious bureaucrat, retrieved a piece of thin paper, and read aloud the latest news. A mimeographed bulletin was distributed by the resistance daily, giving us news broadcasts from the BBC and other sources. Since we did not have radios, this was our only contact with the outside world. The news slowly, slowly became better for the Allies.

The Jewish community of Agrinion consisted of eight families who lived in different parts of the city. They maintained friendly relations with each other and used to get together only once a year, on Yom Kippur. On that day, the families of Eliezer, Yiossoula, Revi, Elia Mizan, Sava Mizan, Leon Matsas, and Isaak Matsas went to the house of Nissim Mionis, who knew how to read Hebrew and read the prayer book. The only one who did not participate in this religious observance was Nissim's brother Yonas, a teacher and member of the Communist Party, and one of the five leaders of EAM in the Agrinion area. The Eliezers, who were members of EAM, had a dog that was very popular among resistance sympathizers. His name was Hitler.

We maintained contact with my parents' families but, unfortunately, I am the only one of my family who did not see our relatives again. Sometime in 1942, my mother decided to visit her sisters in Ioannina as well as her parents and brother in Albania. Since we lost our young maid, Mother gave me some lessons in cooking and house cleaning before she left. She took my sister with her.

People used to travel about in those days by either civilian buses, which used to break down very often, or Italian convoys, which my parents preferred. Tens of thousands of people from Athens and Thessaloniki were starving and traveled to the villages to exchange clothing for food. The Italians allowed a great number of civilians to board their trucks and buses because they felt confident the partisans would not attack such a convoy. My mother stayed for almost two months in Ioannina and Albania. My father also took the opportunity to visit his relatives in Ioannina for a few days.

In Agrinion, all the hotels were occupied by the Italian forces, the people had to rent beds in private houses. Many Jews who knew my parents preferred to stay in our home, not so much because they did not have to pay anything, but because they were afraid that someone would steal their money, gold, or other belongings if they rented a place. Practically every night we had guests. One night we had 12 people who had to sleep on the floor. My parents enjoyed having all these very appreciative guests who kept them in touch with what was happening in Athens or Ioannina.

One time, an old lady by the name Matsa came. I suspect she was the grandmother of Makis Matsas of the family that owned a record company. She told us how their bus made a detour and found themselves in a partisan camp. She kept saying, "What good boys were the young men ...." This was the first time I heard of the young idealistic partisans who, later, helped to save our lives during the war and whom I admired and loved.

Sometime in 1942, the heads of Jewish families were requested to go to the Italian police and register with them. The Italian sergeant in charge of this formality reassured everyone that, as long as the Italians were in Agrinion, nothing was going to happen to the Jews. This special attention to the Jews should have alerted everyone, but it did not. My father also registered our family. We all obeyed the law and soon forgot this little event without grasping the hidden significance of such a registration.

I know of only three families in the Italian Zone of occupation who did not obey the Italian request for registration of the Jews. They were Makis Solomon of Preveza and his parents. They closed their shop and moved to Vonitsa, a small

III. Author's Memoirs

town nearby. I do not know whether they had false identity cards or whether they opened another shop there.

Two other families from Preveza, the family of Solomon Gani and that of Daniel Zafou, also moved to Vonitsa. Six months later, when they saw that nothing happened to the Jews of Preveza, they returned to the city only to be taken by the Germans on March 25, 1944.

By the beginning of 1943, Agrinion had proportionately contributed more partisans to ELAS than any other Greek city. A spirit of defiance prevailed in our area. Many times, my mother prepared baskets of cookies which friends of ours, especially Maria Dimadi, smuggled to a partisan hospital.

One day we received a horseload of wheat we bought from a villager. The man who made the delivery gave us a message: "Inside this bag is a gun and ammunition to be given to Christos Bokoros." In a few minutes, I was transporting this precious cargo in a basket filled with different items. On the way to Bokoros' house I passed close to many enemy soldiers, and I felt proud of my "mission." I did not realize that what I did was dangerous until I delivered the gun and bullets to Christos's sister Kiki and saw the expression of fear in her face!

The Bokoros family were our best friends in Agrinion because they were relatives of one of my father's bank colleagues in Preveza. They gave me a small plot of land on their farm outside Agrinion, and I planted potatoes on it. The problem was that the potatoes needed a lot of water, which I had to lift by hand from a well and then transport to the field. In addition, the farm was a couple of miles away from the city in the village of Zapanti. My potatoes were the smallest potatoes I had ever seen! I did not appreciate it then, but much later I realized that every time I went to water my potatoes, I was in fact leaving occupied Agrinion and going to free, partisan-controlled territory. On that road there was no need for identity cards. I did not even have one, and neither the Italians nor the Germans established a roadblock!

In April 1943, we heard of the deportation of the Jews of Thessaloniki, and we realized the same thing could happen to us. My father asked the director of the bank to allow him to take his annual leave whenever it would be necessary for us to leave the city. The director reassured my father that the Jews of Thessaloniki were "different." (It was rumored in Agrinion that the Papayannis family, to which the director belonged, was one of those who converted to Christianity in 1821.)

In May 1943, the family of Polizos, our neighbors and members of the resistance, had visitors. I remember them as a very elegant-looking couple with a beautiful teenage daughter. We heard rumors that they were rich Jews from Thessaloniki who had come to Agrinion to avoid the anti-Jewish regulations the Germans had imposed in their zone of occupation. They avoided any contact with our community and left the city in a few days. We did not even think that we should also leave the city. We acted as if we were indeed different than they in the eyes of the Germans.

Italy surrendered in September 1943. German troops entered Agrinion to replace the Italian garrison. Members of the resistance made a great effort to collect Italian war material, while the Germans tried to prevent them from doing so.

One day, while I was on the back balcony of our apartment, I saw a German soldier with a drawn pistol chasing and shooting at a young man carrying a bag. The man entered our yard, passed through the first-floor apartment, and went out through the back window located directly under my balcony. The German also entered our yard, climbed the outside concrete stairs, entered our house (the door was open), ran through the corridor to the balcony and, in front of my bewildered eyes, aimed his pistol at the young man who was running below and pressed the trigger. Nothing happened. The gun jammed. The resistance fighter escaped unharmed while the German looked straight into my eyes to see, I think, whether I was happy with his failure or not. I was petrified. The German soldier left without uttering a word and looking at his gun in disgust.

In September 1943, we were unhappy with the arrival of the Germans in Agrinion because we did not know that, if Italy had not capitulated, all Greek Jews were to have been arrested by the Italian army and interned in a concentration camp. The purpose of the innocent-looking registration by the Italian police was nothing but the first step toward our destruction. I learned this from a history book thirty years later.

With the arrival of the Germans and the knowledge that the Jews of Thessaloniki had been deported, we should have left the city and gone to the free countryside. Yet we remained

III. Author's Memoirs

in the comfort of our home! One day the Germans occupied one room in the house of our friend, Kalydopoulos, across the street from our house. His mother asked me to go and stay with her until her son, the director of the Bank of Agriculture, came home. There I met a young German soldier who looked very nice, and we soon became "friends." Since he did not know Greek and I did not know German, I thought we had found some common ground of communication by playing with the word "good." We established the fact that we both knew how to say good in Greek, Latin, German, French, Spanish and Italian. (I also knew how to say "good" in Hebrew, but I was smart enough to be quiet about it.) Our expertise in linguistics made us both smile! I misunderstood only one thing. While I was thinking of the word good, he was thinking in terms of good people. I found that out as soon as I said, "English—good." He instantly changed. He became mad and slapped me on the face. It seems that even in September of 1943 I did not know what kind of beasts even the best-looking Germans were. After this experience, I should have asked my parents to leave the city. Yet, in spite of all my rhetoric, I did not ask them, let alone insist on abandoning our home.

The Italians, when they were in power, were so afraid of the Greek resistance movement that they fortified every house they occupied in the city. The Germans did not approve of the fortifications surrounding the buildings occupied by the Italian troops. They decided to deal with the partisans in the area in a decisive manner. One hundred twenty-eight elite German soldiers moved in the direction of the resistance in Thermos, about thirty miles from Agrinion. The partisans were informed by their underground sources, and they ambushed the German column. They destroyed the first and last truck of the convoy. The German troops were left at the mercy of the partisans on the winding mountain road. Only one wounded German motorcyclist returned to the city alive, but he later died.

After the war ended, we learned that for this successful partisan operation and others, credit was due to our friend and neighbor Maria Dimadi, who belonged to one of the most prominent families of the city. She had started her resistance activities first by collecting cookies and many other things for resistance hospitals. When the Germans arrived, since she had studied in Germany, she was asked to become an interpreter for the German commander of Agrinion. Eventually she became, it is rumored, the commander's mistress, and thus enjoyed his protection. (On the very last night the Germans abandoned Agrinion, the Greek officers of the Security Battalions executed her because she knew too much about their collaboration with the Germans. The resistance warned her that night to leave the city. She went to her house to get a pair of flat shoes and was arrested.)[300]

In September 1943, we suspected that things could get worse for us very soon. Father's request to receive his annual leave on a day's notice was approved. We hid whatever religious items and books we possessed in the bank's archives. (The Germans requisitioned the bank building and transferred everything, including our Hebrew prayer books and megillah, to the nearby Bank of Agriculture building, where we found everything intact after the war.) Influenced by the spirit of revolution which permeated Agrinion, we were determined not to obey any rules that would be considered discriminatory against the Jews. Yet we remained in the city!

At the end of September 1943, Yonas Mionis told my father that Nissim Mionis, who had gone to Athens to buy merchandise, returned immediately to Agrinion when he discovered that the three big Jewish stores where he would usually shop were closed. "Everyone here is getting ready to go," Yonas continued. "My brother said that we should not tell you too soon because, since you do not have a shop to take care of, you might leave before the others do. I did not agree with this. That's why I tell you. Tomorrow morning, I leave the city." As soon as Father came with the news, we immediately contacted the owner of the house, who wanted to live in our place. We distributed our household goods among our friends and neighbors. In my father's bank, one room was used for storing food provisions, which the bank distributed monthly to its employees. Dimitris Pipiringos, who was in charge of the distribution, accepted a quantity of oil, wheat and corn from my father. Dimitris understood that he would give the food to persons who would visit him periodically with written instructions from us. We made the same agreement with Yannis Exarhos, Andreas Papadopoulos, Michael Bellos, and

---

300 Philippas Geladopoulos, *Maria Dimadi* (Athens: Nestoras, 1982), 156.

III. Author's Memoirs

Costas Maniakis. (It was impossible at that time to predict that within a few months all these people, with the exception of Maniakis whose son was a partisan, would become members of the notorious Security Battalions. One of our friends, Yannis Exarhos, a captain of the reserves, became an officer of the Security Battalion of Agrinion. My high school principal, Pantazis, gave a speech in the main square of Agrinion, exhorting the Greek youth to "imitate the German youth!")

After we distributed everything that we did not intend to take with us, we started packing in waterproof bags made from military tents whatever clothing, food, utensils, medicines, etc., we needed to establish a new household. I was even sent to the dentist to have a troublesome tooth extracted since there were no health facilities where we were going. Within a few days, we were ready to leave. At that point, we realized that we did not know where to go. We were not politically mature, and we did not realize the political polarization taking place among the Greeks. We did not know that people were supposed to be either "right" or "left." We wanted to be "neutral and anti-German," and this was a nonexistent position. Yannis Exarhos suggested that we go to Arta and from there to the mountains, which were occupied by the nationalist EDES. Our friend Christos Bokoros invited us to stay in his house for a day or two and leave the city with horses he would provide. We decided to follow his plan, which placed us with EAM-ELAS. My father visited our neighbor Maniakis and told him that "tomorrow we go to partisan territory. Make sure that nobody goes to tell the Germans about it." He was especially suspicious of a very religious woman living next door. Maniakis assured my father that nobody would make a wrong move.

On October 2, 1943, a porter with a pushcart transferred all our bags to the house of Bokoros. Mother, Ninetta, and I went there a few minutes later. Father went to the bank to transfer his papers and money to the bank director. On our way to Bokoros's house, we were approached by a bus driver, Zaharopoulos, who knew us. He said in a low voice, "You know, Mrs. Matsas, all the Jews of Athens went into hiding. I was going to visit you to tell you about it." "Thank you very much," Mother replied. "We are leaving right this minute."

There was a great deal of turmoil in Bokoros's house. Many people came and went. A battle was taking place between the Germans and the partisans, and there were no horses available for civilian use. To make matters worse, a German soldier entered the house, looked around and left without saying anything. Many times, Greek collaborators disguised themselves as German soldiers. This unexpected, suspicious visit alarmed both my mother and our hosts.

Thomas Bokoros went to the bank to find Father. When he saw how busy Father was, he went to the director's office and, in a demanding tone, asked him to forget about formalities and permit Father to leave immediately; otherwise, he told the director, "If anything happens, I will hold you responsible for it." The director, who knew that Bokoros was a resistance leader, agreed to let Father go without even counting the money being transferred to him. Father left the bank, on a supposed twenty-day leave of absence.

Since there were no horses available, Thomas and his brothers developed a different plan. They made the necessary arrangements with Mr. Psilopoulos, who had a car powered by wood fuel in which he transported passengers to Houni, a village thirty miles from Agrinion. The following day, Sunday, October 3, 1943, Psilopoulos's "gazozene" parked in front of Bokoros's house. We loaded our bags on top of the car and, with a few more passengers, we departed in style for Houni. The car stopped for a few seconds, and my mother noticed one of the Eliezer brothers. She called him over and told him, "We are leaving. Don't wait. Get out of the city."

A few minutes later, we were stopped at the German roadblock. The guards accepted the raisins and cigarettes Psilopoulos offered them, and we left occupied territory forever. If my father's bureaucratic tendencies had delayed our departure just two more days, I am sure this story would not have been written.

On October 5, two days after we left Agrinion, two Germans visited the bank and asked to see my father. I am sure this was not a courtesy visit! They were told that he was on leave. Judging this German action on the basis of similar actions in other cities, there is a good chance that they intended to arrest Father and hold him as hostage until the day they arrested the rest of the community. If this assumption is correct, we saved ourselves at the very last minute! If Father were arrested, I am positive my mother would have never abandoned him.

There were three other Jews in Agrinion in October 1943: Mimis Cohen, who had been born in Ioannina, his wife and

III. Author's Memoirs

newborn baby. Mimis had worked as an interpreter for the Italian police. Some interpreters were true heroes of the resistance. He was not one of them. When he first came to Agrinion, he became friendly with us and offered to give me mandolin lessons. When Father learned what his work was, he asked him to go back to Ioannina or, if he stayed, not to come back to our house. The Eliezer brothers were instructed by the resistance to lure Mimis Cohen to the outskirts of Agrinion. Mimis was extremely careful. He and his family lived in the Italian police station. We knew of another Jewish man who had worked for the Italians in the same capacity of interpreter and informer. EAM agents lured him out of the city, and nobody saw him again.

The collapse of Italy left Mimis in a most perilous position. On the one hand, he could not go to free territory like we did. On the other hand, he did not have the means to hide in Athens. Nobody in our community thought of informing him about our impending exodus from the city. He remained in Agrinion and operated a dance school! A friend of ours, Sanio Exarhou, who was wronged by him when he was in his position of power, knew that he was Jewish. Sanio, a sister of an officer of the Security Battalion of Agrinion, stopped him on the street one day and told him, "For the sake of Mrs. Matsas, I will not report you to the Germans."

In 1992 an Israeli researcher, Yitzhak Kerem, informed me that he was writing the story of a war hero. "A double agent who studied medicine in Italy: Mimis Cohen of Ioannina!" I had a hard time stopping Yitzhak from creating another myth!

October 8, 1943, the Greek newspapers published the following orders:

1. All Jews residing in German-occupied territories are to go without delay to their permanent homes in which they resided as of June 1, 1943.
2. It is forbidden for Jews to abandon their residence or change residence.
3. Jews residing in Athens and its suburbs have to present themselves within five days to the Jewish religious community of Athens and register. In areas outside of Athens, this declaration has to be made to the Greek public and community offices there.

The Illusion of Safety

4. Jews who do not comply with this order will be executed. Non-Jews who hide Jews, offer them shelter or help them escape will be transferred to a concentration camp, unless a more severe punishment is given them.
5. Jews of foreign nationality have to present themselves on October 18, at 8:00 a.m., to the Jewish community of Athens and submit their passports. Outside of Athens, this declaration will be made to the above-mentioned Greek authorities.
6. The Jewish religious community of Athens is appointed as the only representative of all the Jews of Greece. It should, without delay, appoint a council of elders and commence its functions.
7. After the registration, all male Jews above the age of 14 have to present themselves every other day to the above office.
8. It is forbidden for Jews to be on the street and public squares from 5:00 p.m. to 7:00 a.m.
9. The Greek police is directed to supervise the execution of the above order and arrest any Jews who do not comply with it, or any persons who assist them in disregarding this order.
10. The above order considers as Jews persons who are descendants of at least three generations of ancestors of the Jewish race, regardless of the religion to which they belong at present.

The Supreme Commander of the Security Battalions
and the Greek Police Brigadier of Security Battalions
Lieutenant General of Police

When this order was issued in Agrinion, the Germans did not find there any Jews ready to comply with their wishes. In this way, the community of Agrinion occupies a unique position of defiance among the Jewish communities of occupied Europe. It is the only community in which not even one member ever registered with the Germans or was deported by them. On October 23, 1943, the German consul in Patras sent the following note to the German embassy in Athens, regarding the Jews of Agrinion: "I have the honor to respectfully report that after the local press printed the order of the obligatory registration of the Jews, they disappeared. It is said that they went to the mountains."[301]

In retrospect, we should have left the city when the Italians requested our registration. It was extremely easy to leave while it was legal to do so. All those who assisted us were not in danger, because they had not done anything illegal.

As for our exhilarating trip to freedom on October 3, when our car entered free territory, we all sighed with relief. In a few minutes we were stopped by an armed soldier dressed in a shabby uniform. We exchanged warm greetings with him. We knew him well. He was a cabinetmaker, and he had polished our furniture. The word ELAS was embroidered on his cap. I thought I discovered a spelling mistake since ELLAS, meaning Greece, is written with two Ls. Fortunately, I kept my mouth shut. Later I found out that ELAS stood for National Popular Resistance Army.

We passed the village of Agios Vlassis, where we saw Leon Revi, and arrived in Houni. The road ended near an unfinished bridge. A beautiful fountain stood nearby. It had been erected by the Italians at a time when enemy soldiers were not afraid to be stationed so far from Agrinion.

My father explained to the driver that he wanted to go to a village located some distance from the road. The driver understood and suggested the village of Psilovrahos, a three-hour hike from Houni. He arranged with local villagers to provide transportation for us. After a while, we were on our way with two horses and a donkey. Mother and Ninetta, my five-year-old sister, were placed in "nests" created between the bags loaded onto the horses, while Father and I walked. We felt great, the weather was excellent, and we were surrounded by beautiful scenery. We were in free territory and felt more like carefree tourists than oppressed, escaping Jews.

We finally approached the village of Psilovrahos, with a population of 300, spread on the side of a mountain. There were numerous fruit trees and evergreens, firs and pines. One could barely see the houses dotting the landscape all the way down to the Megdova River. On the other side of the river, one could see the village of Episcopi. In the distance, other villages were

---

301 P. K. Enepekidis, "The Secret Archives of the SS," *To Vima,* article 17, August 1966.

visible, nestling on the slopes of other mountains. The houses were pretty, well-kept, and at a distance from each other, surrounded by fruit trees and vegetable gardens. The cascading waters of a noisy stream were running parallel to our path. Soon we arrived at the center of the village among friendly people. One offered us a room in his house for a modest rental fee. The room had a fireplace, but no furniture except for a few wooden stools. There was no electricity or running water, bathroom or toilet. We soon found out that the forest and open fields were to become our toilets. We were provided with a small barrel and a rope. Father practiced how to secure the barrel on his back with the help of the rope. We walked for ten minutes to go to a beautiful, tree-shaded spring to get crystal clear water.

Our landlord, Georgios Papaioannou, allowed us to use his firewood for the fireplace. We bought sawhorses and boards to create beds. On them we placed mattresses filled with straw. The sheets, blankets and pillows we brought with us made up two beds. At night a quiet darkness descended on the village and flickering lights could be seen from a great distance.

It did not take long to realize that our meticulous preparation for life in a village was ill-planned and lacked many essential items. Fortunately, what we lacked in utensils or knowledge we compensated for with money for purchases and a willingness to learn. The villagers showed a great deal of good will, and they never refused to give us any household implement they could spare. We had to improvise continuously. Mother had the hardest time of all of us. How can one cook without a kitchen? How and where does one clean the dishes? How do you take a bath without a bathroom? We had to answer these questions, and we did to the best our imaginations allowed.

We kept in touch with Agrinion. A villager contacted Dimitrios Pipiringos at the bank and returned with two horseloads of provisions. Pipiringos, in order to help us, ignored the German order forbidding any assistance to Jews and disobeyed the bank director, who asked him to refrain from doing anything unlawful on our behalf. We felt we were well prepared to spend the winter without experiencing too many difficulties.

We maintained contact with our relatives in Ioannina by establishing our own mail service. Father sent a letter with a villager to Eugenia Papadopoulou, a colleague of his in Agrinion. She in turn mailed the letter to her brother Grigori in Ioannina. Then he delivered it in person to our relatives. The reverse route brought letters back to us. We were very distressed to learn that none of them had followed our example. In turn, they were unable to understand the reasons prompting our departure. The differences between our views and theirs were that we were not willing to accept any form of discrimination against the Jews, while they were persuaded that registering with the Germans was just a formality. In Ioannina they did not have to wear the yellow star or report to the community offices. We did not trust the Germans. Our friends and relatives were convinced that strict obedience to the Germans would provide safety for all. In a way, they trusted the Germans as we had trusted the Italians the year before.

A letter we received from Moshe Matsas, a first cousin of my father, demonstrates the false sense of security of the Jewish community of Ioannina. Moshe, in his letter, was reassuring us that everybody was well. He also informed us that he was going to bring supplies to us by traveling from Ioannina to Agrinion on board a German military car. It was obvious that he wanted to prove to us that the Germans could not possibly be bad if they provided transportation for Jews while they were in the middle of a war.

Father's efforts to persuade our relatives to leave the city were directed toward his brother-in-law, Dr. Nissim Samuel. To emphasize how strongly we felt about abandoning the city and going to free territory, my parents thought of a plan whereby a villager would go to Ioannina and bring my grandparents to Psilovrahos. Unfortunately, subsequent events prevented this plan from being carried out.

The villagers were very religious, and everybody went to church every Sunday where a kind priest, Papadimitris, officiated. We thought it would be better for us if we did not seem different, and so we went to church like everyone else. Our only difference was that we did not make the sign of the cross nor take communion at the end of the service.

Papadimitris became a good friend of ours. We told him that we were Jews, and he liked to come every Sunday after the service to our home where Mother prepared Turkish coffee for him. Coffee was a very rare delicacy, and mother was the only one in the village who possessed it. The same was true for sugar, rice, tea, soap, and quinine. All five items were used as medicines, which Mother dispensed as a sign of goodwill without accepting anything in return. She provided many "medical services" for the villagers. Sugar mixed with boiled ouzo was for all respiratory infections; rice and tea were the cure for all intestinal ailments; soap for all dermatological diseases; and quinine for malaria. In the village, people were divided into two categories: those (most) who had already malaria, and the very few who were about to suffer from it. We belonged to the second category. There were no real medicines, nurses, or doctors. The people of the village were born, grew old and died without the help of the medical profession. Our landlady was nine months pregnant, but she continued working in the fields with her husband. One day she came back earlier than usual. She carried with her the newborn baby, which had been delivered in the field.

The school consisted of one large room that accommodated all four classes of the elementary school. The teacher, Vasilis Arhimandritis, tried his best, but he did not have enough books, any notebooks or any other educational materials. Ninetta enrolled in the first grade. I copied the first-grade book for her.

Since he was not receiving any salary, the teacher closed the school and decided to go on foot to his village in the free mountains in Ipiros. My father was educated, and he could have become the teacher and kept the school open. I am sure that we would not have starved the way we did. The villagers would have felt sorry for us, and they would have helped us. We all made a big mistake not to suggest this idea. Even when the teacher Vasilis was in the village, if my father taught under his supervision, we would have had the best elementary school in the free mountains of Greece.

Once a week the village butcher would slaughter a goat or a cow. All those who had money would buy meat. The people had few animals, and only those animals that were sick were sold to the butcher.

Every night we listened anxiously to the voice of EPON (the National Greek Youth Organization). A bullhorn taken from an old gramophone was used as an amplifier by a youth who virtually shouted the news. The partisans established an excellent system of communications by the use of telephones.

III. Author's Memoirs

If they did not have enough cable, they used barbed wire from the fences. Wherever there were no telephones, as in our village, runners were used. After a few months, I was used as a runner between Psilovrahos and the nearby village of Agalianos.

Travel permits were issued for movement within the free territories. To move into the occupied cities, people were issued identity cards by the German authorities. The president of Psilovrahos issued birth certificates for my parents. The certificates, accompanied by my parents' photographs, were sent to Agrinion for processing. Soon my parents received valid German identity cards. In the process, the names were modified to conceal their Jewish origin. Leon was changed to Leonidas and Esther to Eftyhia. Peculiarly enough, the German identity cards did not mention religion, whereas, the Greek cards still do to this very day. The false documents gave us a feeling of security, given the remote possibility that we might be captured by the Germans or their collaborators.

My father's German identity card. The cards were issued to all the villagers of Psilovrahos. The president of the village took the papers to Agrinion, where the Germans put their official stamp. Father's own handwriting is recognizable to me.

At the end of October 1943, two Jews, Elias Krispis and Solomon Ovadias from Chalkis, came to our village and rented a room in our house. They, like many other Jewish men, believed that the Germans did not plan to harm in any way women, children, or old people. Their families were left behind while they tried to stay away from the Germans.[302] We gave a little party in their honor. The landlord was invited too. We lit a few candles for light, and Father made an excellent fire in our fireplace. It was a major social event.

The following day the landlord told us that, since we liked to have a warm room as we had the night before, we should get the wood from the forest by ourselves! Firewood was difficult to find, and our small blunt axe made things even worse. The first day I went to find firewood, I located a tree without leaves. I thought it was dead. I went to work! I was actually trying to cut down a fig tree which, at the end of October, no longer had any leaves. (In 1976 I saw the tree again. The point where I cut the branch could still be seen.) In spite of our minor problems, we all enjoyed our life in the village. We felt as if we were on a great vacation. I took my schoolbooks with me, but I never opened them while we were in the mountains.

This illusion of the "great vacation" soon ended. On November 5, we had an unexpected visitor. Yonas Mionis, a political leader of the resistance, came from Agios Vlassis with information that a large German column was advancing toward our general area. In a few minutes the church bell sounded the alarm, while the "voice of EPON" asked all men to attend a meeting at the school. At that meeting the reserve soldiers of ELAS and any others who wished to volunteer were ordered to go to Agios Vlassis where weapons and ammunition would be distributed. The partisans planned to resist the German advance. Late in the afternoon a group of 15 aroused men left our village for battle. Yonas Mionis, who knew the military situation better than anyone else, thought we should all leave the village early in the morning and go to higher ground. He expected the Germans to be in the village the following day.

Although the villagers felt safe with the Germans, we knew that under no circumstances should we fall into their hands. Our situation was even more perilous than that of the Jews

---

302 Their logic did not make any sense since they were aware of the fact that in Thessaloniki the Germans deported the entire family and not only men. The only other excuse they had was that the deportations were preceded by the induction of young men to "slave workers" groups. No such labor battalions were formed yet!

III. Author's Memoirs

who remained in the cities and followed the German orders. As long as they obeyed the Germans, they remained unmolested, while we were fugitives and, therefore, according to German law, condemned to death. The order was absolutely explicit on this point, and we realized its significance.

We prepared to take with us whatever clothing and food could be loaded on a small donkey and leave everything else in the room. That night was the worst one in my memory. Overzealous boys kept sounding the nerve-racking alarm all night long. A nightmare tormented me throughout the night. I had a dream that the safety of all the villages depended on a rope that was held by the men, one at a time. When my turn came to hold it, I failed, and so I placed the entire population of the area in jeopardy!

In the middle of the night, a distant explosion was heard. The partisan commander of Agios Vlassis realized he did not have enough forces to resist the Germans. The reserve ELAS reinforcements were coming too slowly. He blew up the guns and ammunition to prevent their capture by the Germans.

Early the next morning our group of seven Jews, together with two loaded donkeys and a villager, approached the top of the mountain. We found shelter in the house of Triantafyllis. The location was remote and at a distance from all trails that could be of any interest to the Germans. The house of Triantafyllis was located between corn and wheat fields on the right and a forest of large oak trees on the left. Father and Triantafyllis became good friends when our host mentioned that his daughter was working as a maid for someone who was a friend and colleague of my father. Our host's son Spyros established an instant restaurant for his guests.

Meanwhile, the German column kept moving ahead undisturbed in spite of the fact that the partisans had dynamited the road at key points and blown up a bridge at Potamoula. A few hours after our departure, German patrols were already in Psilovrahos.

On the first day away from the village, I was responsible for a false alarm that sent our group flying in all directions. I saw a long line of men and horses approaching on the trail. I yelled, "The Germans are here!" Everyone ran into the forest except for Father, who hid behind a rock, while Spyros went to see who these people were. They were only civilians returning to their village. This incident made our hosts aware of how much we feared the Germans. They suggested we spend the day in a nearby cave and return to their home at night. We accepted the suggestion, but Krispis, Ovadias, and Mionis preferred to go to another village behind the mountain.

Spyros led us to the cave of Arapokefalos, which was on the side of a hill near a stream passing through a fir forest. We explored the cave and enjoyed the beauty of the stalactites and stalagmites. The cave was very big, but since we did not have any light with us, we advanced only as far as the filtering light from the entrance allowed us to see. On the left side of the cave, we saw a flat surface, like an alcove, large enough to accommodate all four of us. We placed a heavy blanket on it and sat down. We told stories and relaxed as we waited for the time to pass. Sometime later we heard footsteps in front of the cave and then someone calling, "Mr. Matsas! Mr. Leon Matsas, come out!" We were terrified because we did not expect anyone. We kept very quiet. "Mr. Matsas, it's me, Spyros, come out!" the man continued. We were afraid we had been betrayed. He insisted on calling us. We were afraid our tormentors might throw a grenade into the cave. Father finally decided that we should go out. It took us a few seconds to get used to the sunlight before we recognized Spyros. Standing close by in this wilderness were two well-tailored men, one of whom had a suitcase.

Mother scrutinized the older of the two men, and before we were introduced, she told my father in French, "He looks very Jewish. If we are caught with him, we will all be lost." The man looked at my mother and in a bitter tone of voice replied in impeccable French, "You look more Jewish than I!" Had we become uncivilized like the Germans? I wondered. Everyone remained silent for a few seconds. Mother blushed, embarrassed, and obviously regretted the episode. The old man also regretted his outburst. As a man who was used to controlling his emotions, he turned to Father and discussed something else. No one mentioned this encounter again.

The old man was Aaron Romano, a multimillionaire shipowner, and his companion was Alexander Levi, the former owner of a private bank. They were in Agios Vlassis, where they were told about us, and they had walked to Psilovrahos accompanied by Oreozyl Levi, Alexander's wife. She became so tired from walking that she decided to stay in the village rather than follow the men who kept looking for us, following our trail

III. Author's Memoirs

all the way to the cave of Arapokefalos. Romano, who did not know Greek, exhibited a boundless capacity to endure suffering with fortitude and resignation. He preferred hunger than disclose the fact that he had gold with him.

The following day we decided not to stay in the cave any longer, as it had been very easy for Spyros to find us. We found shelter under a large protruding rock. Another flat rock served as a sofa on which we placed blankets for comfort. Branches of fir trees were placed in front, leaning on the rock overhead. We created a new hiding place which protected us from rain, wind and unwelcome visitors. Romano and Levi stayed in the Triantafyllis house. Ovadias, Krispis, and Mionis decided that the next village was not any safer than the Triantafyllis house and returned the next day. They became lost and passed in front of our hiding place. We called them, and they could not find us. Our camouflage was perfect. We felt like children playing hide and seek! We had to direct their steps to find us. At night we were 14 people sleeping on the floor in one room dominated by a huge fireplace. The elder Triantafyllis lay next to the fireplace. Half asleep, he would clear his throat every so often and spit on the fire.

For eight days we survived in the forest, and for eight nights we slept in the room of Triantafyllis. We all slept peacefully, except my father, who in the middle of the second night witnessed a puzzling episode. Someone knocked gently. Old Triantafyllis answered the door opening it less than an inch. A heavy wooden bar was in place, not allowing any further opening. In spite of the bitter cold, he did not allow his guest in, and yet he carried on with him or them a lengthy quiet conversation. Eventually the door was closed. Father could not sleep any longer that night nor the following nights. He kept his thoughts secret and decided to sleep during the day and keep guard at night. In many conversations during the following 46 years, he told me he did not want to alarm anybody. He also did not want to see Mionis, Ovadias, and Krispis leave again. He wondered whether the "guest" was a criminal operating on his own or a potential informer. He lay at night next to Mionis, who was an armed and experienced fighter. He would be ready to deal with Greek criminals. Father figured that a German squad would need an hour and a half to reach our solitary house, and that they could not possibly arrive before sunrise. By that time, we were all dispersed in the forest.

My father was greatly disturbed by this incident and many thoughts crossed his mind. My father originally thought, as he told me, to report this very important incident to the partisans. It was obvious that Triantafyllis was a friend of ours, who did not agree to anything that was proposed to him that night.

At the same time, it was also very suspicious. There were two possibilities - either the Germans had agents in our village, or a villager wanted to blackmail us. Either way, the partisans would have to interrogate Triantafyllis. Triantafyllis would not want to betray another villager. The partisans could even threaten him with execution unless he told them who was the man and what he wanted. The usual way was for the man under interrogation to dig his own grave until he talked. So, my father never reported the incident to anyone.

For me this adventure was an unforgettable experience. For the first time I saw heavy fog climbing up the mountain toward us and enjoyed the stillness of the dense forest. During the time we were in Arapokefalos, a German unit remained in the village while the main force advanced. German soldiers slept in our room and stole some of our goods. One of them found a red book and made a great fuss about it. He threw it into the mud and stepped on it as he yelled, "Communista!" Communista!" This little incident made the rounds of the village, and our popularity fell to its lowest point. The villagers, who loved the organizations of EAM-ELAS-EPON, did not know they were communist led.

A man from Agrinion who was in the village eventually picked up the book and discovered that, in spite of its red cover, it was only a Greek-English dictionary! Oreozyl Levi, who spoke German fluently, talked with the German officers and interpreted for them. She claimed that she stopped the Germans from sending a patrol to the upper village by telling them there were no other houses beyond the church.

One woman discovered the telephone cable the advancing German units left behind and realized she had many uses for it! With the help of two stones, she cut it, and after she had collected as much as she wanted, she cut it again. Without realizing it, she became a saboteur. A villager who was an army veteran explained to her what she had done, took her wire, and

III. Author's Memoirs

restored the German communications before any reprisals took place.

Many years later, I found out what really happened in November 1943. The commander of ELAS, General Stefanos Sarafis wrote:

> A German force of more than 600 men, with vehicles and artillery, advanced from Agrinion toward Agios Vlassis. There it clashed with the 13th Division troops, and its advance was held up for 24 hours.
>
> It crossed the Sidera bridge, clashed with ELAS forces south of Frankista on the 7th, and finally pushed toward Kalismeno. It again clashed with ELAS forces and, after burning part of the center of Karpenissi and several villages, returned to Agrinion on November 13.[303]

As soon as the Germans left, we returned to our room in the village. We were appalled by the disorder we found and especially by the near-total disappearance of our food supplies. The landlord told us the Germans had stolen everything. While it is possible that the Germans took some things, the room was in our landlord's hands before the Germans arrived and after they left, and he was the real thief, as we later found out. Ninetta continued playing with the daughters of our landlord, Georgios Papaioannou, and they told her how their life had improved lately. "We have things we never had before: candles, candy, and macaroni!" When my mother heard this, she became furious. She went downstairs and thoroughly searched their house, finding many of our missing things. She took whatever was obviously ours and accused the landlord of stealing. We decided, after much thought, not to press charges against him in the "People's Court" of the resistance. We did not want to be responsible for a death penalty, which would most certainly have been imposed on him. (We knew that a partisan had been executed for stealing a chicken!) He, however, became angry with us and asked us to leave our room. He most probably hid our supplies away from his house,

---

[303] Major General Stefanos Sarafis, *Greek Resistance Army* (Humanities Press, 1981), 437.

because Mother retrieved very little. Another reason I suspect him is the fact that the Germans did not engage in looting our village. When the villagers were asked to submit a list of the items they lost, most of them listed things like "a bottle of wine, including the bottle" or "a bottle of ouzo, including the bottle." Bottles were very scarce in Psilovrahos, and thus more valuable than wine or ouzo.

The winter was about to begin, and we were without enough food or shelter. A family by the name Yovanos from Agrinion, who lived in a house just below the church, was about to return to the city. Father arranged with Dimitrios Serpanos, the owner of the house, to give us their room. Mr. Yovanos had deposited large amounts of grain with Andrea Bouloumbassis, the richest man of the village. An agreement was made with Mr. Yovanos to give us 100 kilos of corn and to receive the same amount from our supplies in the bank. If this transaction proved successful, Yovanos agreed to continue giving us more supplies in exchange for equal amounts, which he would withdraw from our supplies in Agrinion.

We received the 100 kilos of corn, but the greed and malice of Andrea Bouloumbassis sabotaged our plans and condemned our family to starvation. Bouloumbassis forced Yovanos either to take his supplies with him immediately or to sell them to him. Yovanos was forced to sell them, and we thus lost the last opportunity to receive supplies from any source, with the exception of a small can of olive oil, which a villager brought to us from Pipiringos. We made an inventory of our supplies and realized that the situation was desperate. In the meantime, conditions in the occupied cities had become worse, and the villagers did not visit Agrinion anymore.

Even the villagers did not have enough food. The terraces where they planted wheat and corn were filled with rocks. They normally worked on road projects to supplement their income, or they received assistance from relatives who went to the cities or immigrated to America. The war put an end to these sources of income. Still, every family had a few goats, chickens or pigs, and some had a cow or two. All of a sudden, we became the poorest of all. Even our money would soon lose all its value because of hyperinflation. The Germans printed enormous amounts of it. Our 4,000,000 drachmas would not even buy a loaf of bread.

III. Author's Memoirs

Our new stone house had two rooms. We occupied one; the other was a cafe. A trap door connected our room with the cellar beneath it. The floor was made of flagstones. Father made a secret compartment under a flagstone where he could hide books and valuable documents in case of an emergency.

The previous tenant, Mr. Yovanos, had constructed a primitive outhouse for his wife and daughters nearby in an abandoned field. On the day the Yovanos family departed, the Tserpelis boys destroyed the outhouse. Evidently it spoiled their view. Father found a secluded spot, placed two big square stones near each other, and used this as his permanent toilet. Mother was very fast. She used to go behind our house when she knew that no one was around. Ninetta and I changed spots every day in the unused fields near the house.

The Jewish community of Psilovrahos became smaller when Yonas Mionis went back to his duties, while Ovadias and Krispis decided to go and hide in Athens rather than be subjected to German raids.

We constructed an oven on the side of the house. On a base of flagstones, the round clay cover could bake bread or pies. We also collected a large quantity of firewood by making a special expedition to the nearby forest. We were assisted by a laborer who was paid the usual amount of one kilo of corn for one day's work and a former Italian soldier who passed by our village and worked for a few hours for a cup of soup. The poor laborer, I was told, died at the age of forty. He was always overworked and underpaid. The phantom of starvation was already in the village.

One day, Father bought a goat (this was before the money lost all its value). The villager who sold her persuaded Father to buy it by telling him the goat was pregnant and that in a few months we would have two goats as well as milk. Unfortunately, the goat was sold because she was very sick. The villager sold her just in time. When the goat's illness reached the point that even ignorant city people like us were able to understand, we rushed her to the butcher. While we did not mind eating the meat of a sick animal, the idea of eating a dead animal revolted us. Aaron Romano asked my father what he had done with the fetus. When he was told that we threw it away in the forest, he rushed with father, before any dog or other animal ate it, and retrieved it. With my father's permission, he gave it to Oreozyl Levi to prepare it for dinner.

The multimillionaire, the banker, and the Athenian socialite had a feast that evening! Usually, they ate even less than we did. They started losing weight in an alarming way, and they felt that we should have shared what we had with them. My mother, more so than my father, refused to give away anything, and this did not help our relations with them.

Mother refused to share our meager supplies, first because of her feelings of self-preservation, and second because she correctly suspected that these wealthy people had gold with them but preferred to starve rather than reveal its existence. In fact, just four months later, Aaron Romano gave my mother gold to buy food for them when she was going to Agrinion. After she came back, she returned the gold to Romano.

Oreozyl Levi tried in vain to persuade the villagers who lived in the upper village that they should help them with some food. She told them that the Germans wanted to send troops to search their houses when they saw smoke coming out of the forest. She also told the German officers that there were no houses there, just some poor shepherds. Even if they felt any gratitude toward her, it was not translated into food, which was desperately needed. The question arises as to why the Germans did not ask an elegant lady like Oreozyl Levi what she was doing in a poor, forsaken village by herself in the middle of winter. It is impossible to believe that they did not suspect she was Jewish. Yet they treated her with great politeness, perhaps following instructions designed to lure all Jews back into the clutches of the Gestapo in the cities.

Father and Aaron Romano used a wooden stool as a board on which they drew squares to play backgammon. Father used little stones for pieces, and Romano selected acorns, the fruit of the oak trees, of which there were a great number everywhere. Years later I found out that Indians and Africans remove the hard shell of the acorns and eat the soft interior, which is very nutritious. If only we had known more! The villagers did not have this knowledge either, though the few pigs of Psilovrahos ate acorns with no ill effect.

As for the meat from our sick goat, we never thought of the obvious fact that all meat inspectors would have rejected it. On the contrary, we intended to use this meat as our sole source of protein for the next six months. The goat must have been very agile and very old. It was impossible to chew any part of the meat. Even if it were cut into small pieces, it had to be

III. Author's Memoirs

swallowed whole because it was like small pieces of leather. We preserved the meat in a wooden barrel by using large amounts of salt. Our intention was to eat a small piece each week. There was no more meat for sale in the village.

Aaron Romano knew the villagers were suspicious of everything foreign. He told us that, in the beginning, he pretended to be the mute uncle of the Levis, rather than disclose the fact that his mother tongue was Turkish. He spoke with the Levis in French. In the marginal existence of village life, every little thing counted, material or psychological, and made the difference between life and death. My mother was liked by the village women, and this brought us an egg or an onion, while Oreozyl Levi was disliked because she acted "superior." Acting this way did not bring any food. Mother taught the village women embroidery, sewing, and cooking. She had great ability as a teacher.

She spent many hours a week in the house of the former village president, Dimitrios Tsoulos, who, in his great desire to have a son, produced seven lovely daughters. They were all appreciative students of my mother since each one of them was eager to prepare her dowry and learn the ways of cultured women in the cities. The youngest daughter Martha was a classmate of my sister.

The partisans provided food for themselves with a form of taxation that was the responsibility of ETA. They asked Father to become the ETA man of the village, and he accepted the job. Psilovrahos was so poor that the collected items were insignificant. Father, though, enjoyed the idea that he officially, at least, was a partisan with ELAS.

On November 25, 1943, the military governor of Greece issued an order confiscating all assets of Jews of Greek nationality who had not registered with the authorities:

> Assets are considered all items and rights representing monetary value, real estate, rents, farm income, corporate agreements, demands of every type, stocks and bonds. All confiscated assets will be given to the Greek State for management.[304]

---

304 National Archives No. 82, File No. 8401.

This meant that we lost the house we owned in Athens and anything the bank owed Father for his work from 1922 to 1943.

In the middle of December 1943, the news of a German attack sounded the alarm again. This time we did not consider the matter as seriously as we had previously. In retrospect, complacency and an illusion of safety proved to be worse than fear. Father and I forgot all our principles of freedom and resistance and, at a critical point, we abandoned both Mother and Ninetta.

Oreozyl Levi, who did not want to venture into the mountains and caves, persuaded Mother that the Germans were harmless. Mother did not want to leave our remaining supplies for fear of losing them to the villagers, if not to the Germans, and agreed to stay. Father and I did not object. So, as the Germans were approaching the village, Romano, Levi (with the suitcase), Father, and I hiked the slope leading to the cave of Arapokefalos, while Oreozyl, Mother, and Ninetta remained in our room.

A neighbor of ours, Barbayiorgos, a retired policeman whose son was a partisan, believed we had all made a mistake. He went to our house and in an authoritarian manner told the women not to stay in the village. "How do you know whether the German unit which will occupy the village will be the same one that did not do any harm to Oreozyl Levi last time? How do you know that they will believe you are from this village? Or isn't it possible that they have orders to arrest any suspicious-looking people?" In a few minutes Mother, with Oreozyl and Ninetta, locked the house and began the journey toward the upper village. Fortunately for everyone, the Germans did not even enter Psilovrahos on this raid. Their column could be seen advancing by the shores of the Megdova River. Fifteen partisans who came to the village got ready to fire at the Germans from a great distance. The villagers persuaded them that their firing would be ineffective and would only bring disaster to the civilians. The partisans promptly agreed to accept the hospitality of the villagers until the Germans left the area.

Another partisan unit, however, of the 13th ELAS Division, attacked the German mechanized force on the

III. Author's Memoirs

Agrinion-Agios Vlassis Road. They destroyed four vehicles, killing 25 Germans and wounding one.[305]

Winter arrived, and it was cold! It was especially so for me, since I wore shorts. We had a pair of woolen leg protectors extending from knee to ankle. Mother attached these to my pants and, although my appearance was grotesque, my legs were not cold anymore. We also had problems with our shoes. Ninetta was given a pair of pigskin slippers. My feet outgrew my shoes, and so I began wearing my galoshes without any shoes inside. Since we had lost our candles, we had no light at night. Father, though, made a discovery. Close to the shoe repair shop were small pieces of rubber from discarded tires used to make the soles of shoes. Father collected many pieces of rubber. Then, with the help of a wire, a piece of tin can, and a nail, he made a container that was hung in our fireplace. During dinner we had light. The smell of the burning rubber was horrible, but darkness was worse. (During my family's 1976 visit to the village, Mr. Serpanos graciously allowed us to see the room and the basement, which both witnessed some of the most important moments in my life. I remembered my father's lighting "system," and, as I described it, I bent and looked inside the fireplace. To everyone's surprise, the nail was still there where my father had placed it 33 years before.)

I was in charge of collecting small branches and other wood for our ever-increasing needs for the fireplace and the oven. My other duties included getting water from the spring or from a stream whose water descended rapidly just behind the church. Since we did not have enough pots for water storage, I had to go to the stream quite often. This meant passing through the village cemetery, which I did not mind during the day. At night, however, I had to hide my fears, especially during the first days after a funeral when a small flame from an oil lamp could be seen flickering in the darkness. I could have avoided all this if I had chosen a shortcut and got the water at a point below the cemetery. That is something I never did. It would have been unhealthy and revolting.

In the winter of 1943-1944, our main preoccupation was food and how to stretch what little we had for as long as possible. One day a British military mission passed through

---

305 Sarafis, *Greek Resistance Army*, 348.

our village. Father tried to practice his English, and he was given four multivitamin tablets by a British soldier; we did not eat anything else on that day. Our regular diet during this period consisted of corn flour soup and a pie made of corn flour mixed with dandelions and other wild vegetables I collected in the fields. They were so bitter that the animals could not eat them. Mother had to boil them three times and throw away the water before the bitterness was eliminated. The vitamins were also eliminated in this way. Cellulose is not normally digested, but the human body can adapt itself and utilize it. These wild vegetables really eliminated our hunger. Our stomachs were full, in spite of the fact that we were losing weight.

Every Sunday, after the religious service, boiled wheat was offered by a different family each week in memory of their dead. The wheat was placed in our cupped hands and we ate it slowly. It took many months before a little boy approached me and in a resentful voice said, "You eat here every week, but you never bring a tray of wheat like all the other families." None of the adults ever made any comment. (One year later, during the civil war, when all the villagers of Psilovrahos were lodged in a warehouse in Agrinion, we distributed loaves of bread to the entire village as a token of gratitude for all the things they did for us while we were among them.)

In the middle of our self-imposed food rationing, we received a letter from my uncle, Dr. Nissim Samuel, from Ioannina. His letter, dated January 12, 1944, was written partly in code, in case it was intercepted by the Germans:

Dear Brother and Sister,

We have received an old letter of yours from your vacation home. We wish a speedy recovery to our dear Nelly. John feels better from his diabetes, thanks to his discipline in following his diet and the instructions of his doctors. All our relatives here are well, send you many kisses, and want to receive a letter from you.

We received three letters from Delvino within the last month. Our children Gracia and Annoula kiss you. Waiting good news from you.

                        Love,
                        Nissim

III. Author's Memoirs

The way we interpreted the main points was this: "We hope that the war will end soon, victoriously. The Jews of Ioannina feel better after the impact of the German restrictions and, by obeying their orders to the letter, they are well."

We naturally welcomed this good news, and in our pitiful surroundings a new debate arose. Why should we suffer and run risks in the mountains instead of staying in the city like so many others? This debate, as we found out later, took place in hundreds of Jewish households in villages and hiding places. Many Jews returned to normal life and their familiar surroundings. The Germans did not take any measures against them, and this encouraged many more hard-pressed Jews to return home.

After the war, we found out that the German general who was stationed in Ioannina promised the Jews of the city that "As long as I am in charge here, nothing will happen to you." The Jews of Ioannina did not have to wear the yellow star nor present themselves anywhere every two days as they did in Athens. It is possible that the German general was an honest man, but his superiors sent him someplace else before they arrested the Jewish community. According to Yossas Matsas, a few days prior to their arrest, a high German official arrived by seaplane in Lake Pamvotis of Ioannina. It was Kurt Waldheim, the future secretary General of the United Nations and future President of Austria. He was in charge of looting the gold and jewelry of the Jews after their deportation while they were in Larissa on their way to Auschwitz.

In our case, the doubts about leaving Agrinion lasted only momentarily. Father and I declared that we would not, under any circumstances, return to occupied territory. So, I decided to become a hunter! Flagstones were precariously supported by sticks in an inclined position. A few grains of wheat or corn were used as bait. A bird would try to eat the grain, and if it disturbed the stick, the flagstone would fall on it. During the whole winter, I caught only one skinny sparrow. I did not witness the success of my trap. The children of our neighbor Tserpelis did. They could have kept the bird if they wanted, but it was known in the village that we were starving. They gave it to me. We had a feast! Father used a wire to make a rotisserie, and then he roasted the bird to perfection. We even ate the bones! Another time we ate healthy meat was when a villager gave Father a few ounces of pork. It must have been

Christmas. Traditionally, the villagers would slaughter a pig at Christmas and a lamb at Easter. This was the first time we ate pork. Father said, "Let's pretend it's chicken!"

On January 30, 1944, we received a letter from Eugenia Papadopoulou from Agrinion:

> Dear Esther and Leon,
> Happy New Year. I wrote another letter to you but was not able to find a person to give it to you. I don't know where you are, and I tore it up. Well! After such a long time, Nikos brought me a letter from Ioannina. They tell me, "Grigoris went to the house of Esther's sister Eftyhia and she told him that all her relatives are very well. They did not leave and only her brother in Albania lost a lot of money. The relatives of Leon are also very well. Eftyhia said that she was going to write to you but she must have been afraid and she did not.
> How are you? We miss you and think of you. Maybe you should not have left. Your clothes are all right. Kiss the children and especially my golden Ninetta for me.
> Greetings from Andreas.
> Love,
> Eugenia

"Maybe you should not have left." We repeated these words openly and, in our thoughts, over and over again. We thought of them when we ate and in the chill of the night. It took a few days before we regained our equilibrium and returned to our obstinacy and refusal to accept good living in exchange for our freedom. We preferred the rags of free Greece to the velvet gowns in German-occupied territory! I remember I thought I would have felt defeated and humiliated had I returned to my school when the Germans were still in the city.

What surprises me now as I write this account in 2020 is the following: My father sent a villager to Mr. Pipiringos in the bank to collect some of our food supplies. He returned without any supplies, and he gave us a letter. He did not bring any food to us. The same thing happened with a second villager that my father sent to the bank. Again, we did not receive any food and only received a letter. We were so preoccupied with the letters and the question of whether to stay or to return to the city, that we did not even ask these men why they did not bring us any

III. Author's Memoirs

of our food. We continued to starve and even after we returned to the free city, we never found out if Mr. Pipiringos gave them any supplies for us. We were just so happy to be alive!

In our village, in addition to Jews, there were also Italian ex-servicemen. When they first arrived, they were in a terrible state of appearance and health. The partisans exchanged uniforms with captured Italians and Germans, or they would simply take their clothes and boots. Mother had to give them some clothing. One had dysentery, and my parents did their best with our meager resources to help him survive. One decided to become a barber, and the other, as soon as he recovered, a tailor. In appreciation for our help, the tailor made an overcoat for me out of a military blanket we had. It was the most ill-fitting garment ever created. I wish I had a picture of myself wearing that coat, the short trousers with the woolen additions, and my galoshes or, later on, shoes which were made of canvas on top and concentric lines of nylon rope from a parachute on the bottom. There was a third Italian in the village briefly. He became a nurse in the partisan hospital in Tatarna.

One night we heard the motor of a plane flying at low altitude. The following morning, we discovered a great number of leaflets with the picture of the prime minister of the Greek government-in-exile, George Papandreou. We found also a package of leaflets which had not been opened. The arrival of all this paper pleased us immensely. We were able to have toilet paper again! The following are the important points of the leaflets: "... The civil war among our partisans in the Greek mountains are shadows which would not blemish the glory of all our people who suffer the inhuman tyranny of both Germans and Bulgarians. They are the barbarians of Europe and the Balkans, who offer victims to the altar of freedom." The leaflet reinforced our view that Greece was going to be liberated soon. All we had to do was make sure we remained alive to see the day of liberation.

Sometime in February 1944, Father and the teacher Vasilis had a brilliant idea. They decided to go to the British mission in Priantsa and ask for financial assistance. Their rationale was the following: Father and Vasilis were both employees who did not receive any salary. Inflation had decimated their savings. They did not have land, animals, or even a room of their own. Romano and the Levis were also suffering. Since no one knew for sure whether they had any gold with them, they were told about the plan. It was suggested that Oreozyl Levi should go with them since the old men were not fit for such a trip. Father and Vasilis were misunderstood, and I witnessed an argument which had sexual overtones and barely disguised Romano's jealousy. I could not believe there were subjects other than food, war, and freedom. Father and Vasilis went to Priantsa by themselves.

A British major listened to them but refused to extend any financial help. A villager in Priantsa gave Father a comb made out of wood as a gift. Our only comb had been broken and then lost, and its replacement would have been worth the trip if it were not for the fact that Father became ill. During the journey they had to cross the Agrafiotis River. The current was swift, and the water cold. Father returned with great pain in his legs. Nobody was able to help him in Psilovrahos, and Mother decided to go to the partisan hospital in Tatarna and ask for medicine there.

The following morning Mother and I, supplied with a few pieces of vegetable pie, started our trip to Tatarna. We passed the villages of Sidera and Agios Vassilios and reached Kremasta, where there was a spectacular gorge, narrow, and awe-inspiring with vertical granite cliffs on both sides. Three rivers, the Megdova, Agrafiotis and Acheloos, joined as they flowed thundering between the cliffs of Kremasta. A primitive aerial tramway consisting of a box attached with a pulley to an overhead cable provided the means to cross from one side to the other. This is the exact spot which, several years later, was selected for the construction of the biggest hydroelectric dam in Greece. On our way to Tatarna, we also had to cross the Agrafiotis River. Mother and I held hands as we started walking on the round pebbles, which we could see through the crystal-clear waters. Since there were no roads in sight, we hiked on narrow trails which sometimes were not passable even for horses, let alone carriages. None of the villagers in these mountains possessed anything with wheels. Except for one at Sidera, there were no bridges over the rivers or streams. The only evidence of a man-made road was in Valtos, near Tatarna. It was a wide stretch of about fifty feet of cobblestones, which could have been the exposed part of a Roman road. There were no signs to mark the trails or the

III. Author's Memoirs

names of the villages. It was extremely easy to get lost and walk for hours in the wrong direction.

Tatarna was a beautiful, affluent village. We arrived in the center of it immediately after the execution of a suspected German agent. I felt no sympathy for his fate, and I was glad he had been captured and executed. The hospital was in the large monastery of Tatarna. It was to Dr. Panopoulos, its director, that we tried to explain the symptoms of Father's illness. He wanted to help us, and he gave us a number of pills for Father. As we were about to leave, he asked me if I liked to sing and whether I knew many songs. In a few minutes, I was escorted into the main room of the monastery, where there were at least fifty lightly wounded or convalescing partisans. With great enthusiasm, I gave the first song recital of my life. The ELAS songs were most inspiring. The melodies were haunting, and the lyrics spoke of what is precious to any man or woman who loves freedom and justice.

These beautiful songs created great patriotic enthusiasm. Young people flocked to EAM-ELAS by the thousands. They believed that as soon as the war was over a new world would be born, one without ignorance, poverty, and injustice. This idealism of EAM-ELAS influenced the people deeply, and it created the most favorable conditions for fugitives like us.

[A few years ago, I received a telephone call from Yad Vashem, the Holocaust memorial museum in Jerusalem. A lady told me that Yad Vashem collects songs that were sung by Jews during the Second World War. She knew about my recital at age 14 in the Tatarna Hospital.

She asked me how many Jews were partisans of ELAS and if they all sang these songs. I said 650, and I believe all of them knew the songs. Then with great hesitation in her voice she said, "Do you still remember them?" I said, "I do, because these are beautiful songs that I still sing when I am by myself."

She arranged the details and a wonderful CD was produced via a telephone interview with me. I translated each song from Greek into English, and I sang it in Greek. It was my first and last song production!]

Once the recital was over, Mother and I had to think again of the little details of everyday living. We found shelter for the night in a house in Tatarna, and for the first time in months I had a nutritious meal. My stomach was too weak, and I vomited. My mother reciprocated our hosts' kindness by preparing "minestrone," or Italian noodles, and cooking them. Everybody liked this new food so much that they asked us to stay there for a few days to prepare more. We naturally had to refuse because of Father's illness. The following morning the hostess gave us a piece of bread and cheese. We decided to share this food with Father and Ninetta, so we did not eat it.

On our return to Psilovrahos, we were joyously welcomed by them. In a few days, Father's legs were fine, but he became dizzy and was unable to stand. Again, we did not know how to help him. We needed medical advice, and someone suggested that it was easier to go to Agios Vlassis, where there were partisan physicians.

Mother and I were on the march again. We hiked to Houni and then continued on the road to Agios Vlassis. Parts of the road had been destroyed by the partisans in their attempt to slow the German advance in November. In Agios Vlassis, we met the partisan medical team, which consisted of a dentist and two Jewish physicians from Thessaloniki. Unfortunately, I don't remember their names. One of the two physicians was an obstetrician. He promised to visit Psilovrahos in three days and examine Father. On our way back, we passed a butcher shop where a partisan worked. Mother begged for a piece of meat, and she was successful. We returned home with the head of a lamb. Meanwhile, Father had become well on his own. This was fortunate, as the physician never came; a battle with the Germans forced him to go to a different area.

In the middle of March 1944, a minor incident took place in our home that illustrates the degree of hunger we were experiencing. We were having lunch, and Father threw a small piece of cornbread on the floor near an emaciated cat which belonged to a neighbor. I jumped instantly and got the cornbread before the cat did. I yelled at my father, "You give food to a strange cat while we are starving? No wonder she comes here so often." This little episode made us all realize that I, at least, was slowly descending to the lower depths of civilization, reaching the level where food dominates one's thoughts.

We made a new inventory of our supplies. They were diminishing at a faster rate than we originally anticipated. Mother insisted that she should go to Agrinion and bring some of our supplies back from there. Father and I were against this plan because we were afraid for her safety.

III. Author's Memoirs

A few days later the village was filled with a great deal of excitement. A company of as many as sixty partisans arrived to stay for a period of twenty days. They were of all ages and backgrounds, from idealistic university students to patriotic villagers. They were dressed in uniforms from four armies: Greek, British, Italian, and German. Some were dressed partially in civilian clothes, and one wore a black tuxedo jacket. Their boots were in different states of disrepair. They had walked long distances on rough terrain. Some wore pigskin sandals.

They occupied the school and a few rooms in adjacent houses. They cooked their meals in the kitchen of the Tsoulos family. Oreozyl Levi and I asked the partisan commander if they could help us with our food situation. By March 1944, we definitely showed signs of malnutrition. The commander brought up the subject of sharing their food with us at their usual meeting that same day. The partisans voted in our favor. Each family was given the ration of one partisan. We were overjoyed. Twice a day when the bugle sounded the familiar tune, I ran and stood in line with the partisans. Their main food consisted of corn soup with a little olive oil and corn bread. They were not well fed either. We decided to divide the food we received, which was supposed to be eaten by only one person into four portions. In this way, we would save our own supplies and subsist on what we received from the partisans for as long as they stayed in the village.

In March 1944, a campaign of terror was instigated in Agrinion against all resistance sympathizers. A mass execution of 200 left no doubt about the seriousness of the situation. Mother kept insisting that we needed supplies and that we would die from starvation. I refused to go with her on this trip, and she decided to go by herself.

On March 31, she began the 12-hour hike to Agrinion. Three days later she returned, totally exhausted and deeply depressed. In addition, the acrylic veneer on her upper bridge had accidentally broken, changing her appearance for the worse. "They arrested them," she told us. "The Jews of Arta, Preveza and Ioannina are in the tobacco warehouses of Papapetrou in Agrinion."

Our anger was great. Our contempt and hate for the Germans had no limits. We could not suppress our disappointment toward our friends and relatives for having trusted the Germans. We were angry with their weak, cowardly, unsophisticated, servile, fatalistic leaders. The arrest had violated the sanctity, preciousness, and happiness of our relatives. We did not know that deportation meant more than a degrading experience. I remember we were only afraid that we would not see my grandparents again. They were very old.

After we calmed down, Mother told us what happened during her journey. "A few kilometers beyond Agios Vlassis I met our friends, Mr. and Mrs. Svolis. They did not recognize me. [They were Christians. He was my math teacher.] When I told them who I was and that I was going to Agrinion, they both said, 'Go back, Mrs. Matsas. Don't you know that all the Jews of Arta, Preveza and Ioannina are inside the tobacco warehouses of Papapetrou?' I explained to them our lack of food, and they advised me to go to Kamaroula, a village on the outskirts of Agrinion, and ask their godfather, Christos Zambaras, to go to the city to bring us food. I thanked them and kept going toward Agrinion. On the bridge of Potamoula, the partisans have a control point. The man in charge was Joseph Lahanas. When he understood who I was, he asked me if I knew what had happened. After that we both cried, because he was sure his parents in Arta were also arrested. 'I am not going to let you go any further,' he said. I explained to him my plan, and he agreed that it was a sensible one. I put my resistance identity card under a rock and kept only my German one. In Kamaroula, I found the Zambaras house. It was in the main square, and it had a mail box in front of it, as described by Svolis. I knocked at the front door and when it was finally opened, I realized that the women in the house were in a state of panic. 'The Germans,' one of them said, 'knocked on this door only a few minutes ago. Nobody comes to the front door. We thought the Germans came again.'

"She pointed in the distance at a group of German soldiers. Once I told them who I was, they told me to wear a village scarf, lie down and pretend that I was a sick cousin from Psilovrahos if the Germans came again. In a few minutes, they brought their brother, who was the village teacher. I explained to him what I wanted, and he agreed to go to the bank in Agrinion and bring back a horseload of supplies. 'In the meantime,' he said, 'My sister will take you to our house in the fields, where my deaf-mute aunt is living.' His sister took me to the little house, ten minutes away, while he mounted his horse and went to Agrinion. In a few hours, which seemed like an eternity, he came back with an unloaded horse. 'I am sorry,' he said. 'I went to the bank and talked with the director, Papayannis, who is my godfather. As soon as he heard that you were in Kamaroula he became very concerned: "It is a pity," said Papayannis. "Get her out of there immediately." He called Pipiringos and Eugenia Papadopoulou into his office and, after a small discussion, they decided that it was too risky to transfer food out of the bank and put it on a horse. The second request I made was carried out. Eugenia went to the house of Exarhos and brought me tea, matches, sugar and quinine. I put them in my pockets and I left Agrinion.' I was unhappy," Mother continued, "for failing to bring any food, but at the same time I was moved by the bravery of Zambaras and the devotion of our friends in Agrinion." [Exarhos, an officer of the Security Battalion, and other German collaborators were imprisoned by the partisans as soon as Agrinion was liberated.]

Mother continued, "Zambaras did not even consider the country house safe. We started walking toward Potamoula. It was getting dark, and the partisans did not allow any movement at night. We eventually went to the lonely church of Prophet Elias, atop a hill. 'My grandfather built it,' Christos said. We spent the night there without blankets, food, or water. The wind was blowing hard, and every noise scared me. Early in the morning Christos showed me the way toward Agios Vlassis. I thanked him and went on my way.

"In Potamoula, I saw Joseph Lahana again. We fell into each other's arms and cried. [Lahana's entire family perished. He later died during Israel's War of Independence.] We thought it would be better if none of the villagers knew that the Jews in the nearby cities were arrested. After all, we always tried to give the impression that there was no difference between Christians and Jews, except for the sign of the cross!"

We decided to tell this news only to Romano and the Levis, who reacted the same way we did. A few days later, Oreozyl Levi contacted General Sarafis of ELAS, with whom she was acquainted, and obtained a position for her husband as a typist at the command headquarters in Frankista. Once again, we were the only Jews remaining in the village.

Father, who was very methodical in his thinking, noticed that my teacher Svolis had an unusual Christian surname, which, however, was common among the Jews of Ioannina. He sent Mother to his *koumbaros* (godfather) Zambaras, and although the name Zambaras was not a common one among Christians, it was a nickname for the Levi family of Ioannina. The director of the bank, Papayannis, was Zambaras's godfather (Papayannis was known as a descendent of Jews). Perhaps the Jewish survivors of the massacre of 1821 maintained ties with each other by becoming godparents. In an amazing coincidence, and perhaps without being aware of it, the descendants of the Jews who survived the massacre of 1821 were helping other Jews survive the massacre of 1944.

Mother needed time to recuperate, and we tried to comfort her. We did not have the means to celebrate Passover, but we went to the church for Easter. On Good Friday, Papadimitris gave an excellent religious service, but he was not satisfied by the response of his congregation. He turned to his parishioners and, with a voice filled with emotion, pleaded, "Don't you feel moved by the crucified Jesus? His suffering doesn't touch your hearts?" He kept asking similar questions until his words started producing the desired effect. Many women started crying, and many people started looking at us without love. On Easter Sunday, Papadimitris came to our house as he did every Sunday. Only this time it was obvious that he felt a little uneasy. Something was disturbing him. "About Friday night," he said, "I had to talk in a way that I didn't want to, especially because you were there. But it is my job, you understand. I am supposed to talk like that." We understood.

That same day I saw Panos, my four-year-old friend, who used to adore me. This time he did not run to me as usual. He stared at me with suspicion. I asked him what was wrong. He replied, "You crucified Jesus Christ." To this day I feel pain remembering the words of the little boy. (In 1976, I was told that Panos became a teacher of theology.)

On Monday, the service was supposed to take place in the old church of the Virgin Mary, used only once a year for this purpose. Whenever I went to the spring for water, I was able to see the church, small and white, on top of a gigantic granite hill. There was no direct trail leading to the church, which was located next to a precipice. At the bottom of the precipice, large rocks of all shapes were thrown one on top of the other, covering an enormous area. Many hiding places could be found there, and the villagers used to hide their supplies there during

III. Author's Memoirs

the German raids. This rocky area was the result of an avalanche caused by a tremendous earthquake, which split the hill in two. Half the hill was still standing, the little church crowning its top.

The villagers did not know when the catastrophe took place. The only thing they knew was that the houses at the side of the hill had been buried by the rocks and that roosters could be heard for a few days after the houses disappeared. Maybe Psilovrahos, which means "tall rock," was named after this rock of the Virgin Mary. Psilovrahos, the new village, was built near the site of the lost one, whose name was Sovolak.

Around 10:00 in the morning, the people of the village began their ascent up the mountain. They passed by the fountain of the upper village before turning left. In a few minutes everyone, including us, was on a plateau where the beautiful little church was standing. I had the feeling of being on an imaginary balcony with a spectacular view all around me. There was a lot of singing and dancing. Even we forgot about the war and its misery. The life of the villagers was totally interwoven with the church and the religious holidays. With religion, the people were able to forget the past, ignore the present, and be hopeful about the future.

The arrest of the Jews in Ioannina, Arta, and Preveza shattered all our hopes for a speedy Allied victory. We tried to keep a proper perspective on our lives, but the fear of what might be happening to our friends and relatives at the hands of the Germans was not something we could easily bear.

The various possibilities of the outcome intruded into our quiet hours, but our imaginations, even at the wildest and most pessimistic moments, never approached the real truth, as eventually became known to the entire world when Allied troops entered the concentration camps. We knew about the Allied victories in Russia and North Africa. We were sure that the Germans were losing the war. Because of that we could not understand what forced the Germans to deport the Jews of isolated communities like those of Arta, Preveza, and Ioannina. We felt this should be immediately reported to the Allies and to the Jewish organizations of the free world. We had no doubt that, once informed, the democracies would find the means to persuade the Germans to return the people to their homes.

Father began to write. He composed three letters. One was to be sent to the British military mission, another to the Jewish community of Egypt, and, finally, a message to his brother-in-law who lived in Alexandria, Egypt. The letters were written on April 20, 1944. After the war, we found out that this was ten days after the majority of the people we were attempting to save were already dead.

On April 21, Mother and I, armed with these papers and provided with our usual vegetable pie, felt like new versions of Don Quixote who were about to right the wrongs suffered by the Jews. We were on the march, ill fed, ill clothed, and wearing primitive shoes, attempting to alter the fate of people and influence history. Our naivete was matched only by our determination.

The trail we followed was carved on the precipitous side of a mountain overlooking the Megdova River. At one point the trail all of a sudden disappeared because of a storm. The familiar, smooth, vertical line of a small dry waterfall starting at the top of the mountain had intersected our path, continuing all the way down to the river. We were afraid to cross the waterfall, our shoes being slippery. We would have had to find another route if it were not for a partisan who arrived, dug his boots into the slope, and helped us cross the precipice. He was returning to his unit and accompanied us to Kremasta.

At Kremasta, all three of us entered the *kareli* (a box with two open sides and a pulley which moved, suspended from an overhead cable). The wooden box was swinging sideways, and after we let it loose it started rolling down until it came to a stop. At this point the partisan's overcoat fell onto a rock at the very edge of the cliff that rose vertically from the river below. The partisan held me by the hand and actually dropped me next to his overcoat. I threw the coat back to him. As for me, I had to take the next ride after I pulled the *kareli* back to my side of the river. Once secure inside the box, I let it roll toward the center. At this point the people on the other side of the river were supposed to pull the *kareli*. The rope, however, had become detached, and I had no choice but to pull myself over. I had reached the center of the river when I realized that the *kareli* could not move forward because the rope, attached to the back of the box, became entangled on the rocks. It was windy, and the box was swinging violently over the abyss. I looked down at the quiet-looking waters, and my legs trembled. I had to return to the starting point, disengage the rope, and start all over again. But when I moved to the center of the river, the rope became stuck all over again.

On the opposite side, an audience was attracted by my acrobatic performance. They were all trying to give me instructions by yelling at the same time. The roar of the river made any communication impossible. I continued my efforts, and I must have eventually done something right as I finally reached the other side, exhausted, and with the palms of my hands bleeding from pulling on the rough cable.

The partisans maintained a squad of men there to control the movement of people from the province of Valtos to that of Trihonidos. The man in charge was none other than our baker, Yiannis, from Agrinion. When he heard where we were going, he asked us to give greetings to a woman named Chrysoula who lived there. The trip from Kremasta to Priantsa was exciting. We had to climb the steep side of the Kremasta gorge and, when we reached the top, we were utterly exhausted, hungry, and thirsty. We saw an isolated house, and almost instinctively our feet took us to it. There, a lone woman let us know, by the way she looked at us, that she did not like ELAS. (We were in former EDES-occupied territory.) My mother asked her politely to give us something to eat. She replied that she had absolutely nothing to give us. Mother became furious. She told her: "What? You mean you don't have any corn flour or milk?" Mother entered the two-room house. Within seconds she found corn flour, milk, and olive oil; completely ignoring the woman, she prepared and cooked a meal for us. The partisan did not say a word, but he was grateful to my mother's aggressive spirit. The woman eventually became more friendly when she realized that we did not ask for much. After lunch, the partisan left us, and we continued our trip alone. The last obstacle we had to cross was the Agrafiotis River, which we did like old veterans.

In Priantsa, we were shown the large house of the British mission, and also the house where Chrysoula was staying. We met her, and she told us she had become the girlfriend of the English major. Unfortunately, they had recently argued, and she warned us that he was not in a good mood. When she noticed my clothes, she gave me the remaining material from a pair of khaki woolen trousers. She had made a pair of shorts from them. She also gave us a bottle of scotch for our common friend, Yiannis. We visited the British military mission, and the interpreter, Kontis, arranged for us to meet the major the following morning.

A walk through the village persuaded us that Priantsa was definitely more affluent than Psilovrahos. We noticed that many people wore shirts and dresses made out of parachute material. Not far away was a large flat area the size of a few football fields, where parachute drops were taking place. We also were impressed by a group of pretty girls, wearing a lot of makeup, on horseback. We learned that they were prostitutes who "worked" for the British! This most probably was both patriotic and profitable for them! (In Agrinion, the price Italian soldiers were willing to pay for the same service fluctuated between a half and a whole loaf of bread.)

The village was small, and our arrival did not pass unnoticed. We received an invitation to stay in the house of Maria Papazekou, who lived near the warehouse of the British mission. She was a wonderful woman with three lovely children and a maid. Her husband was a wealthy man from Amphilohia who rose to a leadership position in the resistance. Maria Papazekou was lonely in Priantsa, and she asked us to leave Psilovrahos and come to live in her house for the duration of the war. We were treated very well and enjoyed not only the good food and pleasant company, but also the great spectacle of parachute drops. We heard the familiar noise of low-flying aircraft passing overhead. The flat area below was marked with fires at regular intervals. Then we saw the long and narrow barrels attached to the parachutes slowly descending to the ground.

The night would have been remembered as a most pleasant one if it were not for the great commotion which interrupted our sleep shortly after midnight. We rushed out, sleepy and half dressed. We saw partisans rushing into the nearby warehouse and then heard someone yell, "Fire in the stockade!" It may have been a case of sabotage. That house was a munitions dump filled with deadly explosives, ammunition, and weapons. I ran back into the house, grabbed the sleeping three-year-old boy, and rushed down the hill to take cover from the explosion, which was sure to take place. Mother, with another child, was on the ground next to me. Fortunately, nothing happened; the partisans managed to extinguish the fire. We went back to bed absolutely convinced that we should not leave our house in Psilovrahos. (After the liberation of

III. Author's Memoirs

Greece, I heard that Captain Papazekos was executed. I never saw his family again.)

On April 22, 1944, at 10:00 a.m., we were supposed to meet the members of the British mission. We arrived for our meeting a little earlier and had the opportunity to witness the incredible sight of a British officer giving bread to his horse. My expression of shock, and my general appearance, must have impressed the officer just as much because he immediately offered me a slice of white bread without saying anything. I had not seen white bread for over four years, and its whiteness transcended nutrition. It offered hopes for peace and freedom. I carefully saved it in my bag.

We were ushered into a big conference room with an enormous table in the center of it. British officers and an interpreter were seated around it. We were offered two chairs. They were all immaculately dressed. The interpreter presented our case and my father's letters. We received their response in a few minutes. The major said, "I am sorry about the arrest of your friends and relatives. I lost my sister's family during the air raids of London, and I know how bad it is. We will send the messages to Egypt." Mother wanted to talk directly to him, and she asked if he spoke French. At this time, I knew very little French, and I did not understand the whole conversation. A few minutes later, I saw my mother crying and, although I did know the exact words that had brought on the tears, I started crying too.

After the war, we found out that neither the Jewish community of Egypt nor my uncle Elie Gani received our messages. It is obvious to me now that the British knew what was taking place in Europe, and they realized how futile it would have been to give our message to the free Jews. If our effort to reach the Allies failed, those of others did not.

On March 27, 1944, the American ambassador to Egypt, Lincoln MacVeagh, dispatched a six-page report to Washington on the plight of the Greek Jews. David Wyman, an American professor, wrote in 1984: "The American State Department and the British Foreign Office had no intention of rescuing large numbers of European Jews. On the contrary, they continually feared that Germany might release tens of thousands of Jews into Allied hands."[306]

Wyman concluded that Jews were not saved by the Americans and the British "not because of a lack of workable plans, or insufficient shipping, or that rescue projects would hamper the war effort. The real obstacle was the absence of a strong desire to rescue Jews."[307] It is good that we did not know then that the so-called "civilized world" thought we were expendable. We thought highly of ourselves and never intended to stop our struggle to survive.

As soon as we left the British military mission, we again began thinking of ways to find food. Mother realized that, thanks to the abundance of parachutes in the village, we could somehow provide ourselves with material to exchange in Psilovrahos for food. We visited quite a few houses, and Mother actually begged the village women to give her pieces of the green and khaki silk material as well as rope. The women were eager to help these unusual beggars. Every house had plenty of parachute material they did not know what to do with, so they gave it to us.

On our way back we came across a villager with a donkey loaded with two great baskets of oranges. There were no orange trees in our general area because of the high altitude. We were greatly surprised to see this cargo. He told us he had been on the road for two days, and that his destination was the British mission in Priantsa. Mother asked him to give us one orange, as we had not had any for over a year. He refused until Mother told him a white lie. She confessed to him that she was pregnant. In Greece the wishes of expectant mothers are respected. He gladly gave her an orange, which we kept in our bag.

After a while we sensed that we were in unfamiliar territory. We kept walking in the hope of finding a house or a traveler, but in vain. It became dark and we were in unknown, wide-open countryside. We saw a light flickering in the distance. It seemed to be close by, and we started calling for help. Somebody responded from a small hill to our left and two

---

306 David Wyman, *The Abandonment of the Jews* (New York: Pantheon Books, 1984), x.

307 Ibid., 158.

villagers approached us. They were surprised to hear that the distant light made us call for help. "The light is far away," they said. "You have to cross the river to get there." They invited us to their home. It was the most primitive home I have ever spent a night in. It consisted of one room with a packed earth floor. The walls were made of clay plastered over wood and tree branches. It had a thatched roof. A fireplace dominated the room, and its fire enabled us to see in the twilight. In this room we saw five children, the mother, and an old grandfather. One of the children was sick with a cold. Mother decided to open the bottle of whiskey we were supposed to give to Yiannis and gave three teaspoons of warm whiskey to the sick boy. Somehow the boy felt better, to the great pleasure of everyone. They served dinner consisting of freshly made cornbread and cottage cheese. For sleeping, they spread heavy homemade blankets on the floor and the room was transformed into a bedroom. There were no pillows, and the blankets, as I discovered in the morning, were filthy. In spite of this poverty, the people maintained their humanity, dignity, and generosity. They gave us breakfast consisting of cornbread and buttermilk. Later they showed us the way to Kremasta.

In a few hours, we found ourselves on a plateau overlooking Kremasta. We were able to see the spectacular gorge and hear the thundering roar of the river. But we were lost again. We could not find the trail leading to the houses below. At one point we saw partisans running below and looking up at us. From our height they looked like little puppets. Suddenly they started firing their guns. We heard the noise of whistling bullets. One of the men made a sign with his hand, pointing to our left, and we thought he was directing us that way. We followed his directions, while I, naively, felt sorry that they wasted so many bullets, just to attract our attention and help us find the right path. We soon found the trail winding its way down the hill toward the springs of Kremasta. At one point where the trail made a sharp turn between rocks, we found ourselves surrounded by partisans who were hiding behind the rocks, their guns pointed at us. We had actually fallen into an ambush! The leader of the group was none other but our friend Yiannis, to whom we were bringing the bottle of whiskey.

When he saw us, he became pale and nervous, and he kept gesticulating in a way only a Greek would understand: he was reprimanding himself. He kept saying, "What did I try to do?"

Had the partisans been better sharpshooters, we would have lost our lives. They were alerted to be on the lookout for a man and a woman, German agents, who had escaped from a partisan detention center. When they saw that we were obviously unfamiliar with the area, they felt certain we were the German agents. When the bullets failed to hit us, they decided to ambush us. We went to their guardhouse, where they opened the bottle we brought and offered drinks to everybody to celebrate their failure as marksmen.

On the same day, we crossed the river and bypassed the point where the trail was cut by making a wide detour, arriving home safe and sound. We told Father and Ninetta about our adventures as we feasted on the stale slice of bread and orange. We devoured the orange peels as well.

The arrest of the Jews made us doubt that the Allies would win the war soon. Would the Germans devote their time and resources to capture Jewish women and children if they were losing? Would they use precious trains to transport civilians? Was it possible the war would last much longer? Would it be won by the Germans? Hitler mentioned secret weapons so many times. Couldn't these secret weapons upset the balance of power and turn victory into defeat for the Allies? [The Germans developed V-1 and V-2 missiles and jet fighter planes. Otto Hahn, a German, split the atom.]

We were going to be prepared for a long siege in our beautiful free mountains. Even if the Germans won the war, we were determined never to surrender. As if our thoughts were read by others, the teacher of Agalianos gave us a book to read. It was the story of a Jewish family who converted to Christianity. If Germany won, we would have become the "new Marranos."

The villagers, after three years of occupation, did not have any clothes left except old rags and whatever they could make by themselves. This presented us with an opportunity for trade. We had a few sheets and two mattresses made of a very strong fabric. We could manage without the sheets. We could eliminate our wooden beds and sleep on the floor. Also, we had additional changes of clothing we could do without. Mother was not a seamstress, but she had an elementary knowledge of how to make shirts and pants. The parachute material we brought from Priantsa could be used for blouses. Nylon ropes provided thread for Mother's sewing "laboratory." Everything had to be sewn by hand. Since we did not have buttons, she used pieces of small cord that could be tied together in strategic locations, especially for the pants. The sheets and mattresses were not appropriate for clothing, for their stripes of different colors patterned white or gray backgrounds. Without dyeing the cloth, the garments looked as if they belonged to prisoners. Father began experimenting with different plants and discovered that leaves from walnut trees, which were in great abundance, could permanently dye the fabrics and give them a soft brown color, even though the stripes were still visible.

Another ambitious plan involved selling Father's two suits. Since no one in the village could afford them, we thought of selling lottery tickets worth one kilo of wheat or corn each. When fifty tickets were sold, the one with the winning ticket would get one of the two suits. We soon gave up the idea, because we feared the resistance organization would frown on capitalistic ventures of this sort. We decided to keep the suits in reserve and borrow merchandise from our friends in the village of Paliokerassia, where most of the Jews from Agrinion had gone.

Paliokerassia was about an eight-hour walk from our home. Mother and I were on the road again! On our way to Paliokerassia, while in a dense forest, we heard people who were lost calling for help. We responded by yelling back, "This way! This way!" Soon, out of the forest came none else but my Jewish classmate from Agrinion, Lazaros Mionis, and his father. It was a most exciting reunion. They were returning to their village from a trip to Paliokerassia.

Many times, real life is more exciting than fiction. So many things happened to me in the mountains from October 1943 to October 1944 that I still consider that year the most meaningful of my life. In Paliokerassia, we met the families of Savas Mizan, Elias Mizan, Leon Revi, and Yosoula Yesoua and his nephew Peppos Issis. They were very glad to see us and tried to make our stay in their village a pleasant one. We explained to them what we wanted. Their generosity overwhelmed us. "Take anything you want!" responded Savas, Elias, and Leon. They took us to their homes and showed us what they had. Mother selected material for two jackets, three blouses, and two scarves. She explained to me later, "I did not ask for more because I saw they did not have enough for themselves."

The Illusion of Safety

They had all left Agrinion as we had, a few days before the publication of the German order of October 8, 1943. Some left by taxi. Others left on foot, while their belongings were transported by horses. Nobody faced the slightest difficulty in leaving the city. They took with them as much merchandise as they could manage, but they had not been able to resupply themselves, and their reserves were reduced considerably. We were told not to ask Yosoula Yesoua for help because he was in need more than anyone else. He had five children, two of whom suffered from a chronic eye disease, and a sick wife. Peppos Issis, Yosoula's nephew, was twenty at the time. He was a sensitive man who did not wish to continue being a burden to his uncle. He became a partisan of ELAS.[308]

In the same village of Paliokerassia, we found Kiki and Theodora Bokorou, our friends from Agrinion. They had abandoned the city, and their brothers had joined ELAS. Kiki found the time to teach me a beautiful resistance song.

Back in Psilovrahos, we prepared ourselves for a prolonged stay. It could be years before the war was over! Next to our house were arid and totally unproductive fields. We were given permission to cultivate them. Father and I went to work. The terrain looked as if a torrential rain had removed all the soil and left behind only rocks and pebbles. A supporting wall created a terrace. We removed as many stones as possible and were ready to fertilize the field. I took a big bag and visited many houses. I asked permission to take one bagful of manure from each stable. Nobody refused. I carried the manure and spread it on our field. Since we never cleaned our outer garments, I became the most unpopular person in my family for a few days. The smell of manure had permeated my clothes and my body.

We borrowed a pick to loosen the dry soil. Soon we sowed the seeds we were given for growing beans, onions, lettuce, and tomatoes. [In 1976, I was glad to see that our vegetable garden

---

308 At one time during 1944, Issis was a guard in a detention camp. Ten men were executed by the partisans. A year later this had tragic consequences for Issis. He was arrested, together with all the other partisans who had guarded the camp. Although it was proven that he had remained in the camp guarding other prisoners while the execution took place, they were all sentenced to death and were executed by firing squad.

was still under cultivation, while the rest of the field was worse than ever!] Since we had the pick, I thought it would be a good idea to create a hiding place in our basement for our supplies in case of a German raid. Our plan was to store bags of clothing and food in a hole, cover it over with earth and flagstones, and place thorny bushes on top. I started digging what could be the equivalent of a tomb. I did the digging when the cafe in the next room was closed. The earth that was excavated was spread evenly along the back wall of the basement. I collected a lot of thorny bushes to place around the hole to prevent the advance of any inquisitive person. In the event that we had to hide our supplies and abandon the house, we would be ready in record time. Even if the house were burned, the earth would have protected our supplies.

Until April 1944, the only health problems we had were Father's pains and aches. Then all of a sudden, we all developed the classic symptoms of malaria, with intense attacks of chills, fever, sweats, and great weakness. The fever occurred every 72 hours, so in between we each tried to do everything we were supposed to do prior to the next attack. Fortunately, we had quinine, and that helped us overcome this dreadful disease.

The further we advanced toward summer and salvation, the closer we courted disaster. Our food reserves were diminishing at an alarming rate. The villagers could not afford to buy any clothing before the harvest. Mother was given some food for knitting a dress for the only affluent lady of the village, the wife of Andreas Bouloumbassis. She received one half-kilo of butter and one kilo of cheese as payment. It took over a month of hard work to knit that dress![309] There were many good people in the village who tried to help us. Serpanos allowed us to stay in the room without rent once the money we

---

[309] In 1963, while my parents were preparing to immigrate to the United States, they had an unexpected visitor, Andreas Bouloumbassis. After the customary greetings, he told them, "I was very sick in the hospital, and I was not sure I would get out of there alive. I promised Jesus that if I lived, I would find you and ask you to forgive me for letting you almost die from hunger. In the name of God, please forgive me!" Andreas is the man who prevented Yovanos from giving us the food supplies that he had in the village in exchange for our supplies in Agrinion.

had became worthless. (We paid him after the war ended.) Areti Papaioannou would occasionally give us eggs or onions or salt without letting her husband know about it. Others gave us a piece of cornbread or some dried figs. Barbayiorgos gave me a shovel and an old axe to chop wood. Every day I had to go to his house to get a small branch of kindling to help get our fire going, for by morning there was nothing but cold ashes in our fireplace. The villagers knew how to keep the fire going day and night.

Dimitrios Tsoulos gave us a basin made from the trunk of a large tree. We used this for bathing and, after Mother cleaned it, for mixing flour and water to make bread or for mixing corn flour and wild vegetables to make our "pie." I discovered another use for the basin. It could be used as a boat in a nearby artificial pond! I put my sister inside the boat and moved it in the pond by pushing it. I found that the greatest depth was no more than three feet. Word of my adventure went back to Tsoulos, who had more respect for the basin than I did; unfortunately, he politely asked Mother to return it to him. Mother, who had to improvise without the basin, never found out the real reason for the loss of such a precious appliance.

Life in the village was a lot of fun. There were singing parties and village festivals near the spring. We attended everything, always hoping that someone would offer us something to eat. One time two young women who lived near our house invited me, alone, for dinner. One had a brother and the other a husband who were partisans. After a glorious meal, I entertained them by singing every song I knew. In contrast, Bouloumbassis once invited us, Aaron Romano, and the Levis to a party. My expectations were great, but they offered us absolutely nothing to eat. There was music from an old gramophone, and Father danced with Oreozyl Levi. I will never forgive them for not giving us at least a piece of bread or some walnuts or dried figs as I had expected.

Occasionally Father and I went to the Megdova River and swam in the part that was just two or three feet deep. The river had fish, the famous *pestropha* [trout], as I read in a book years later! One time a villager gave us a small fish, and another time there was a great commotion in the village when a partisan went fishing with dynamite and actually blew off his hand. They had to give him first aid and transport him to the nearest hospital while he was screaming in pain.

III. Author's Memoirs

All this meant that we could have eliminated hunger by finding ways to catch fish. We had everything we needed to make nets. It seems that we were stupid city folk, because we never even thought of that, and we did not try to catch turtles near the pond. One time a squirrel came to our room. Instead of trying to kill it, we helped it get out. The little bird caught in my trap was the only exception. We remained unimaginative and hungry, city people.

One day Father found out that the lettuce was ripe in a nearby garden. He had picked up a couple of heads when suddenly the owner appeared. They both said nothing, and Father, red with shame, did not abandon his loot, but brought it home. He decided not to do it again. That was no different than what happened to me on a bitterly cold and snowy day. I could not find any wood for our fireplace. Near the church was an uninhabited house with a decorative wooden fence around it. I took as many pieces of wood from this fence as we needed to avoid freezing to death. Somebody told the owner, who in turn told my father that all I had to do was ask him for firewood. He would have given it to us with pleasure. Perhaps he would have, but in the meantime I made sure we survived no matter what. I regret that I did not tell this kind man that I saw two other boys getting wood from the fence before I decided to take a few pieces myself.

Another time Father collected wild, unripe pears, which we ate. We realized again how valuable the food was that the partisans had given us for twenty days, which helped extend our reserves. The day came, however, when our house did not have any more corn, wheat, or anything else that we ordinarily ate. Georgios Tsoulos, the leader of the village EAM and who knew of our plight, asked me to climb his mulberry tree and collect as many of the sweet black berries as I wanted. I did this, and that was the only food we ate for four days. On the fourth day, we all developed diarrhea. Since we did not have a bathroom and we did not have enough time to run to the fields, we were forced for the first time to use our basement as a bathroom.

Even though we were starving, we did not take anything from the supplies that father collected for the partisans - we would never touch their provisions.

We discontinued the fruit and only drank tea. When we felt better, but on the verge of collapse, Mother thought that the only thing we had which could be exchanged for food was our sugar. Nobody else had sugar in 1944. Mother and I, in spite of our weakness, managed to walk down the mountain, cross the Megdova River, and go to the village of Episcopi, which was a little more affluent than ours. We went from house to house and exchanged one cup of sugar for five cups of the homemade cereal called *trahana*. This was the turning point in our struggle against starvation. The *trahana*, which is composed of wheat flour mixed with milk and then dried in the sun, saved our lives. Revitalized by this nutritious food and encouraged by the success of our exchange of sugar for *trahana*, we decided to repeat our effort in richer surroundings.

Armed with our homemade garments and other fabrics, we went to the wealthy village of Tatarna. We again visited the partisan hospital, and I remember how impressed I was when I saw the three daughters of the new director, Dr. Thanos Papatheodorou. Their appearance contrasted dramatically with that of my sister or any other village girl. With their pretty clothes, stylish hairdos, and carefree ways, they looked as if they belonged to a different world. The villagers were eager to exchange wheat and other produce for clothing. Since milk was impossible to transfer or prevent from spoiling, we made *trahana* with the assistance of the woman who operated a watermill, which ground wheat or corn into flour. We made enough to fill two twenty-pound bags.

The nephew of this woman was about to get married to a girl who lived in a village close to ours, and he invited us to spend the night in his house. The following morning, we would be able to join the wedding party. The prospective groom was literally dressed in rags. He was probably the most handsome and the poorest man in his village. Mother did her best to mend his clothing and improve his appearance. The wedding party consisted of about ten young men, including the groom, riding horses, with Mother and myself walking. The groom and a friend of his loaded our bags of *trahana* onto their horses, and the journey began. We were under the impression that we were going to move with the slow speed of a normal caravan. To our dismay, the horsemen started trotting and we kept running behind them. By the time we reached the Agrafiotis River, the horsemen had already crossed it. The river was swollen because of a recent rain, and we knew we would not be able to cross it on foot. We looked in despair at the distant horsemen, who were trotting in a cloud of dust, carrying our precious supplies with them.

At this point the bridegroom stopped, looked back and then, like a knight, turned his horse around and came to our rescue. He crossed the river twice, carrying first me and then Mother behind his saddle. His companions were waiting. We retrieved our bags and continued the trip on our own. We were extremely happy because there was no doubt in our minds that with our supplies, our greatest enemy, starvation, was beaten, and our survival assured.

At this point a long line of partisans on horseback and on foot came our way. Some of them joked; others used the moment for a bit of political propaganda. They made comments such as these: "People will not carry loads this way in our future society," or "Wake up, slaves. Break your bonds!" We managed to smile and exchange greetings with almost every man in the column as we continued moving in the opposite direction.

The harvest brought an abundance of food. The vegetable gardens and the fruit trees satisfied every appetite. We continued our expeditions and exchanges, collecting everything we needed for the following winter and even the one after that. To prevent losing everything again in case the Germans launched another one of their search-and-destroy missions, we left a substantial amount of supplies with trustworthy villagers in Tatarna. Experience had made us wise.

Once our basic needs were met, we started thinking of the better things in life! In Greece, politics dominate most discussions. Soon Father and Mother had an argument. A communist nucleus had been organized in the village, and Father attended its meetings. Mother was opposed to communist views, and after many discussions she got angry, took Ninetta with her, and went to the baths of Kremasta. In a few days, a villager passed through Psilovrahos and gave us a list of items my mother needed. The next day I was on my way to the baths, which were credited with many miraculous cures. In the case of my mother, the mineral water proved to be extremely beneficial. She had suffered from an ear infection for as long as she could remember, and while many physicians had failed to improve the condition, the sulfuric waters of Kremasta cured her permanently!

The Illusion of Safety

In the summer, Kremasta was filled with partisans recuperating from wounds or diseases. I vacationed there for just a few days. One day in August, the head of the partisan unit that had fired upon us a few months before, Yiannis, asked all recuperating partisans and civilians to go to their units and homes because the Germans were on the march again. In a few hours, we were back in Psilovrahos.

The village was in a state of alert which did not at all resemble the apathy that had prevailed during the attacks of November and December 1943. This time the partisans ordered the total evacuation of the villages. Although these measures implied greater danger, we were extremely pleased that the Jews would not be the only ones who had to hide this time. Everybody was trying to hide everything that could not be taken with them. Father and Barbayiorgos concealed a few bags of supplies in hiding places among the fallen rocks covering the area of the old village. I opened the trap door in our room and moved all our food supplies into the ditch in the basement. I covered everything with earth and flagstones and then spread thorny bushes over the area. Father put books and other incriminating papers into the other hiding place, under a flagstone. Mother baked bread and prepared whatever we were going to need for the next few days.

The Germans were approaching the village of Houni when we joined the long procession of villagers who, together with their animals, were climbing the slopes leading to the most inaccessible place I ever saw, a mountaintop called Kamaria. We walked for over two hours until we reached a high plateau overlooking the Megdova River and the surrounding villages. All the villagers camped on the flat, stony terrain. It did not take us long to realize that our preparations were again inadequate. For our water supply, we had provided only a military canteen. It was hot, and we were very thirsty. The nearest source of water was a spring down the side of the mountain over an extremely precipitous trail. I took our empty flask and returned an hour and a half later, carrying the pitiful quantity of three glasses of water. At night it was chilly, and Father borrowed a blanket which proved to be a source of misery for us later, as it was filled with lice.

The Germans approached the area, and it became dangerous to go for water, since an enemy typically places ambushes near water sources. Many villagers tried in vain to discover other sources of water in our immediate area. In the meantime, the German column kept advancing. Rifle shots were heard, and panic broke out because the villagers thought we were being fired upon. What actually happened was that a partisan unit had taken positions on a hill on the opposite side of the river and ambushed the German column. The rifle shots were followed by machine gun fire, accompanied by mortar shelling. When the German mountain artillery joined the battle, everybody was petrified.

Vasilis Arhimandritis, the teacher, was aware of the particular danger we faced if a German patrol arrived. He also knew that he, as a teacher, could become a hostage. He asked us to join him and his wife in a hideout he discovered away from the villagers' encampment. It was a secluded spot offering a spectacular view of the village of Episcopi and the surrounding countryside. Mother managed to grab a passing goat and milked her, providing us with some nutrition. On that day, we witnessed from our eagle's nest a facet of German inhumanity. We saw a line of soldiers advancing. One or two of them entered a house, and in a few minutes smoke came out of it. Others entered the next house and the next until all the houses were on fire. The distance from the houses made them look like toys, and the smoke looked like wisps of smoke from cigarettes. We wondered whether our house was about to meet the same fate.

This did not happen, thanks to the brave intervention of an old man, Vasilis Bouloumbassis. He saw from a distance that two houses on our side of the river were burning. That made him furious because it was obvious that they were starting to burn Psilovrahos, too. Without telling anybody and moving almost instinctively, he went down to the deserted village. He hid behind a rock and observed two Germans and their two horses as they moved toward his house. He knew that if he did not do anything, the house would be burned. He started running with an insane fury toward his house. In the absolute stillness of the village, the noise that was made on the rocky paths did not escape the two soldiers. They looked up the trail and caught a glimpse of a man with a stick in his hands, which perhaps looked to them like a gun, and with a beard that, even though it was white, looked like the typical beard of a partisan.

The two Germans who were so nonchalantly burning houses started running toward the river and the safety of their unit as fast as they could. They even abandoned their two horses and supplies. This explains why Psilovrahos was one of the few villages spared the fate of so many others. We stayed in our hiding place for a few more days before the Germans left, and the whole village returned to its peaceful pursuits.

We saw part of the war, but like the soldiers on the front line, we did not know in detail what really happened. Only in 1981 did I read about the events of August 1944:

> On August 6, another column with a large force of tanks and artillery advanced from Agrinion towards Agios Vlassis. After a battle, it captured the village and burned it. It then advanced westwards and captured Houni and Sidera. There was a further battle with the 13th Division troops, who were finally forced to retire as they were in danger of being surrounded. The Germans captured and burned East and West Frankista, and Marathia.
>
> On the 11th, at Kerasovo, they were attacked as they entered the village by reinforcements sent from General Headquarters. They then began to withdraw. On the 13th they crossed the Sidera Bridge, and on the 14th pulled back to Houni. Here they were attacked by our troops, and on the evening of the 14th, withdrew to Agios Vlassis.[310]

In August 1944, all the news bulletins talked about the Allied victories on all fronts. We witnessed the immense power of the Allied air force when I counted almost 600 planes flying overhead. I still don't know what the target was. Maybe it was the Ploesti oil fields in Romania. In the meantime, "our targets" were the thousands of lice that made us itch all over.

Ninetta's abundant curly hair was filled with lice. Every louse we caught was squeezed between our thumbnails, making a familiar little crushing sound. In spite of our efforts, we were unable to cope with the great number of lice and their eggs, which were deposited on every hair and in all the folds of clothing. Ninetta's hair was cut off completely. We borrowed a big metal barrel the villagers used for moonshining and carried

---

310 Sarafis, Greek Resistance Army, 452.

our clothing to a nearby stream. We started a fire to boil our clothes in the water. As soon as one bunch of clothing was finished, another pot full of laundry was boiled. Eventually all clothing and blankets were disinfected and placed on rocks to dry, while all four of us were dressed in clean underwear and nothing else, until the fierce August sun dried everything.

My parents, Leon and Esther Matsas, on the day they returned from Psilovrahos to the liberated city of Agrinion in October, 1944.

In the following weeks, we collected more wheat and corn from Tatarna and other places. The good news that the Germans had withdrawn from Agrinion reached us, as usual, through the "voice" of the youth organization. Mother and Father decided to go to the city first to find a house since the one in which our furniture had been stored was occupied by the landlords. We knew the landlord was an enemy of EAM and that we could easily reclaim the house for ourselves, but we decided against it. Once my parents entered liberated Agrinion, the first thing they did was to have a photograph of themselves taken. We still have this picture, in which Father looks wild and Mother depressed.

Since my parents had difficulties finding a house, Ninetta and I were left in the village longer than anyone anticipated and without any adult supervision. The bread, which was made before my parents left, was not baked well and became moldy. Our room was dark, and we did not realize that the bread was spoiled. We kept eating it though with every passing day, the bread was getting worse, and we were progressively becoming sicker from food poisoning.

A villager gave me a pot of grape juice. Instead of drinking it, my love for sweets gave me the idea of making syrup or marmalade from it, to eat with our bread. I boiled the juice until most of it evaporated; what remained created a thick, sticky, distasteful mess which destroyed our only cooking pot. I tried to clean the pot quite unsuccessfully, and then proceeded to cook some vegetables in it. The bad taste from the burned dish, combined with my inexperience as a cook and my forgetting to use salt or olive oil, made my creation totally inedible. Since there was nothing else, we ate more spoiled bread. The Red Cross distributed some sort of canned fish, and we were given a big spoonful of something that smelled like fish, which was the only nutritious thing we had for many days.

The fact that we, the underprivileged of the village, were soon to be restored to our previous middle-class status did not escape the children of our neighbor Tserpelis. When I went out in the yard, they accused me of having dirtied the entire countryside by defecating all over the place. The accusation was true, and I did not deny it. Was it my fault if the village houses did not have any toilets? The older boy went so far as to attack me with a knife. Sick as I was, I fought back and managed to take his knife, although in the process I cut myself. I was lucky that the younger brother did not join the fight. It was hard to believe that these same boys only a few months before had taken pity on us and given us the little sparrow caught in one of my traps.

Ninetta and I became progressively worse, and by the time my parents returned, we were approaching an inglorious end. We were soon, however, restored to good health, thanks to the fact that we stopped eating the spoiled bread and enjoyed all kinds of delicacies my mother brought from the city.

Finding a house to rent in Agrinion proved to be difficult. Finally, the EAM committee for finding shelter located a house

III. Author's Memoirs

for us, which had until recently been occupied by German soldiers.

When my parents went to Agrinion, the ETA organization ordered my father to become the director of the immense warehouses of Papastratos. They fell into the hands of the partisans still filled to capacity with German supplies. Father accepted out of gratitude for the assistance we received from EAM-ELAS. The head of ETA lent him a magnificent white horse to help us with the transfer of our things from the village to the city. By then we had so much wheat and corn that we needed many horses for its transfer. Father conceived the idea of transferring food the same way you transfer money. He delivered our wheat and corn to his ETA replacement in Psilovrahos, and he received a receipt. In a few days we said farewell to the village of Psilovrahos and left for our new house in Agrinion.

I departed first with Barbayiorgos and his donkey, loaded with apples, walnuts, and other supplies. On the way to Agrinion, I witnessed the dramatic changes which had taken place since the time Psilopoulos's taxi brought us to Houni. The road was destroyed at several points. Houses were burned. Bridges were blown up. Gravesites on the side of the road indicated the places where people, killed by the Germans or the partisans, were buried in a hurry. We spent the night at a point halfway between Psilovrahos and Agrinion, where Barbayiorgos was godfather of our host. In Agrinion, we saw the big tomb where 200 people executed by the Germans were buried. For a whole year, I had been dreaming of the day I would return to the free city of Agrinion. I thought it was going to be an extremely joyful and happy event. Yet my joy was not at all as great as I had imagined it would be.

My parents and Ninetta arrived two days later. Father presented his unusual receipt to the partisan warehouse, and he was given the wheat and corn which was rightfully ours. For the transfer of the grain to our house, I escorted a German prisoner who used a wheelbarrow several times. My mother treated the German very well, giving him raisins and cookies, thinking that perhaps someone in Germany was doing the same for her sisters.

The city people did not have enough food, and we gave gifts of food to all our friends, including the family of Exarhos, who was imprisoned by the partisans. I was a frequent guest in their home, since they had been our next-door neighbors and had two sons who were my friends. Mrs. Exarhos was trying to find out if I knew whether the prisoners were going to be executed, while Michalis, one of her sons, showed me an anti-Semitic cartoon which depicted the Statue of Liberty holding an ugly Jew in her arms. The caption under it said, "Get rid of the Jew and you will be free." I realized then how in one year we had moved in different directions. Our friendship ended.

Transferring food with the prisoner and making gifts to people who were considered reactionaries did not escape the highly alert resistance sympathizers. Father's activities were investigated and, of course, he was proclaimed innocent, although nobody knows what happened to all the food he "deposited" in Psilovrahos. Becoming an ETA official had bad consequences for his career, for in a few months the German collaborators came out of Agrinion's prisons and started their rule of terror.

After the war, the school allowed me and a few others to take an examination, so I would not lose a year. I moved to the next class with my classmates and continued high school in Agrinion. Our friends returned all the things we had given them for safekeeping, including clothing, furniture, and books. There were only two minor exceptions. Eugenia Papadopoulou kept or used some of the items my mother entrusted to her, and when she was asked about the missing things she said, "I took nothing by comparison. You should have seen what people took in Ioannina." A lot of things were taken by our former landlady, a very religious woman. She told me, "The Germans did very well!" I replied, "Congratulations to you, with your long crucifix." She withdrew, deeply ashamed.

Life returned to normal, and all the Jewish families returned to their usual pursuits. The wife of Yosoulas and the sister of Mionis did not return. They both died at an early age because of lack of medical care. Everyone else was safe, and it is possible that the Jewish community of Agrinion was the only one in occupied Europe whose members never obeyed any German regulations and survived the war.

My mother's family in Albania was alive and well. We were told that a convoy of German trucks carried away the merchandise from my uncle Semos Kohen's large shop in Agioi Saranda. He and his family moved to partisan controlled areas. My grandparents, Joseph and Gracia, remained in Delvino,

III. Author's Memoirs

and German personnel occupied part of their house making it their headquarters. The Germans made some alterations in the kitchen and discovered the gold my grandfather had hidden there. When the German forces withdrew from Delvino at the end of the war, they blew up and burned their headquarters. My grandparents lost everything.

Once regular transportation was established between Athens and Ioannina, a trickle of Jews who were not taken away by the Germans started passing through Agrinion. There were mostly partisans of ELAS. Some were civilians. We started forming in our minds what could be considered a roll call of survivors. It is incredible that even at the end of 1944 none of these people had any idea of what had happened to their families once they had been transferred beyond the borders of Greece. My uncle from Albania wrote: "I have reliable information that our sisters live in a city in Poland." In March 1945, Nissim Mionis returned from Athens with information about the fate of the deported Jews, which later proved to be correct. Revecca Mizan told me at the time, "He is a mean man. Of course, he can talk like that. He does not have brothers and sisters who were arrested by the Germans."

One day in the cinema, I saw a chilling "World Report" newsreel showing the American and British entry into the concentration camps. This was my first contact with an unbelievable reality. I saw Eisenhower visiting a camp. There were thousands of bodies on the ground. It was spring there. The corpses looked fresh. I could not believe that those people had died after the liberation! Slowly and painfully we were given glimpses of what happened to our relatives on the day they were arrested.

At the time of the arrest, a neighbor asked my Aunt Annetta of Ioannina, "Where do you think they will take you?" "I don't know," she replied. "We are in God's hands now." Then she offered her friend a box of jewelry and said, "Give this to my sister, Esther Matsas." But she changed her mind and said, "I will take them with me. We will need them."

A German officer lived in the home of my uncle, Dr. Nissim Samuel. On March 24 he asked my aunt Eftyhia to prepare a festive dinner for the family, himself, and a Greek woman, Mrs. Stavropoulou. The officer made a toast and added, "Who knows who lives or who dies tomorrow?" The next day, early in the morning, the Germans came to arrest the Samuel family.

Eftyhia knocked at the door of the officer, and when he opened it, she asked him, "We too have to go?" The officer did not reply, closed the door, and in a few minutes left the house to go to his office. Dr. Samuel was not fast enough, and a soldier punched him and threw him down the stairs. Eftyhia, who was nine months pregnant, was wearing shoes with high heels. Mrs. Kostadima, a Christian neighbor, approached, took off her flat shoes and gave them to Eftyhia. "Please take them," she said. "You are pregnant. You can't walk on high heels." In their surprise and haste they did not take their little girl Enni with them. Mrs. Stavropoulou, who could have saved Enni, rushed out with the little girl, saying politely, "Mrs. Samuel, you forgot Enni. Here she is." These few words condemned lovely Enni to death.

We learned all these details of the arrest of my mother's sisters Eftyhia and Annetta and their families from my mother who went to Ioannina after the war and met her sisters' neighbors.

This knowledge and my own experiences made such an impression on me that after the war, when I was 14, I wrote my first manuscript, "One Year in the Mountains." At the time, I did not know then that the Jews who "were taken by the Germans" were killed by them. Now, in retrospect, I realize that, just like many authors in the field of Holocaust literature, I wanted to tell the world what had happened from my perspective. I may have been one of the first in Greece to record our survival story.

When I reflect upon my childhood, now knowing that the Germans killed the Jewish children below the age of 16, it saddens and angers me greatly that I lost all my friends and classmates from the Jewish schools I attended in three cities: Ioannina, Arta, and Preveza.[311] In Preveza, after passing the difficult examination to enter the public high school, I was the only Jew in my class. Before I completed the school year, we moved to Agrinion where I continued in high school. It was here in Agrinion, where the events of the war affected our family of

---

311 During this time, many attended school only through the fourth grade. Only 10% of students would pass the exam for high school which was 8 years long starting in 5th grade. Only about 10% of high school graduates would continue their studies in the university.

III. Author's Memoirs

four personally, and we had the opportunity to escape and survive.

The Illusion of Safety would not have been written if it were not for a series of events in my life, which I will describe, that enabled and motivated me to write this book. Entering the University of Athens and coming to the United States were most important.

After the war in 1947, I completed high school and received my diploma. Then, I prepared to go to Athens to pursue my studies. Going from Agrinion to Athens was not simple and presented some difficulties related to politics. Greece was embroiled in a civil war at that time. The police in Agrinion refused to give me the necessary permit to leave the city. I appealed to the chief of police, who, in the presence of Mr. Ksinos, the leader of the fascist organization "X," reminded me of my past in the mountains of EAM-ELAS.

I knew that Mr. Ksinos was the advisor to the chief of police who was new to the city of Agrinion. I also knew that he did not like my father because he sent one of his followers, a clerk in the bank of agriculture, to my father's office. This clerk, displaying a revolver in his belt, told my father in an impolite way, "The other Jews give to our organization a lot of money. How much are you going to give us?" My father, who was very proud and not easily intimidated, threw him out of his office.

When I was refused the permit, I could have mentioned to the chief of police that his predecessor Commander Iliopoulos was a good friend of my father. (He did not collaborate with the Germans. He kept items that we entrusted with him, including my mandolin, and he returned them after the war. The most important thing was that the partisans did not arrest him. Iliopoulos became afraid that other partisans might arrest him, and he asked my father to give him the money he needed to go with his family out of Agrinion. My father did.)

I was too proud to ask for a favor. I also knew that I did not do anything wrong in the free mountains. I had the right to go to Athens.

By that time, I was street wise in the politics of Greece. I knew that the fascist leader, Mr. Ksinos, and my high school principal, Mr. Pantazis, had been imprisoned by the partisans and liberated by the British. I said, "You don't know anything about me. The only person who knows me is my high school principal." My reply made them look at each other and smile!

Then the chief of police said, "If you can bring a paper from Mr. Pantazis certifying that you are all right, I will give you the permit."

I went to visit Principal Pantazis at his home. He liked me because I was one of his best students in the subjects he taught: Latin, ancient Greek, and modern Greek. After my request, he composed a beautiful letter that ended with the statement, "He has nationalist feelings and Christian ethics." He shook my hand and, although he knew I was Jewish, added, "Go with the blessings of Jesus Christ and Virgin Mary."

I was moved, for he was my favorite teacher; however, I could not understand why he admired the Germans. In class, he had once mentioned the Dreyfus affair and said the best things about the Jews. Thanks to his letter, which was placed in my file, I was not only able to go to Athens to pursue my studies at the university, but also it helped me to become an officer in the Greek army.

In 1948, I passed the difficult entrance exam for the Dental School. There were 820 candidates for 30 positions. I was thrilled to be accepted as number 17.

In 1951, during a trip with the School of Archeology to Crete and Egypt, I made one of the most important decisions of my life. I decided to start learning English on my own, using the book "English Without a Teacher," in my spare time during my military service.

I graduated in 1953 from dental school and then served my obligatory army service as a dental officer for three years. I served in Corinth, Chios, Athens, and Veria.

In Veria, I served in a hospital as a dentist and as an assistant to the director. Oddly enough, the military chaplain loved me because I ordered the soldier at the gate to present arms when he passed and because I maintained quiet and order when he delivered his sermons. The chaplain was very surprised when I told him that I was Jewish.

Almost one year after I started working there, the hospital was to be closed for unknown reasons. We were not to accept any more medical patients; however, one evening a soldier was brought to us. He had attempted suicide and needed medical care. The physician who was in charge said that he had to transfer him to the closest hospital one hour away in Kozani. I told the physician that by the time he went to Kozani he would die. He said that he knew that, but he had to follow his orders.

III. Author's Memoirs

I said, "I take over." Against all army regulations, I sent the patient by taxi to a local clinic and saved his life.

After my stay in Veria, I was transferred to the beautiful city of Patras where I met again Iakovos Frizis, the son of Colonel Mordechai Frizis. He was a soldier there, and we became good friends.

Most likely because of my excellent record for the past two years in the army, I was promoted and transferred to the Military Academy of Athens. This was the highest position for a reserve dental officer and a great honor for me. I enjoyed being in Athens because I was able to stay with my family who lived there.

At the pyramids of Giza. 1951.

I am near Veria in 1954.

The Illusion of Safety

My graduation ceremony as a dentist in the University of Athens.

In Chios during infantry officers training.

III. Author's Memoirs

One day, I reported to General Laspias, the commander of the Military Academy of Athens. It was a Friday afternoon. He told me that the Military Academy did not have a dentist for the last six months because the dentist was a patient in a psychiatric hospital. He continued, "Early Monday morning the cadets are going to participate in an amphibious exercise, and the weather is predicted to be bad. Many of them will try to avoid this exercise, and they will claim that they have problems with their teeth. I want you to prepare the office and treat their dental problems by Monday morning."

In Thessaloniki (on the left) with two medical officers.

I started saying, "But Sir . . ." He looked at me as if he wanted to kill me, and I continued with, "Yes Sir. Is there anything else?" He said, "No." I saluted, and I left. My first thought was, did he make the dentist crazy? The second thought was – if I am not for myself, who is going to be for me? I went to the medical and dental building, and I met the director, a physician with the rank of Colonel. He was a very kind man, and he welcomed me warmly. I asked his assistant to notify all cadet units and tell them that the dental office will accept all those who wanted to see the dentist at 9 am Saturday.

I found out in what hospital was the dentist. I went there; nobody could find the dentist.

On Saturday morning, I went to the Military Academy. I checked the dental office and gathered the tools I needed. By 8:45 am, I was ready.

The office was on the second floor. I heard marching footsteps, "1, 2 – 1, 2," and I looked outside the window. I saw the cadets coming in large groups, left and right. Their boots were quite noisy.

My strategy for dealing with so many patients was to eliminate any dental pain and to treat any dental infection. I started promptly at 9 am. To my great surprise, at 10 am, I had an unexpected visitor. General Laspias himself. I heard the sound of many boots coming to attention. The General took a look around, said nothing and left.

I worked all day Saturday and Sunday. I remember I performed five extractions. Normally, I would give three-day exemptions from duty to soldiers who had a tooth extracted. But, in this situation, I gave them gauze in case of bleeding, pills for pain and antibiotics in case of infection and they were returned to duty. Nobody had any excuse to avoid the exercise.

In a couple of weeks, I asked General Laspias to give me a one-week vacation. He gave me two weeks, and I went by boat – first class to Rhodes and Corfu!

On the way back from Rhodes, I went to the back deck of the boat at night to gaze at the water. I saw three young Greek men and a young German. I was told that the German man was an archaeologist. While he was admiring the sea, I heard the three others discussing how they could easily throw him overboard. I immediately approached them and, in a calm voice, I told them, "I hate the Germans much more than you do, but this man is innocent. He is very young, and he was not a soldier ten years ago. In addition, he is an archaeologist which means to me that he loves Greece. That's why he is here. You don't want to do that." One of them said, "You are right." And we all left.

In Athens, I enjoyed working in the Military Academy. In the evenings, I studied English at the American Institute. Mr. Nanos, the Director, tested my language skills and enrolled me in the fourth year of the six-year Institute.

As I made progress in learning English, I got the idea to go to America to improve my dental education. I applied to many dental schools and was accepted by Georgetown University. I believe that the dean, Admiral Rowe, was impressed by the fact that I served as the dentist of the Military Academy of Athens. He, himself, was the commander of the Dental Corp of the American Navy prior to his retirement.

My family in 1956 while I served in the Military Academy of Athens.

Four months before I departed for America, I told my sister Ninetta that, in case I liked America and decided to stay there, I did not want to be separated from her. "How about if I teach you English," I suggested. She was an excellent student and eight years younger than me. She agreed to cooperate with me and each month, I taught her the book of each year of the American Institute. On the fourth month, Mr. Nanos gave her a placement test and, to my great surprise, enrolled her in the fifth year of the Institute. She surpassed her great teacher – myself.

In order to come to the United States, I needed to obtain a student visa and, before that, I had to pass an oral examination by the American consul in Athens. This was the first time that

I spoke in English with an American. I am surprised that I passed.

After serving my three-year obligatory service in the army, I was discharged and prepared myself for the trip to America. I went to a travel agency, and I bought a ticket for the Italian Ocean Liner "Saturnia" leaving from Patras for New York City.

My mother did not want to say goodbye to me in Athens. She wanted to go to Patras one day earlier. "Saturnia" was too big to dock in the port, and the passengers had to be transferred with small boats to the ocean liner.

On board the "Saturnia." My arrival in New York City with Greek immigrants. I am first on the right. 1956.

My mother persuaded the captain of one of these boats to allow her to come with me to the "Saturnia." On the ocean liner, she stopped an officer and, speaking with him in Italian, asked permission to let her see the big cabin where I was going to be with other Greek men on my way to America for the next two weeks. Only at the last minute, she decided to embrace me and say goodbye as if she knew that she was not going to see me or even hear my voice on a telephone for the next very long and difficult five years. As for me, seeing the immigrants with limited means who did not know any English, I was truly

III. Author's Memoirs

feeling sorry for them. I did not know that soon I would be worse than they - totally alone and very poor.

On August 27, 1956, we saw the skyline of New York. I hate crowds, and I couldn't understand why everyone was moving to the port or left side of the liner. I went to the right side, and most probably I am the only visitor to New York City who missed the beautiful and inspiring Statue of Liberty.

After my first five days in New York, I fell in love with the United States and its people. Since the medical degree from the University of Athens was accepted, I thought that my dental degree would be accepted too. I was wrong. I had to go back to dental school for three more years after my year at Georgetown. My desire to stay here was so strong that I decided to accept this new difficult challenge and ultimately bring my sister and my parents to the United States.

While I worked in the summer of 1957 as a dental technician, I heard that candidates for dental school had to prove their manual dexterity. I decided to prove that to myself, although I was a dentist and a good one since 1953. I carved in wax a kneeling mother with a baby in her arms. When I showed it to a nurse, she was so moved that she made the sign of the cross. I still have the statue. I was now confident that I had good manual dexterity.

In April 1960, I was working in the laboratory of Howard University Dental School when my friend and classmate, Ray Oliver, developed abdominal pain and went to the Oral Surgery Department. One hour later I went to see him. He was in bed with great pain. When he told me where the pain was, I told him that he had appendicitis and should go to the hospital next door. He did. When the professor of oral surgery came back to see him, he was informed that I had told Ray to leave. The professor became furious with me and said he was going to expel me from the school the next day. It was less than two months before graduation!

The next day a student warned me about the professor's threats, and I ran to the hospital to see what happened to Ray. When I arrived, the doctors congratulated me. They had to operate immediately on Ray to prevent peritonitis. "You saved his life!" they told me. I became a hero!

Upon graduation, I was offered the position of clinical instructor of oral medicine, and later I became an assistant professor.

Ninetta came to America in 1959 on a student visa to attend George Washington University. That same year, I fell in love at first sight with my beloved Eleanor, and we married in 1960. In 1961, five years after I left Greece, I was finally able to go back to Greece, tired but very optimistic about the future. In Athens, I had a very emotional reunion with my parents. In 1962, I opened my private dental office in Maryland. My parents came for Ninetta's wedding in 1963. Every summer my parents were able to return to their home in Athens and enjoy beautiful vacations all over Europe and Israel.

Going back to my roots, I realized how lucky I was and how easily I could have ended up in Poland instead of Psilovrahos. Psilovrahos will remain as a monument to a special period in my life. At age 14, I wrote about our experiences in the mountains in a manuscript entitled, "One Year in the Mountains." My literature teacher, Panos Papachristos, kept it for six months but refused to make any comment on it. My father created a hiding place for it under our heavy dining room table. It remained there until 1963 when my parents were getting ready to come to the United States. The thought that some Greek policeman or customs inspector in Greece or the United States would see that we were in the mountains with the partisans of ELAS, whom I admired and whose songs I loved, forced them to burn my memoirs in the backyard of our house in Athens, where my parents had moved in 1952. My first literary work became a victim of the Cold War! Later on, I wrote, in Greek, "Jewish Contributions to Civilization." This was published in serial form by the Jewish newspaper of Athens, *Israeliticon Vima*.

At the height of the Greek Civil War, the people of many neighboring villages, including those of Psilovrahos, were relocated to Agrinion. My parents asked our friendly baker (who as a Partisan commander in Kremasta almost killed my mother and me by mistake) to prepare bread for us. We ordered large loaves of bread for all the families of Psilovrahos. With my friend Sam Mionis, we delivered the bread in baskets to the villagers who were living in the tobacco warehouse nearby. In this small way, we expressed our warm feelings for them.

Our contact with the village remained strong. My father had maintained close relations with the villagers of Psilovrahos after the war. In the National Bank of Greece in Agrinion, where he became a manager, everyone gave a warm

III. Author's Memoirs

welcome to the clients who were from "Mr. Matsas' village." Father was among the first who contributed to the fund for the renovation of "our" church. When he visited Psilovrahos one time, he was surrounded by so many friendly villagers that a politician campaigning for the Greek parliament became alarmed, thinking that father was his opponent!

The first time I went back to Psilovrahos was in 1951, at the end of the civil war. I wanted to take pictures of the village, the river, and the cave. My parents did not want me to go because of the political tensions still in the air, so they hid the camera. I found it and replaced it with another box, so they would not realize that I had left for the village, being able to see the "camera" in its place. In the village, there were many army officers, and all the villagers who were former friends of EAM-ELAS had become members of the anti-communist paramilitary forces. Since I was a university student from Athens, a lieutenant wanted to know why I was there. When I told him that I came as a tourist, he wanted me to give him an exact account of what I was doing during all the hours I spent in his area.

When I told him that I was going to visit the cave of Arapokefalos, which he did not even know existed, he did not want to let me out of his sight. He asked if he could come with me to the cave the next day. I welcomed his company.

After meeting all my friends and sleeping in the house of Tsoulos, early the next morning the lieutenant and Spyros Triantafillis, both heavily armed, accompanied me on the steep hike to the cave. They entered the cave the way they do in war movies, which made me realize that they suspected I was going to meet somebody there. When they saw nobody, we took pictures immortalizing my expedition.

Spyros spread the rumor that the main reason I returned to the village was to find a treasure Romano and the Levis had buried there. Rumors don't fade away! In 1991, my sister Ninetta visited Psilovrahos. There were no more than ten people living in the village. They all gave her a warm welcome. One of them told her, "Your brother came here; you come here. Are you looking for the treasure?" My sister replied, "Yes, you are right, and I found it." She pointed to the men and women who surrounded her and continued, "I found it in the hearts of these people who helped my family in our hour of need."

The Illusion of Safety

Posing (with gun) in front of the cave. Psilovrahos, 1951.

In Psilovrahos, 1951.

The Tsoulos family and me in 1951.

    The war ended for most people, but not for us. I remember that I disliked holidays. Every year since the war ended, Jewish holidays made me uneasy, when our family, my parents, my sister and I would be alone with the specter of dead grandparents, aunts, uncles, and other relatives and friends all around us. Christian holidays made me uneasy too, especially Easter, which produces a higher degree of awareness of Jews on the part of the Christians, especially in Greece. The only

III. Author's Memoirs

holiday I really enjoy now is Thanksgiving, which transcends the narrow limits and prejudices of all religions.

With friends in front of the house in which my family lived in 1943-1944. Photo 1951.

The wild beauty of Psilovrahos. Photo from 1951.

The Illusion of Safety

In 1976, I found myself again in the beautiful mountains of Greece. This time I was accompanied by my beloved American wife, Eleanor, and my daughters Linda and Alice, who were 10 and 8. We took a bus from Agrinion and stopped close to the area where the Megdova river once flowed (a dam was built to form a large artificial lake in the 1950's). Then we hiked the steep path going up to Psilovrahos. Our visit to Psilovrahos on April 15 coincided with the first day of Passover, which for me

With my two daughters, George Papaioannou, and young Panos in the village. 1976.

The Megdova river (now a lake), view from Psilovrahos.

III. Author's Memoirs

is the celebration of a revolt by Jewish slaves and their subsequent exodus from Egypt.

The rocky, steep, practically nonexistent path was difficult to negotiate. I had to carry three handbags and also hold Alice's hand. At one point I stopped, feeling very tired, and told my children: "Today perhaps you are getting the most valuable lesson in your lives. By climbing this mountain, we celebrate our own family's exodus, which for us was more important than the Exodus was for the Jews of Egypt. If the exodus from Egypt had failed, the Jews would have remained slaves. If we had failed in our exodus on October 3, 1943, we would have been killed by the Germans. Personal freedom is the most precious possession you have, and you have to fight for it, if necessary, in order to preserve it." Following the Jewish tradition that allows Jews to add to the story of Passover anything that they feel is important for their family, this reference to the exodus is recited every year in the houses of Linda and Alice during the Passover seder.

For the whole year we lived in Psilovrahos, we took for granted the wild beauty of the province of Trihonida and did not pay any attention to some of the stones of our own house, which had carvings of animals or geometric designs and

In 1976, I discover the nail my father placed in 1943.

Stone carvings, from a previous civilization, on our home during the war.

belonged to a higher civilization that had flourished in the same area over 2,000 years earlier. Eleanor noticed these stones with their beautiful designs, which we missed in 1943-44! The only thing we cared about then was freedom and food.

Dr. Papatheodorou and his wife Popi, with my family in our reunion in 1976. (The doctor was the director of the ELAS hospital in Tatarna.)

Ninetta Feldman, my sister, in front of the house in Psilovrahos in her 1991 visit.

In 2007, Eleanor, Alice, her husband Maury, and I visited Psilovrahos again. Fewer and fewer people remained in the village. The houses were destroyed from the periodic earthquakes and disrepair, and perhaps the next time I visit

III. Author's Memoirs

there nobody will shed the warm tears I saw when these people realized that my deep affection for them was genuine and lasting. The cemetery will be there, and I will see the names of the prominent citizens of 1943-1944, such as the authoritarian Barbayiorgos, the self-respecting Tsoulos, and the earnest Tserpelis, who once distributed Red Cross supplies on the basis that 0.25 was five times more than 0.5 in spite of my strong protests. Nobody knew the distribution was unfair. Everyone respected him, as he was the only one who knew how to give injections with a syringe and needle he had from the time he was in the army in the war of 1921!

Alice and Maury visited Psilovrahos a second time in 2016 with their daughters Leanne and Danielle. They tried to visit our abandoned house, but it suffered much structural damage from recent earthquakes. Leanne, who was 16, carefully entered the house by herself to attempt to take a photograph. Just as we did in 1976, she saw the nail that my father placed in the fireplace in 1943. The nail was still there!

At this point, I should like to mention an incident which also made a deep impression on me. It is another situation where I narrowly escaped being killed as a target of anti-Semitism. This unbelievable attempt to murder Alice and myself happened 50 years after the beginning of the Holocaust, the greatest crime ever committed, where even the youngest children were killed. Men who knew nothing about us wanted to kill us just because they thought we were Jews.

For many years, my wife Eleanor and I volunteered every October for the program "Dental Volunteers for Israel" in Kibbutz Ein Shemer. In October 1990, my daughter Alice came instead of Eleanor. On Yom Kippur, as there was no bus transportation in Israel, Alice and I went for a walk on the nearby road connecting Israel with the West Bank. On our return to the Kibbutz, we were walking on the left side of the road. There were no cars in sight. I heard a distant sound which was getting louder and I thought it was a low flying airplane. When it became really loud, I thought the plane was going to make an emergency landing on the road. I did not have time to take a look. I pushed Alice two steps out of the road and leaped after her. A Palestinian car passed exactly on the spot where we had been one second before.

They were going to ram and kill us! I knew that the car was an Arab car because the license plate was green. The car was going more than 100 miles per hour. It was a miracle that we survived!

My instinctive two-step lifesaving movement out of the path of the speeding car brought to mind my thoughts and experiences from 1943-1944. During that time, we jumped from our comfortable existence in Agrinion to an unknown future in the free beautiful and wild Greek mountains.

I conclude with the belief that my year in the mountains shaped my values more profoundly than any school I ever attended. This experience influenced my ideals for human rights, social justice, freedom of expression, and pursuit of happiness. At the beginning, I felt as if I was on a wonderful vacation. Later on, when we were starving and we had to hide from the Germans in a cave, I realized the immense injustice that was done to the Jews. A big "Why?" remains alive in my mind to this day.

Epilogue

Men who are good desire nothing for themselves, which they do not also desire for the rest of mankind.

—BARUCH SPINOZA

Criminals

The destruction of the Greek Jews could not possibly have been achieved by the Germans acting alone. They were assisted by Greek policemen, civil servants, members of the Security Battalions, and traitors. Were any of them punished for their deeds? Three Greek-Christian traitors were condemned to death! They were Kirkor Boudourian, Laskaris Papanaoum, and police officer Adam. They were, however, condemned to death in absentia. Long before, they collected the treasure they stole from the Jews and moved to West Germany.[312] Colonel Poulos and his deputy were among the very few war criminals to be executed in Greece after the war.[313]

Thousands of other Greek collaborators of the Germans were never brought to trial. In the Public Records of London, a report from Greece mentions the names of German collaborators who had been "especially active in persecuting the Jews."[314]

---

[312] Molho, *In Memoriam,* 325.

[313] Mark Mazower, *Inside Hitler's Greece* (New Haven: Yale University Press, 1993), 339.

[314] Public Records Office, London, No. FO 371.

The U.S. naval attaché in Athens reported:

> The trial of the important Greek collaborators of the Germans ended on May 31, 1945 ... The trial of three Quisling prime ministers and the ministers who served under them ended yesterday. Condemned to death are General Tsolakoglou and Messrs Gotsamanis and Tsironikos, the latter two in absentia...
> The liberal and leftist press is highly critical. They point out that ... thanks to the assistance rendered the enemy by those on trial, some 500,000 Greeks are now dead. *To Vima* is emphatic in denouncing what it says amounts to a "travesty of justice."[315]

The only ones who paid for their crimes were the Greek-Jewish traitors because the Greek Jews insisted that they should be tried and punished. Even these criminals were aware of how benevolent the climate in Greece was to traitors in the aftermath of the war. Otherwise, they would not have returned to Greece, but would have tried to change their identity and disappear among the millions of homeless people who roamed the world in those years.

Vital Hasson made an agreement with officials of the Italian consulate in Thessaloniki. He would close his eyes and let the Italians save as many Jews as they wished, and in exchange they would allow him to escape when the right time arrived. Both sides honored their agreement, and the Italians provided Hasson with a car and the necessary papers which enabled him to go from Greece to Italian-occupied Albania. In the city of Koritsa, Hasson, his wife, his child, and another woman (his mistress) were arrested by the Italians and interned in an Albanian camp. When Italy surrendered on September 8, 1943, they were released. Hasson had enough money to buy a boat, cross the Adriatic, and land in Bari, Italy.[316]

Hasson was seen in Bari by Dr. Richard Kohen, a well-known Thessaloniki dentist, who reported Hasson's identity to

---

315 National Archives, Washington, DC, 055 135246.
316 Molho, *In Memoriam*, 322.

Epilogue

the Allied authorities. This criminal was in custody for a few days, but was later released. A World Jewish Congress representative wrote to Washington: "We are at a loss to understand this leniency, and steps should be immediately taken at your end in order to have him placed under arrest until the time comes to meting out to him the severe punishment which he has so richly deserved."[317]

Hasson went from Bari to Alexandria, Egypt. There he moved about as a free man until he was recognized by a refugee from Thessaloniki. The British police arrested him, and as soon as Greece was liberated, he was transferred to Athens. In Athens, nobody cared to prosecute him, and he was released. Most of Greece at that time was ruled by former German collaborators. Hasson the traitor felt so safe in the Greek atmosphere of 1945 that he did not hesitate to return to Thessaloniki, where he had committed his crimes. A group of Jews who returned from Poland beat him up and delivered him to the Greek police, who locked him in the Pavlos Melas prison.

The other traitors, Jacques Alballa, Leon Sion (Topouz), Edgar Kounio, Ino and Pepo Recanati, and Daniel Kohen also returned to Greece. The Jewish organizations forced the Greek government to arrest and punish them. Their trial took place in June 1947. Witnesses for the prosecution included Pepo Carasso, who told the court how Hasson discovered him and six members of his family in a remote suburb where they were hiding. Hasson without hesitation arrested them. Only Pepo Carasso survived. The most moving witness was Albert Talbi, who described how in June 1944 he had to leave his hiding place in order to find medicine for his seriously ill seven-year-old daughter. He was recognized by Daniel Kohen. Soon the Germans arrested the whole family. Again, Albert Talbi was the only one who survived. Upon hearing his story, many Jews in the audience attempted to lynch the prisoners. The police kept them back with difficulty. Hasson was condemned to death and was executed by firing squad.

Ino Recanati was also condemned to death. He attempted suicide, was declared insane, and was transferred to a mental asylum. Pepo Recanati and Daniel Kohen were condemned to

---

[317] Franklin D. Roosevelt Library, War Refugee Board Collection Container No. 26.

life in prison. Leon Sion (or Topouz) was condemned to life in prison. Alballa was condemned to 15 years in prison, while Edgar Kounio was condemned to eight years in prison.[318]

The German Criminals

Thousands of Germans, in large or small ways, placed themselves at the service of the impersonal machine which led the Jews to the chimneys of the camps. The great majority of them believe that they did nothing wrong. They followed orders and, in fact, did not murder any Jew. Yet, by their mere presence, they helped in the destruction of innocent people and, in this respect, they are criminals although they remain anonymous and without any fear or guilt feelings.

What about the major criminals? Alois Brunner lived freely in Syria. Dieter Wisliceny, commander of the German police RSHA and one of the main culprits in the drama of the Greek Jews, was captured in Germany as a result of pressure by the International Court of Justice. He was sent to Prague, where he was tried, convicted and hanged.[319]

Maximilian Merten, the military commander of Macedonia and the worst criminal of the German zone of occupation in Greece, remained free. He had collected an enormous amount of gold and jewelry from his victims, which he transported to Germany as part of his personal luggage. It is rumored that another great quantity of precious items was left by Merten in Greece in the hands of his Greek collaborators. He practiced law freely in Germany and in 1957 did not hesitate to return to Greece to recover his fortune. He claimed he visited Greece on legal business for a client. He was arrested on April 26, 1957. Two hundred witnesses testified against him. He was accused in the execution of 600 Greek Christians and for sending 9,000 Greek Jews to slave labor camps; for the extortion of 5,000 gold sovereigns from the Jewish community of Thessaloniki with the false promise that the Jews would be exempt from the application of the Nuremberg laws; for the destruction of the

---

318 Molho, *In Memoriam,* 327.
319 Ibid., 326.

Epilogue

Jewish cemetery of Thessaloniki; for numerous thefts; and, finally, for the deportation of 56,000 Jews to the death camps.

Twenty months later, on March 5, 1959, the trial began. People unsuccessfully attempted to lynch Merten. During Merten's trial in Athens, a letter from Salzburg was read. It described how, when he left Greece, Merten took with him a trunk filled with jewelry, gold, and diamonds and entrusted it to a woman named Frau Eiser. Later, Merten built a luxurious villa, most probably by selling part of his loot.[320] He was found guilty and sentenced to 25 years in prison. The Greek government, in a shameful effort to save Merten, passed a special law No. 4016 allowing him to obtain his freedom.

The Jewish community of Thessaloniki demanded that at least the 5,000 gold sovereigns Merten received from the community be returned. Even this failed. A Lufthansa plane was waiting to transfer Merten to Germany and freedom.

Some of the principal Bulgarian criminals who organized the arrest and deportation of the Jews in the Bulgarian zone of occupation were Captain Meltser in Kavalla, Daskalof in Serres, Gikof in Xanthe, Natsalnik in Komotini, and Moudrof in Drama, who was a lawyer and leader of the bandits called Comitatzides. Their whereabouts are unknown.[321]

Beyond the Archives

In 1975, I was greatly surprised to find out that the U.S. State Department was advised by noble human beings like Consul Berry as to how to save thousands of Greek Jews with a minimum of effort or resources. I was also shocked by the realization that Consul Berry's superior did not take any action or follow any recommendation sent to him by Consul Berry.

His superior was like the mayor of a city who received information that the water supply of his city was poisoned. Instead of sounding the alarm and telling everyone not to drink the poisoned water, he did nothing. He just received reports from the various precincts detailing how many died in one precinct and how many died in the other. He filed the reports

---

[320] Novitch, *Le Passage des Barbares* (Athens: Dodos, 1985), 15.
[321] *Chronika,* Athens, April 1982, 9.

away, while the people who trusted him died. I had wanted to know who Consul Berry's superior was, who exhibited this monstrous behavior. Did he have parents, a wife, or children? How did Consul Berry feel about his superior's indifference? Did he confront him after the war?

The State Department informed me that Consul Berry retired and lived permanently in Istanbul, Turkey. At the same time, I was informed that, by paying an hourly fee, I could find out who had received a particular report, what action was taken (if any) and by whom, until the report was sent to the archives. It was that simple. I could find out who was indirectly responsible for the death of my relatives.

That night I had a dream. My 126 close relatives lived in an old apartment building. In the middle of the night, neighbors noticed that the building started burning. They informed the chief of the fire department close by. He could have pressed a button to have sounded the alarm in the old building. He did not even have to send the fire engines, since the building was old. He did not press the alarm button, which would have forced my relatives to wake up and get out of the burning building. Instead, he watched the conflagration with a sadistic smile on his face. I killed him. Fortunately, it was only a dream. The following day I threw away my letter requesting the Diplomatic Branch, National Archives and Records Administration in Washington, DC, to begin the search for the man for whom I felt such utter contempt.

Monuments, Memorials and Museums

As time passes, more people feel the need to honor the memory of the Greek Jews who so needlessly perished. The Jewish community of Thessaloniki erected a beautiful monument honoring the victims of the Holocaust. On September 3, 1986, the mayor of Thessaloniki renamed a square in the center of the city the "Square of the Jewish Martyrs." On April 5, 1987, the Jewish community of Larissa erected its own Holocaust memorial in a newly created square, which the civil authorities called "Square of the Jewish Martyrs of Occupation." The Jewish communities of Greece erected a monument in Leanokladi, honoring the 500 Greek-Jewish slave laborers who worked on the rail system of this

Epilogue

area. In September 1988, in Sikourio-Larissa, a monument was erected on the spot where the Germans executed 67 ELAS partisans. Among the names of these heroes are seven Jews:

Algoussis, Salvator
Felous, Markos
Feretzi, Albertos
Feretzi, Moissis
Feretzi, Sadon
Maissi, Simantov
Sasson, David

Mayor Xariliou in Rhodes decided that Prince Square would be renamed "The Square of the Jewish Martyr" in honor of the Rhodian Jews who suffered terrible death in the German concentration camps. In Chalkis, the birthplace of Mordechai Frizis, there is a bust of the heroic colonel in a prominent square as well as the statue of Frizis on horseback, which was initiated and funds raised by Greek-American Stefanos Becharas of Michigan. A bust of Frizis is also located in the war museum in Athens. There are also Holocaust memorials in Ioannina, Corfu, Athens, and other cities in Greece.

Museums also serve the purpose of educating the public about the Holocaust and as a place for remembering the communities and the people who lived in them. In Greece, there are Jewish museums in Athens, Thessaloniki, and Rhodes. In New York City, the synagogue and museum of Kehila Kedosha Janina honors the memory of the Jews of Greece under its director Marcia Ikonomopoulos. It has an extensive archival collection and runs annual Jewish heritage tours to Greece through the Association of Friends of Greek Jewry.[322]

---

[322] Kehila Kedosha Janina Synagogue and Museum - website address www.kkjsm.org.

Survivors

Law is an invention of the strong to chain and rule the weak.

— JEAN-JACQUES ROUSSEAU

The rapid advance of the Russian army in Romania and Bulgaria forced the German army of occupation in Greece and Albania to withdraw to the north. Since the Germans retreated in an orderly fashion, without any fighting, Greek cities survived the war virtually undamaged.

When the Jews came out of hiding in the cities or returned from the mountains, they either found everything they left with trusted Christian friends or they were told by their dishonest "friends" that "The Germans confiscated all." There was nothing that could be done. Of course, there were cases where the Germans did confiscate everything.

In the provinces, emptied Jewish neighborhoods provided shelter to villagers who were forced to come to the city after the Germans destroyed their homes during their search-and-destroy campaigns. It is estimated that 3,700 villages were totally or partially destroyed by bombardments and fire. Over 1,200,000 Greeks became homeless.[323]

After October 30, 1944, there were no more hidden Jews in Greece. They started making their appearance as if reborn. In Thessaloniki there were about seventy Jews (married mostly to Christian women). The Pardo family also came out of hiding. Another 400 Jews arrived in Thessaloniki from the villages where they had found shelter. Many Jewish partisans returned to their cities.

This is what happened in Ioannina. Out of 1,860 Jews who were living there before the war, only the Vehoropoulos family of four returned to the city from the mountains. A dozen partisans returned to Ioannina to find their Jewish neighborhoods filled with villagers who were occupying Jewish homes, sometimes one family per room. All Jewish homes had been looted systematically, and all Jewish shops, artisan

---

323 Molho, *In Memoriam*, 334.

Epilogue

workshops and offices were empty of any merchandise and occupied by strangers.

In Ioannina, the Germans accumulated all valuable merchandise and household goods in a big warehouse, but they did not have enough time to transfer these to Germany. The resistance organization had other plans. They distributed, to each Jew who was present in Ioannina at that time, the equivalent of thirty gold sovereigns in merchandise. An exception was made in the case of my father. Although he was not physically present in Ioannina, he was given his share because he was considered a partisan director of the warehouses in Agrinion.

The Jewish ELAS partisans guarded this big warehouse, hoping that the Jews of Ioannina who would return from captivity would find something to help them restart their lives. However, the communist leaders of EAM-ELAS preferred to confiscate all this fortune. Nothing remained for the 163 survivors who returned from the concentration camps.

In the next few months, the survivors of the camps arrived in Ioannina. They were sick, dispirited and totally destitute. The community increased to 163 people. One could not find a room, even in his or her own house. They had to beg, insist, complain and argue in order to get a room in their family homes, which were filled with a great number of strangers who resented the reappearance of even one person who could be their potential landlord.

One sole survivor returned to her large house, and the only room she was given was a closet under the staircase which was used for the storage of charcoal. She cleaned the place, installed a light, and this became her home.[324]

Another survivor, the only one from her family, returned to her house in Ioannina. The lady who occupied her home, opened the door and recognized her as the owner of the house. Instead of embracing her and welcoming her home, she almost fainted and then raising her hands, looked towards the heavens and said, "*Panagia mou* [Virgin Mary]! Why are you doing this to me?!" – as told to me by Dr. Mimis Cohen.

---

[324] On my visit to Ioannina, I visited this woman to give her a gift from her relative, Leon Revi of Agrinion.

It is estimated that 1,500 Greek Jews returned from the concentration camps. The first to arrive in Greece in May 1945 was Leon Batis. He told many people what had happened in the camps. Nobody believed him; they thought he was insane. This was the first time the Greek Jews were told about the existence of the gas chambers, the crematoria and the death camps. The price of ignorance had been an enormous one.

Soon, in all the movie houses, Greek Jews saw newsreels of Allied troops liberating the camps. They all kept speculating about what they could have done had they ever suspected the real meaning of the "resettlement in the East."

It was extremely hard to believe that, in a few short minutes, all their relatives were dead. Perhaps the fact that there was no illness or accident, mourning or funeral, religious services or even cemetery tombs made it much more difficult for them to comprehend that they would never see anyone again. Once the last of the "hostages," as they were called, returned, none others followed.

Among the survivors were a few instances in which two and three sisters or two brothers returned. There was not, in Ioannina at least, even one couple of husband and wife or parent and child who returned from captivity.

The "new" Jewish community of Ioannina was composed of people not younger than 18 nor older than forty. No children, no old people, no families, except one. Every evening they went to the outdoor cafes, if the weather permitted, and socialized once again among themselves. They formed large groups of seemingly happy, laughing people who would sit for hours in the cafes by the lake, sipping a lemonade or dancing to the popular tangos of the period.

The Christians all around them were in small, quiet groups, and they would often look at the "happy" Jewish men and women with a sadness that perhaps reflected compassion mixed with subconscious feelings of guilt.

During the occupation, the big synagogue on Max Nordau Street had been transformed into a horse stable by the Germans. The first priority of the community was to clean the place which they associated with many happy or sad events that reminded them of their lost families. Mayor Demetrios

Epilogue

Vlahlides saved the sacred scrolls and returned them to the Jewish community.[325]

The 163 survivors gathered in the synagogue to hold services for their dead. There was no rabbi. Someone intoned the words of the memorial blessing: "Yithkadal, Veyithkadash shemei raba," but it was impossible for him to continue. An unrestrained sobbing was shaking everyone in the place. The 163 survivors were weeping and mourning for the loss of their parents, their children, their brothers and sisters, their sweethearts and their friends. Many of them must have wondered if there were a God and, if so, where was He when their precious parents and children entered the gates of Auschwitz.

In order to survive, they had to find capital to open small shops and artisan workshops. The only assets they could use were the hundreds of houses and shops that had belonged to their parents. All of a sudden, these real estate holdings went on the market. They were sold easily at a small fraction of their real value. In one case a house was sold for the price of a refrigerator!

Thousands of Christians all over Greece acquired properties for prices next to nothing, and perhaps they were grateful to the Germans for getting rid of their Jewish competitors and also giving them, indirectly, the property the Jews left behind.

Soon the survivors started marrying each other and wondered whether they would want to raise families in their ancestral cities. The "wandering Jew" was on the road again. Many immigrated to Palestine; others went to the United States or South America. Some of those who wanted to immigrate to the United States were unable to do so if they had saved themselves by joining the resistance forces of EAM-ELAS. For example, Joseph Kohen of Ioannina, who joined ETA of ELAS and lost his entire family, in spite of the fact that he was a well-to-do merchant without any political affiliation, was refused entry to the United States. He remarried in Greece, and eventually his son came to the United States.

Many of those who became partisans of ELAS suffered a worse fate. Joseph Issis was executed, and Mihalis Valais of

---

325 Rachel Dalven, *The Jews of Ioannina* (New York, 1990).

Ioannina was beaten to death. Others, like Moissis Sakis, lost their jobs.

My first cousin, Sam Meyer, who had not even been a partisan was also punished. He was a dairyman selling milk products. A policeman, who refused to pay what he owed him, created a communist file for Sam. So, when Sam was drafted into the Greek army, he was exiled to the island of Makronisos, which was filled with soldiers who were former members of EAM-ELAS. His superiors realized he had been exiled by mistake. He was given a cane and asked to join those who beat the resistance soldiers at night in their tents. Sam refused to do so. They placed him in a communications unit.

Fortunately, many former partisans took advantage of a law allowing them to leave Greece for Palestine provided they signed a paper renouncing their right to return to Greece as permanent residents. In Palestine, they joined the Haganah and participated in the Israeli War of Independence.

In Greece, out of a Jewish population of 10,371 in 1947, there were only 5,260 left in 1959, in spite of the great natural increase from the children who were born to the newly married couples. Another additional movement took place, bringing Jews from small cities and even Thessaloniki to Athens. Many Jewish communities disappeared completely. In Arta and Preveza, the only Jewish person who remained was a man in Arta who became a Christian. The synagogues and the Jewish schools were replaced by new buildings. In Preveza, a commemorative plaque was placed on the building that replaced the synagogue. In Veria, the city where Apostle Paul preached to the Jewish community, there is not even one Jew remaining. In many other cities, there is no longer any trace of the former Jewish community.

The Rescuers

In spite of the dangers, many individuals did save Jews during the Holocaust. In 1963, Yad Vashem, the World Holocaust Remembrance Center, began to officially honor those non-Jews who, without any financial motive and at great risk to themselves, helped Jews to survive. These people were nominated as a tribute by those whom they had saved.

Epilogue

There have been many rescuers representing many countries. As of January 1, 2020, Yad Vashem has honored 357 Greek citizens for their heroism and named them the Righteous Among the Nations. Several of their stories are described in my book. To learn more, one can go to the Yad Vashem website – www.yadvashem.org.

The author with Dr. Michel Negrin. He became a physician partisan of EDES.

What Happened to Some of the Survivors

Dr. Michel Negrin, who saved the ten wounded German prisoners, became an ophthalmologist in Athens. At the peak of his medical career, he died. Before his death, he instructed his wife Mireille to donate all the equipment in his clinic to a village in Israel. The Michel Negrin Clinic was providing treatment in Ginot Shomron.

Solomon Matsas, who escaped from the camp at Larissa, was killed three years after the liberation during the civil war while he served as a soldier in the Greek army.

Markos Ganis, the young boy who joined the partisans after the battle of southern Mt. Olympus, went to live in Israel.

Moissis Alballa, who was taken to the mountains as a baby, was a prominent optometrist in Santa Monica, California.

Rosa Pardo Asser, who as a young girl lived for 18 months hidden in a house in the center of German-occupied

Thessaloniki, was luckier than Anne Frank of Amsterdam. She survived the war and lived in Athens.

Lazaros Mionis, who went to the mountains of Valtou, lived in Athens.

Joseph Stroumtsa, the son of the president of the Jewish community of Veria, is a retired dentist and lives in Thessaloniki.

Joseph Yohanas of Patras lived with his family outside Baltimore, Maryland, and worked in the men's clothing department of Saks Fifth Avenue.

Emmanuel Velellis, whose brothers were killed by the partisans of ELAS, lived with his wife and two daughters in Baltimore, Maryland.

Mimi Assael, who was transferred from Thessaloniki to Athens as an Italian prisoner, lived in Seattle, Washington.

Sam Meyer, whose life was spared when a Jewish partisan asked him to recite the "Shemah," died in 1977, in spite of efforts by the National Institutes of Health in Maryland to save him from a rare illness.

Eliasaf Matsas, who escaped from the Germans in Perama and became a partisan, lived in Beersheva, Israel. He was the father of five children and had many grandchildren.

Yesoua Matsas, who escaped from the camp at Larissa and became a partisan, was the father of four children and many grandchildren. He also lived in Beersheva, Israel.

Albertos Negrin, for whom the Second World War lasted for 16 years, died in 1992. He was the proud father of one engineer and one architect and the grandfather of four lovely girls. He lived in Ioannina, where he was born.

Isaak Koulias, who crossed the Aegean and swam to the Turkish shore when his boat capsized, lived with his family in Baltimore, Maryland.

Rachel Kamonto, whose brother was betrayed to the Germans by his bank colleague, moved to Israel and lived in Tel Aviv.

Jeanette Vehoropoulou, who escaped Ioannina on the day of arrest, moved after the war to Geneva, Switzerland, where she married the Sephardic cantor of that city.

Leon Batis, the first Greek Jew to return to Greece from the camps, became a successful merchant in Athens. I remember that in his shop he had an enormous framed

Epilogue

photograph of himself, taken on the day of his arrival in Athens.

Dr. Errikos Levis was active in the Greek army as a physician. He died in 2005 and is buried near Washington, DC near the tombs of my parents.

Makis Solomon, the only Greek Jew I knew who did not trust even the Italians, married Anna Mioni, the sister of my classmate Lazaros. They lived in Athens.

Sam Matsas, who prompted some of the Ioannina Jews to disobey the Germans and save themselves, became an industrialist. One of his sons became a physician in Athens. Sam died suddenly in 1985.

Yonas Mionis, who was one of the leaders of EAM, immigrated to Israel where he was active in politics as a leader of the Communist Party until his death a few years later.

Dr. Manolis Aruh, the physician-fighter of the II Division of ELAS, survived the war but lost all 35 members of his immediate family. He practiced medicine in Athens.

Moshe Yomtov, who served as a partisan in the same unit with Dr. Manolis Aruh, lived in Ramat Gan, Israel. Both lost their families, and they maintained close relations with each other. They both started their letters to each other with the words "Dear brother…"

Salvator Bakolas, a partisan in the unit of Nikiforos, completed his studies as a chemist after the war and lived in Athens. He married my cousin, Dora Kohen, from Corfu.

Ido Simsi or Maccabee, of the II Division of ELAS, lived in Israel.

Christos Bokoros, the resistance leader to whom I delivered a gun and ammunition in 1943, was drafted as an officer of the Greek army and was killed in 1948 during the civil war.

Thomas Bokoros, who organized our escape to the mountains, was the president of the Archaeological Society of Agrinion when I met him in 1976. He later died at the age of 58.

Matika Taboch of Veria, who witnessed the looting of the Jews in Palatitsa, married my cousin Yesoua Matsas and lived in Beersheva, Israel.

Joseph Matsas, who fought the SS battalion on southern Mt. Olympus, wrote many booklets and articles about the Jews of Ioannina. He also gave lectures about the Jewish participation in the Greek forces during the Second World War. He died in Athens in 1986.

From a lecture by Joseph Matsas published in 1991 by the *Journal of the Hellenic Diaspora*, I found out that the partisans Solon Abraam Levi, Sam Leon Gavrielidis, and Joseph Lahanas survived the war, went to Israel, and died during its War of Independence in 1948.[326] On July 18, 2010, I learned from Ms. Dorit Perry of Jerusalem, a researcher of the Israeli Army's unit responsible for detection of missing and deceased soldiers, the following:

> "Joseph Lahanas fell on June 3, 1948 in the battle in the City of Jenin. In this battle fifty soldiers died and they were buried in a mass grave on Mount Herzl in Jerusalem. Recently, we discovered a 1952 letter from his brother Gershon and his sister Zimbola who moved to France before the Second World War. They were looking for Joseph. We located the children of his brother Gershon, who lived in France and they were excited to hear these details. They have lived all their lives in France and knew neither their grandparents Nissim and Esther nor their uncle Joseph or when and how he died."

The partisans Leon and Fani Florentin moved to America and lived in Seattle, Washington, with their two children.

Iakovos Frizis, son of Colonel Mordechai Frizis, studied political science and became an employee of the National Bank of Greece. He lives in Athens.

Sotiris Papastratis, the "short guerrilla" who supervised the embarkation of those who crossed the Aegean to Turkey, continued his law practice in Athens. Yad Vashem honored him

---

326 Solon Abraam Levi was the brother of Lola Matsa, grandmother of the Greek translator of the *Illusion of Safety*, Mihalis Matsas. Joseph Lahanas was the commander of the bridge of Potamoula who stopped my mother from entering Agrinion.
Lecture by Joseph Matsas, "The Participation of the Greek Jews in the National Resistance,1940-1944." *Journal of the Hellenic Diaspora*, Vol. 17.1, 1991 (NewYork: Pella Publishing Company, Inc.).

Epilogue

with the Righteous Among the Nations award in 1988 for saving eight Jewish families from Chalkis.

Lazarus Azarias, the agriculture specialist who, with his organizational ability, helped solve the problem of providing food for the partisans of ELAS, was condemned to death in absentia after the Second World War. He went into hiding in friendly houses. He later joined one of the first groups who attempted to enter Palestine illegally. He was captured by the British and transferred to a prison camp in Cyprus. Azarias organized the life of the Jewish inmates and married Rachel Kohen, a former partisan of ELAS from Volos.

When he finally was allowed to go to Israel, Azarias started his new life as a porter of milk in the Tnuva Company. His ability was soon recognized. He produced the "Azaria" cheese from milk powder imported from the United States at a time of food shortages, and he eventually became the general director of Tnuva. In 1972, he died of a heart attack, leaving his wife and two children, both scientists.[327]

Mimis Kohen, the Italian interpreter, moved to Athens. His wife was killed during the civil war. Mimis and his son immigrated to Israel in 1948.

Rebecca Matsas Gani, my aunt, is the little girl in the large family portrait of my grandparents' family. This portrait was found crumpled in the street after the looting of her ancestral home during the war. She married Elie Gani of Alexandria, Egypt before WWII and settled in Egypt. This saved her life.

The Gani family was very prosperous and happy in Egypt. In 1956, Gamal Abdel Nasser, the President of Egypt, decided to throw out all of the Jews of Egypt. Rebecca and her family lost their wealth and made their way to Paris.

In Paris, her husband started a costume jewelry business. Unfortunately, Eli died young and Rebecca became a poor widow at the age of 49 with four children. She was a strong woman who managed to take over her husband's business and become successful.

Her four children received the best possible education, and she lived a long life, dying at age 96 in 2013. She is survived by her family including nine grandchildren and thirteen great-grandchildren.

---

[327] Moissis Sakis, letter to the author, August 28, 1977.

Rebecca Gani with her three boys, Clement, Makis and Charles, in Alexandria, Egypt. Rene-Claire was born later in Paris, France.

My grandparents and uncle, who were living in Albania, died after the war. In 1991, we were able to bring from Albania to the United States my aunt Julie, her three children, Pepo, Gracia, and Enni, and their families: a total of 33 people. Actually, we brought four more people related to one of our relatives by marriage.

Among the 33 relatives was my cousin Enni's son Renato Margariti who now works in New York as a radiology technician. When he was a little boy in Albania, he was close to dying from an intestinal parasitic infection. His father sent me the name of the parasite. No doctor here would write a prescription without seeing the patient. I went to a medical library, where I researched the problem and discovered the treatment. I wrote and filled a prescription for the medicine, and I translated the instructions into Greek. I mailed the medication to Albania, but the local doctors refused to use it. When Orestes, Renato's father, saw that his son was going to die, he gave him the medicine and then sent me a letter thanking me for saving his son's life. In a few days, I received

Renato Margariti

Epilogue

another request for another child; Orestes gave the medicine to him, and we saved his life. The medicine cost $1.80 in 1971!

My sister Ninetta, for whom I made her first schoolbook, received a bachelor's degree in psychology and a master's degree in education. She is a retired science teacher living in Bethesda, Maryland. Her late husband, Lloyd Feldman, was an official of the Labor Department. They have one daughter and three grandchildren. One is a teacher, and the other two are high school students.

As for myself, I retired from my dental practice in 1995 after my daughters were married. My older daughter, Linda, is a pediatrician who is married to a physician, Dr. Ira Berger. They have three children, one in medical school, and the other two in college. My younger daughter, Alice, is an educator who is married to an attorney, Morris Garten. They have two daughters who are in college. My original dream was realized in this beautiful and great country that I love very much.

As I finish this manuscript, I am tormented with the thought that the Holocaust was not an inescapable natural disaster, but a preventable historic event. I am convinced that tens of thousands of Greek Jews would not have died if the United States and Great Britain had refused to remain silent and instead exposed the German secret plans for the "Final Solution." This murderous silence undermined the basic moral foundation of the Western Allies forever.

The Illusion of Safety

The Holocaust memorial in Corfu, Greece. (Photo by Linda Berger.)

Bibliographical Essay
By Professor Steven Bowman

Dr. Matsas has produced a manuscript that is a tribute to personal memory. He has caught the essence of a problem of the Second World War and the resultant destruction of innocent Jewish communities. He has assembled his account from his own undirected readings and from the memoirs of participants of that tragic period. He has given us a firsthand account of the tragedy of Greek Jewry.

The following essay will address the question of modern scholarship. Is his story accurate in the wider perspective of the historical discipline? True, his memoirs tell the story of participants, but does an individual understand the greater story? The tragedy of Greek Jewry is relatively unknown, and is generally unappreciated within the wider context of the Holocaust of European Jewry. The Greek Jewish story can only be compared to that of Yugoslavia if we restrict our framework to the Holocaust of Sephardic Jews. It can only be compared to Hungarian Jewry if we analyze and compare the process of destruction. If we apply the criteria of Dr. Matsas, we have to admit that Greek Jewry constitutes a unique story in the vast encyclopedia of the Holocaust. This tragic story he tells with the passion and anger of a survivor.

The reader of Dr. Matsas's collection will be able to test his thesis in the following English-language works of scholars who have pursued parallel research in the professional archives of bureaucrats of numerous countries. It is their records that historians research to prove their theses. Yet these records, which are the stuff of modern history, are wanting in the passion of action which in fact makes history. Hence, their studies, which are a useful support to his arguments and which clarify the motives and methodologies of the destructive process, stand anemic alongside the passion of activist memoirs that tell the story from the grassroots level.

It would be anomalous to implant modern scholarly research into the author's story. Rather, the present essay will guide the interested reader to the scholarship and other sources available in English that analyze the documents and motives of the various participants and victims of this unique story Dr. Matsas has assembled for history.

There are many actors in the story of the Second World War in Greece. The first question raised by the author is: who knew and said nothing? This question has been researched by David Wyman in his challenging study, *The Abandonment of the Jews: American Policy and the Holocaust, 1941-1945* (New York, 1984). The ongoing disaster was already known by western states, as has been shown by Walter Laqueur in several seminal studies: *The Terrible Secret: An Investigation into the Suppression of Information about Hitler's "Final Solution"* (London, 1980), and with R. Breitman, *Breaking the Silence* (New York, 1986).

The vicissitudes of Greek history during the war have been studied most recently by Mark Mazower in his innovative social and economic history of the war years, *Inside Hitler's Greece: The Experience of Occupation 1941-44* (New Haven, 1993). His study is the first scholarly account to break new ground in the general study of Greek Jewry, and it supersedes the classical work of Michael Molho and Joseph Nehama, *In Memoriam* (originally published in 1948), which the author has used extensively in its Greek translation. So, John Louis Hondros's study *Occupation and Resistance: The Greek Agony 1941-44* (New York, 1983), while breaking new ground for the study of World War II Greece in his detailed reading of German army records in the National Archives (Washington, DC), based his chapter on the Jews on the out-of-date material in Molho-Nehama, *In Memoriam*. At the same time, a beginning in the revision of the Jewish story was presented by Steven Bowman, "Jews in Wartime Greece," *Jewish Social Studies* 48 (1986), 45-62; "Jews in Wartime Greece: A Select Annotated Bibliography" in *Greece in the 1940s: A Bibliographic Companion,* edited by John O. Iatrides (Hanover and London, 1981); several entries in the *Encyclopedia of the Holocaust* (e.g., Greece, Athens, Thessaloniki, Thrace, etc.), and essays in the memoirs of Marco Nahon and Daniel Bennahmias (below). An earlier bibliography was prepared by Philip Friedman, "The Jews of Greece During the Second World War (A Bibliographic Survey)," *The Joshua Starr Memorial Volume* (New York, 1953), 241-248; a number of his entries have been superseded by further research.

Bibliographical Essay

The other two participants in the enslavement of Greece were the Bulgarians and the Italians. The fate of the Jews in each occupied zone differed according to the predilections of the *ethnoi* (autonomous linguistic-religious groups) involved. The Bulgarians were selfish and divided their Jews into two groups: old subjects and new conquests. The fate of the latter included the Jews of occupied Thrace and was analyzed by Frederick B. Chary, *The Bulgarian Jews and the Final Solution, 1940-1944* (Pittsburgh, 1972), and earlier by Alexander Matkowski, "The Destruction of Macedonian and Thracian Jews," *Yad Vashem Studies* III (1959), and his book-length study *A History of the Jews of Macedonia* (Skopje, 1982). An early insight into the tragedy of Thrace is the memoir of Nadejda S. Vasileva, "On the Catastrophe of the Thracian Jews," *Yad Vashem Studies* III (1959), 295-302.

In the Italian zone we now have the recent study by Jonathan Steinberg, *All or Nothing: The Axis and the Holocaust 194-1-43* (London and New York, 1990), which is based on a detailed analysis of Italian and German military documents. The earlier study of Meir Michaelis, *Mussolini and the Jewish Question in Italy 1922-1945* (Oxford, 1978), is seminal for an understanding of the fascist attitude toward the Jews. Leon Poliakov and Jacques Sahille, eds., *Jews under the Italian Occupation* (Paris, 1955), were the first non-Greeks to point out the Italian role in the Greek story. The memoir of an Italian diplomat in Thessaloniki has been recently published by Joseph Rochlitz and Menachem Shelach, "Excerpts from Thessaloniki Diary of Lucillo Merci (February-August 1943)," *Yad Vashem Studies* VIII (1987), 293-323. A number of studies have been made, with considerable documentary detail, by Daniel Carpi of Tel Aviv University in a host of studies, including: "Notes on the History of the Jews in Greece during the Holocaust Period: The Attitude of the Italians (1941-1943)," *Festschrift in Honor of Dr. Gregory S. Wise* (Tel Aviv, 1981), 25-62 [the Italian documents are available in *Michael* VII (Tel Aviv, 1981)]; his *Between Mussolini and Hitler: The Jews and the Italian Authorities in France and Tunisia* (Hanover and London, 1994) provides the background study for the destruction of the Greek-Jewish colony in Paris.

The attitude of Greek citizens has been defended by Alexander Kitroeff based on documents in American archives ["Documents: The Jews in Greece, 1941-1944: Eyewitness

Accounts," *Journal of the Hellenic Diaspora* XII (1985), 5-32], Though the latter material is somewhat wanting in its total approach to the problem, the effort by bystanders is appreciated; nevertheless, this Greek action was late in terms of actual numbers of individuals saved. On the other hand, people acted as individuals and should be honored for their choice. The bottom line is that the Germans were intent on killing Greek Jews because they were Jews, and they were assisted by some Greek Christians and various Jews in the process. The role of German diplomats was described in detail by Christopher Browning, *The Final Solution and the German Foreign Office: A Study of Referat D III of Abteilung Deutschland 1940-1943* (New York, 1978). A comparison of the German and Italian armies is the thesis of Jonathan Steinberg's study, *All or Nothing* (cited above). The strange career of Kurt Waldheim was well exposed by Robert Edwin Herzstein, *Waldheim: The Missing Years* (New York, 1988).

Many Greek Jews survived with the assistance of Greek Christians either in the mountains or in the cities. In addition, those of the official government and the official church are to be recognized for their actions as options representing the free choice of individuals in a period of terror, and so the latter have been honored by Yad Vashem in Jerusalem. More righteous Greek Gentiles have been honored in recent years. Cf. Steven Bowman, "Greek Jews and Christians During World War II," *Remembering the Future: Jews and Christians During and After the Holocaust,* Theme I (Oxford, 1988). The first study of the role of the Greek resistance is in L. S. Stavrianos, "The Jews of Greece," *Journal of Central European Affairs,"* 3 (1948), 256-81. Further material on the Jews in the Greek resistance can be found in Steven Bowman, "Joseph Matsas and the Greek Resistance," *Journal of the Hellenic Diaspora,* 17 (1991). The latter contains the only public statement by Joseph Matsas on the subject; this lecture was first summarized by Michael Matsas, "How the West Helped Destruction of Greek Jewry," *The Jewish Week* (Washington, DC), 13-19 1978, pp. 48 and 70. Dr. Matsas has presented his thesis in a number of newspaper articles, including *The Jerusalem Post.*

Two countries that could save Jews through diplomatic action were Spain and Turkey. Haim Avni explored the Spanish archives for material on Greek Jews who could claim

Bibliographical Essay

Spanish citizenship. Their story is recounted in his *Spain, The Jews, and Franco* (Philadelphia, 1982). His earlier study was specifically focused on Greece ("Spanish Nationals in Greece and Their Fate during the Holocaust," *Yad Vashem Studies* VIII (1970), 31-68. Recently, a biased study of Turkey's efforts was presented by Stanford J. Shaw, *Turkey and The Holocaust* (New York, 1993); the latter suffers from a vitriolic antipathy to the Greeks and an apologetic panegyric of the Turks. The reader should know that Turkey's record is more balanced, given the pressures it was under from both Allied and Axis diplomats as well as the threat of Axis armies on its European border [cf. Bernard Wasserstein, *Britain and the Jews of Europe, 1939-19U5* (Oxford, 1979)]. Earlier efforts notwithstanding, Turkey (and Spain as well) became more aggressive in the rescue of Greek Jews only late in the war and after the establishment of the War Refugee Board in the United States.

Dr. Matsas is the first researcher in Greek Jewish history to enter into the hospitable labyrinth of the Franklin D. Roosevelt Archives in Hyde Park, New York. There he uncovered the records of the War Refugee Board that dealt with the problem of Greek Jewry. He has also rediscovered the missing reports about Greek Jewish affairs of Ambassador Lincoln MacVeagh, sent from Egypt to President Roosevelt. These reports are conspicuously absent from the otherwise well-edited volume of John 0. Iatrides, *Ambassador MacVeagh Reports: Greece, 19B3-19U7* (Princeton, 1980).

Dr. Matsas also presents the hitherto unknown reports of American diplomats in Turkey who debriefed Jewish refugees from Greece and added to these debriefing reports corroborating material received from British officials and from a number of Palestinian agents who assisted these refugees to continue their journey to Palestine. The Istanbul chapter of Greek Jewish rescue has not yet been told in English. We are grateful to his pioneering research in this area.

The English reader can now experience the Holocaust of Greek Jewry in the memoirs of Dr. Albert Menasse, *Birkenau /Auschwitz II /. How 72,000 Greek Jews Perished* (New York, 1947), excerpts of which were translated from the Greek version for the present study; Dr. Marco Nahon, *Birkenau: The Camp of Death* (Tuscaloosa, AL, 1989), memorializes the community of Didimotiho (Demotika) ; Rebecca Camhi Fromer,

The Holocaust Odyssey of Daniel Bennahmias, Sonderkommando (Tuscaloosa, AL, 1998) is the first published participant Greek voice in English on the revolt in Auschwitz [Dr. Menasse records one testimony in his memoir] (above) and should balance the propagandistic essay of Isaac Kabelli, "The Resistance of the Greek Jews," *YIVO* 18 (1953) [the author was *persona non grata* among the American diaspora of Greek Jews due to his service in the Athens Judenrat. The exaggerations in the essay may be part of his postwar apology], and Errikos Sevillias, *Athens-Auschwitz* (Athens, 1983). The first collection of memoirs, originally published in French (still preferable) is now available in a posthumous English translation: Miriam Novitch, *The Passage of Barbarians* (Hull, England, 1989). Isaac Jack Levy translated with commentary *And the World Stood Silent: Sephardic Poetry of the Holocaust* (Urbana and Chicago, 1989).

The first scholarly report on postwar Thessaloniki is Cecil Roth's "The Last Days of Jewish Thessaloniki," *Commentary*, 10 (July, 1950), 49-55; his report is a sequel to Hal Lehrman's "Greece: Unused Cakes of Soap," *Commentary* 7 (May, 1947), 48-52. Roth's castigation of Rabbi Koretz, which follows popular sentiment, was countered in the study of Nathan Eck, "New Light on the Charges against the Last Grand Rabbi of Thessaloniki," *Yad Vashem Bulletin* 17 (1965), 9-15 and 19 (1966), 28-35. The controversial question of Rabbi Koretz was reexamined somewhat apologetically by Joseph Ben, "Jewish Leadership in Greece during the Holocaust" in *Patterns of Jewish Leadership in Nazi Europe, 1933-1945* (Jerusalem, 1979), 335-352.

Rae Dalven recounted the tragedy in Ioannina in her *The Jews of Ioannina* (Philadelphia, 1990) and more fully in "The Holocaust in Ioannina," *Journal of Modern Greek Studies* (1984), 87-103. The recent Ph.D. dissertation by Annette Fromm adds more details on the Ioannina community: "We Are Few: Folklore and Ethnic Identity of the Jewish Community of Ioannina, Greece," Folklore Institute, Indiana University (1992). Joshua Plaut's rabbinic thesis at the Hebrew Union College—Jewish Institute of Religion (1986), recently published as *Greek Jewry in the Twentieth Century, 1913-1983* (Madison, London, 1996), attempts to cover the provincial towns of Jewish Greece throughout the twentieth century. It includes a number of interviews with survivors.

Bibliographical Essay

The question of the end of Cretan Jewry remains an almost unresolved mystery. However, a number of seminal research papers have been published by Judith Humphrey of Cambridge, England, in *the Bulletin of Judeo-Greek Studies,* the latter edited by Nicholas de Lange and Judith Humphrey. Her conclusion, based on an analysis of Greek, British and German documents is that the *SS Tanais,* which transported the remaining Jews of Crete—a number had already been executed by the Germans as part of their hostage policy—was most likely torpedoed by a British submarine.

A memorial to the Jews of Rhodes and Kos has recently been translated into English: Hizkia Franko, *The Jewish Martyrs of Rhodes and Kos* (Paris, 1993). This work, originally published in Elizabethville, Congo, in 1952, is an attempt to list all the Jewish inhabitants of these two unhappy islands [cf. Steven Bowman, "Could the Dodekanisi Jews Have Been Saved?" *Newsletter* of The Jewish Museum of Greece, no. 26 (Winter, 1989)]. Marc Angel provided a survey of the Rhodes community in his *The Jews of Rhodes* (New York, 1980). The moving story of a group of Czech Zionists who spent the war in Italian-occupied Rhodes before being deported to Auschwitz is in John Bierman's *Odyssey: The Last Great Escape from Nazi-Dominated Europe* (New York, 1984). The Corfu community was studied by Pearl Liba Preschel, "The Jews of Corfu" in her unpublished Ph.D. dissertation (New York University, 1984).

Needless to say, there is a vast bibliography of memoirs in Greek, Hebrew, French and other languages dealing with the various experiences of Greek Jews during the war. More work needs to be done, but Dr. Matsas's collection of memoirs will be seen, in the long run, as a seminal collection that retells the overall story of the Greek Jewish experience from the perspective of the participant and the victim. Its publication some 50 years after the Second World War will probably be the last major collection to be derived directly from those who experienced the war period in person. Henceforth we shall have to rely on previously collected but unpublished memoirs, archival documentation, and reinterpretations of the materials made available. Hence, Dr. Matsas's study may be the final call of Greek Jewry in its own voice.

— *STEVEN BOWMAN*
University of Cincinnati, 1997

Made in the USA
Middletown, DE
05 February 2025

70196572R00267